DEVELOPED FOR COMMON CORE STATE STANDARDS

TEACHER EDITION

Level B

# Vocabulary Surge

## Unleashing the Power of Word Parts™

MAT: LATIN ROOT WITH AFFIXES

voc al ize

re ing claim ed pro

ANGLO-SAXON LATIN GREEK

95% GROUP INC.

*95 percent of students reading at grade level . . . an achievable goal*

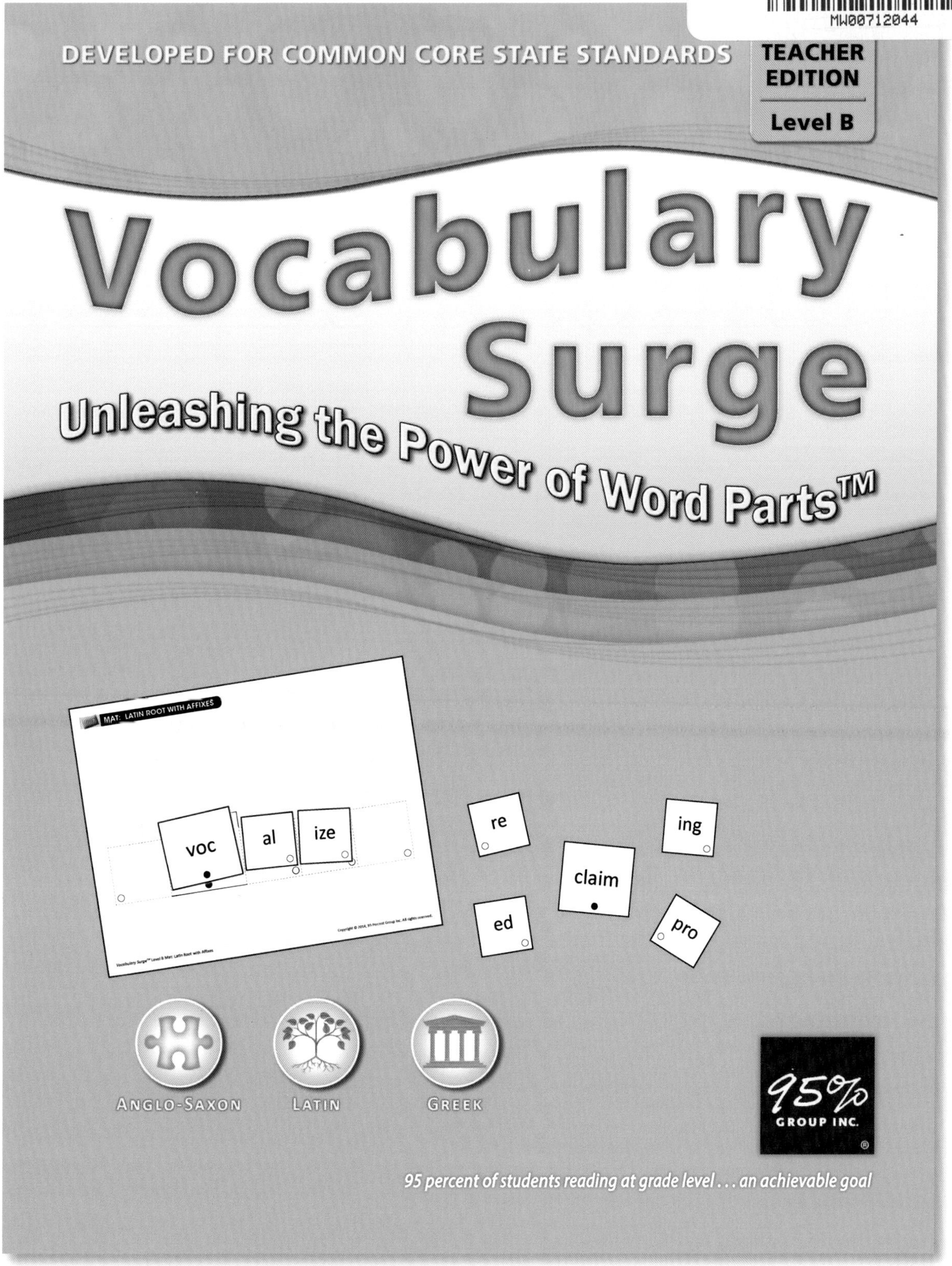

475 Half Day Road, Suite 350 • Lincolnshire, IL 60069
847-499-8200 • www.95percentgroup.com

# *Vocabulary Surge: Unleashing the Power of Word Parts™, Level B*

## *What is it?*

A series of 15-minute daily lessons that teach students how to break words into parts, hypothesize the meanings of unknown word parts, and check meaning in context. Students learn the meaning of common affixes, Latin Roots, and Greek Combining Forms.

## *Why was it developed?*

Memorizing vocabulary lists is not enough! As the rigor of the text increases to meet the demands of the Common Core State Standards, students will encounter more complex vocabulary words. ***Vocabulary Surge™*** was developed to teach students a systematic process to independently figure out the meaning of an unknown word by breaking it into meaningful parts. In order for students to learn 2,000-3,000 new words per year, they need to be skilled at figuring out the meaning of unfamiliar words as they come to them in text. That is exactly what ***Vocabulary Surge*** teaches.

## *Who is it for?*

***Vocabulary Surge™, Level B*** is a supplement for classroom teachers in grades 3–8 who provide instruction in Language Arts in upper elementary, middle school, and junior high. It can also be used by teachers who work with students receiving special education, English Language Learners, and intervention groups.

## *How does it work?*

Through the use of a 10-day lesson plan taught for 15-minutes per day, students are introduced to the meaning of common affixes, Latin Roots, and Greek Combining Forms. The concepts are further reinforced through activity-based exercises and word building with mats and cards.

## *What does it include?*

Everything you need is included, from the Teacher's Edition to downloadable student materials, mats, and word cards.

The Teacher's Edition features colorful lesson plans with symbols guiding the step-by-step process throughout the 10-day plan *(note: Affix Lesson plan is 5-days)*.

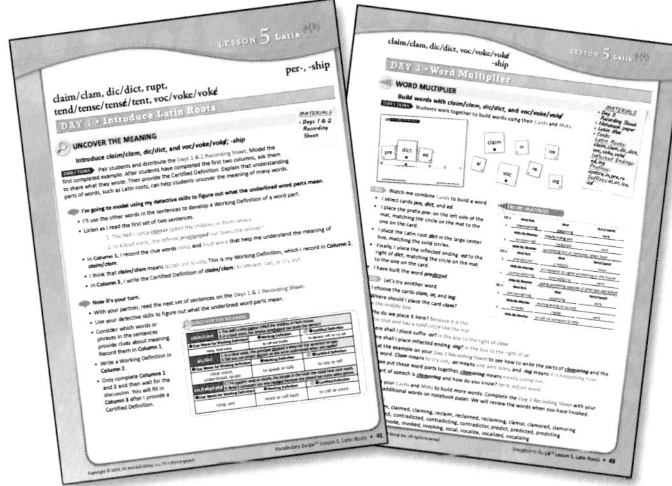

**DAY 1 • Introduce Word Parts**

UNCOVER THE MEANING

**DAY 2 • Deepen the Meaning**

CHECK MEANING

**DAY 3 • Word Multiplier**

WORD MULTIPLIER

**DAY 4 • Demonstrate Meaning**

BUILD MEANING

**DAY 5 • Introduce Word Parts**

UNCOVER THE MEANING

**DAY 6 • Deepen the Meaning**

CHECK MEANING

**DAY 7 • Word Multiplier**

WORD MULTIPLIER

**DAY 8 • Demonstrate Meaning**

BUILD MEANING

**DAY 9 • Review What You Learned**

REVIEW THE MEANING

CHECK MEANING

**DAY 10 • 2nd Day Review**

MAKE CONNECTIONS

MORPHEME MADNESS CHALLENGE

Student materials include colorful recording sheets, mats, and word cards for engaging, activity-based learning.

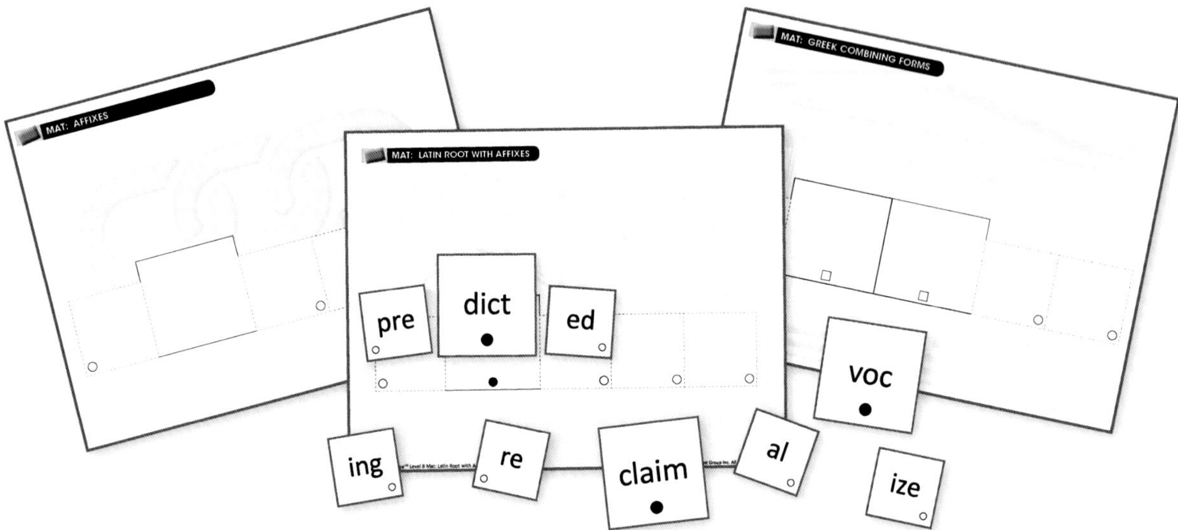


**Mats and Word Cards**

**Seven Types of Word Cards (368 Total)**

| Size | Symbol | | Number of Cards |
|---|---|---|---|
| Large | group<br>Lesson 3 | Bases | 48 |
| | claim<br>● | Latin Roots | 126 |
| | photo<br>□ | Greek Combining Forms | 55 |
| Medium | re<br>○ | Prefixes | 64 |
| | ize<br>○ | Suffixes | 69 |
| | ed<br>○ | Inflected Endings | 4 |
| Small | i | Connecting Letters | 2 |

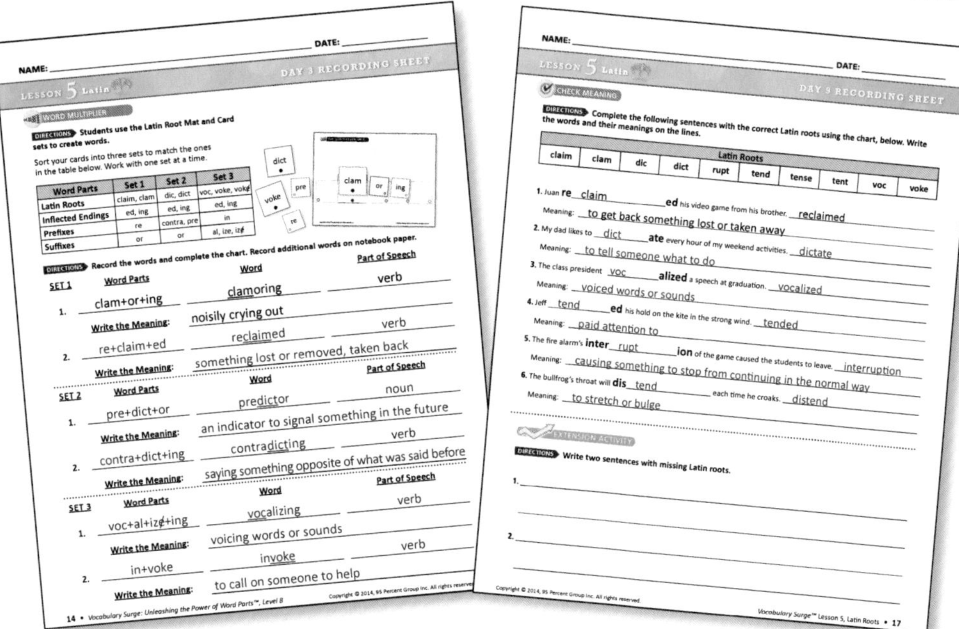

NAME: ______________________ DATE: __________

LESSON 5 Latin — DAY 3 RECORDING SHEET

WORD MULTIPLIER

DIRECTIONS Students use the Latin Root Mat and Card sets to create words.

Sort your cards into three sets to match the ones in the table below. Work with one set at a time.

| Word Parts | Set 1 | Set 2 | Set 3 |
|---|---|---|---|
| Latin Roots | claim, clam | dic, dict | voc, voke, voké |
| Inflected Endings | ed, ing | ed, ing | ed, ing |
| Prefixes | re | contra, pre | in |
| Suffixes | or | or | al, ize, izé |

DIRECTIONS Record the words and complete the chart. Record additional words on notebook paper.

SET 1 — Word Parts / Word / Part of Speech

1. clam+or+ing — clamoring — verb
   Write the Meaning: noisily crying out
2. re+claim+ed — reclaimed — verb
   Write the Meaning: something lost or removed, taken back

SET 2 — Word Parts / Word / Part of Speech

1. pre+dict+or — predictor — noun
   Write the Meaning: an indicator to signal something in the future
2. contra+dict+ing — contradicting — verb
   Write the Meaning: saying something opposite of what was said before

SET 3 — Word Parts / Word / Part of Speech

1. voc+al+izé+ing — vocalizing — verb
   Write the Meaning: voicing words or sounds
2. in+voke — invoke — verb
   Write the Meaning: to call on someone to help

14 • Vocabulary Surge: Unleashing the Power of Word Parts™, Level B — Copyright © 2014, 95 Percent Group Inc. All rights reserved.

NAME: ______________________ DATE: __________

LESSON 5 Latin — DAY 9 RECORDING SHEET

CHECK MEANING

DIRECTIONS Complete the following sentences with the correct Latin roots using the chart, below. Write the words and their meanings on the lines.

| Latin Roots | | | | | | | | | |
|---|---|---|---|---|---|---|---|---|---|
| claim | clam | dic | dict | rupt | tend | tense | tent | voc | voke |

1. Juan **re** claim **ed** his video game from his brother. reclaimed
   Meaning: to get back something lost or taken away
2. My dad likes to dict **ate** every hour of my weekend activities. dictate
   Meaning: to tell someone what to do
3. The class president voc **alized** a speech at graduation. vocalized
   Meaning: voiced words or sounds
4. Jeff tend **ed** his hold on the kite in the strong wind. tended
   Meaning: paid attention to
5. The fire alarm's **inter** rupt **ion** of the game caused the students to leave. interruption
   Meaning: causing something to stop from continuing in the normal way
6. The bullfrog's throat will **dis** tend each time he croaks. distend
   Meaning: to stretch or bulge

EXTENSION ACTIVITY

DIRECTIONS Write two sentences with missing Latin roots.

1. ______________________
2. ______________________

Copyright © 2014, 95 Percent Group Inc. All rights reserved. — Vocabulary Surge™ Lesson 5, Latin Roots • 17

**Student Recording Sheets**

## *What are the Benefits?*

- Dramatic surge in vocabulary using word-part meanings
- More accurate decoding
- Improved fluency and comprehension
- Acceleration in rate of learning words independently
- Increase in word consciousness about importance of word origin to determining meaning and spelling
- Teacher's Guide includes lessons and materials for 30 weeks of instruction and downloadable student materials

> ***"Fourth graders are supposed to be learning 2,000–3,000 new words per year, which is about 8 words per day. This product is a really great way for my students to pick up that extra vocabulary."***
>
> **– Robyn, Teacher in Pennsylvania**

Written and published by
95 Percent Group Inc.
Susan L. Hall, EdD, Founder and President
475 Half Day Road, Suite 350
Lincolnshire, IL 60069
www.95percentgroup.com



**Art Credits:** Cover, ©iStockphoto.com/Anastasiya Bugayova, ©iStockphoto.com/jjaakk, ©iStockphoto.com/usetrick

# Acknowledgments

95 Percent Group would like to thank Marcia Henry, Ph.D., author of ***Unlocking Literacy: Effective Decoding & Spelling Instruction***, for serving as content expert for ***Vocabulary Surge B: Unleashing the Power of Word Parts™***. Her expertise and guidance were pivotal in the development of this product.

95 Percent Group would also like to thank the following educators who participated in the pilot of ***Vocabulary Surge B: Unleashing the Power of Word Parts™***.

Polly Breen

Kate Cummmings

Robyn DiSabato

Jennifer Kilfoy

Laura Louis

Ed Martinson

Teri Mudd

Deborah Rupiperd

Omar Urias

Dustin Vaught

Melonie Wolf

# Table of Contents



 

# Vocabulary Surge™, Level B

## INTRODUCTION

### Why Was This Product Developed?

*Vocabulary Surge*™ is designed to address a pressing academic issue: Students whose vocabulary is limited are unable to comprehend complex text. Many students—not just English Language Learners (ELLs)—lag behind in reading comprehension and fluency because of low vocabulary skills. For many years, educators have voiced concerns about their students' diminishing vocabulary levels caused by many factors, including a reduced interest in pleasure reading outside of school. A large majority of students do not have the vocabulary levels required to be able to comprehend complex literary text, and they are impaired in understanding text in the content areas of science, social studies, and even math.

The urgency of our students' low vocabulary levels will become evident with the implementation of the Common Core State Standards (CCSS). Reading Standard 10 states that students should be reading complex literary and informational text independently and proficiently. The rigor of curriculum text is expected to increase to meet the levels demonstrated in the text exemplars in Appendix B of the CCSS. Complex text will assuredly contain more difficult multisyllabic words starting in 2nd grade and continuing through high school. The increased emphasis on informational text will also mean that students will be exposed to unfamiliar science and social studies content words. As we gravitate toward more complex text and more informational text, the shortfall in our students' vocabulary skills will surface as a root problem holding students back from comprehending text.

Many students have no idea how to figure out the meaning of an unknown word in context and choose to skip the infrequent but highly important multisyllabic words they encounter. This impairs text comprehension because often it's the meaning of the infrequent words that is critical to constructing meaning from the sentence or paragraph. Teaching students a process for figuring out the meaning of unknown words can leverage their comprehension even more than teaching specific words. To draw from a common analogy, teaching a student the meaning of one word at a time is like giving a hungry person a fish whereas teaching a student the skills to figure out any unknown word is teaching HOW to fish.

*Vocabulary Surge*™ provides teachers with a process for figuring out the meaning of unknown words, which increases students' vocabulary skills, expands their vocabulary, and improves their reading comprehension. This leads to more proficient reading and ultimately a more enjoyable and rewarding reading experience.

## PRODUCT DESCRIPTION

### Moving Beyond Vocabulary Lists

Most instruction addresses the issue of unknown words by providing a list of 8–20 vocabulary words and instructing teachers to preteach these vocabulary words before students read. Using morphemes, or the meaning parts in a word, is one of the best ways to comprehend an unknown word. Researchers have found that a 5th grade student's understanding of word parts, or knowledge of morphology, is a better indicator of reading comprehension than his or her vocabulary level (Kieffer et al, 2007). While teaching the meaning of key words before, during, and after reading is beneficial, this is only one step. No matter how many words are selected to teach, students are always going to encounter unknown words in text. Looking words up in a dictionary has been shown to have limited usefulness because a definition often includes additional unknown words. To help students become successful readers, *Vocabulary Surge*™ asks students to be detectives and uncover the smallest word part with meaning in order to comprehend a word. To do this, students need **a process** and **knowledge of the meaning of the most common word parts.**

> *Morpheme:*
> The smallest meaningful part of a word

Teaching the meaning of selected vocabulary words is not enough to equip our students to be successful in reading more complex text. It's impossible to close the vocabulary gap that exists for many students through teaching 8–20 words per week. According to Michael Graves (2006), comprehensive vocabulary instruction includes four components:

1. teaching specific vocabulary words,
2. supporting wide reading to learn words from independent reading,
3. learning words independently from context, and
4. word consciousness.

This product fits with the third component—it's about how a student can learn unknown words from context.

## Morphemes and Meaning

Most multisyllabic words contain several morphemes that each contribute to the meaning. *Vocabulary Surge*™ offers instruction on the different types of morphemes:

- Prefixes
- Suffixes
- Anglo-Saxon Base Words
- Latin Roots
- Greek Combining Forms

It's important to note that morphemes are not always the same as syllables, as in this example with the word *contradict*:

- Syllables: (3) con-tra-dict
- Morphemes: (2) the prefix *contra-* + the Latin root *dict*
- Meaning: *contra-* means the opposite of, and *dict* means to say or tell; *contradict* means to say or tell the opposite

To be successful in figuring out the meanings of unknown words, it's advantageous to know the meaning of at least some of the word so the part that's unfamiliar can be isolated. For example, if you know what the prefix *pre-* and the suffix *-tion* mean, it's easier to figure out the meaning of the word *prediction* in context in the following sentence: *The weatherman's prediction of rain was accurate.*

## Morpheme Scope and Sequence

The range and sequence of morphemes was carefully considered in *Vocabulary Surge*™ in order to make students successful detectives in uncovering meaning. Marcia Henry, Ph.D., author of *Unlocking Literacy: Effective Decoding & Spelling Instruction*, served as a consultant to 95 Percent Group on the development of this product. Dr. Henry served as a content expert and reviewed instruction for each layer of language and lesson content. Dr. Henry's lists of the most common morphemes by layer of language were a key reference in determining the sequence, scope, and meanings of the morphemes. Lessons were also written for (not simply aligned with) the Common Core State Standards; a correlation chart can be found online.

### Scope

Level B teaches some common affixes (prefixes and suffixes), Latin Roots, and Greek Combining Forms. It is important that students first learn the morphemes that most commonly appear in words so that students can uncover the meaning of many words, leading to an exponential growth in vocabulary and a feeling of success as readers. Level B is a follow-up to Level A, but it is not necessary to start with Level A. The focus of Level A is on helping students develop a strong understanding of how Anglo-Saxon base word can be combined to make multisyllabic compound words. The other focus is on using inflected endings with base words (ed, ing, s/es), as well as simple affixes added to Anglo-Saxon words. The Latin layer of language is introduced and simple Latin Roots are covered. The Greek layer is only introduced as a contrast to the Anglo-Saxon and Latin layers of language. Understanding that words can be separated into smaller word parts that contain meaning is a crucial concept for students to master before moving on to more complex Latin Roots and Greek Combining Forms. Level B reviews concepts introduced in Level A and then delves deeper into more difficult Latin Roots and affixes, as well as expanding Greek Combining Form lessons to include affixes.

 

### Sequence

The scope or range of morphemes within each level is only the first step. Within each level, morphemes are organized into meaningful clusters. Each lesson contains morphemes whose meanings are related in some way. For example, the suffixes *-cian, -ian,* and *-ese* are taught as a group because their meanings are about a citizen of a country or location (e.g. American, Chicagoan, or Japanese).

The same idea is evident in the grouping of the Latin Roots *pict* and *scribe*, which have meanings related to painting or writing. In the first day when a new set of roots is introduced, students are encouraged to be detectives to uncover the meanings. The grouping of roots taught in the same lesson is important because comparing and contrasting helps students learn and retain morpheme meanings.

| Latin root | Certified Definition |
|---|---|
| pict | to paint |
| scribe | to write |

### Prerequisite Skills

Because this product does not teach students how to decode words or pronounce them, the ability to decode multisyllable words is a prerequisite for *Vocabulary Surge*™ lessons. Students who don't know how to divide multisyllable words into syllables and pronounce each part based on knowledge about the vowel sound in different types of syllables would benefit from instruction with 95 Percent Group's *Multisyllable Routine Cards*. *Vocabulary Surge*™ is a perfect complement to follow *Multisyllable Routine Cards*.

## Product Benefits

- **Teaches students a process for figuring out the meaning of an unknown word in context**
  A common practice in morphology instruction is to begin the lesson by defining a word part and expecting students to memorize it. Instead, *Vocabulary Surge*™ asks students to be detectives and uncover the meaning in context, making them responsible and engaged in their learning. Each lesson provides students with sentences containing words with a target morpheme; pairs or small groups of students develop a Working Definition, or hypothesis, about what the target part means. Students share their Working Definitions and discuss them before the teacher provides a Certified Definition for students to record. The steps in the discovery process *Vocabulary Surge*™ uses to teach students to figure out an unknown word while reading independently are:
  - Break the word into its meaningful parts,
  - Develop a hypothesis of meaning from context and knowledge of word parts, and
  - Check whether the hypothesis makes sense against the context and background knowledge.
- **Presents the word parts, or morphemes, in order of frequency**
  Level B includes instruction on 37 common prefixes and suffixes and uses additional easier prefixes and suffixes that are likely to be known to students; if students need explicit instruction in these easier affixes, review lessons are provided online. In total, 65 prefixes and 65 suffixes are used in the Level B lessons. The lessons provide explicit instruction on 51 Latin Roots and 37 Greek Combining Forms.
- **Teaches the word parts, or morphemes, in clusters based on related meanings**
  Many programs teach morphemes in order from the most common to the least common. *Vocabulary Surge*™ places the parts in clusters by meaning to enable more efficient learning. Grouping by related meanings allows students to attach new morphemes to the schema they already have for similar meaningful word parts.
- **Reminds students of proper pronunciation of syllables when dropping vowels through special cards with a slash through the vowel letter**
  *Vocabulary Surge*™ includes duplicate Latin Root cards where the final e is slashed to remind students to properly pronounce the syllable's long vowel sound when the final e is dropped before a suffix beginning with a vowel. For example, the final e in the word *incline* is dropped before adding the inflected ending *-ed*. The word *inclined* is built with the following cards: in + clin∕e + ed. Similarly, there are duplicate cards for some suffixes where the initial vowel is slashed for proper spelling of words with multiple suffixes. An example is the word *corporation*, which is built with the following cards: corp + or + at∕e + ion. Showing the suffix *-ate* spelled as *-at* may confuse students about the accurate pronunciation of the long vowel sound in the syllable.

- **Can be taught as a supplement to whole class for 15 minutes daily, in small groups, or both**
  Teachers have a lot of choices in how to use *Vocabulary Surge™* lessons. It can be taught whole class as a supplement to the curriculum if most students need instruction and practice with word parts. The lessons can also be used in small groups if only some students need instruction and practice with word parts. A third approach is a combination of teaching some parts whole class and then following up in small groups with selected students for the remaining parts of the lesson. In this combination approach, Days 1 and 5 could be taught whole class, which are the days when the new morphemes are introduced. Days 2–4 and 6–8 are practice days, and these activities could be used in small groups with some students instead of the whole class. Days 9 and 10 provide multiple opportunities to review the approximately six morphemes taught in the ten-day lesson.

| Combination Approach of Whole Class and Small Group Instruction | |
|---|---|
| **Day 1, Day 5: Introduce Morphemes** | Whole class |
| **Days 2–4 and 6–8: Practice Morphemes** | Small groups |
| **Days 9 & 10: Review** | Whole class or small group |

  Although Level B contains lessons that would take approximately 30 weeks if taught in increments of 15 minutes daily, there is flexibility about how the lessons are used. They can be accelerated by dedicating more time daily, or teachers can determine that they don't need to teach all the lessons.

- **Is a cost-effective and flexible program**
  Schools and teachers have options on how to match their budget for *Vocabulary Surge™*.

  **Teacher's Guide with Online Student Materials** A school can purchase one copy of the Teacher's Guide for each classroom teacher. Teachers use the license key in each teacher's guide to access the Student Recording Sheets, Mats, and Cards.

  **Teacher Kit and Student Kit** Schools can purchase other materials in kits, including
  - Teacher Mats and Cards for introducing each layer of language
  - Student Edition (worksheets)
  - Student Mats and Cards (10 sets for a classroom)

- **Designed for flexible use in many different grade levels.**
  *Vocabulary Surge™* was developed with the understanding that students' abilities and instructional needs vary. Level A is appropriate for students in grades 1–3 and can be used with older students who are unfamiliar with the layers of the English language and would benefit from this instruction. Level B is designed to address the skills identified in the Common Core standards in grades 3 and up with a focus on grades 4 and 5.

## HOW TO USE LEVEL B

Level B introduces the concept of base words from the Anglo-Saxon layer of our language, the oldest and most basic layer. The first four lessons teach how multisyllabic words are constructed in the Anglo-Saxon layer through adding Latin prefixes and suffixes to base words. The following concepts are included:

- Teach 28 common prefixes and 8 suffixes, and use a total of 65 prefixes and 65 suffixes including the simplest ones previously known (or reviewed with online review lessons)
- Teach and practice using 51 of the most common Latin Roots
- Teach and practice 37 Greek Combining Forms

| Book B Lessons | | |
|---|---|---|
| **Layer of Language** | **Lessons** | **Number of Morphemes** |
| **Anglo-Saxon and Affix Lessons** | **1–4** | 28 prefixes, 8 suffixes |
| **Latin Lessons** | **5–13** | 51 common Latin Roots |
| **Greek Lessons** | **14–17** | 37 Greek Combining Forms |

## LESSON LAYOUT

The four affix lessons are taught using a five-day format. The twelve Latin and Greek lessons have a ten-day lesson plan format.

| Overview of the Latin and Greek Ten-day Lesson Plan Format | |
|---|---|
| **Introduction** | **Introduce each layer of language using mats and cards** |
| **First Set of Morphemes** | |
| **Day 1** | Introduce new set of 2–4 morphemes and ask students to discover meaning |
| **Day 2** | Deepen the meaning of the morphemes taught on Day 1 |
| **Day 3** | Apply knowledge through building words (called "Multiplier") |
| **Day 4** | Demonstrate understanding of morphemes |
| **Second Set of Morphemes** | |
| **Day 5** | Introduce new set of 2–4 morphemes and ask students to discover meaning |
| **Day 6** | Deepen the meaning of the morphemes taught on Day 5 |
| **Day 7** | Apply knowledge through building words (called "Multiplier") |
| **Day 8** | Demonstrate understanding of morphemes |
| **Review** | |
| **Day 9** | Review and apply all 6-8 morphemes of lesson |
| **Day 10** | Apply all knowledge including a "Morpheme Madness" activity with word building |

### Introduce Layer of Language Using Mats and Cards

Teachers who piloted this program provided feedback about how effective our multisensory manipulatives are in teaching the lessons, especially the mats and word cards. Using manipulatives creates an experience that makes an abstract concept concrete for students. One of the goals of *Vocabulary Surge*™ is that students will learn that multisyllable words in the English language are created differently depending upon the layer of the language.

- Anglo-Saxon words can be made into multisyllabic words by either combining two completely separate base words or adding one or more affixes to a base word. These are free morphemes and can each stand alone, yet when combined in a compound word they mean something different.
- Latin words are formed by a Latin root and at least one affix. Latin words must have a root and at least one prefix or suffix, although they can have more than one affix.
- Greek words are multisyllabic words that contain different parts called Greek Combining Forms. Each part has a meaning. Greek words don't follow a predictable structure such as the Latin format of a root in the middle surrounded by affixes. For example, the Greek combining form *photo* can appear in alternate positions in a word such as in the words *photosynthesis* or *telephoto*.

**Teacher Mats and Cards** Before each layer of language is taught, the teacher first introduces it by explaining how a word in that layer of language is built (or which parts are needed). The teacher models building words using the Teacher Mat and Cards. Each mat has boxes that delineate the word parts required for the layer of language. Cards are placed over the boxes. Note that meaning is not the focus of these introductory mat lessons, only the structure of each layer of language so students understand the concept of how words are built. Meaning is the focus for the lessons within each layer of language.

## Latin and Greek Lesson
## Days 1 & 5: Uncover the Meaning
### Step 1 Introduce Morphemes

The goal of this day is for students to learn a set of new morphemes. Students are introduced to a new set of morphemes and asked to follow the *Uncover the Meaning Routine* and to determine each morpheme's meaning by completing the *Uncover the Meaning Student Worksheet. Vocabulary Surge*™ intentionally uses a discovery process rather than explicitly telling students the morpheme definition in order to provide students with a process of how to figure out the meaning of the unknown word part through using context and knowledge of known word parts. By discovering, or uncovering, the meaning of the morpheme in context, students are engaged in the learning process and are then able to apply this same process in their own independent reading.

**Background Colors**
There are three different background colors. Affix lessons are green, Latin are turquoise blue, and Greek are royal blue.

**Header**
On the first day of the lesson the Latin Roots included in the 10-day lesson are listed, including the various spellings of the root.

**Materials**
On the yellow sticky note all materials needed for the lesson are listed. Word cards are divided into two categories for those that the teacher needs for modeling as well as those students will need for the You Do.

LESSON 5 Latin

claim/clam, dic/dict, rupt, tend/tense/tens~~e~~/tent, voc/voke/vok~~e~~ per-, -sh

DAY 1 • Introduce Latin Roots

UNCOVER THE MEANING

MATERIALS
• Days 1 & 2 Recording Sheet

**Introduce *claim/clam, dic/dict,* and *voc/voke/vok~~e~~; -ship***

DIRECTIONS Pair students and distribute the Days 1 & 2 Recording Sheet. Model the first completed example. After students have completed the first two columns, ask them to share what they wrote. Then provide the Certified Definition. Explain that understanding parts of words, such as Latin roots, can help students uncover the meaning of many words.

**I'm going to model using my detective skills to figure out what the underlined word parts mean.**

- I'll use the other words in the sentences to develop a Working Definition of a word part.
- Listen as I read the first set of two sentences.
  1. The bell's noisy ***clamor*** called the children in from recess.
  2. In a loud voice, the referee ***proclaimed*** our team the winner!
- In **Column 1**, I record the clue words noisy and loud voice that help me understand the meaning of ***claim/clam***.
- I think that ***claim/clam*** means to call out loudly. This is my Working Definition, which I record in Co
- In **Column 3**, I write the Certified Definition of ***claim/clam***: to declare, call, or cry out.

**Now it's your turn.**

- With your partner, read the next set of sentences on the Days 1 & 2 Recording Sheet.
- Use your detective skills to figure out what the underlined word parts mean.
- Consider which words or phrases in the sentences provide clues about meaning. Record them in **Column 1**.
- Write a Working Definit... in **Column 2**
- ...complete **Columns 1** and **2** and then wait for the ...cussion. You will fill in ...lumn **3** after I provide a ...tified Definition.

UNCOVER THE MEANING

| claim/clam | 1. The bell's noisy clamor called the children in from recess. 2. In a loud voice, the referee proclaimed our team the winner! | |
|---|---|---|
| ❶Clue Words for Working Definition | ❷Working Definition | ❸Certified Definition |
| noisy, loud voice | to call out loudly | to declare, call, or cry out |
| **dic/dict** | 1. In a clear voice, the principal dictated a letter for the secretary to type. 2. Did you use proper diction so you were understood when you spoke? | |
| ❶Clue Words for Working Definition | ❷Working Definition | ❸Certified Definition |
| clear voice, understood, spoke | to speak or talk | to say or tell |
| **voc/voke/vok~~e~~** | 1. The vocalist sang so clearly, the people in the back row could hear each word. 2. Bette's computer use was revoked because she played too many video games. | |
| ❶Clue Words for Working Definition | ❷Working Definition | ❸Certified Definition |
| sang, use | voice or call back | to call or voice |

**Teacher Instructions**
Directions to the teacher are provided after the red arrow. Teacher dialogue is provided after purple speech bubbles or I DO, WE DO, or YOU DO headings.

**Purple Band**
The purple band indicates the section of the lesson. Icons appear to the left, including a magnifying glass for Uncover the Meaning and speech bubbles for student dialogue during the Build Meaning section.

**Student Edition Insert**
In the Teacher's Guide there are inserts of the student's pages with possible answers shown in red font.

 

## Latin and Greek Lesson
## Days 2 & 6: Deepen the Meaning

The purpose of Days 2 and 6 is to help students deepen their understanding of the new Latin Roots or Greek Combining Forms they learned in the first day. This is accomplished by having them use word cards to understand how words change as different prefixes and suffixes are added. In the I DO and WE DO sections, the teacher models using a common root and changing the affixes. Then in the YOU DO section students build words and record them on the Days 2 & 6 Recording Sheet.

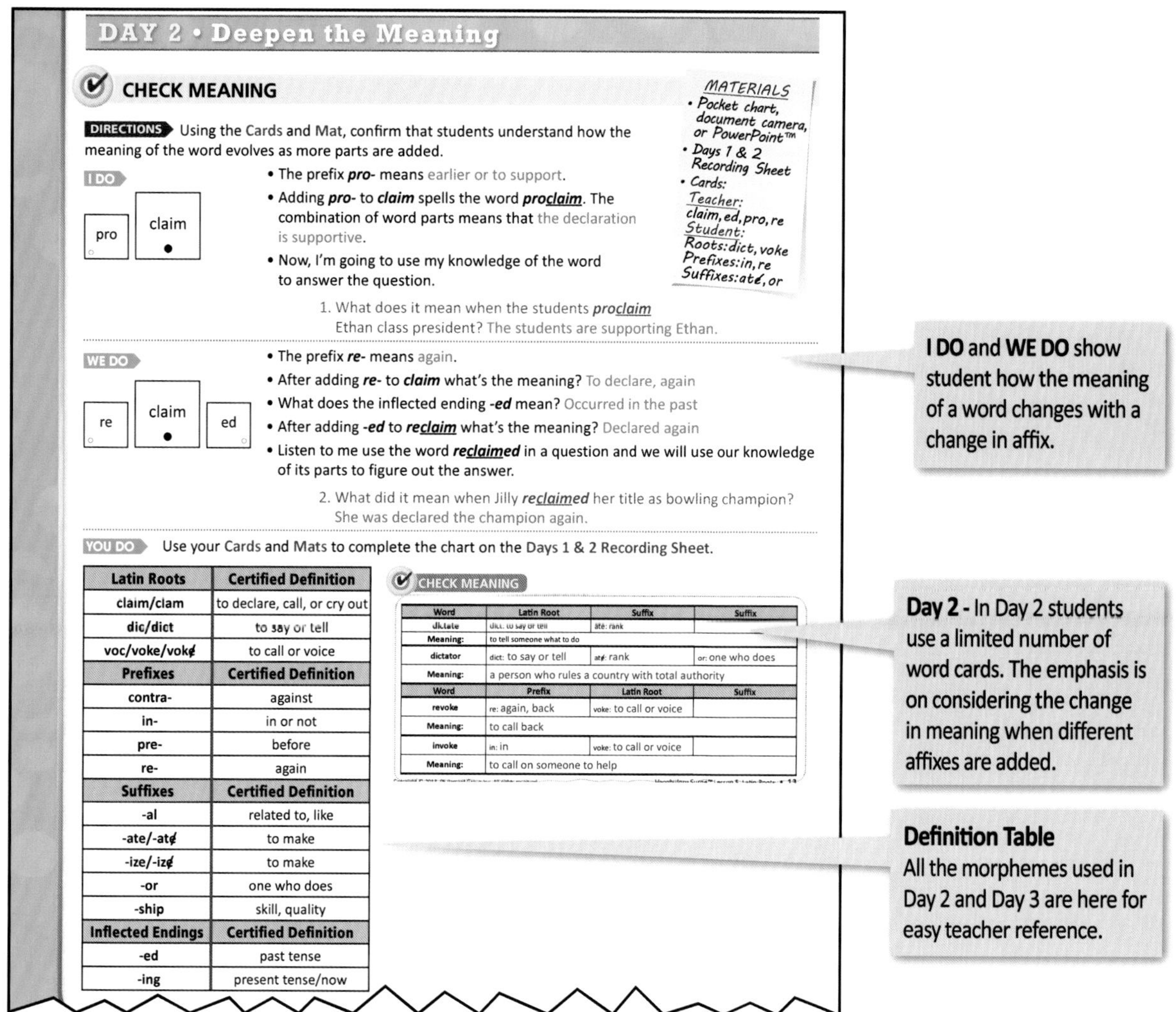

**DAY 2 • Deepen the Meaning**

**CHECK MEANING**

MATERIALS
- Pocket chart, document camera, or PowerPoint™
- Days 1 & 2 Recording Sheet
- Cards:
  Teacher: claim, ed, pro, re
  Student: Roots: dict, voke; Prefixes: in, re; Suffixes: at~~e~~, or

**DIRECTIONS** Using the Cards and Mat, confirm that students understand how the meaning of the word evolves as more parts are added.

**I DO** [pro] [claim]
- The prefix ***pro-*** means earlier or to support.
- Adding ***pro-*** to ***claim*** spells the word ***proclaim***. The combination of word parts means that the declaration is supportive.
- Now, I'm going to use my knowledge of the word to answer the question.

1. What does it mean when the students *proclaim* Ethan class president? The students are supporting Ethan.

**WE DO** [re] [claim] [ed]
- The prefix ***re-*** means again.
- After adding ***re-*** to ***claim*** what's the meaning? To declare, again
- What does the inflected ending ***-ed*** mean? Occurred in the past
- After adding ***-ed*** to ***reclaim*** what's the meaning? Declared again
- Listen to me use the word ***reclaimed*** in a question and we will use our knowledge of its parts to figure out the answer.

2. What did it mean when Jilly ***reclaimed*** her title as bowling champion? She was declared the champion again.

**YOU DO** Use your Cards and Mats to complete the chart on the Days 1 & 2 Recording Sheet.

| Latin Roots | Certified Definition |
|---|---|
| claim/clam | to declare, call, or cry out |
| dic/dict | to say or tell |
| voc/voke/vok~~e~~ | to call or voice |
| **Prefixes** | **Certified Definition** |
| contra- | against |
| in- | in or not |
| pre- | before |
| re- | again |
| **Suffixes** | **Certified Definition** |
| -al | related to, like |
| -ate/-at~~e~~ | to make |
| -ize/-iz~~e~~ | to make |
| -or | one who does |
| -ship | skill, quality |
| **Inflected Endings** | **Certified Definition** |
| -ed | past tense |
| -ing | present tense/now |

**CHECK MEANING**

| Word | Latin Root | Suffix | Suffix |
|---|---|---|---|
| dictate | dict: to say or tell | ate: rank | |
| Meaning: | to tell someone what to do | | |
| dictator | dict: to say or tell | at~~e~~: rank | or: one who does |
| Meaning: | a person who rules a country with total authority | | |
| **Word** | **Prefix** | **Latin Root** | **Suffix** |
| revoke | re: again, back | voke: to call or voice | |
| Meaning: | to call back | | |
| invoke | in: in | voke: to call or voice | |
| Meaning: | to call on someone to help | | |

**I DO** and **WE DO** show student how the meaning of a word changes with a change in affix.
**Day 2** - In Day 2 students use a limited number of word cards. The emphasis is on considering the change in meaning when different affixes are added.
**Definition Table**
All the morphemes used in Day 2 and Day 3 are here for easy teacher reference.

## Latin and Greek Lesson
## Days 3 & 7: Multiplier

The goal of this day is for students to practice the meaning of the morpheme by applying it to more words that contain the word part. This will not only deepen knowledge of the meaning of the morpheme but will also enable the student to learn to generalize from the words used in the first day's lesson to a larger set of words.

Students are asked to practice and apply the target morphemes they learned as well as morphemes they've learned in earlier lessons by building words. Students can work independently or in pairs or small groups to follow the Multiplier Routine by completing the Multiplier Student Worksheet. To focus the lesson on target morphemes, students are given Mats and Cards of specific prefixes, suffixes, and sometimes connective letters (for Latin and Greek lessons) to build words. The students build words using the mats and a limited number of word cards. The cards are divided into between two and four sets so that they have no more than ten cards at a time, and often only about five or six. The Teacher's Guide includes charts with words that students might build as well as the definitions as they relate to the target morpheme. This activity includes writing and is a good opportunity to teach spelling rules, some of which are included in the Teacher's Guide.

After students work together using the Mat and Cards to practice building words, they record their words on the Recording Sheet.

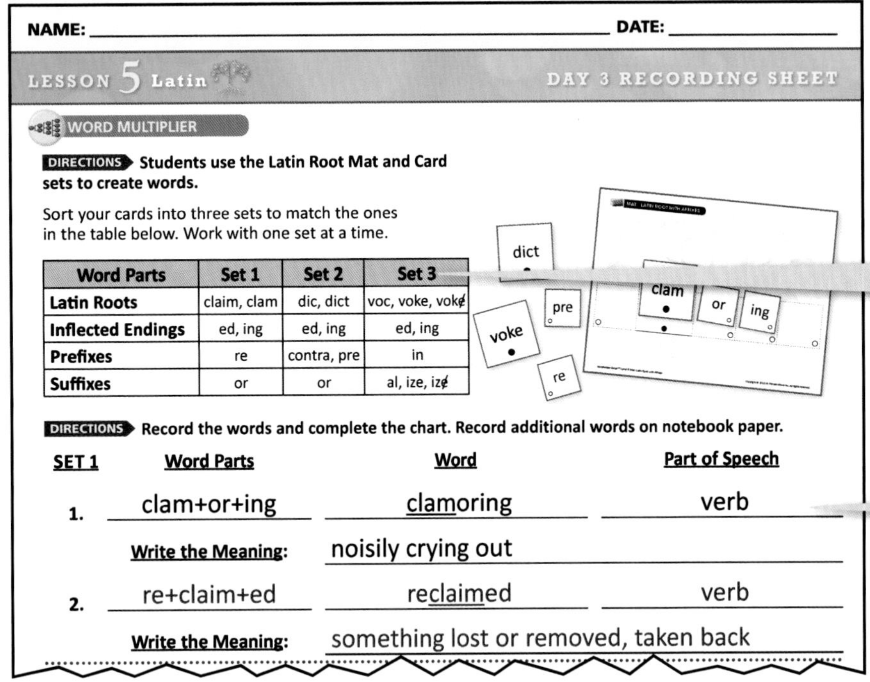
NAME: ______ DATE: ______

LESSON 5 Latin — DAY 3 RECORDING SHEET

WORD MULTIPLIER

DIRECTIONS Students use the Latin Root Mat and Card sets to create words.

Sort your cards into three sets to match the ones in the table below. Work with one set at a time.

| Word Parts | Set 1 | Set 2 | Set 3 |
|---|---|---|---|
| Latin Roots | claim, clam | dic, dict | voc, voke, vok~~e~~ |
| Inflected Endings | ed, ing | ed, ing | ed, ing |
| Prefixes | re | contra, pre | in |
| Suffixes | or | or | al, ize, iz~~e~~ |



DIRECTIONS Record the words and complete the chart. Record additional words on notebook paper.

SET 1 — Word Parts — Word — Part of Speech

1. clam+or+ing — clamoring — verb

Write the Meaning: noisily crying out

2. re+claim+ed — reclaimed — verb

Write the Meaning: something lost or removed, taken back

**Multiplier Sets**
Cards are divided into two and four sets so there are no more than 10 cards at a time.

**Student Recording Sheet Multiplier** Students use the Latin Root Mat and Card sets to create words and complete the chart.

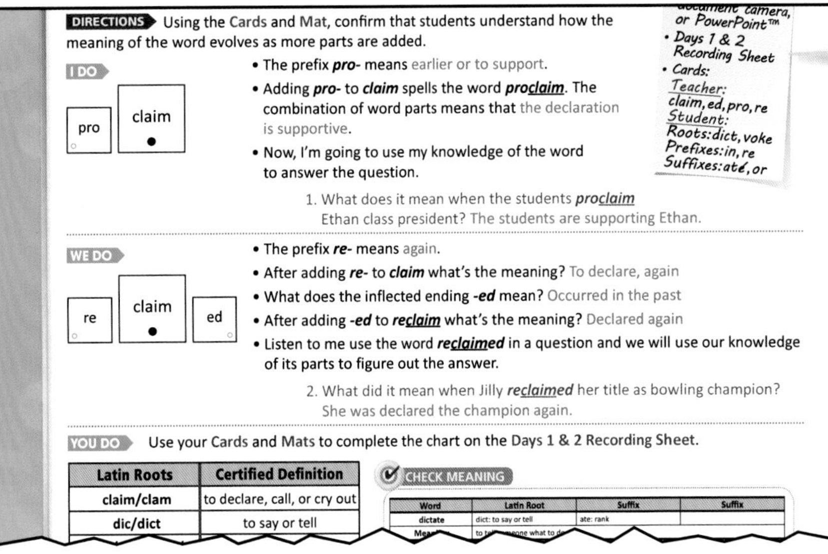
DIRECTIONS Using the Cards and Mat, confirm that students understand how the meaning of the word evolves as more parts are added.

I DO

- The prefix *pro-* means earlier or to support.
- Adding *pro-* to *claim* spells the word *proclaim*. The combination of word parts means that the declaration is supportive.
- Now, I'm going to use my knowledge of the word to answer the question.

1. What does it mean when the students *proclaim* Ethan class president? The students are supporting Ethan.

WE DO

- The prefix *re-* means again.
- After adding *re-* to *claim* what's the meaning? To declare, again
- What does the inflected ending *-ed* mean? Occurred in the past
- After adding *-ed* to *reclaim* what's the meaning? Declared again
- Listen to me use the word *reclaimed* in a question and we will use our knowledge of its parts to figure out the answer.

2. What did it mean when Jilly *reclaimed* her title as bowling champion? She was declared the champion again.

YOU DO Use your Cards and Mats to complete the chart on the Days 1 & 2 Recording Sheet.

| Latin Roots | Certified Definition |
|---|---|
| claim/clam | to declare, call, or cry out |
| dic/dict | to say or tell |



**I DO and WE DO**
Modeling of word building with mats and cards before students build words.

**Possible Words**
This list includes words that can be built with the limited sets (set 1, set 2, etc.).

## Definitions Provided in Teacher's Guide *(found on Day 2)*

| Latin Roots | Certified Definition |
|---|---|
| claim/clam | to declare, call, or cry out |
| dic/dict | to say or tell |
| voc/voke/vok~~e~~ | to call or voice |
| **Prefixes** | **Certified Definition** |
| contra- | against |
| in- | in or not |

## Possible Words *(found on Day 4)*

**Possible Words:**
**claim/clam:** claim, claimed, claiming, reclaim, reclaimed, reclaiming, clamor, clamored, clamoring
**dic/dict:** contradict, contradicted, contradicting, contradictor, predict, predicted, predicting
**voc/voke/vok~~e~~:** invoke, invoked, invoking, vocal, vocalize, vocalized, vocalizing

 

## Latin and Greek Lesson
## Days 4 & 8: Demonstrate Meaning

Similar to the ideas suggested in the book *Bringing Words to Life* by Isabel Beck and colleagues, on Days 4 and 8 students work with sentences that require them to apply the meanings of the target morpheme. Teachers read sentences aloud for students to think about and answer orally. By engaging all students in generating an answer, they are thinking about the meaning of the new morpheme as used in the context of the sentence.

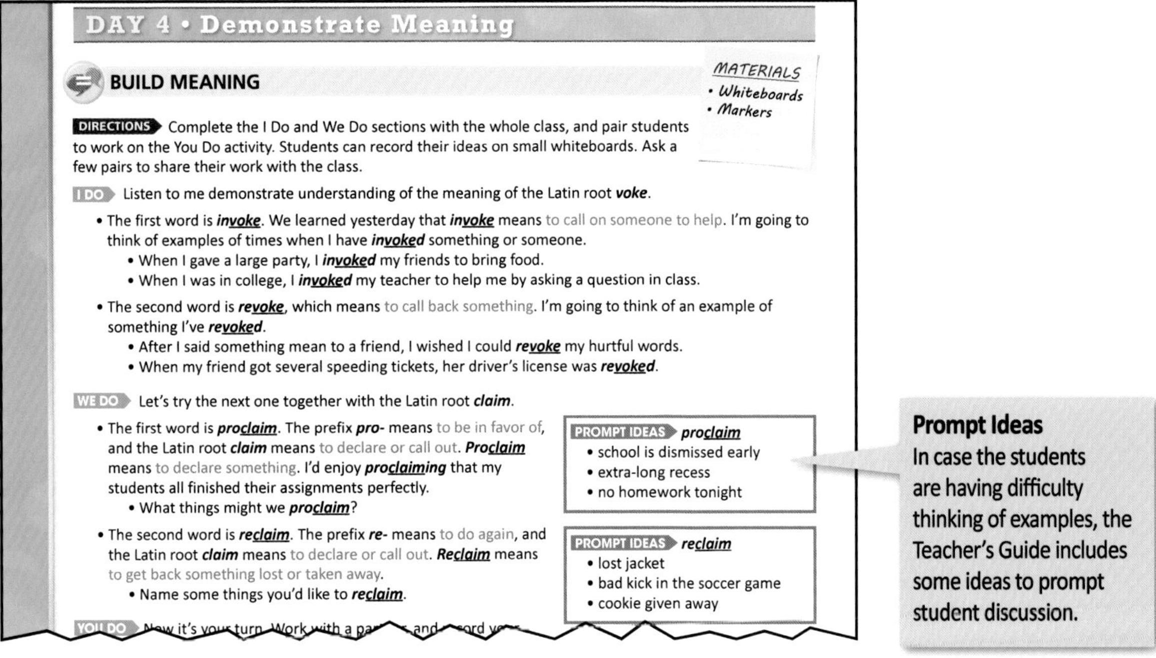

**DAY 4 • Demonstrate Meaning**

**BUILD MEANING**

*MATERIALS*
- *Whiteboards*
- *Markers*

DIRECTIONS Complete the I Do and We Do sections with the whole class, and pair students to work on the You Do activity. Students can record their ideas on small whiteboards. Ask a few pairs to share their work with the class.

I DO Listen to me demonstrate understanding of the meaning of the Latin root *voke*.

- The first word is ***invoke***. We learned yesterday that ***invoke*** means to call on someone to help. I'm going to think of examples of times when I have ***invoked*** something or someone.
  - When I gave a large party, I ***invoked*** my friends to bring food.
  - When I was in college, I ***invoked*** my teacher to help me by asking a question in class.
- The second word is ***revoke***, which means to call back something. I'm going to think of an example of something I've ***revoked***.
  - After I said something mean to a friend, I wished I could ***revoke*** my hurtful words.
  - When my friend got several speeding tickets, her driver's license was ***revoked***.

WE DO Let's try the next one together with the Latin root ***claim***.

- The first word is ***proclaim***. The prefix ***pro-*** means to be in favor of, and the Latin root ***claim*** means to declare or call out. ***Proclaim*** means to declare something. I'd enjoy ***proclaiming*** that my students all finished their assignments perfectly.
  - What things might we ***proclaim***?
- The second word is ***reclaim***. The prefix ***re-*** means to do again, and the Latin root ***claim*** means to declare or call out. ***Reclaim*** means to get back something lost or taken away.
  - Name some things you'd like to ***reclaim***.

PROMPT IDEAS ***proclaim***
- school is dismissed early
- extra-long recess
- no homework tonight

PROMPT IDEAS ***reclaim***
- lost jacket
- bad kick in the soccer game
- cookie given away

YOU DO Now it's your turn. Work with a pa... and ...ord y...

**Prompt Ideas**
In case the students are having difficulty thinking of examples, the Teacher's Guide includes some ideas to prompt student discussion.

## Latin and Greek Lesson
## Day 9: Review What You Learned

In order for students to review the 6–8 roots taught previously in the lesson, there are two activities in Day 9. In the first activity the teacher reviews the meaning of each morpheme featured in the lesson.

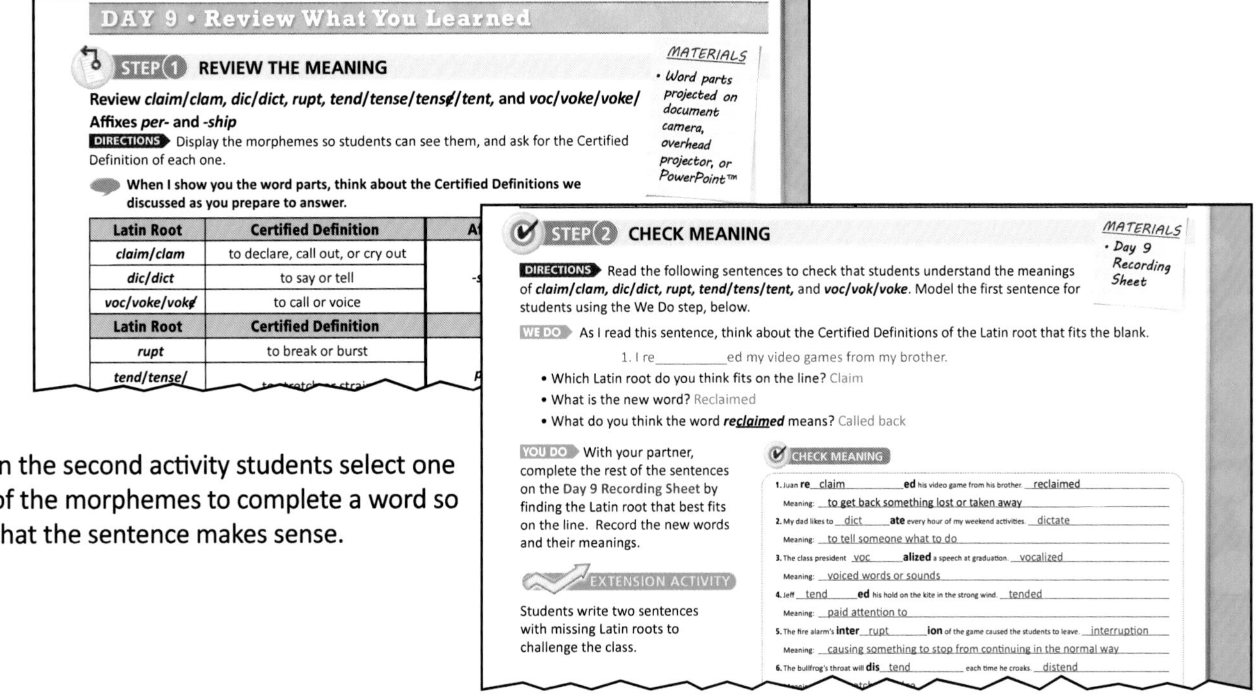

**DAY 9 • Review What You Learned**

**STEP 1 REVIEW THE MEANING**

*MATERIALS*
- *Word parts projected on document camera, overhead projector, or PowerPoint™*

**Review *claim/clam, dic/dict, rupt, tend/tense/tens/tent,* and *voc/voke/vok/* Affixes *per-* and *-ship***

DIRECTIONS Display the morphemes so students can see them, and ask for the Certified Definition of each one.

**When I show you the word parts, think about the Certified Definitions we discussed as you prepare to answer.**

| Latin Root | Certified Definition |
|---|---|
| *claim/clam* | to declare, call out, or cry out |
| *dic/dict* | to say or tell |
| *voc/voke/vok* | to call or voice |
| **Latin Root** | **Certified Definition** |
| *rupt* | to break or burst |
| *tend/tense/* | to stretch or strai... |

**STEP 2 CHECK MEANING**

*MATERIALS*
- *Day 9 Recording Sheet*

DIRECTIONS Read the following sentences to check that students understand the meanings of ***claim/clam, dic/dict, rupt, tend/tens/tent,*** and ***voc/vok/voke***. Model the first sentence for students using the We Do step, below.

WE DO As I read this sentence, think about the Certified Definitions of the Latin root that fits the blank.

1. I re__________ed my video games from my brother.

- Which Latin root do you think fits on the line? Claim
- What is the new word? Reclaimed
- What do you think the word ***reclaimed*** means? Called back

YOU DO With your partner, complete the rest of the sentences on the Day 9 Recording Sheet by finding the Latin root that best fits on the line. Record the new words and their meanings.

EXTENSION ACTIVITY

Students write two sentences with missing Latin roots to challenge the class.

CHECK MEANING

1. Juan re__claim__ed his video game from his brother. __reclaimed__
   Meaning: __to get back something lost or taken away__
2. My dad likes to __dict__ate every hour of my weekend activities. __dictate__
   Meaning: __to tell someone what to do__
3. The class president __voc__alized a speech at graduation. __vocalized__
   Meaning: __voiced words or sounds__
4. Jeff __tend__ed his hold on the kite in the strong wind. __tended__
   Meaning: __paid attention to__
5. The fire alarm's inter__rupt__ion of the game caused the students to leave. __interruption__
   Meaning: __causing something to stop from continuing in the normal way__
6. The bullfrog's throat will dis__tend__ each time he croaks. __distend__

In the second activity students select one of the morphemes to complete a word so that the sentence makes sense.

## Latin and Greek Lesson

## Day 10: 2nd Review Day

Day 10 is a culminating review day. Students are provided a list of eighteen words that contain the morphemes taught in the lesson. They select from this list and write five sentences that each contain at least one of the eighteen words.

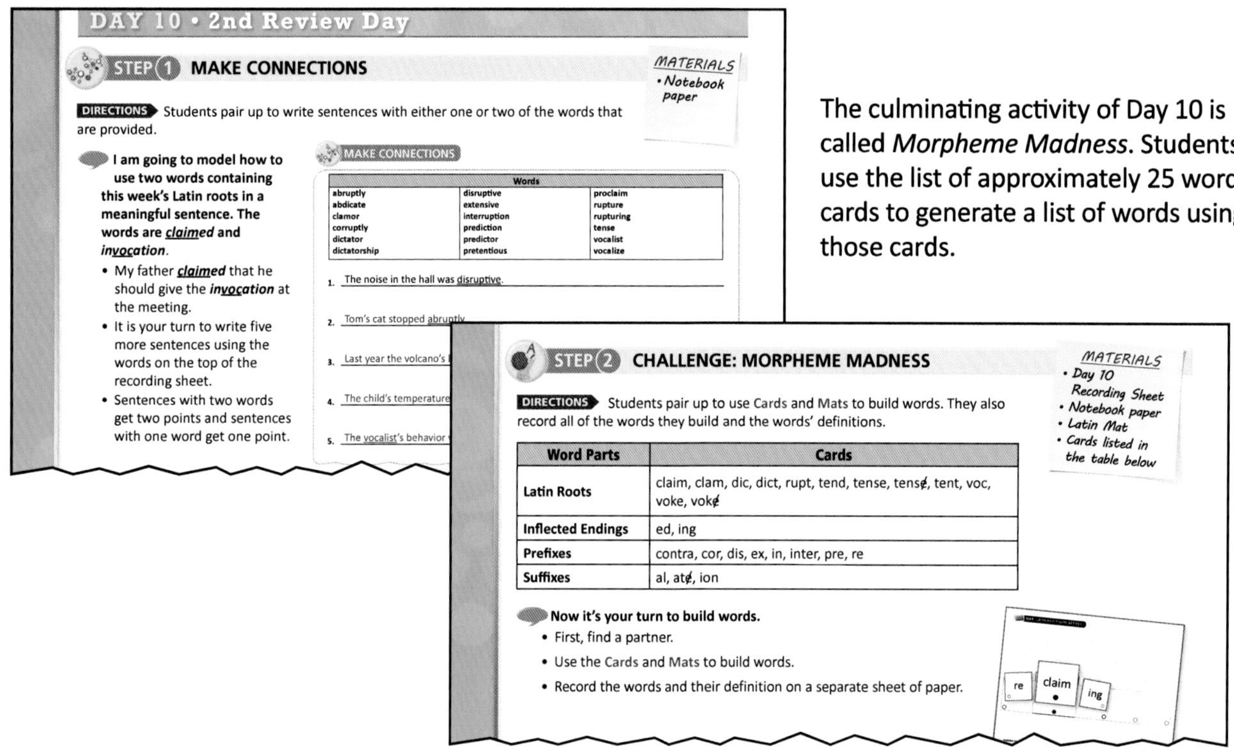

DAY 10 • 2nd Review Day

STEP 1 MAKE CONNECTIONS

MATERIALS
• Notebook paper

DIRECTIONS Students pair up to write sentences with either one or two of the words that are provided.

I am going to model how to use two words containing this week's Latin roots in a meaningful sentence. The words are *claimed* and *invocation*.

- My father ***claimed*** that he should give the ***invocation*** at the meeting.
- It is your turn to write five more sentences using the words on the top of the recording sheet.
- Sentences with two words get two points and sentences with one word get one point.

MAKE CONNECTIONS

| Words | | |
|---|---|---|
| abruptly | disruptive | proclaim |
| abdicate | extensive | rupture |
| clamor | interruption | rupturing |
| corruptly | prediction | tense |
| dictator | predictor | vocalist |
| dictatorship | pretentious | vocalize |

1. The noise in the hall was disruptive.
2. Tom's cat stopped abruptly
3. Last year the volcano's
4. The child's temperature
5. The vocalist's behavior

STEP 2 CHALLENGE: MORPHEME MADNESS

MATERIALS
• Day 10 Recording Sheet
• Notebook paper
• Latin Mat
• Cards listed in the table below

DIRECTIONS Students pair up to use Cards and Mats to build words. They also record all of the words they build and the words' definitions.

| Word Parts | Cards |
|---|---|
| Latin Roots | claim, clam, dic, dict, rupt, tend, tense, tensé, tent, voc, voke, voké |
| Inflected Endings | ed, ing |
| Prefixes | contra, cor, dis, ex, in, inter, pre, re |
| Suffixes | al, até, ion |

Now it's your turn to build words.

- First, find a partner.
- Use the Cards and Mats to build words.
- Record the words and their definition on a separate sheet of paper.



The culminating activity of Day 10 is called *Morpheme Madness*. Students use the list of approximately 25 word cards to generate a list of words using those cards.

## Affix Lesson

## Day 1: Introduce Suffixes

The Latin and Greek lessons follow the format described above. The Affix lessons, which are lessons 1–4, follow an alternate format. Instead of a ten-day lesson where two sets of roots are studied for four days each with two review days, these lessons are five days in length. Additionally the affixes are typically introduced and studied for one day and then the fifth day is a review of all of them.

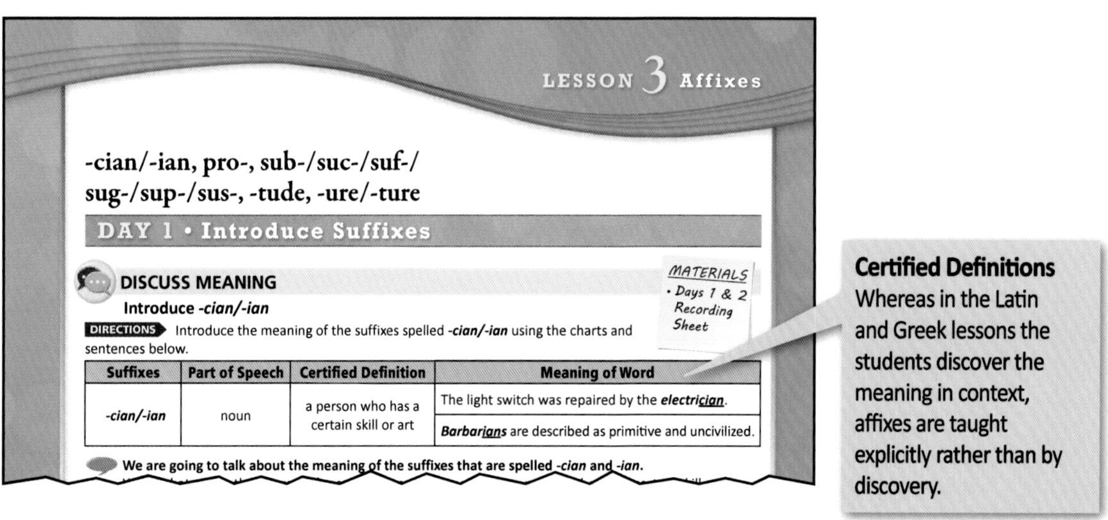

LESSON 3 Affixes

-cian/-ian, pro-, sub-/suc-/suf-/sug-/sup-/sus-, -tude, -ure/-ture

DAY 1 • Introduce Suffixes

DISCUSS MEANING

Introduce *-cian/-ian*

MATERIALS
• Days 1 & 2 Recording Sheet

DIRECTIONS Introduce the meaning of the suffixes spelled *-cian/-ian* using the charts and sentences below.

| Suffixes | Part of Speech | Certified Definition | Meaning of Word |
|---|---|---|---|
| *-cian/-ian* | noun | a person who has a certain skill or art | The light switch was repaired by the ***electrician***. |
| | | | ***Barbarians*** are described as primitive and uncivilized. |

We are going to talk about the meaning of the suffixes that are spelled *-cian* and *-ian*.

**Certified Definitions**

Whereas in the Latin and Greek lessons the students discover the meaning in context, affixes are taught explicitly rather than by discovery.

 

## Affix Lesson
## Day 2: Discuss Meaning

The format of the Day 2 activity differs depending upon the root and how students can learn the meaning best. This is an example of Day 2 where students define the word and finish a partially completed sentence.

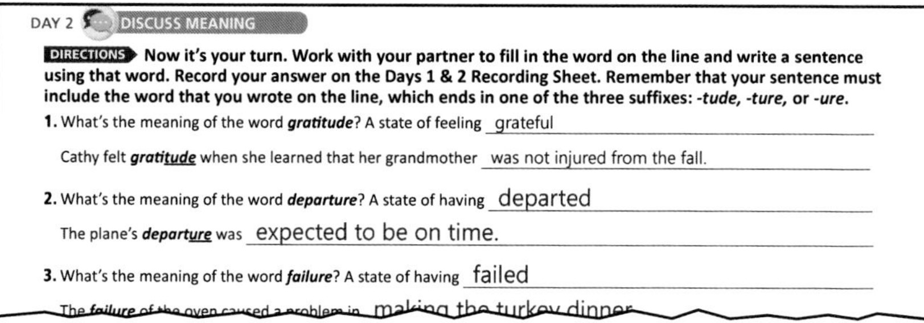
DAY 2 DISCUSS MEANING

**DIRECTIONS** **Now it's your turn. Work with your partner to fill in the word on the line and write a sentence using that word. Record your answer on the Days 1 & 2 Recording Sheet. Remember that your sentence must include the word that you wrote on the line, which ends in one of the three suffixes: *-tude, -ture,* or *-ure*.**

1. What's the meaning of the word ***gratitude***? A state of feeling grateful

   Cathy felt ***gratitude*** when she learned that her grandmother was not injured from the fall.

2. What's the meaning of the word ***departure***? A state of having departed

   The plane's ***departure*** was expected to be on time.

3. What's the meaning of the word ***failure***? A state of having failed

   The ***failure*** of the oven caused a problem in making the turkey dinner

## Affix Lesson
## Day 3: Discuss Meaning

Below is an example of a Day 3 activity where students select the correct word from a list of words provided.

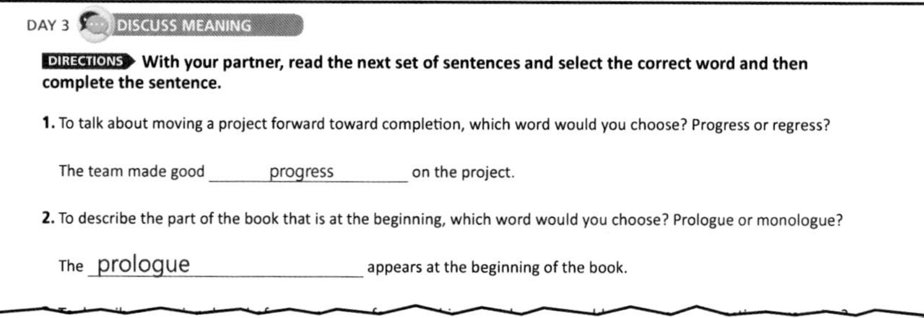
DAY 3 DISCUSS MEANING

**DIRECTIONS** **With your partner, read the next set of sentences and select the correct word and then complete the sentence.**

1. To talk about moving a project forward toward completion, which word would you choose? Progress or regress?

   The team made good progress on the project.

2. To describe the part of the book that is at the beginning, which word would you choose? Prologue or monologue?

   The prologue appears at the beginning of the book.

## Affix Lesson
## Day 4: Discuss Meaning

Activities on this day vary based on the meaning of the affix. Below is an example of a Day 4 activity where the focus is on the meaning of *sub-*, which is *under*. They are instructed to begin their definition with the word *under*.

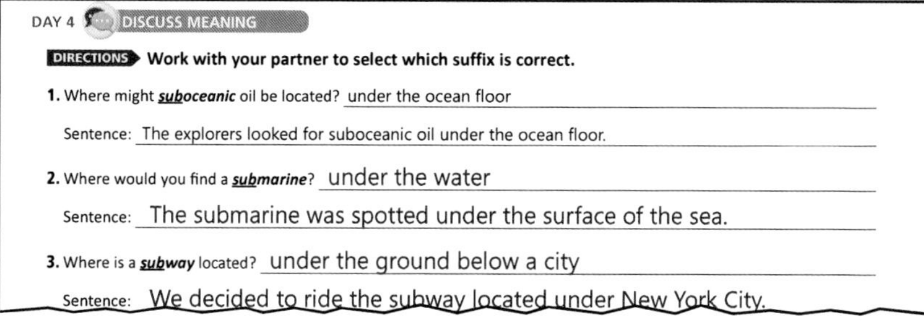
DAY 4 DISCUSS MEANING

**DIRECTIONS** **Work with your partner to select which suffix is correct.**

1. Where might ***suboceanic*** oil be located? under the ocean floor

   Sentence: The explorers looked for suboceanic oil under the ocean floor.

2. Where would you find a ***submarine***? under the water

   Sentence: The submarine was spotted under the surface of the sea.

3. Where is a ***subway*** located? under the ground below a city

   Sentence: We decided to ride the subway located under New York City.

## Affix Lesson
## Day 5: Multiplier

Below is an example of a Day 5 activity where students pair up to use cards and mats to build words.

**DIRECTIONS** **Pair up to use Cards and Mats to build words. Record your words and their meanings.**

| Word Parts | Cards |
|---|---|
| **Bases** | class, fail, floor, group, guard, long, magic, merge, mix, moist, music, plot, press, soil, way (plus country name, Egypt) |
| **Prefixes** | pro, sub, suc, suf, sug, sup, sus |
| **Suffixes** | cian, ian, tude, ure, ture |

Egypt ian

| Word Parts | Word | Part of Speech | Meaning |
|---|---|---|---|
| sub+class | subclass | noun | a class below another class |
| moist+ure | moisture | noun | a state of being moist |
| guard+ian | guardian | noun | a person whose job is to protect someone or something |

## BRIEF OVERVIEW OF THE RESEARCH SUPPORTING THE PRODUCT

### Vocabulary and Morphology

Many experts have written about the vocabulary gap that many students experience and its devastating consequences for their reading achievement. Students reading on grade level learn between 2,000 and 3,000 new words per year. Many students enter kindergarten with a vocabulary that is already behind, and the gap widens as they fail to learn as many words as their peers. In most curriculums teachers provide instruction on 10–20 vocabulary words per week, which would mean students are taught the meanings of approximately 300–600 vocabulary words per academic year. Therefore, they learn most words through context. According to Anderson and Nagy (1992), for many students "the word learning task is enormous".

Not all strategies for learning words are equally effective. Researchers examined the strategies that successful learners use naturally to discover how to help those who are behind in word learning. Teaching individual words is one of the four components but clearly not the one that will result in the highest number of words learned. Of the three other components Graves lists, teaching students how to learn the meaning of unknown words in context is critically important. One of the most important things students can do to figure out a new word is to break it into parts, identify the parts they know, hypothesize a meaning for the unknown piece, and confirm it in context. According to Kieffer and Lesaux (2007), "when it comes to teaching vocabulary, a little knowledge of root words, prefixes, and suffixes goes a long way." (page 134)

Morphology is the study of the meaning-based parts of the language. When students incorporate knowledge of morphemes to make new words it has been described as similar to stringing beads. Yet this traditional view of morphology is under examination, and some researchers propose a newer, more complex cognitive approach that is broader than simply combining parts to make more words. In Jarmulowicz and Taran's article, they propose that morphology cannot be isolated from semantics, syntax, or phonology. They propose that "because morphemes are units of meaning, morphology and the study of the mental lexicon are interconnected." (page 57)

Two definitions of morphological awareness researchers offer are:

- "the awareness of morphemic structure of words and the ability to reflect on that structure" – Wolter and Green (2013), page 27.
- "morphological awareness refers to the ability to consider and manipulate consciously the smallest units of meaning in language." – Apel (2013), page 42.

Morphological awareness (MA) is a metalinguistic skill, and according to Apel (2013), includes several subskills. MA includes an awareness of:

- Spoken and printed forms of morphemes
- The meaning that adding affixes brings to base words (e.g., how *–ed* causes a verb to refer to the past tense or how *re-* means something occurred again)
- The manner in which printed affixes connect to base words (how some suffixes require a consonant to be doubled or dropped when attached to a base word in written form)
- The relation between base words and their inflected or derived forms (knowing that a variety of words are related because they share the same base word, such as act, action, react, and activity)

The research about morphological awareness is that it "develops across time, beginning as early as the kindergarten years and progressing across the elementary school years." (Apel, 2013, page 43) Researcher Virginia Berninger and colleagues have found that students make the most growth in morphological awareness between first and third grade but continue to develop across grades four to six. Kirby et al. (2012) found that morphological awareness can facilitate word-level reading, reading fluency, and reading comprehension. MA influences reading fluency because it supports increasing reading speed.

### Research Findings on the Relationship Between Morphology and Reading Comprehension

There is a reciprocal relationship between vocabulary and reading comprehension. Researcher Keith Stanovich is credited with discussing that the more words a student knows, the better his or her comprehension is likely to be. Additionally when a student's text comprehension is high, it's likely that he or she is learning more vocabulary words from reading. Kieffer and Lesaux (2007) discuss how morphology is related to reading comprehension and how a student's knowledge of morphology is an even stronger predictor of their overall reading comprehension than their vocabulary level.

> We found that morphology was related to reading comprehension in both fourth and fifth grade, and became more important as students grew older. Students with greater understanding of morphology also have higher reading comprehension scores when holding constant their word reading fluency . . . . Students' understanding of morphology was a better predictor of reading comprehension than their vocabulary level. (page 138)

They concluded that breaking down words into meaningful parts is important for both Spanish-speaking ELLs and their native English-speaking classmates.

## Instructional Implications

Many researchers advocate that teaching morphology is a powerful component of reading instruction. Some of the most compelling statements from researchers follow:

> Although there are many ways in which students can understand morphology, the ability to use morphology to attack novel words is the most promising for improving reading comprehension. (Kieffer and Lesaux, 2013, pg. 137)

> The conclusion that students with greater understanding of morphology are more successful at learning academic vocabulary and comprehending text is a strong argument for including morphology instruction in language and literacy programs, especially in urban settings. (Kieffer and Lesaux, 2013, page 139)

Kieffer and Lesaux suggest four guiding principles for instruction. Each is shown below along with comments about how *Vocabulary Surge*™ aligns with these principles.

### Principle 1: Teach morphology in the context of rich, explicit vocabulary instruction.

Instruction should include introducing words in meaningful contexts, providing multiple exposures to the words, and involving students in deep processing of the words' meanings. In *Vocabulary Surge*™ lessons where new morphemes are taught, students are provided words in context of sentences and asked to "Uncover the Meaning." They have to work with the words to develop a hypothesis called a "Working Definition," and then they record the "Certified Definition" when provided by the teacher. There are multiple exposures to the morpheme in many other words, and they engage in thought-provoking and interactive follow-up through the "Multiplier," completing sentences, and categorizing by part of speech.

### Principle 2: Teach students to use morphology as a cognitive strategy with explicit steps.

Researchers Kieffer and Lesaux recommend a 4-step process for teaching morphology. Students:

1. Recognize that they don't know the word or don't have a deep understanding of the word.
2. Analyze the word for morphemes they recognize (both roots and suffixes). May be more difficult if the word is not transparent, particularly if it requires a change in both sound and spelling.
3. Hypothesize a meaning for the word based on the word parts.
4. Check the hypothesis against the context.

*Vocabulary Surge*™ follows this process. Students have to figure out the meaning of an unknown word by using knowledge of previously taught affixes and identifying the meaning of the root or combining forms. They develop hypotheses called "Working Definitions", and state which clues in the context led to the hypothesis.

### Principle 3: Teach the underlying morphological knowledge needed in two ways – both explicitly and in context.

There are three types of knowledge students need to know to use morphology effectively: knowledge of prefixes and suffixes, knowledge of how words get transformed, and knowledge of roots. They say that "students' abilities to extract roots from derived words can be a powerful strategy for acquiring new vocabulary, but only if students know the meanings of the roots" (page 141). In *Vocabulary Surge*™ students first try to uncover the meanings of the morphemes in context, and then they are explicitly taught. The meanings of the most common affixes, roots, and Greek Combining Forms are taught in a carefully planned sequence to assure student success in reading new words.

**Principle 4: For students with developed knowledge of Spanish, teach morphology in relation to cognate instruction.**
Teachers working with students whose primary language is Spanish can make cognate connections during instruction with *Vocabulary Surge*™.

## HISTORY OF THE ENGLISH LANGUAGE

### Old English: 450–1150 C.E.

The Old English period of the language was from 450 to 1150 C.E. when a variety of Germanic groups settled in parts of England. These groups included the Angles, the Saxons, and the Jutes. Anglo-Saxon was the dominant language used during this extensive period. The language focused on words for the events of daily life and objects or people who were part of that life. This period continued until the time of the Norman Conquest when William the Conqueror left Normandy and successfully invaded England, bringing with him the French language. Although the Norman-French language was the official language, English continued as the language of the people. In spite of the fact that the Norman French language never caught on, English did evolve during this period. Latin-based words entered the English language at this time.

### Middle English: 1150–1500

There were substantial changes in English during this shorter period when the language went from predominantly Anglo-Saxon words to an influx of French and Latin words. One expert estimated that more than ten thousand French words were transferred into the English language (Henry, 2010). Some compound words were created with a combination of Anglo and French words. Latin affixes were added to both Anglo-Saxon Base Words and Latin Roots, thereby expanding the number of words exponentially. The French words described food, government, and the arts and brought entirely new spelling patterns to English in words like beautiful, cuisine, baguette, etc. The printing press was developed during this time so there was more attention to consistent spellings.

### Modern English: 1500 to present

English continues to expand during this period, which is known principally for adopting pronunciation and spelling conventions of the melting pot of words adopted into the language. In the early part of this period the "Great Vowel Shift" occurred during which some of the pronunciations from Shakespeare's days were converted. As Marcia Henry (2010) explains in her book, the vowel sound in the word *house* was originally pronounced "hoos," was then converted to /ō/ as in "hose", and finally in the 20th century it became /ou/. As the number of printed books increased, Noah Webster published his first dictionary in the 1780s, and attention focused increasingly on the standardization of spelling. The English language continues to expand today as new words are created. Consider how many technology words didn't exist until quite recently. "Google" is a now used as a verb meaning to search on the internet, "technophobia" has recently emerged, a "blog" is a short informal piece posted on the internet, and "friend" is now used as a verb when expanding one's contacts on a social networking site. As words are incorporated into our language, they eventually are added to the dictionary.

## The Anglo-Saxon Layer of Language

Anglo-Saxon words tend to be short, one-syllable words that describe common, everyday things. Some Anglo-Saxon words are:

- Nature: sky, sun, moon, God, water, man, woman
- Body parts: head, nose, ear, tongue, knee, foot, leg, heart
- Animals: cow, horse, sheep, deer
- Trees: oak, beach, ash

 

The spellings are often irregular, which is problematic because there is a heavy concentration of these words in text that first and second grade students read. Some of the unusual spelling features of these words are silent letters (kn, gn, etc.), vowel teams, consonant digraphs, and dipthongs. Multisyllable words are created by combining two simple words in a compound word (horsefly) or by adding an affix. Anglo-Saxon words also have inflected endings (s, ed, ing).

When the Latin layer entered English, some of the pronunciations and spellings changed (Lever, 2007). One example of a change is that at one time some Anglo-Saxon words had a letter *h* at the beginning of the word, especially in front of the letters *w*, *l*, and *r* (hw, hl, and hr). For example, the word *what* was spelled h-w-a-e-t. The word *ring* was spelled h-r-i-n-g, and the initial /h/ sound was pronounced; the word was /h/ /r/ /i/ /ng/. In some cases the letters were relocated. The word *bird* was spelled b-r-i-d. The letter *r* was relocated in the word.

## The Latin Layer of Language

Latin is the language that is the basis of romance languages such as French and Spanish. It includes words that are completely different from the Anglo-Saxon layer. Although the Anglo-Saxon words tend to be short, one-syllable words, Latin words are multisyllabic because they must include a root and at least one affix (a prefix or a suffix). Anglo-Saxon words describe common things; in contrast, Latin words include more advanced content words found in social science, physical science, and literature.

The spelling of Latin words is more predictable and easier than Anglo-Saxon in many cases. Vowel teams rarely appear in Latin Roots, yet can appear in some suffixes such as *-ion*, *-ial*, or *-ient*. The primary syllable type found in Latin words is closed, whereas Anglo-Saxon words can include any of the six syllable types.

There are a few other notable spelling and pronunciation complexities of Latin words. One spelling complexity is that the final letter in a Latin morpheme often changes depending upon the letters at the juncture between the affix and the root. For example, the final consonant of a Latin prefix can change to sound better when combined with the root. An example of this is when the prefix in the word *inlegal* is changed to *illegal* because it sounds better and is easier to pronounce. There are also many rules for changing letters before adding a suffix ending; sometimes the final consonant is doubled, a final letter is changed from y to i, or a final silent e is dropped before adding an ending that starts with a vowel. One of the most complex aspects of Latin words is that the stressed syllable can change, which can result in a change in pronunciation. An example of this is when the word *medical* changes to *medicinal*.

## The Greek Layer of Language

Greek words are formed by combining two or more morphemes to make a word. Greek morphemes are known as Greek Combining Forms and can appear in multiple positions in the word (biography, antibiotic). This is in contrast to Latin words that have a bound root that cannot stand alone and is positioned in the middle if there is both a prefix and a suffix. Although the construction of Greek words is similar to compounding an Anglo-Saxon word, one important difference is that the Greek Combining Forms don't stand alone like base words in Anglo-Saxon do; for example, *tele* and *photo* (telephoto) don't stand alone while *air* and *plane* (airplane) do.

A large majority of Greek words that have been incorporated into English relate to science, including medicine, and mathematics. There are several distinct spellings that signal the word's Greek origin, including the letters *ch* for /k/, *ph* for /f/, and *y* for /ĭ/ or /ī/. Example words that include these spellings are photosynthesis, chronic, geophysical and psychology. There are many mathematical words that incorporate the Greek Combining Forms for numbers including, mono (1), di (2), tri (3), etc. Other common Greek Combining Forms are *bio* (life), *mania* (madness), *ology/logy* (the study of), *phobia* (irrational fear or hatred), *syn* (together or with), and *graph* (written or drawn).

## REFERENCES

Apel, K, et. al., (2013). Using multiple measures of morphological awareness to assess its relation to reading. *Topics in Language Disorders*, 33, No. 1, 42-56.

Graves, Michael (2006). *The Vocabulary Book: Learning and Instruction*. (New York, NY: Teacher's College Press)

Henry, Marcia (2010). *Unlocking Literacy: Effective Decoding & Spelling Instruction*. 2nd edition. (Baltimore, MD: Paul H. Brookes)

Jarmulowicz, L. and Taran, V. (2013). Lexical morphology: structure, process, and development. *Topics in Language Disorders*, 33, No. 1, 57-72.

Kieffer, M. and Lesaux, N., (2007). Breaking down words to build meaning: morphology, vocabulary, and reading comprehension in the urban classroom. *The Reading Teacher*, 61 (2), pages 134-144.

Kirby, J. R., et.al. (2012). Children's morphological awareness and reading ability. *Reading Writing: An Interdisciplinary Journal*, 24, 389-410.

Lever, Seth. (2007). *Inventing English*. Columbia University Press, NY, NY.

Wolter, J, and Green, L. (2013). Morphological awareness intervention in school-age children with language and literacy deficits: a case study. *Topics in Language Disorders*, 33, No. 1, 27-41.

# Affix Mat

## Introduction

MATERIALS
- Whiteboards and markers
- Affix Mat
- Cards:

Teacher:
Lesson 3 cards: class, group, mix, moist, impress
Prefixes: re, un
Suffix: ify

### Introduce the Mat for use with Latin Affixes

**The English language is several layers of language that were combined over time. We're going to talk about how those layers affect our language, and how we'll use a mat and word cards to study the layers of language.**

**First let's talk about the layers of language.**

- There are three main layers of the English language. They are Anglo-Saxon, Latin, and Greek.
- The oldest layer of the English language is the Anglo-Saxon layer. This first layer contains simple short words for everyday things like the words *bird, girl, mother, pig, sheep,* and *moon*. Although these everyday words are some of the earliest words spoken and read in books, many of these Anglo-Saxon words have unusual spellings that don't follow the rules of other words.
- One of the ways to build a longer word is to combine two short words into a compound word. Although each of these words can stand alone, they are combined to make compound words such as *cowboy, birdhouse, airplane,* and *hotdog*.
- There is a second way to build longer words with Anglo-Saxon simple words. Instead of putting two stand-alone words together to form a compound word, it's possible to add a Latin prefix in front of an Anglo-Saxon word or a suffix behind an Anglo-Saxon word. The Latin layer was the second layer, and over time English speakers began to add the Latin prefixes and suffixes to Anglo-Saxon words to build even more words.
- When a Latin prefix is added to an Anglo-Saxon base word, the meaning of the word changes. For example, the Latin prefix ***mid-*** can be added to the Anglo-Saxon word ***day*** to create the new word ***midday***. When ***mid-*** is added to the beginning of ***night*** it creates the word ***midnight***; the prefix ***-mid*** means middle, and ***midnight*** means middle of the night.
- Suffixes can also be added to the end of Anglo-Saxon words. The suffix ***-ful*** means full of. When ***-ful*** is added to the Anglo-Saxon word ***hope***, the new word is ***hopeful*** and it means full of hope.

**Now let's talk about the mat and word cards we'll use.**

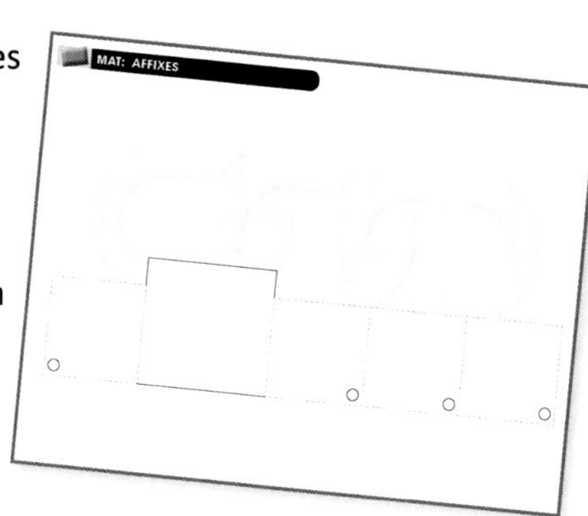


- Look at this mat. There is an image in the background. What does it look like? Links that are hooked together. That's to remind us that when we build words, word parts are connected to make larger words. The meanings are also connected together.
- Now look at the boxes on the mat. Are they all the same size? No That's right, there is one large box and smaller boxes on each side of it.
- Look inside the boxes at the dots. Are they all the same? No The large box doesn't have a dot. The smaller box in front of it has a small circle in the bottom left corner to remind us that it

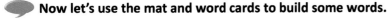

comes before the large box. This is where a prefix goes. The smaller box on the right side of the large box also has a circle that is not filled in and is located in the bottom right corner to remind us that this comes after the large box. This is where a suffix goes. Notice that there can be more than one suffix in the words we'll be building.

**Now let's use the mat and word cards to build some words.**

I DO • Watch me build the word ***ungroup***.

- The Anglo-Saxon word ***group*** is the base word. It goes in the large box in the center of the Affix Mat. The prefix ***un-*** comes first in the word, so it comes first on this Mat. I place it in the box to the left of the word ***group***, matching the open circle on the card to the one on the Mat. The new word is ***ungroup***. The word means not to group.
- I can build some more words on the mat. Unclass, unmix, unmoist, unimpress
- Let's brainstorm a list of words that contain the prefix ***un-***. Unable, unaware, unclean, unfair, unfit, unhappy, unknown, unlike, unlucky, unsafe, unusual, or unwise

WE DO Help me build the word ***reclassify*** on this Affix Mat.

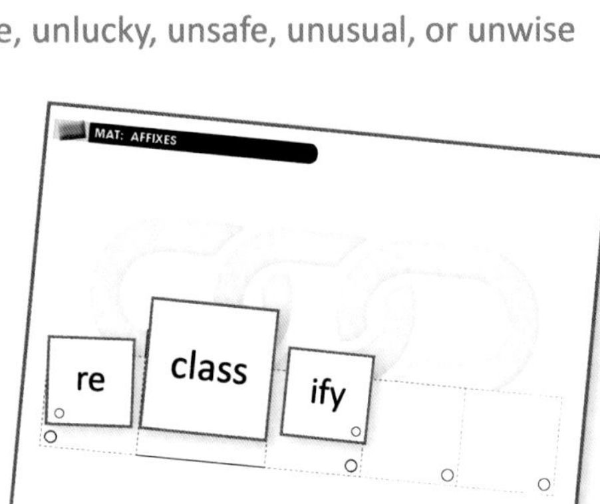


- Where shall I place the word ***class***? In the large center box
- Why do I place it there? Because it is the base word
- Where shall I place the prefix card ***re-***? In the box on the left side of the mat
- Why do I place it there? Because it is a prefix and the circle on the card matches the circle on the mat
- What word have I built so far? Reclass
- Where shall I place the card ***-ify***? In the box on the right side of the mat, next to mark
- Why do I place it there? Because it is a suffix and the circle on the card matches the circle on the mat
- What word have I built so far? Reclassify

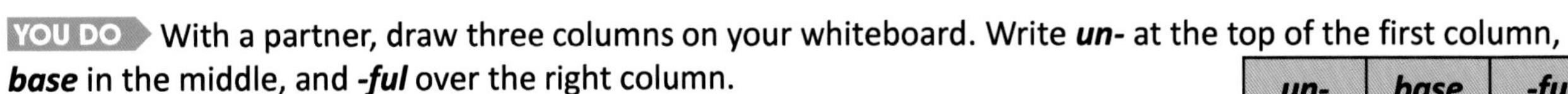

YOU DO With a partner, draw three columns on your whiteboard. Write ***un-*** at the top of the first column, ***base*** in the middle, and ***-ful*** over the right column.

| *un-* | *base* | *-ful* |
|---|---|---|
| un | clean | |

- What's the definition of the prefix ***un-***? Not
- What's the definition of the suffix ***-ful***. Full of
- Write some two syllable words you know that include either the prefix ***un-*** or the suffix ***-ful***. Let's do the first one together. For the word ***unclean***, the prefix ***un-*** is in the first column and the base ***clean*** is in the middle.
- Now take turns reading the words with your partner.
- Share the meanings and your list of words with the class.

---

- You will be using this Affix Mat and Cards in the next four lessons.

PROMPT IDEAS Prefix ***un-***
- unable, uncertain, unfair, unfit, unhappy, unjust, unknown, unlucky, unrest, unsafe, unskilled, unusual, unwise

PROMPT IDEAS Suffix ***-ful***
- Awful, bashful, beautiful, careful, doubtful, forgetful, grateful, harmful, hateful, hopeful, painful, truthful, wishful

 

# -an/-ian, -ary/-ery/-ory, -ese, -cious/-ious/-ous/-tious

## DAY 1 • Introduce Suffixes

MATERIALS
• Days 1 & 2 Recording Sheet

### DISCUSS MEANING

**Introduce *-an/-ian,* and *-ese***

**DIRECTIONS** Introduce the meaning of the suffixes spelled ***-an/-ian,*** and ***-ese*** using the charts and sentences below.

| Suffix | Part of Speech | Certified Definition | Meaning of Word |
|---|---|---|---|
| ***-an/-ian/-ese*** | noun or adjective | a person or describing a person | An ***American*** is a citizen of the United States. |

**We are going to talk about the meaning of the suffixes that are spelled *-an/-ian* and *-ese*.**

- Most of the time these three suffixes refer to the nation, city, or region where a person was born. Examples include American, Minnesotan, or Chinese. When the name of a country, city, or region ends in a vowel letter, sometimes the vowel is dropped before adding the suffix. For example, America ends in the vowel letter *a* so the final *a* is dropped before adding the suffix ***-an***, which begins with a vowel. There are no rules about how to choose which of the three suffixes to use.
- Words with the suffix ***-an*** and ***-ian*** also can refer to a descriptive word about a person. Examples include humanitarian, suburban, or vegetarian.
- Words such as ***American*** can be used either as a noun or an adjective.

**I DO** Listen as I read these sentences using the word ***American***.

- **Noun.** I am proud to be an ***American***.
- **Adjective.** We learned about the ***American*** culture during the 1920s.

**WE DO** Let's do the next ones together. After listening to each sentence, answer whether the focus word is a noun or an adjective.

- The ***Japanese*** suffered a major Tsunami in 2012. Is ***Japanese*** a noun or an adjective? Noun
- The ***Bostonian*** pride was evident at the Red Sox game. Is ***Bostonian*** a noun or an adjective? Adjective
- The ***vegetarian*** menu included many soups. Is ***vegetarian*** a noun or an adjective? Adjective
- The ***humanitarians*** are leading a march on Capitol Hill. Is ***humanitarians*** a noun or an adjective? Noun

**YOU DO** Listen to the sentence and then answer two questions. In the sentence is the focus word a noun or adjective? What does the word with the suffix ***-an, -ian,*** or ***-ese*** mean in the sentence?

- The ***Chinese*** New Year was celebrated with a huge parade. Is ***Chinese*** a noun or adjective in this sentence? Adjective What is the meaning of ***Chinese*** in this sentence? It is relating to the country of China.

Now it's your turn. Work with your partner to determine if the underlined word is used as an adjective or a noun in the sentence. Then write the meaning of the word. Record your answers on the **Days 1 & 2 Recording Sheet**.

**DISCUSS MEANING**

1. The Chinese New Year was celebrated with a huge parade? Chinese
   Is Chinese a noun or adjective in this sentence? Adjective
   What is the meaning of Chinese in this sentence? It is relating to the country of China.
2. The Canadians cheered aggressively for their hockey team. Is Canadians a noun or adjective? noun
   Write a meaning for the word Canadians in this sentence. citizens of Canada
3. The family lived in a suburban neighborhood. Is suburban a noun or adjective? adjective
   Write a meaning for the word suburban in this sentence. a neighborhood that is located in the suburbs
4. The Austrian hiker was very fit. Is Austrian a noun or adjective? adjective
   Write a meaning for the word Austrian in this sentence. a citizen of Austria
5. The delicious pasta dish was made by an Italian. Is Italian a noun or adjective? noun
   Write a meaning for the word Italian in this sentence. a citizen of Italy
6. The Veteran's Day holiday honors those who served our country. Is Veteran a noun or adjective? adjective
   Write a meaning for the word Veteran in this sentence. a former soldier

# DAY 2 • Introduce Suffixes

## DISCUSS MEANING

### Introduce *-ary/-ery/-ory*

MATERIALS
- Days 1 & 2 Recording Sheet

**DIRECTIONS** Introduce the meaning of the suffixes spelled ***-ary/-ery,*** and ***-ory*** using the charts and sentences below.

| Suffix | Part of Speech | Certified Definition | Meaning of Word |
|---|---|---|---|
| *-ary/-ery/ -ory* | noun or adjective | relating to, quality, or place where | A person who is not afraid shows ***bravery***. |

**We are going to talk about the two meanings of the suffix spelled *-ary/-ery/-ory*.**

- When the suffixes ***-ant*** and ***-ent*** are at the end of a noun, the word refers to a person or thing. Examples include the words ***adolescent, agent, informant, lieutenant,*** and ***resident***.
- These suffixes can mean several different things. One meaning is a place where something is made or happens. Examples include the words ***bakery, refinery,*** or ***hatchery***.
- Other times when these three suffixes appear in a noun, it is not about a place but the meaning is less clear. Examples include the words ***category, memory,*** and ***territory***.
- Finally, these three suffixes can also appear in adjectives where the meaning is often a description of a behavior. Examples include the words ***compulsory, mandatory,*** or ***satisfactory***.

**I DO** I'll read two sentences and identify the word with one of the suffixes we're studying at the end of the word. Then I'll tell you whether the word with the suffix ***-ary/-ery/-ory*** is a noun or an adjective.

- The rare fish were hatched in a ***fishery***. Is ***fishery*** a noun or an adjective?
  - A ***fishery*** is a place where fish are bred. It is a noun in this sentence.
- The confused referee gave ***contradictory*** calls. Is ***contradictory*** a noun or adjective?
  - ***Contradictory*** means opposite or inconsistent. It is an adjective in this sentence.

**WE DO** Listen as I read these sentences. Be prepared to tell me whether the focus word with the suffixes ***-ary/-ery/-ory*** is a noun or an adjective in the sentence.

- The cougar's ***predatory*** behavior worried the smaller animals. Is ***predatory*** a noun or adjective? Adjective
- The goal was to place objects in the proper ***category***. Is ***category*** a noun or adjective? Noun
- My grandmother's ***memory*** was starting to fail. Is ***memory*** a noun or adjective? Noun
- Attendance at the meeting was ***compulsory***. Is ***compulsory*** a noun or adjective? Adjective

**YOU DO** With your partner, write five sentences each of which includes one word from the list below. The first three sentences must include one word from each of the three categories. The last two sentences can use any other words you select. Record your sentences on a **Days 1 & 2 Recording Sheet**.

DISCUSS MEANING

| Nouns | | Adjectives |
|---|---|---|
| Column 1 - Places | Column 2 - Other | Column 3 - Descriptive Words |
| armory, bakery, confectionary, hatchery, nursery, refinery, tannery | category, directory, history, inventory, memory, territory | advisory, auditory, compulsory, contradictory, defamatory, exclamatory, mandatory, predatory, satisfactory, sensory supervisory |

Include word from Column 1
1. The smells from the bakery were wonderful.

Include word from Column 2
2. We looked for a directory of stores in the mall.

Include word from Column 3
3. Jack's statement was defamatory about Suzie's character.

Include word from any column
4. My grandmother had a huge inventory of buttons.

Include word from any column
5. We felt sensory overload at the theme park.

 

## -cious/-ious/-ous/-tious

## DAY 3 • Introduce Suffixes

### DISCUSS MEANING

MATERIALS
- Days 3 & 4 Recording Sheet

#### Introduce *-cious/-ious/-ous/-tious*

**DIRECTIONS** Introduce the meaning of the suffixes spelled ***-ous, -cious, -ious,*** and ***-tious*** using the charts and sentences below.

| Suffix | Part of Speech | Certified Definition | Meaning of Word |
|---|---|---|---|
| *-cious/ -ious/ -ous/ -tious* | adjective | Possessing, full of, having | The ***mysterious*** box was full of mystery. |

**We are going to talk about the meanings of the suffixes spelled *-cious/-ious/-ous/-tious*.** These suffixes, which are found in adjectives, mean possessing, full of, or having.

**I DO** Listen as I generate adjectives that contain the suffix ***-cious, -ious, -ous,*** or ***-tious***.

1. If someone has a lot of fame, I'd change fame to ***famous*** to make it an adjective. Famous person
2. If a letter raises ***suspicion***, I'd change ***suspicion*** to ***suspicious*** to make it an adjective. Suspicious letter

**WE DO** Let's do the next ones together.

- If someone has an illness that can be caught by others, which is the correct phrase? Infectious illness, or infect illness? Infectious illness
- If something has to be done with caution, which is the correct phrase? Cautious step, or caution step? Cautious step
- If someone is speculating on the answer, which is the correct phrase? Speculating answer, or speculatory answer? Speculatory answer

**YOU DO** Listen to this sentence and select the phrase that is correct.

1. If you wanted to describe someone who is well known, which phrase would be correct?
   a. He is fame.
   b. He is famous.

- Now it's your turn. Work with your partner to select which sentence is correct. Circle your answer on the **Days 3 & 4 Recording Sheet.**

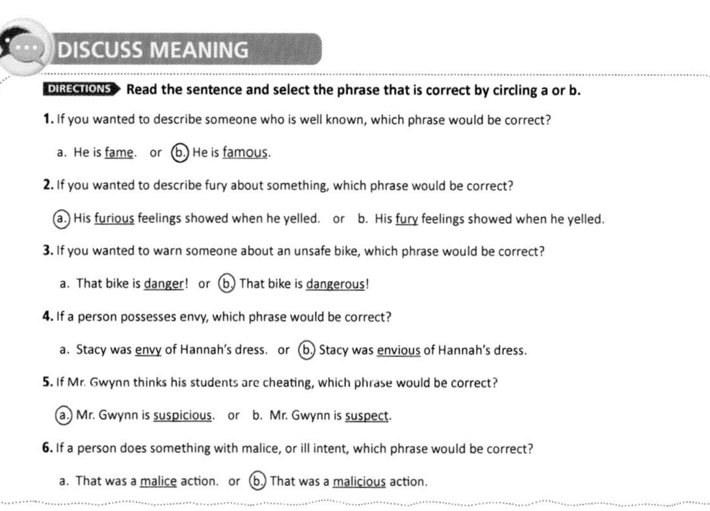

DISCUSS MEANING

**DIRECTIONS** **Read the sentence and select the phrase that is correct by circling a or b.**

1. If you wanted to describe someone who is well known, which phrase would be correct?
   a. He is fame. or (b.) He is famous.
2. If you wanted to describe fury about something, which phrase would be correct?
   (a.) His furious feelings showed when he yelled. or b. His fury feelings showed when he yelled.
3. If you wanted to warn someone about an unsafe bike, which phrase would be correct?
   a. That bike is danger! or (b.) That bike is dangerous!
4. If a person possesses envy, which phrase would be correct?
   a. Stacy was envy of Hannah's dress. or (b.) Stacy was envious of Hannah's dress.
5. If Mr. Gwynn thinks his students are cheating, which phrase would be correct?
   (a.) Mr. Gwynn is suspicious. or b. Mr. Gwynn is suspect.
6. If a person does something with malice, or ill intent, which phrase would be correct?
   a. That was a malice action. or (b.) That was a malicious action.

**-an/-ian, -ary/-ery/-ory, -ese, -cious/-ious/-ous/-tious**

# DAY 4 • Review Suffixes

## DISCUSS MEANING

MATERIALS
- Days 3 & 4 Recording Sheet

**DIRECTIONS** Review the meaning of the suffixes using the chart and sentences below.

| Suffix | Part of Speech | Certified Definition |
|---|---|---|
| -an/-ian | noun or adjective | a person, or describing a person |
| -ary/-ery/-ory | adjective | relating to, quality, or place where |
| -ese | noun or adjective | a person, or describing a person |
| -cious/-ious/-ous/-tious | adjective | possessing, full of, or having |

**Now we'll review the ten suffixes *-an/-ian, -ary/-ery/-ory, -ese, -cious/-ious/-ous/-tious*.**

**I DO** Listen as I determine which suffix is the correct one.

1. To change the word ***mystery*** to describe something related to intrigue, which suffix is correct?
   - The options are ***-ious, -ese, -an***. -ious
   - What is the new word? Mysterious

**WE DO** Let's do the next one together. Choose the suffix and say the new word.

- To change the word ***danger*** to fit in this phrase "the _______ gangster", which suffix is correct?
  ***-ary, -ster, -ous*** *-ous* Say the word: dangerous
- To change the word ***Austria*** to fit in this phrase "the _______ team", which suffix is correct?
  ***-ese, -an, -ous*** *-ian* Say the word: Austrian
- To change the word ***civil*** to fit in this phrase "the lawful ________", which suffix is correct?
  ***-ese, -ian, -ory*** *-ian* Say the word: civilian
- To change the word ***bake*** to fit in this phrase "the popular ______", which suffix is correct?
  ***-ese, -ious, -ery*** *-ery* Say the word: bakery

**YOU DO** Listen to the question and think of which option is correct.

- To change the word ***Sudan*** to describe something related to the country, which suffix is correct?
  - The options are -or, -ese, -an -ese
  - What's the new word? Sudanese

Now it's your turn. Work with your partner to select which suffix is correct. Record your answer on the **Days 3 & 4 Recording Sheet.**

**DISCUSS MEANING**

**DIRECTIONS** **Work with your partner to select which suffix is correct and write the word.**

1. To change the word ***Sudan*** to describe something related to the country, which suffix is correct?
   *-or, -ese, -an* -ese Sudanese
2. To change the word ***fame*** to fit in this phrase "the __________ actress", which is the correct suffix?
   *-ese, -ous, -ian* -ous famous
3. To change the word ***sense*** to fit in this phrase "the _________ experience", which is the correct suffix?
   *ese, -ory, -ory* -ory sensory
4. To change the word ***danger*** to fit in this phrase "the _________ gangster", which is the correct suffix?
   *-ary, -ster, -ous* -ous dangerous
5. To change the word ***Japan*** to fit in this phrase "some _________ sushi", which suffix do you use?
   *-ese, -cious, -tious* -ese Japanese
6. To change the word ***joy*** to mean full of happiness, which is the correct suffix?
   *-cious, -ese, -ous* -ous joyous

 

# -an/-ian, -ary/-ery/-ory, -ese-, -cious/-ious/-ous/-tious

## DAY 5 • Review

### WORD MULTIPLIER

MATERIALS
- Day 5 Recording Sheet
- Affixes Mat
- Cards listed in the table below

**DIRECTIONS** Students work together to build words using their **Cards** and **Mats**. They also record all of the words they build and the words' definitions on the **Day 5 Recording Sheet**.

| Word Parts | Cards |
|---|---|
| **Suffixes** | an, ary, cious, ery, ese, ian, ious, ory, ous, tious |
| **Bases** | fish, hatch |
| **Latin Roots** | fact, judic, puls, sens, tent |
| **Place Names** | America, Japan |
| **Prefixes** | com, pre |
| **Connecting Letter** | i |

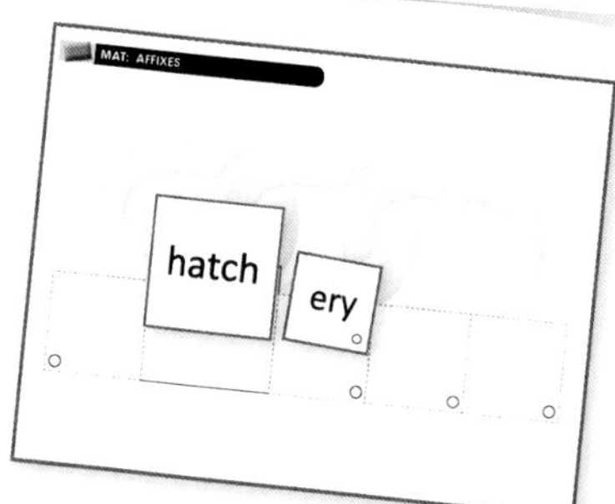


**Now it's your turn to build words.**
- First, find a partner.
- Use the **Cards** and **Mats** to build words.
- Record the words and their definitions on the **Day 5 Recording Sheet**.

WORD MULTIPLIER

| Word Parts | Word | Meaning |
|---|---|---|
| sub+class | subclass | a class below another class |
| hatch + ery | hatchery | a place where animals hatch |
| America + an | American | a citizen of America |
| fact + ory | factory | a place where goods are manufactured |
| pre + tent + ious | pretentious | an attitude of self-importance, sometimes undeserved |
| judic + iary | judiciary | a system of courts of justice in a country |
| com + puls + ory | compulsory | required |
| sens + ory | sensory | relating to the senses (hearing, sight, smell, taste, or touch) |
| Japan + ese | Japanese | a citizen of Japan |

# -ance/-ence, -ancy/-ency, -ant/-ent, -ile, -ine, -ster

## DAY 1 • Introduce Suffixes

MATERIALS
- Days 1 & 2 Recording Sheet

### DISCUSS MEANING

**Introduce *-ance/-ence* and *-ancy/-ency***

**DIRECTIONS** Introduce the meaning of the suffixes spelled ***-ance/-ence*** and ***-ancy/-ency*** using the charts and sentences below.

| Suffix | Part of Speech | Certified Definition | Meaning of Word |
|---|---|---|---|
| ***-ance/-ence***<br>***-ancy/-ency*** | noun | the state or quality of something | ***Fluency*** is the ability to do something in a smooth, flowing manner. |

**We are going to talk about the meaning of the suffixes that are spelled *-ance/-ence* and *-ancy/-ency*.**

- Words that end in these four suffixes are nouns, and they refer to a state or quality of something.
- When someone is ***hesitant*** to do something, he is in a state of ***hesitancy***.
- To change the word ***hesitant***, I drop the ***-ant*** ending and add either the suffix ***-ance*** or ***-ancy***; both endings work with some words, and sometimes only one ending works.

**I DO** Listen as I read these sentences using the nouns ***arrogant*** and ***dominant***.

- **Arrogant**. The word that means a state or quality of being ***arrogant*** is ***arrogance***.
  - Carol is ***arrogant*** about her speech. Her ***arrogance*** bothers her friends.
- **Dominant.** The word that means a state or quality of being ***dominant*** is ***dominance*** or ***dominancy***.
  - Juan is the team's ***dominant*** outside hitter. His ***dominance*** shows in the volleyball game statistics.

**WE DO** Let's do the next ones together. Say the noun or nouns that answer the question.

- What's a word that means a state or quality of being ***brilliant***? brilliance or brilliancy
- What's a word that means a state or quality of being ***insistent***? insistence
- What's a word that means a state or quality of being ***relevant***? relevance or relevancy
- What's a word that means a state or quality of being ***intolerant***? intolerance

**YOU DO** Listen to the question and think of what word fits. Then use it in a sentence.

- What's the word that means a state or quality of being ***dependent***? ***dependence*** or ***dependency***
- Use the word ***dependency*** in a sentence about the puppy's need for its mother.
  1. Naomi's ***dependent*** puppy was still in the stage of ***dependency*** on the mother dog.

Now it's your turn. Get your **Days 1 & 2 Recording Sheet** and let's review the directions.

**DISCUSS MEANING**

**DIRECTIONS In the sentences below there are two blanks, and a pair of words. With your partner, determine which word fits in each blank and fill them in to complete the sentence.**

1. **dependent**: (adj.) relying on someone else for help — **dependency**: (n.) the state of being independent

   Naomi's dependent puppy was still in the stage of dependency on the mother dog.
2. **confident**: (adj.) sure of oneself — **confidence**: (n.) the state of being confident

   John's confidence in Josie's work resulted from her confident manner.
3. **patient**: (adj.) being calm even with delays — **patience**: (n.) the state of being patient

   Mom's patience was about to run out after she had been patient all day.
4. **tolerant**: (adj.) allowing or permitting — **tolerance**: (n.) the state of being tolerant

   The coach's tolerant rules about being late for practice showed his tolerance for tardiness.
5. **elegant**: (adj.) having excellent quality — **elegance**: (n.) a state of elegant quality

   Joan's elegant gold dress showed her sense of elegance.
6. **urgent**: (adj.) requiring immediate attention — **urgency**: (n.) a state of requiring immediate attention

   There is an urgency to call the veterinarian to get the horse urgent care for his leg.

# -ant/-ent

## DAY 2 • Introduce Suffixes

### DISCUSS MEANING

MATERIALS
- Days 1 & 2 Recording Sheet

**Introduce *-ant/-ent***

**DIRECTIONS** Introduce the meaning of the suffixes spelled ***-ant*** and ***-ent*** using the charts and sentences below.

| Suffix | Part of Speech | Certified Definition | Meaning of Word |
|---|---|---|---|
| *-ant/-ent* | noun | a person or thing | A person who is a ***servant***. |
| | adjective | a state or quality | Something that can be seen through is ***transparent***. |

**We are going to talk about the two meanings of the suffix spelled *-ant/-ent*.**

- When the suffixes ***-ant*** and ***-ent*** are at the end of a noun, the word refers to a person or thing. Examples include adolescent, agent, informant, lieutenant, and resident.
- When the suffix ***-ent*** and ***-ant*** appear at the end of an adjective, the word describes a state of something. Examples include abundant, arrogant, flippant, indulgent, and affluent.

**I DO** Listen as I read these sentences using the adjectives ***decadent*** and ***dominant***.

- **Decadent.** The adjective that means a state or quality of ***decadence*** is ***decadent***.
  - Jessica's ***decadent*** habits were self-indulgent. Her ***decadence*** was beyond belief.
- **Resilience.** The adjective that means a state or quality of showing ***resiliency*** is ***resilient***.
  - Bradley was a ***resilient*** shooter. His ***resilience*** paid off as he sunk many baskets in spite of missing often.

**WE DO** Let's do the next ones together. Say the word that answers the question.

- What's the noun for a person who sells ***merchandise***? merchant
- What's the adjective to describe someone ***neglecting*** his duties? negligent
- What's the adjective for a state of ***magnificence***? magnificent
- What's the adjective for feeling a state of ***buoyancy***? buoyant

**YOU DO** Listen to the question and think of what word fits. The word is then used in a sentence.

- What's the noun for a person who ***resides*** in a home? ***resident***
- Use the word ***resident*** in a sentence about a person who lives in an apartment.
  1. The apartment's ***resident*** had a great view of the nearby pond.

Now it's your turn. Work with your partner to fill in the word on the line and write a sentence using that word. Record your answer on the **Days 1 & 2 Recording Sheet**. Remember that your sentence must include the word that you wrote on the line, which ends in one of the two suffixes: ***-ant, -ent***.

**DISCUSS MEANING**

**DIRECTIONS** **Work with a partner to fill in the word on the line and write a sentence using that word.**

1. What's the noun for a person who resides in a home? resident
   Use the word resident in a sentence about a person who lives in an apartment. The apartment's ***resident*** had a great view of the nearby pond.
2. What's the noun for a person who is studying? student
   Write a sentence about a student. The student paid attention.
3. What's the noun for a person who enters a contest? contestant
   Write a sentence about someone who's entered a contest. The game's contestant was excited.
4. What's the adjective for the state of showing violence? violent
   Sentence: His violent behavior got him in trouble.
5. What's the adjective that describes a state of obeying someone else? obedient
   Sentence: The dog was obedient.
6. What's the adjective for a state of inconsistency? inconsistent
   Sentence: His inconsistent dives made him lose points.

# DAY 3 • Introduce Suffixes

## DISCUSS MEANING

MATERIALS
• Days 3 & 4 Recording Sheet

### Introduce *-ile, -ine*

**DIRECTIONS** Introduce the meaning of the suffixes spelled *-ile* and *-ine* using the charts and sentences below.

| Suffix | Part of Speech | Certified Definition | Meaning of Word |
|---|---|---|---|
| *-ile* | noun | person or thing | The blue ***textile*** was used to make a bedspread. |
| | adjective | relating to, suited for, capable of | The butterfly wings are too ***fragile*** to touch. |
| *-ine* | noun | person or thing | Leopards and cheetahs are both ***felines*** because they are part of the cat family. |

**We are going to talk about the two meanings of the suffixes spelled *-ile* or *-ine*.**

- When the suffixes *-ile* or *-ine* appear in nouns, they refer to a person or thing. Examples include automobile, reptile, gasoline, and submarine.
- When the suffix *-ile* appears at the end of an adjective, the word changes to mean relating to, suited for, or capable of. Examples include fragile, sterile, hostile, and versatile. These words describe other things.

**I DO** Listen as I discuss two adjectives that end in the suffix *-ile* or *-ine*. The first word is ***agile***, which means to be quick and well-coordinated. The second word is ***divine***, which is related to religion or a God-like deity.

1. What's an adjective to describe someone who is quick and well-coordinated? ***agile***
   - The ***agile*** doe jumped over the fallen tree branch.
2. What's an adjective describing something related to religion or God? ***divine***
   - The religious scholar had a ***divine*** spirituality.

**WE DO** Let's do the next ones together. After each question you'll hear two options. Select the word that best fits.

- A woman who carried the child from a burning house is known as which noun? Heroine or masculine?
- A hospital operating room that is free of germs is described by which adjective? Sterile or fragile?
- Soil that produces an abundance of crops is described by which adjective? Mobile or fertile?
- Which adjective describes a nation that is not friendly with another nation? Immobile or hostile?

**YOU DO** Now it's your turn.

- With your partner, read the next set of sentences on the **Days 3 & 4 Recording Sheet.**
- In the box you'll see some words listed. Select a word from the box that best completes each sentence. One hint is to consider whether the missing word should be a noun or adjective, which limits the possibilities to one row or the other.

| Words with the Suffix *-ile* or *-ine* | |
|---|---|
| Nouns | heroine, missile, reptile, submarine, tambourine, textile, vaccine |
| Adjectives | agile, divine, feminine, fertile, fragile, hostile, immobile, infantile, masculine, mobile, sterile, versatile |

1. Jeremy was a very versatile ball player since he played soccer and baseball.
2. Sometimes Mary's infantile behavior was like a baby.
3. The settlers preferred to locate near a river where the soil was more fertile.
4. Doctors recommend a vaccine to protect children and older people from getting the flu.
5. The dog owner's choice of a pink bow made the poodle look feminine.
6. After recovering from knee surgery, grandma was amazingly mobile.

-ster

# DAY 4 • Introduce Suffixes

## DISCUSS MEANING

MATERIALS
• Days 3 & 4 Recording Sheet

### Introduce *-ster*

**DIRECTIONS** Introduce the meaning of the suffix spelled ***-ster*** using the chart and sentences below.

| Suffix | Part of Speech | Certified Definition | Meaning of Word |
|---|---|---|---|
| *-ster* | noun | person or thing | The ***monster*** in the movie wasn't scary. |

**Now we'll talk about the meaning of the suffix that is spelled *-ster*.** Words that end in this suffix are nouns, and they refer to a person or thing. Examples include gangster, monster, trickster, and youngster.

**I DO** Listen as I read these sentences using the nouns ***prankster*** and ***hipster***.

1. A person who plays pranks, or practical jokes, on others is known as a ***prankster***.
    - The ***prankster*** placed dried glue on the floor to look like spilled milk.
2. A person who is interested in cool things is often called a ***hipster***.
    - Kristin looked like a ***hipster*** in her fashionable clothes.

**WE DO** Let's do the next ones together. Answer the question with a noun that ends in the suffix ***-ster***.

- If a boy plays tricks, what is he called? A trickster
- When referring to a young child, what term might you use? A youngster
- What might you call someone who loves rock music? A rockster
- What might you call an early automobile for driving on the road? A roadster

**YOU DO** Listen to the question and think of which option is correct.

- To change the word gang to mean someone like Al Capone who was a robber in the 1920s, what suffix do you use?
    - The options are ***-ile***, ***-ine***, ***-ster***. -ster
    - What's the new word? Gangster

Now it's your turn. Work with your partner to select which suffix is correct. Record your answer on the **Days 3 & 4 Recording Sheet.**

DISCUSS MEANING

1. To change the word ***gang*** to mean someone like Al Capone, "a ______" in the 1920s, what suffix do you use? *-ile, -ine, (-ster)* gangster
2. To change the noun ***confidence*** to an adjective to complete this phrase "the ______ contestant" which suffix do you use? *(-ent), -ency, -ile* confident
3. To change the noun ***fluency*** to an adjective to complete this phrase "the ______ reader", which suffix do you use? *-ster, (-ent), -ile* fluent
4. To change the word ***trick*** to mean someone who plays tricks, which suffix do you use? *-ile, -ine, (-ster)* trickster
5. To change the noun ***extravagance*** to an adjective to complete this phrase "the ______ party", which suffix do you use? *-ster, (-ant), -ile* extravagant
6. To change the noun ***mobility*** to an adjective to complete this phrase "the ______ deer", which suffix do you use? *(-ile), -ster, -ine* mobile

# -ance/-ancy, -ant/-ent, -ence/-ency, -ile, -ine, -ster

## DAY 5 • Review

### STEP 1 REVIEW THE MEANING

MATERIALS
• Day 5 Recording Sheet

| Suffix | Certified Definition | Suffix | Certified Definition |
|---|---|---|---|
| *-ant/-ent* | noun: person or thing<br>adjective: a state | *-ile* | noun: person or thing<br>adjective: relating to, suited for, capable of |
| *-ance/-ancy*<br>*-ence/-ency* | noun: a state or quality | *-ine* | noun: person or thing |
| | | *-ster* | noun: one who is associated with, participates in |

**DIRECTIONS** Write five or more sentences with at least one word from the list in each sentence. Record your answer on the **Day 5 Recording Sheet**.

REVIEW THE MEANING

| Words | |
|---|---|
| dormant<br>distance<br>existence<br>fragile<br>gangster | hesitant<br>resilient<br>translucent<br>versatile<br>youngsters |

1. Bonita's class argued over the possible existence of dragons.
2. Pigeons peered through the translucent glass.
3. During the winter bears hibernate in a sleeplike or dormant state.
4. Two youngsters were on the swing set.
5. The distance between the signs was a mile.

### STEP 2 CHALLENGE: MORPHEME MADNESS

MATERIALS
• Notebook paper
• Affixes Mat
• Cards listed in the table below

| Word Parts | Cards |
|---|---|
| **Bases** | hero, trick, young |
| **Latin Roots** | cad, fid, flu, hero, mob, pend, rept, sist, urg |
| **Prefixes** | af, con, de, dis, im |
| **Suffixes** | ance, ancy, ant, ence, ency, ent, ile, ine, ster |

**DIRECTIONS** Students pair up to use **Cards** and **Mats** to build words. They also record all of the words they build and the words' definitions on a sheet of notebook paper.

**Now it's your turn to build words.**

- I take the Latin root ***flu*** and place it in the middle of the mat in the large square.
- Then, I place the suffix ***-ent*** in the small box after ***flu***.
- I have built the word ***fluent***.
- The word fluent means flowing smoothly. Fluent is an adjective.
- I write the word on a separate sheet of notebook paper.

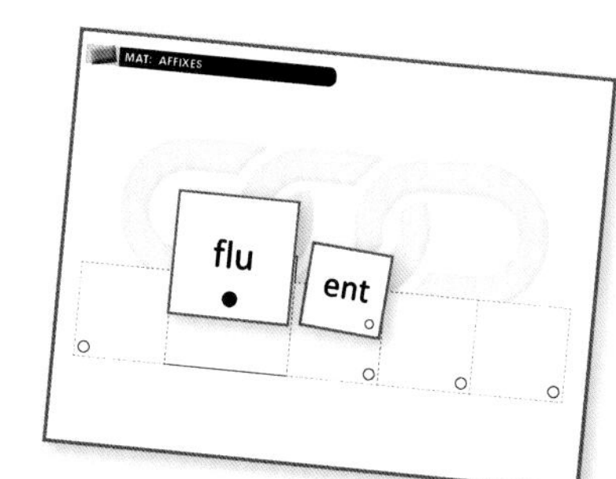


 

# -cian/-ian, pro-, sub-/suc-/suf-/sug-/sup-/sus-, -tude, -ure/-ture

## DAY 1 • Introduce Suffixes

### DISCUSS MEANING

MATERIALS
- Days 1 & 2 Recording Sheet

**Introduce *-cian/-ian***

**DIRECTIONS** Introduce the meaning of the suffixes spelled ***-cian/-ian*** using the charts and sentences below.

| Suffixes | Part of Speech | Certified Definition | Meaning of Word |
|---|---|---|---|
| *-cian/-ian* | noun | a person who has a certain skill or art | The light switch was repaired by the ***electrician***. |
| | | | ***Barbarians*** are described as primitive and uncivilized. |

**We are going to talk about the meaning of the suffixes that are spelled *-cian* and *-ian*.**

- Words that end in these two suffixes are nouns, and they refer to a person who has a certain skill or art.
- When the suffix ***-ian*** is added to the end of **magic** to make ***magician***, the word's meaning changes from the topic of magic to the person who creates it.
- Other examples include *musician, comedian, custodian*, and *librarian*.

**I DO** Listen as I add a suffix to make nouns about people who have a certain skill or art.

- **Comedy.** The word that means a person who entertains audiences with comedy is a ***comedian***.
  - Henrique's friends consider him a ***comedian*** because he tells such funny jokes.
- **Politics.** The word that means a person who is active in government is a ***politician***.
  - Mr. Porter would be a good candidate to run for state senator because he wants to be a ***politician***.

**WE DO** Let's do the next ones together.

- What's the noun for a person who advises people about their **diets**? Dietician
- What's the noun for a person trained to make others look **beautiful**? Beautician
- What's the noun for a person who avoids meats and eats primarily **vegetables**? Vegetarian
- What's the noun for a doctor specializing in children or **pediatrics**? Pediatrician

**YOU DO** Listen to a word and change it by adding one of the two suffixes, ***-cian*** or ***-ian***. Then use the word to complete the sentence. Let's do the first one together.

- The first word is **mathematics**.What's the noun for a person who is an expert in mathematics? Mathematician
- Use the word ***mathematician*** to finish the following sentence:
  1. When David needed help with his math homework, he looked for a mathematician at school.
- Now it's your turn. Work with your partner to write the word that answers the question, and then finish the sentence using that word. Record your answer on the **Days 1 & 2 Recording Sheet**. Remember that your sentence must include the word that you wrote on the line, which ends in one of the two suffixes: ***-cian, -ian***.

**DISCUSS MEANING**

1. Use the word *mathematician* to finish the following sentence:
   When David needed help with his math homework, he looked for a mathematician at school.
2. What's the noun for a person who works in a library? librarian
   **Library.** When I needed help finding books for my research project, I went to see the librarian.
3. What's the noun for a person who is from the country of Egypt? Egyptian
   **Egypt.** In our social studies class, we are studying Egyptian pyramids.
4. What's the noun for a person who plays music? musician
   **Music.** The person carrying the violin is a musician in the orchestra.
5. What's the noun for a person who works with electricity? electrician
   **Electricity.** After the severe storm, we called the electrician to fix the broken outside light.
6. What's the noun for a person who makes others laugh with their comedy? comedian
   **Comedy.** For my uncle's birthday party, we hired a comedian to entertain the guests.

## DAY 2 • Introduce Suffixes

### DISCUSS MEANING

MATERIALS
• Days 1 & 2 Recording Sheet

DIRECTIONS Introduce the meaning of the suffixes spelled ***-tude*** and ***-ure/-ture*** using the charts and sentences below.

| Suffixes | Part of Speech | Certified Definition | Meaning of Word |
|---|---|---|---|
| *-tude* | noun | condition, state, or quality of | There were a ***multitude*** of reasons that the field trip was canceled. |
| *-ure/-ture* | noun | state of, process, function | Jarod's favorite class was English because he loved the ***literature*** the teacher assigned. |

**We are going to talk about the meaning of the suffixes spelled *-tude, -ture,* and *-ure*.**

- The suffix ***-tude*** means a condition, state, or quality of something. One example is the word solitude, which means the state of being solitary or alone. The suffix ***-tude*** appears at the end of nouns. Other examples include *gratitude, aptitude, and attitude.*
- The second suffix can be spelled either ***-ture*** or ***-ure***. It's also found in nouns and it most often means the state of something. One example is the word ***exposure***, which means the state of being exposed. Other examples include *nurture, endure, and structure.*

I DO Listen as I define the nouns ***aptitude*** and ***disclosure*** and read sentences containing these words.

- The first word is ***aptitude***, which means the condition of having an innate talent for something.
  - Jessica's natural ***aptitude*** in science made her a good student in her advanced biology course.
- The next word is ***disclosure***, which means the state of having disclosed, or revealed, something.
  - The criminal's ***disclosure*** about his involvement in the robbery shocked the jury.

WE DO Let's do the next ones together. I'll give you the beginning of a sentence containing a word with one of the suffixes we are studying. We'll complete the sentences together.

- Multitude means the state of having a great number of something.
  Classmates were drawn to Jason, so people say he had a multitude of what? friends
- Composure means the state of being composed, calm, or serene.
  The ballerina's composure was evident in the calm what? look on her face
- Signature means having signed one's name.
  What did the doctor have to provide on the prescription? a signature
- Solitude means the state of being solitary or alone.
  Jarrod prefers solitude so did he choose to work alone or with a partner? alone

YOU DO Answer the question about the meaning of the word. Then complete the sentence. We'll do the first sentence together and then you'll work in groups to finish the rest. Record your answers on the **Days 1 & 2 Recording Sheet**.

- What's the meaning of the word ***gratitude***? A state of feeling grateful
  Cathy felt ***gratitude*** when she learned that her grandmother was not injured from the fall.

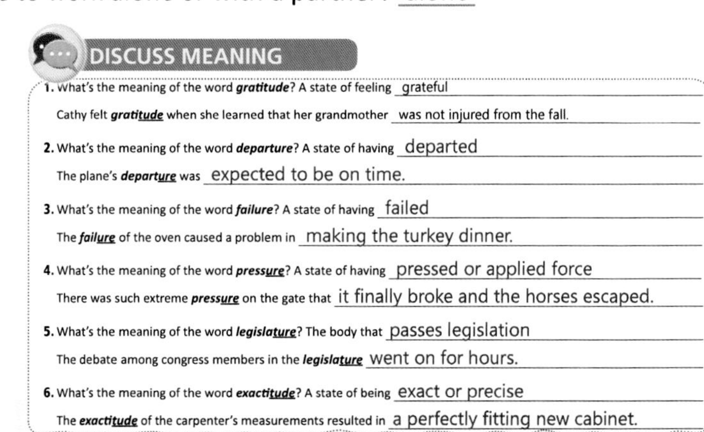

DISCUSS MEANING

1. What's the meaning of the word ***gratitude***? A state of feeling grateful
   Cathy felt ***gratitude*** when she learned that her grandmother was not injured from the fall.
2. What's the meaning of the word ***departure***? A state of having departed
   The plane's ***departure*** was expected to be on time.
3. What's the meaning of the word ***failure***? A state of having failed
   The ***failure*** of the oven caused a problem in making the turkey dinner.
4. What's the meaning of the word ***pressure***? A state of having pressed or applied force
   There was such extreme ***pressure*** on the gate that it finally broke and the horses escaped.
5. What's the meaning of the word ***legislature***? The body that passes legislation
   The debate among congress members in the ***legislature*** went on for hours.
6. What's the meaning of the word ***exactitude***? A state of being exact or precise
   The ***exactitude*** of the carpenter's measurements resulted in a perfectly fitting new cabinet.

pro-

# DAY 3 • Introduce Prefixes

## DISCUSS MEANING

MATERIALS
• Days 3 & 4 Recording Sheet

### Introduce *pro-*

**DIRECTIONS** Introduce the meaning of the prefix spelled ***pro-*** using the charts and sentences below.

| Prefix | Part of Speech | Certified Definition | Meaning of Word |
|---|---|---|---|
| *pro-* | various including nouns and verbs | forward, earlier, or prior to | The ***prologue*** of the book gave the reader a view into why the author wrote it. |

**We are going to talk about the meanings of the prefix spelled *pro-*.**

- The prefix ***pro-***, which appears at the beginning of many nouns, means forward, earlier, or prior to. Examples include the words *project, pronounce, propel,* and *protrude*.
- Even though the meaning of earlier is obvious in some words, in many other words that contain the prefix ***pro-***, that meaning is not as clear. Examples where the connection to earlier is less clear include the words *provide, program,* and *produce*.

**I DO** Listen as I discuss two words, one of which begins with the prefix ***pro-***.

- What does ***propel*** have to do with forward, earlier, or prior to? It means to cause to move forward.
  - Sentence: The quarterback ***propels*** the football down the field to the running back.
- If the prefix ***pro-*** is changed to ***re-***, what does ***repel*** mean? It means to move away.
  - Sentence: The insect spray ***repels*** mosquitos.

**WE DO** Let's do the next ones together. After each question you'll hear two options. Select the word that best fits, and then we'll use that word in a sentence.

- To talk about the shark's teeth extending out from its mouth, which word would you choose? Protrude or intrude? The shark's teeth protrude from its mouth.
- To say that the mother proclaimed riding a bike without a helmet as dangerous, which word would you choose? Proscribe or describe? The mother proscribed riding a bike without a helmet as dangerous.

**YOU DO** Now it's your turn.

- With your partner, read the next set of sentences on the **Days 3 & 4 Recording Sheet**. Select the correct word and then complete the sentence. We'll complete the first one together.
- To talk about moving a project forward toward completion, which word would you choose? Progress or regress?

  The team made good progress on the project.

DISCUSS MEANING

1. To talk about moving a project forward toward completion, which word would you choose? Progress or regress?

   The team made good progress on the project.

2. To describe the part of the book that is at the beginning, which word would you choose? Prologue or monologue?

   The prologue appears at the beginning of the book.

3. To describe an action done to prepare for something, which word would you choose? Proactive or reactive?

   The emergency plan helped the group be proactive.

4. Write a sentence using one of these 3 words: ***progress, prologue,*** or ***proactive***.

   My mother was happy with the **progress** I've made this morning in cleaning up my room.

# DAY 4 • Introduce Prefixes

## DISCUSS MEANING

MATERIALS
• Days 3 & 4 Recording Sheet

**DIRECTIONS** Introduce the meaning of the prefixes spelled ***sub-/suc-/suf-/sug-/sup-/sus-*** using the chart and sentences below.

| Prefixes | Part of Speech | Certified Definition | Meaning of Word |
|---|---|---|---|
| ***sub-/suc-/ suf-/sug-/ sup-/sus-*** | various including nouns and verbs | under, beneath, or below | The purpose of the basement columns was to ***sustain*** the floor by supporting it from below. |

**Now we'll talk about the meaning of the prefix that is spelled *sub-*.**

- The prefix ***sub-***, which appears at the beginning of many nouns, means under, beneath, or below. Examples include the words *subfloor, sublease,* and *submerge*.
- Even though the meaning of under or beneath is obvious in some words, in many other words containing the prefix ***sub-***, that meaning is not as clear. Examples where the connection to beneath is less clear include the words *subtract, submit,* and *subject*.
- The prefix ***sub-*** has five alternate spellings where the letter ***b*** changes to match the first letter in the root or base that follows it. The five alternate spellings are: ***suc-*** before roots beginning with ***c***; ***suf-***before roots beginning with ***f***; ***sug-*** before roots beginning with ***g***; ***sup-*** before roots beginning with ***p***; and ***sus-*** before roots beginning with ***s***.

**I DO** Listen as I discuss two words that begin with the prefix ***sub-***.

1. To ***subvert*** means to undermine, or cause the downfall, of something.
   - Jessie's mean comment was intended to ***subvert*** Lauren's plan with her friends.
2. ***Subterranean*** means something that is underground.
   - The construction of the tunnel was complex because it was ***subterranean***.

**WE DO** Let's do the next ones together.

- What does ***subplot*** have to do with ***under*** or ***beneath***? A plot beneath the main plot
- What does ***subclass*** have to do with ***under*** or ***beneath***? A class that is beneath the main class
- What does ***sublease*** have to do with ***under*** or ***beneath***? A lease that is under the main lease
- What does ***submerge*** have to do with ***under*** or ***beneath***? To put something under water

**YOU DO** Listen to the question and write an answer that starts with the word ***under*** or ***beneath***. Then write a sentence that includes the word with the prefix ***sub-***.

- Where might ***suboceanic*** oil be located? Under the ocean floor
  - Sentence: The explorers looked for suboceanic oil under the ocean floor.

Now it's your turn. Record your answer on the **Days 3 & 4 Recording Sheet**.

**DISCUSS MEANING**

1. Where might ***suboceanic*** oil be located? under the ocean floor
   Sentence: The explorers looked for suboceanic oil under the ocean floor.
2. Where would you find a ***submarine***? under the water
   Sentence: The submarine was spotted under the surface of the sea.
3. Where is a ***subway*** located? under the ground below a city
   Sentence: We decided to ride the subway located under New York City.
4. Where would you find a ***subfloor***? under the main floor
   Sentence: When the house was built, a strong subfloor was added under the main floor.
5. Where would you find ***subsoil***? beneath the main layer of soil
   Sentence: Earthworms dug down into the subsoil beneath the main soil.

 

# -cian/-ian, -tude, -ure/-ture
# pro-, sub-

## DAY 5 • Review

### STEP 1 REVIEW THE MEANING

**MATERIALS**
- Day 5 Recording Sheet

| Suffixes | Certified Definition | Prefixes | Certified Definition |
|---|---|---|---|
| *-cian/-ian* | a person who has a certain skill | *pro-* | forward, earlier, or prior to |
| *-tude* | condition, state or quality of | *sub-/suc-/ suf-/sug-/ sup-/sus-* | under, beneath, or below |
| *-ure/-ture* | state of, process, or function | | |

**DIRECTIONS** Select one of the words in the box to finish each sentence.

REVIEW THE MEANING

| Words with the Prefix *sub-*, or alternate spellings *suc-*, *suf-*, *sug-*, *sup-*, or *sus-* |
|---|
| Words with *sub-*: subgroup, submarine, submerge, subplot, subsoil |
| Words with alternate spelling of *sub-*: succeed, suffer, suggest, supplant, suspect |

1. This winter's strain of flu causes people to ___suffer___ with severe headaches.
2. Jerry's younger sister was afraid to ___submerge___ her head in the pool water.
3. On our science poster we showed robins as a ___subgroup___ of birds.
4. My parents were concerned that the new game might ___supplant___ use of all our old games.
5. When my teacher saw my struggles she wanted to ___suggest___ that I try a different way.
6. The book's complicated ___subplot___ made it hard to follow the main plot.

### STEP 2 CHALLENGE: MORPHEME MADNESS

**MATERIALS**
- Day 5 Recording Sheet
- Notebook paper
- Affixes Mat
- Cards listed in the table below

| Word Parts | Cards |
|---|---|
| Anglo-Saxon Words | class, fail, floor, group, guard, long, magic, merge, mix, moist, music, plot, press, soil, way (plus country name, Egypt) |
| Prefixes | pro, sub, suc, suf, sug, sup, sus |
| Suffixes | cian, ian, tude, ure, ture |

**DIRECTIONS** Students pair up to use **Cards** and **Mats** to build words. They also record all of the words they build and the words' definitions.

**Now it's your turn to build words. I'll do the first one as an example.**

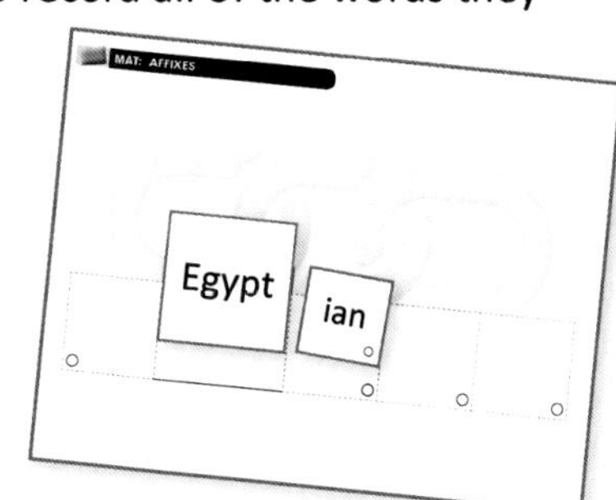


- I take the Anglo-Saxon base word ***Egypt*** and place it in the middle of the mat in the large box.
- Then, I place the suffix ***-ian*** in the small box after ***Egypt***.
- I have built the word ***Egyptian***.
- I write the word on my **Day 5 Recording Sheet**.
- The word ***Egyptian*** means a person from the country of Egypt. Egyptian is a noun.

# -ate, de-, -ive, -ize

## DAY 1 • Introduce Suffixes

### DISCUSS MEANING

MATERIALS
- Days 1 & 2 Recording Sheet

#### Introduce *-ate*

**DIRECTIONS** Introduce the meaning of the suffix spelled ***-ate*** using the charts and sentences below.

| Suffix | Part of Speech | Certified Definition | Meaning of Word |
|---|---|---|---|
| -ate | verb | to cause or make | When the equipment didn't arrive, the worker had to ***deviate*** from his normal process. |

**We are going to talk about the meaning of the suffix spelled *-ate*.**

- The suffix ***-ate*** means to cause or to make. One example is the word ***stimulate***, which means to cause someone or something to act. The suffix ***-ate*** can appear in adjectives or nouns, but we're going to focus on verbs today. Other examples include *hydrate, ventilate, dictate,* or *estimate*.

**I DO** Listen as I define the verbs ***speculate*** and ***eradicate*** and read sentences containing these words.

- The first word is ***speculate***, which means to cause to reflect about something or predict an outcome.
  - The scout leader didn't even want to ***speculate*** how long it would take to clean the sticky marshmallow fingerprints from the cabin following last night's campfire.
- The next word is ***eradicate***, which means to cause to be completely removed from existence.
  - The leader pleaded for action to ***eradicate*** world hunger.

**WE DO** Let's do the next ones together. I'll give you the beginning of a sentence containing a word with the suffix we are studying. We'll complete the sentences together.

- **Illustrate** means to make a drawing or illustration.
  - As part of our science lab report, we had to **illustrate** ________________. the frog's body
- **Initiate** means to cause something to get going.
  - When the coach was late, the team captain was the one to **initiate** ________________. warming up
- **Dedicate** means to commit to something.
  - I was going to have to **dedicate** some of my weekend to ________________. finishing my book project
- **Dominate** means to rule over, or tower above, something or someone.
  - In our group Carol is always the one to **dominate** ________________. the discussion

**YOU DO** Now it's your turn. First answer the question about the meaning of the word. Then complete the sentence. We'll do the first sentence together and then you'll work in groups to finish the rest. Record your answers on the **Days 1 & 2 Recording Sheet.**

- ***Hesitation*** is the act of delaying due to uncertainty. What's the meaning of the verb ***hesitate***? To act with ***hesitation***.
  1. During the hike we saw Matthew ***hesitate*** when he thought he saw a snake.

**DISCUSS MEANING**

1. Hesitation is the act of delaying due to uncertainty. What's the meaning of the verb ***hesitate***? To act with hesitation
   During the hike we saw Matthew hesitate when he thought he saw a snake.
2. Estimation is an approximate calculation. What's the meaning of the verb ***estimate***? To make an estimation
   Our team had to estimate when we didn't have the exact data.
3. Hibernation is spending the winter in a sleeplike state. What's the meaning of the verb ***hibernate***? To go into hibernation
   The bear will hibernate in a cave throughout the winter.
4. Mediation is seeking an agreement between parties. What's the meaning of the verb ***mediate***? To act as a mediator
   Jason stepped up to mediate when his two friends began to argue about the game.
5. Retaliation is the act of getting back at someone for mistreatment. What's the meaning of the verb ***retaliate***? To do something to get back at someone when you are mistreated
   Jeremy worried that the other team might retaliate for last year's landslide win.
6. Vaccination is a shot to prevent illness. What's the meaning of the verb ***vaccinate***? To give a vaccine
   Write a sentence that contains the word ***vaccinate***.

de-

## DAY 2 • Introduce Prefixes

### DISCUSS MEANING

MATERIALS
- Days 1 & 2 Recording Sheet

**DIRECTIONS** Introduce the meaning of the prefix spelled ***de-*** using the charts and sentences below.

| Prefix | Part of Speech | Certified Definition | Meaning of Word |
|---|---|---|---|
| de- | verb | away from or down | The ***decline*** in book sales concerned the author. |

**We are going to talk about the meaning of the prefix spelled *de-*.**
- The prefix ***de-*** appears at the beginning of many nouns and means away from or down. Examples include the words *decay, decline, deplane,* and *deduct*.

**I DO** Listen as I discuss two words, one of which begins with the prefix ***de-***.
- What does ***detract*** have to do with away from or down? It means to take away value or attention.
  a. Sentence: The garbage ***detracts*** from the beautiful view of the coastline.

**WE DO** Let's do the next ones together. After each question you'll hear two options. Select the word that best fits, and then we'll use that word in a sentence.
- What does ***defer*** have to do with away from or down? It means to delay or turn down.
  - Sentence: Jenny wanted to ***defer*** taking down holiday decorations for as long as possible.
- What does ***deduct*** have to do with away from or down? It means to take away.
  - Sentence: We have to ***deduct*** three dollars for expenses.

**YOU DO** Now it's your turn. Using the Affix Mat and Cards, build as many words as you can that begin with the prefix ***-de***. On the table of the **Days 1 & 2 Recording Sheet**, record the word parts, then the whole words, and finally the meaning of the word.

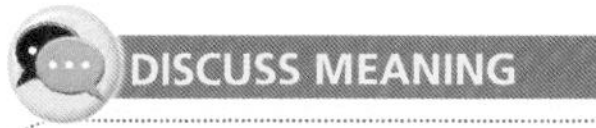

| Word Parts | Word | Meaning |
|---|---|---|
| de+code | decode | to break a code |
| de+plane | deplane | to move away from a plane |
| de+camp | decamp | to take apart, or move away from, camp |
| de+port | deport | to move someone away |

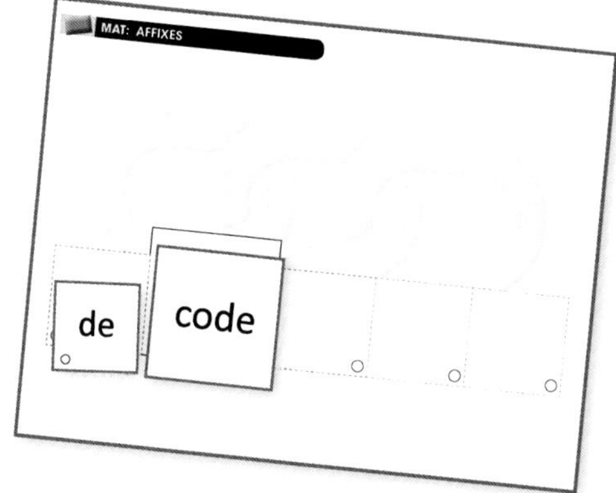

# DAY 3 • Introduce Suffixes

## DISCUSS MEANING

### Introduce *-ive*

**DIRECTIONS** Introduce the meaning of the suffix spelled ***-ive*** using the charts and sentences below.

| Suffix | Part of Speech | Certified Definition | Meaning of Word |
|---|---|---|---|
| -ive | adjective | causing or making | The artist's work was amazingly ***creative***. |

**We are going to talk about the meaning of the suffix spelled *-ive*.**

- The suffix ***-ive***, which is an adjective, means causing or making. In the word *offensive,* the suffix changes the word *offend* to mean to cause someone to feel offense at a comment or action. Examples of other words with the suffix ***-ive*** include the words *massive, assertive, active,* and *negative*.

**I DO** Listen as I discuss two adjectives that end in the suffix ***-ive***. The first word is ***elusive*** and the second word is ***assertive***.

- An adjective to describe someone who doesn't make things clear is ***elusive***.
  - Jane's answer to her mother about where she had been was a bit ***elusive***.
- An adjective to describe someone's behavior that is confidently aggressive or self-assured is ***assertive***.
  - Jarrod was ***assertive*** about why he should be the next soccer team captain.

**YOU DO** Now it's your turn. Look at the **Day 3 Recording Sheet**. Notice the box at the top with pairs of adjectives.

- With a partner, study the pairs of words and discuss which one is a positive adjective that could be used to describe a good characteristic of a person.
- On each line below you'll see lines one through six. There is a pair of words before the sentence; circle the word in the pair that is positive and then fill it into the sentence.
- Reread your completed sentence to make sure it makes sense.

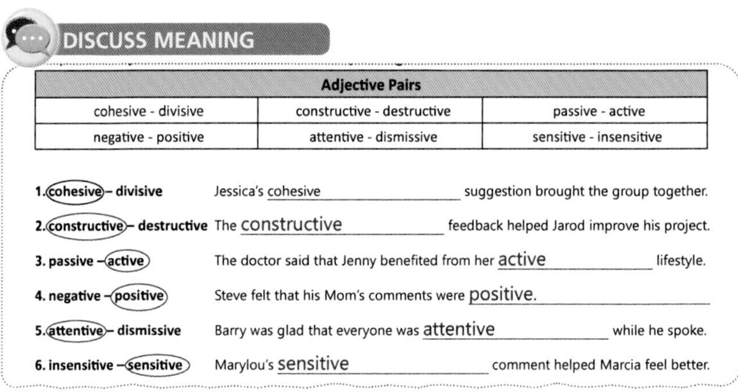

DISCUSS MEANING

| Adjective Pairs | | |
|---|---|---|
| cohesive - divisive | constructive - destructive | passive - active |
| negative - positive | attentive - dismissive | sensitive - insensitive |

1. (cohesive) – divisive  Jessica's cohesive ____ suggestion brought the group together.
2. (constructive) – destructive  The constructive ____ feedback helped Jarod improve his project.
3. passive – (active)  The doctor said that Jenny benefited from her active ____ lifestyle.
4. negative – (positive)  Steve felt that his Mom's comments were positive. ____
5. (attentive) – dismissive  Barry was glad that everyone was attentive ____ while he spoke.
6. insensitive – (sensitive)  Marylou's sensitive ____ comment helped Marcia feel better.

We'll do the first one together. The words are ***cohesive*** and ***divisive***. See where the word ***cohesive*** is circled and then it is filled into the sentence.

1. (cohesive) – divisive  Jessica's cohesive ____ suggestion brought the group together.

Finish the other five sentences.

 

-ize

## DAY 4 • Introduce Suffixes

### DISCUSS MEANING

MATERIALS
• Days 3 & 4 Recording Sheet

**DIRECTIONS** Introduce the meaning of the suffix spelled ***-ize*** using the charts and sentences below.

| Suffix | Part of Speech | Certified Definition | Meaning of Word |
|---|---|---|---|
| -ize | verb | become, change, or make | John goes to a lot of parties because he loves to ***socialize*** with friends. |

**We are going to talk about the meaning of the suffix spelled *-ize*.**

- The suffix ***-ize***, which is a verb, means to become, change, or make. In the word ***dramatize***, the suffix changes the word ***drama*** to mean to express something dramatically or emotionally. Examples of other words with the suffix ***-ize*** include the words *legalize, realize, criticize,* and *formalize*.

**I DO** Listen as I discuss a verb that ends in the suffix ***-ize***. The word is ***socialize***.

- A verb to mean associating or mingling with other people is ***socialize***.
  - Carlos was so shy that he preferred not to go places where he'd have to ***socialize***.

**WE DO** Let's do the next ones together. After each question, answer with the verb that includes the suffix ***-ize*** at the end.

- What is the verb that means to make an apology? apologize
- What is the verb that means to bring organization to something? organize
- What is the verb that means to think of someone as an idol? idolize
- What is the verb that means to voice a criticism? criticize

**YOU DO** Now it's your turn. Look at the **Days 3 & 4 Recording Sheet**. Identify the verb that ends in the suffix ***-ize*** for each item below. First read the phrase and then write the word on the blank line that makes the verb that is described. Remember that your word must end in ***-ize***.

We'll do the first one together.

- What is the verb that means to make soil fertile? fertilize

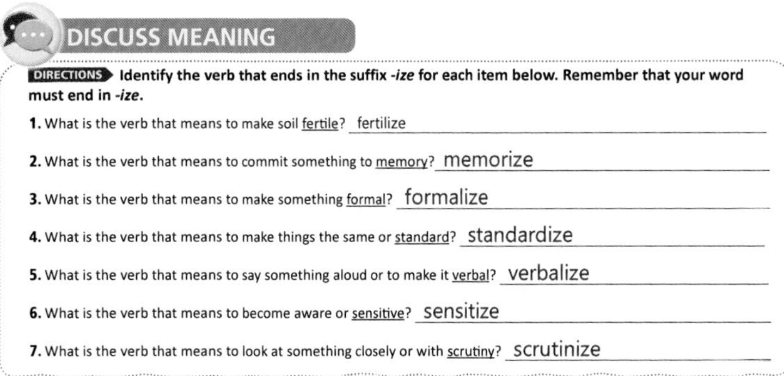

DISCUSS MEANING

**DIRECTIONS** **Identify the verb that ends in the suffix *-ize* for each item below. Remember that your word must end in *-ize*.**

1. What is the verb that means to make soil fertile? fertilize
2. What is the verb that means to commit something to memory? memorize
3. What is the verb that means to make something formal? formalize
4. What is the verb that means to make things the same or standard? standardize
5. What is the verb that means to say something aloud or to make it verbal? verbalize
6. What is the verb that means to become aware or sensitive? sensitize
7. What is the verb that means to look at something closely or with scrutiny? scrutinize

**-ate, de-, -ive, -ize**

# DAY 5 • Review

## STEP 1 REVIEW THE MEANING

MATERIALS
- Day 5 Recording Sheet

**DIRECTIONS** On the **Day 5 Student Recording Sheet** you'll see a box with 8 words, all of which end in the suffix ***-ize***. Select the word from the list that best completes the phrases, and fill it in on the blank line.

We'll do the first one together.

To apologize for a mistake.

**REVIEW THE MEANING**

**DIRECTIONS** Select a word from the list that best completes the phrases.

apologize, criticize, dramatize, familiarize, hypnotize, minimize, realize, socialize

To apologize for a mistake

To hypnotize with a smooth and charming voice

To socialize by having a party

To criticize about things done incorrectly

To realize what was unclear before now

To dramatize the act on stage

To familiarize by studying things closely

To minimize by pretending it's important

## STEP 2 CHALLENGE: MORPHEME MADNESS

MATERIALS
- Day 5 Recording Sheet
- Affixes Mat
- Cards listed in the table below

| Word Parts | Cards |
|---|---|
| **Bases** | act, assert, construct, destruct, domin, erupt, estim, exhaust, formal, idol, illustr, impress, instinct, local, mass, organ, part, pass |
| **Prefixes** | de |
| **Suffixes** | ate, ive, ize |

**DIRECTIONS** Students pair up to use **Cards** and **Mats** to build words. They also record all of the words they build and the words' definitions on the **Day 5 Recording Sheet**.

**Now it's your turn to build words.**

- I take the base ***estim*** and place it in the middle of the mat in the large square.
- Then, I place the suffix ***-ate*** in the small box after ***estim***.
- I have built the word ***estimate***.
- I write the word on my **Day 5 Recording Sheet**.
- The word estimate means to form an approximate judgment

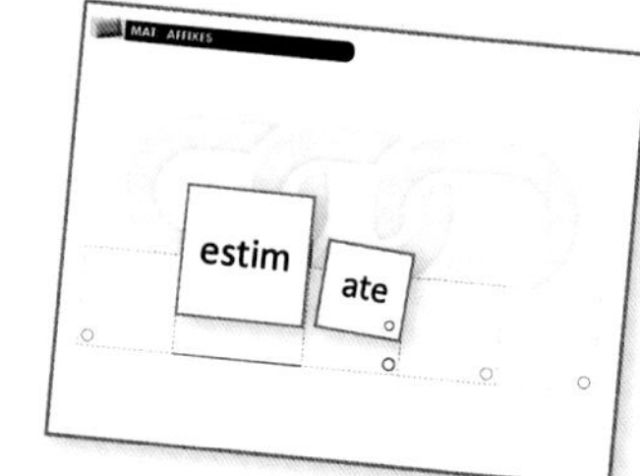


**REVIEW THE MEANING**

| Word Parts | Word | Meaning |
|---|---|---|
| estim+ate | estimate | to form an approximate judgment |
| exhaust+ive | exhaustive | a comprehensive or thorough job |
| organ+ize | organize | to form into a system |
| construct+ive | constructive | to help to improve |
| de+part | depart | to leave |

 

# Latin Mat

## Introduction

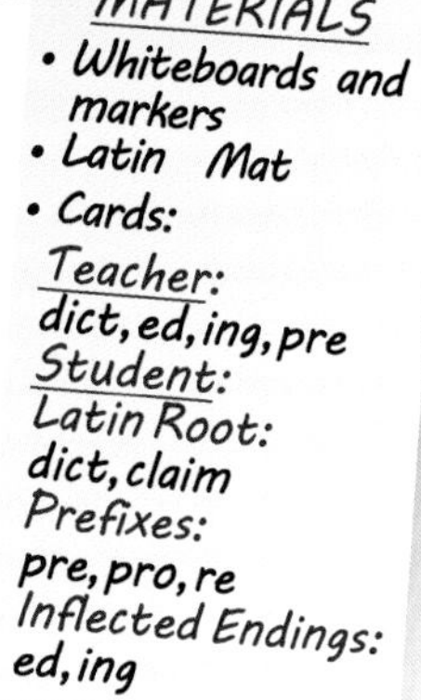

MATERIALS
• Whiteboards and markers
• Latin Mat
• Cards:
Teacher:
dict, ed, ing, pre
Student:
Latin Root:
dict, claim
Prefixes:
pre, pro, re
Inflected Endings:
ed, ing


### Introduce the Latin Mat

**In the past four lessons we've been working with words that have Latin affixes added to simple base words. Starting in the next lesson, we'll study Latin words constructed with Latin roots instead of simple base words.**

**First let's talk about the way words are constructed in the Latin layer of language.**

- The Latin layer was the second layer of language, which was added to the Anglo-Saxon layer long ago when the people who spoke a Latin-based language moved into the regions of English-speaking people.
- Latin words are constructed differently than the words we were building in the first four lessons. In lessons 1 through 4, many of the words were built with a stand-alone base word that had either a prefix or suffix added to it. However, the base word could stand by itself without having a prefix or a suffix.
- What's unique about the Latin layer is that there must be a Latin Root in each word. A Latin Root can't stand alone, and it doesn't make sense by itself. It has to have either a prefix or a suffix to complete the word. It can have both a prefix and a suffix, and sometimes there is more than one of each.
- An example of a Latin Root is ***struct***, which isn't a word. The suffix ***-in*** can be added to the root ***struct*** to make the word ***instruct***. The suffix ***-tion*** can be added to make another word, ***instruction***.

**Now let's talk about the mat and word cards we'll use.**

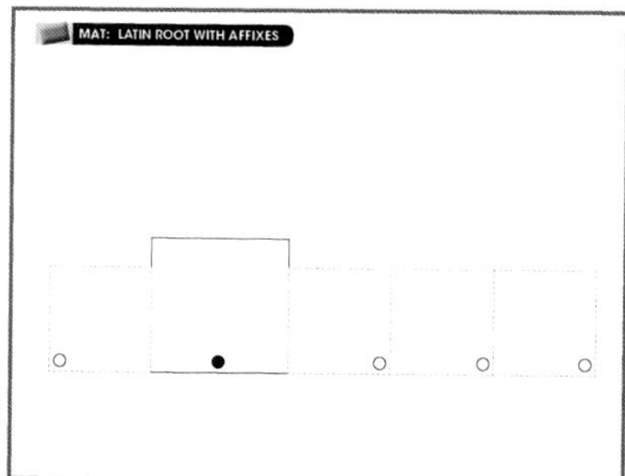


- There is an image in the background. What does it look like? A tree with roots below the ground That's to remind us of the Latin Root. Now look at the boxes on the mat. Are they all the same size? No That's right, there is one large box and smaller boxes on each side of it.
- Look inside the boxes at the dots. Are they all the same? No, there are two types of dots The large box has a dot that is filled in, or solid. The smaller box in front of it has a small circle in the bottom left corner to remind us that it comes before the large box. This is where a prefix goes. There are three smaller boxes on the right side that also have a circle that is not filled in and is located in the bottom right corner to remind us that this comes after the large box. This is where the suffixes go. Notice that there can be more than one suffix in the words we'll be building.

**Now let's use the mat and word cards to build some words.**

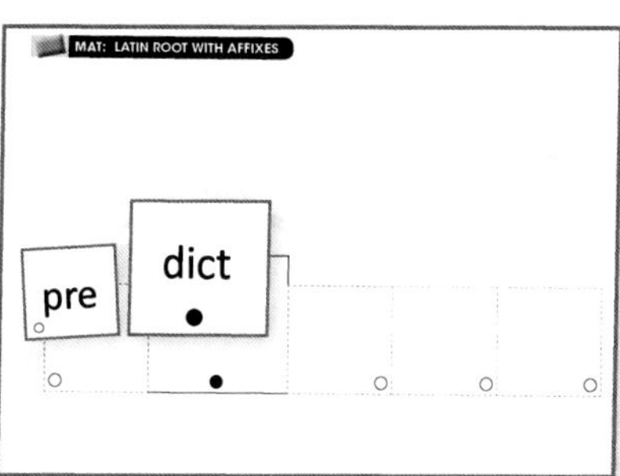


I DO • Watch me build the word ***predict***.

- The Latin Root is ***dict***. It goes in the large box in the center of the Latin Mat. The prefix ***pre-*** comes first in the word, so it comes first on this Mat. I place it in the box to the left of the Latin Root ***dict***, matching the open circle on the card to the one on the Mat. The new word is ***predict***. The word means to tell something before it happens.
- I can build some more words on the mat. *Predict, predicted, predicting*

**WE DO** Help me build the word ***reclaimed*** on this Latin Mat.

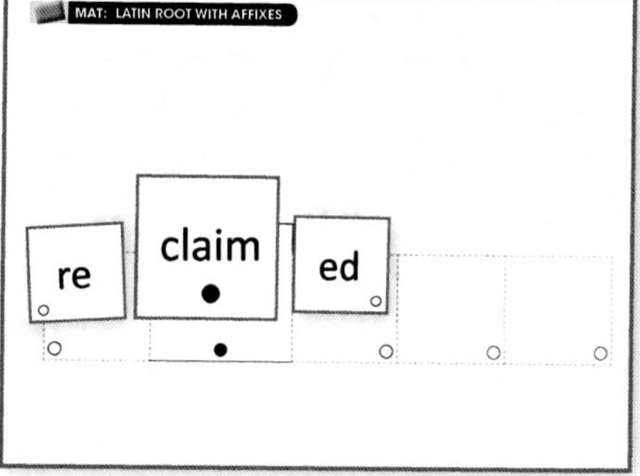


- Where shall I place the word card ***claim***? In the large center box
- Why do I place it there? Because it is the Latin Root
- Where shall I place the prefix card ***re-***? In the box on the left side of the mat
- Why do I place it there? Because it is a prefix and the circle on the card matches the circle on the mat
- What word have I built so far? Reclaim
- Where shall I place the card ***-ed***? In the box on the right side of the mat, next to ***claim***
- Why do I place it there? Because it is a suffix and the circle on the card matches the circle on the mat
- What word have I built so far? Reclaimed

**YOU DO** With a partner, collect the following word cards:

Latin Roots: ***claim***

Prefixes: ***pro, re***

Inflected Ending: ***ed***

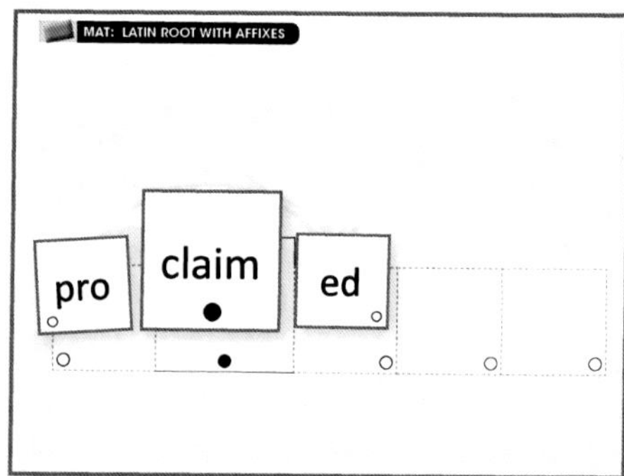


- What's the definition of the prefix ***pro-***? Forward, earlier, or prior to
- What's the definition of the inflected ending ***-ed***? Past tense
- With your partner build the word ***proclaim*** on your Latin Mat.

---

- Let's review your word.
- Where did you place the word card ***claim***? In the large center box
- Why did you place it there? Because it is the Latin Root
- Where is the prefix card ***pro-***? In the box on the left side of the mat
- Why is it placed there? Because it is a prefix and the circle on the card matches the circle on the mat
- Where is the card ***claim***? In the large box in the middle
- Why is it placed there? Because it is a Latin Root and it goes in the middle
- How do you know if it's in the right place? The size of the box is large and the solid circle on the card matches the circle on the mat
- What word have you built so far? Proclaim
- Where did you place the card ***-ed***? In the box on the right side of the mat, next to ***claim***
- Why did you place it there? Because it is a suffix and the circle on the card matches the circle on the mat
- What word have you built so far? Proclaimed
- How would you change the word ***proclaimed*** to ***reclaimed***? By changing the prefix ***pro-*** to ***re-***

---

- You will be using this Latin Mat and Latin Root Cards in the next eight lessons.

 

# claim/clam, dic/dict, rupt, tend/tense/tens~~e~~/tent, voc/voke/vok~~e~~ — per-, -ship

## DAY 1 • Introduce Latin Roots

### UNCOVER THE MEANING

MATERIALS
- Days 1 & 2 Recording Sheet

#### Introduce *claim/clam, dic/dict,* and *voc/voke/vok~~e~~; -ship*

**DIRECTIONS** Pair students and distribute the Days 1 & 2 Recording Sheet. Model the first completed example. After students have completed the first two columns, ask them to share what they wrote. Then provide the Certified Definition. Explain that understanding parts of words, such as Latin roots, can help students uncover the meaning of many words.

**I'm going to model using my detective skills to figure out what the underlined word parts mean.**

- I'll use the other words in the sentences to develop a Working Definition of a word part.
- Listen as I read the first set of two sentences.

    1. The bell's noisy ***clam*or** called the children in from recess.
    2. In a loud voice, the referee ***proclaim*ed** our team the winner!

- In **Column 1**, I record the clue words noisy and loud voice that help me understand the meaning of ***claim/clam***.
- I think that ***claim/clam*** means to call out loudly. This is my Working Definition, which I record in **Column 2**.
- In **Column 3**, I write the Certified Definition of ***claim/clam***: to declare, call, or cry out.

**Now it's your turn.**

- With your partner, read the next set of sentences on the Days 1 & 2 Recording Sheet.
- Use your detective skills to figure out what the underlined word parts mean.
- Consider which words or phrases in the sentences provide clues about meaning. Record them in **Column 1**.
- Write a Working Definition in **Column 2**.
- Only complete **Columns 1** and **2** and then wait for the discussion. You will fill in **Column 3** after I provide a Certified Definition.

UNCOVER THE MEANING

| claim/clam | 1. The bell's noisy clamor called the children in from recess. 2. In a loud voice, the referee proclaimed our team the winner! | |
|---|---|---|
| ❶ Clue Words for Working Definition | ❷ Working Definition | ❸ Certified Definition |
| noisy, loud voice | to call out loudly | to declare, call, or cry out |
| **dic/dict** | 1. In a clear voice, the principal dictated a letter for the secretary to type. 2. Did you use proper diction so you were understood when you spoke? | |
| ❶ Clue Words for Working Definition | ❷ Working Definition | ❸ Certified Definition |
| clear voice, understood, spoke | to speak or talk | to say or tell |
| **voc/voke/vok~~e~~** | 1. The vocalist sang so clearly, the people in the back row could hear each word. 2. Bette's computer use was revoked because she played too many video games. | |
| ❶ Clue Words for Working Definition | ❷ Working Definition | ❸ Certified Definition |
| sang, use | voice or call back | to call or voice |

**claim/clam, dic/dict, voc/voke/voke̸**
**-ship**

# DAY 2 • Deepen the Meaning

## CHECK MEANING

> **MATERIALS**
> - Pocket chart, document camera, or PowerPoint™
> - Days 1 & 2 Recording Sheet
> - Cards:
>   Teacher: claim, ed, pro, re
>   Student: Roots: dict, voke
>   Prefixes: in, re
>   Suffixes: ate, ate̸, or

**DIRECTIONS** Using the **Cards** and **Mat**, confirm that students understand how the meaning of the word evolves as more parts are added.

**I DO**

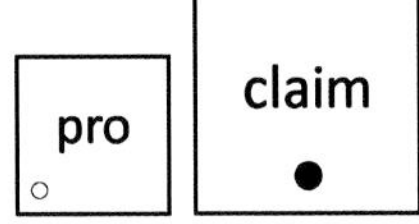


- The prefix ***pro-*** means forward, earlier or to support.
- Adding ***pro-*** to ***claim*** spells the word ***pro<u>claim</u>***. The combination of word parts means that the declaration is supportive.
- Now, I'm going to use my knowledge of the word to answer the question.

1. What does it mean when the students ***pro<u>claim</u>*** Ethan class president? The students are supporting Ethan.

**WE DO**

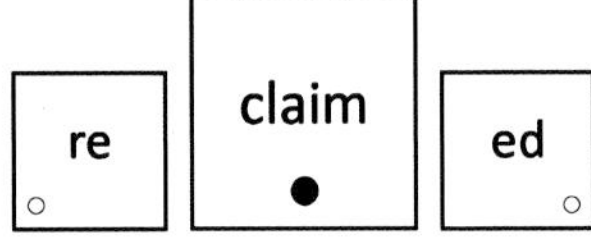


- The prefix ***re-*** means again.
- After adding ***re-*** to ***claim*** what's the meaning? To declare, again
- What does the inflected ending ***-ed*** mean? Occurred in the past
- After adding ***-ed*** to ***re<u>claim</u>*** what's the meaning? Declared again
- Listen to me use the word ***re<u>claim</u>ed*** in a question and we will use our knowledge of its parts to figure out the answer.

2. What did it mean when Jilly ***re<u>claim</u>ed*** her title as bowling champion? She was declared the champion again.

**YOU DO** Use your **Cards** and **Mats** to complete the chart on the **Days 1 & 2 Recording Sheet.**

| Latin Roots | Certified Definition |
|---|---|
| claim/clam | to declare, call, or cry out |
| dic/dict | to say or tell |
| voc/voke/voke̸ | to call or voice |
| **Prefixes** | **Certified Definition** |
| contra- | against |
| in- | in or not |
| pre- | before |
| re- | again |
| **Suffixes** | **Certified Definition** |
| -al | related to, like |
| -ate/-ate̸ | to make |
| -ize/-ize̸ | to make |
| -or | one who does |
| -ship | skill, quality |
| **Inflected Endings** | **Certified Definition** |
| -ed | past tense |
| -ing | present participle |

| Word | Latin Root | Suffix | Suffix |
|---|---|---|---|
| dictate | dict: to say or tell | ate: rank | |
| Meaning: | to tell someone what to do | | |
| dictator | dict: to say or tell | ate̸: rank | or: one who does |
| Meaning: | a person who rules a country with total authority | | |
| **Word** | **Prefix** | **Latin Root** | **Suffix** |
| revoke | re: again, back | voke: to call or voice | |
| Meaning: | to call back | | |
| invoke | in: in | voke: to call or voice | |
| Meaning: | to call on someone to help | | |

# claim/clam, dic/dict, voc/voke/vok~~e~~ -ship

## DAY 3 • Word Multiplier

### WORD MULTIPLIER

**Build words with *claim/clam, dic/dict,* and *voc/voke/vok~~e~~***

**DIRECTIONS** Students work together to build words using their **Cards** and **Mats**.

*MATERIALS*
- Day 3 Recording Sheet
- Notebook paper
- Latin Mat
- Cards:
  Latin Roots: claim, clam, dic, dict, voc, voke, vok~~e~~
  Inflected Endings: ed, ing
  Prefixes: contra, in, pre, re
  Suffixes: al, or, ize, iz~~e~~

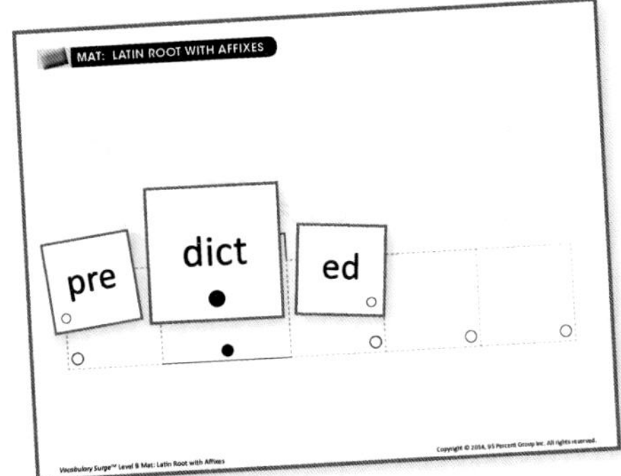


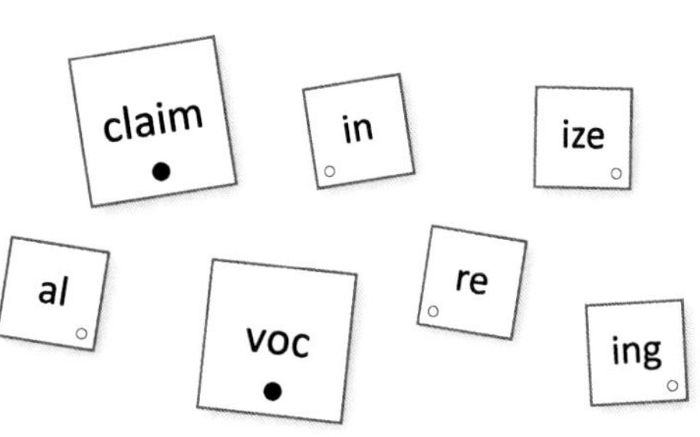


**I DO** Watch me combine **Cards** to build a word.
- I select cards ***pre, dict,*** and ***ed***.
- I place the prefix ***pre-*** on the left side of the mat, matching the circle on the mat to the one on the card.
- I place the Latin root ***dict*** in the large center box, matching the solid circles.
- Finally, I place the inflected ending ***-ed*** to the right of ***dict***, matching the circle on the mat to the one on the card.
- I have built the word ***predicted***.

**WORD MULTIPLIER**

| SET 1 | Word Parts | Word | Part of Speech |
|---|---|---|---|
| 1. | clam+or+ing | clamoring | verb |
| | Write the Meaning: | noisily crying out | |
| 2. | re+claim+ed | reclaimed | verb |
| | Write the Meaning: | something lost or removed, taken back | |
| **SET 2** | **Word Parts** | **Word** | **Part of Speech** |
| 1. | pre+dict+or | predictor | noun |
| | Write the Meaning: | an indicator to signal something in the future | |
| 2. | contra+dict+ing | contradicting | verb |
| | Write the Meaning: | saying something opposite of what was said before | |
| **SET 3** | **Word Parts** | **Word** | **Part of Speech** |
| 1. | voc+al+iz~~e~~+ing | vocalizing | verb |
| | Write the Meaning: | voicing words or sounds | |
| 2. | in+voke | invoke | verb |
| | Write the Meaning: | to call on someone to help | |

**WE DO** Let's try another word.
- I choose the cards ***clam, or,*** and ***ing***.
- Where should I place the card ***clam***? In the middle box
- Why do we place it here? Because it is the Latin root and has a solid circle like the mat
- Where shall I place suffix ***-or***? In the box to the right of ***clam***
- Where shall I place inflected ending ***-ing***? In the box to the right of ***or***
- Look at the example on your **Day 3 Recording Sheet** to see how to write the parts of ***clamoring*** and the whole word. ***Clam*** means to cry out, ***-or*** means one who does, and ***-ing*** means it is happening now.
- When we put these word parts together, ***clamoring*** means noisily crying out.
- What part of speech is ***clamoring*** and how do you know? Verb, action word

**YOU DO** Use your **Cards** and **Mats** to build more words. Complete the **Day 3 Recording Sheet** with your partner. Write additional words on notebook paper. We will review the words when you have finished.

**Possible Words:**
**claim/clam:** claim, claimed, claiming, reclaim, reclaimed, reclaiming, clamor, clamored, clamoring
**dic/dict:** contradict, contradicted, contradicting, contradictor, predict, predicted, predicting
**voc/voke/vok~~e~~:** invoke, invoked, invoking, vocal, vocalize, vocalized, vocalizing

claim/clam, dic/dict, voc/voke/vok~~e~~
-ship

## DAY 4 • Demonstrate Meaning

### BUILD MEANING

MATERIALS
- Whiteboards
- Markers

**DIRECTIONS** Complete the I Do and We Do sections with the whole class, and pair students to work on the You Do activity. Students can record their ideas on small whiteboards. Ask a few pairs to share their work with the class.

**I DO** Listen to me demonstrate understanding of the meaning of the Latin root ***voke***.

- The first word is ***invoke***. We learned yesterday that ***invoke*** means to call on someone to help. I'm going to think of examples of times when I have ***invoked*** something or someone.
  - When I gave a large party, I ***invoked*** my friends to bring food.
  - When I was in college, I ***invoked*** my teacher to help me by asking a question in class.
- The second word is ***revoke***, which means to call back something. I'm going to think of an example of something I've ***revoked***.
  - After I said something mean to a friend, I wished I could ***revoke*** my hurtful words.
  - When my friend got several speeding tickets, her driver's license was ***revoked***.

**WE DO** Let's try the next one together with the Latin root ***claim***.

- The first word is ***proclaim***. The prefix ***pro-*** means to be in favor of, and the Latin root ***claim*** means to declare or call out. ***Proclaim*** means to declare something. I'd enjoy ***proclaiming*** that my students all finished their assignments perfectly.
  - What things might we ***proclaim***?

**PROMPT IDEAS** ***proclaim***
- school is dismissed early
- extra-long recess
- no homework tonight

- The second word is ***reclaim***. The prefix ***re-*** means to do again, and the Latin root ***claim*** means to declare or call out. ***Reclaim*** means to get back something lost or taken away.
  - Name some things you'd like to ***reclaim***.

**PROMPT IDEAS** ***reclaim***
- lost jacket
- bad kick in the soccer game
- cookie given away

**YOU DO** Now it's your turn. Work with a partner, and record your ideas on a whiteboard so you're ready to share with the class. You'll have five minutes to think of examples of two words that contain the Latin root ***dict***.

- The two words are ***predict*** and ***contradict***.
  - What does the prefix ***pre-*** mean? Before What does the root ***dict*** mean? To say or tell What does ***predict*** mean? To tell something before it happens
  - What does the prefix ***contra-*** mean? against What does the root ***dict*** mean? To say or tell What does ***contradict*** mean? To say something that is the opposite of what was said earlier
  - Think of an example of a ***prediction***. It can be one you've actually made or one that is possible.
  - Think of an example of a ***contradiction***. Again, it can be something that you observed or something that could happen.

**PROMPT IDEAS** ***predict***
- weather tomorrow
- gift for an upcoming birthday
- winner of future game

**PROMPT IDEAS** ***contradict***
- feeling good but calling in sick
- saying one thing and doing another
- eating ice cream while on a diet

# rupt, tend/tense/tens~~e~~/tent per-

## DAY 5 • Introduce Latin Roots

### UNCOVER THE MEANING

**Introduce *rupt* and *tend/tense/tens~~e~~/tent; per-***

MATERIALS
- Days 5 & 6 Recording Sheet

**DIRECTIONS** Pair students and distribute the **Days 5 & 6 Recording Sheet**. Model the first completed example. After students have completed the first two columns, ask them to share what they wrote. Then provide the Certified Definition. Explain that understanding parts of words, such as Latin roots, can help students uncover the meaning of many words.

**I'm going to model using my detective skills to figure out what the underlined word parts mean.**

- I'll use the other words in the sentences to develop a Working Definition of a word part.
- Listen as I read the first set of three sentences.
  1. The balloon ***ruptured*** with a loud pop that startled the class.
  2. Last year the earth's crust was ***rupturing*** from the volcano's pressure.
  3. The music stopped ***abruptly***, surprising the audience.
- In **Column 1**, I record the clue words pop, startled, strong surge, stopped, and surprising that help me understand the meaning of ***rupt***.
- I think that ***rupt*** means to crack open or stop suddenly. This is my Working Definition, which I record in **Column 2**.
- In **Column 3**, I will write the Certified Definition of ***rupt***: to break or burst.

**Now it's your turn.**

- With your partner, read the next set of sentences on the **Days 5 & 6 Recording Sheet**.
- Use your detective skills to figure out what the underlined word parts mean.
- Consider which words or phrases in the sentences provide clues about meaning. Record them in **Column 1**.
- Write a Working Definition in **Column 2**.
- Only complete **Columns 1** and **2** and then wait for the discussion. You will fill in **Column 3** after I provide a Certified Definition.

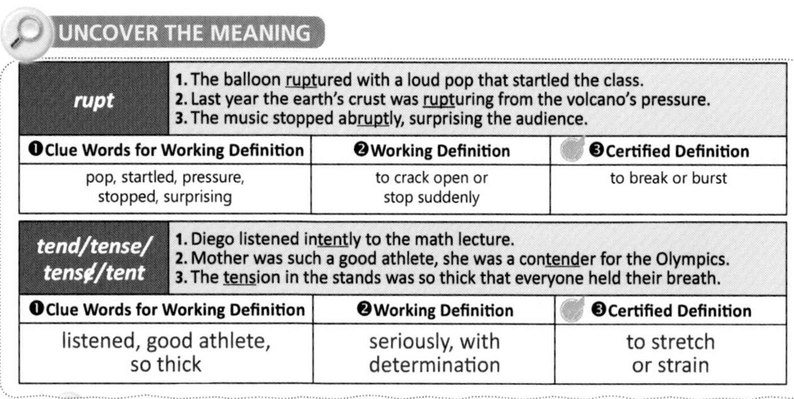

UNCOVER THE MEANING

| *rupt* | 1. The balloon ruptured with a loud pop that startled the class.<br>2. Last year the earth's crust was rupturing from the volcano's pressure.<br>3. The music stopped abruptly, surprising the audience. | |
|---|---|---|
| **❶ Clue Words for Working Definition** | **❷ Working Definition** | **❸ Certified Definition** |
| pop, startled, pressure, stopped, surprising | to crack open or stop suddenly | to break or burst |

| *tend/tense/tens~~e~~/tent* | 1. Diego listened intently to the math lecture.<br>2. Mother was such a good athlete, she was a contender for the Olympics.<br>3. The tension in the stands was so thick that everyone held their breath. | |
|---|---|---|
| **❶ Clue Words for Working Definition** | **❷ Working Definition** | **❸ Certified Definition** |
| listened, good athlete, so thick | seriously, with determination | to stretch or strain |

# DAY 6 • Deepen the Meaning

## CHECK MEANING

MATERIALS
- Pocket chart, document camera, or PowerPoint™
- Days 5 & 6 Recording Sheet
- Cards:
  Teacher: cor, inter, rupt
  Student: Roots: rupt, tense, tensé, tent
  Prefixes: dis, ex
  Suffix: ive

**DIRECTIONS** Using the **Cards** and **Mat**, confirm that students understand how the meaning of the word evolves as more parts are added.

**I DO**

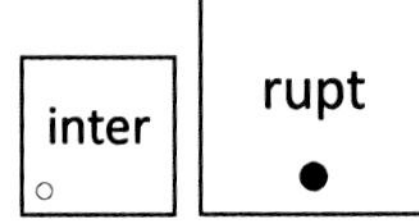

- The prefix ***inter-*** means between.
- Adding ***inter-*** to ***rupt*** spells the word ***interrupt***. The combination of word parts means stopping an activity by breaking in.
- Now I'm going to use my knowledge of the word to answer the question.
  1. What does it mean when I ***interrupt*** a lecture? I break into the lecture.

**WE DO**

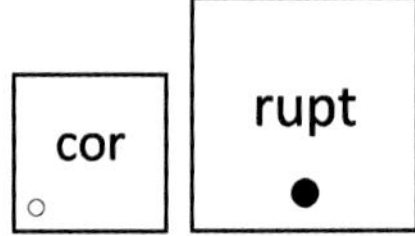

- The prefix ***cor-*** means with.
- After adding ***cor-*** to ***rupt*** what's the meaning? To break trust with or be dishonest
- Listen to me use the word ***corrupt*** in a question and we will use our knowledge of its parts to figure out the answer.
  2. What does it mean when a shop owner is ***corrupt***? He breaks the trust of his customers or cheats them.

**YOU DO** Use your **Cards** and **Mats** to complete the chart on the **Days 5 & 6 Recording Sheet**.

| Latin Roots | Certified Definition |
|---|---|
| rupt | to break or burst |
| tend/tense/ tensé/tent | to stretch or strain |
| **Prefixes** | **Certified Definition** |
| ab- | from, away |
| cor- | together, with |
| dis- | not, apart |
| ex- | out |
| in- | in, on, toward |
| per- | through or completely |
| pre- | before |
| **Suffixes** | **Certified Definition** |
| -ly | like |
| -ion | state of being, quality, or action |
| -ious | characterized by, like |
| -ive | showing a quality |
| **Inflected Endings** | **Certified Definition** |
| -ed | past tense |
| -ing | present participle |

| Word | Prefix | Latin Root | Suffix |
|---|---|---|---|
| extent | ex: out | tent: to stretch or strain | |
| Meaning: | the range to which something reaches | | |
| extensive | ex: out | tensé: to stretch or strain | ive: showing a quality |
| Meaning: | having a wide reach | | |
| disrupt | dis: not | rupt: to break | |
| Meaning: | to stop something from continuing in the normal way | | |
| disruptive | dis: not | rupt: to break | ive: showing a quality |
| Meaning: | causing an interruption or break | | |

# rupt, tend/tense/tens~~e~~/tent
# per-

## DAY 7 • Word Multiplier

### WORD MULTIPLIER

**Build words with *rupt* and *tend/tense/tens~~e~~/tent; per-***

**DIRECTIONS** Students work together to build words using their **Cards** and **Mats**.

MATERIALS
- Day 7 Recording Sheet
- Notebook paper
- Latin Mat
- Cards:
  Latin Roots: rupt, tend, tense, tens~~e~~, tent
  Inflected Endings: ed, ing
  Prefixes: ab, cor, ex, in, per, pre
  Suffixes: ion, ious, ly

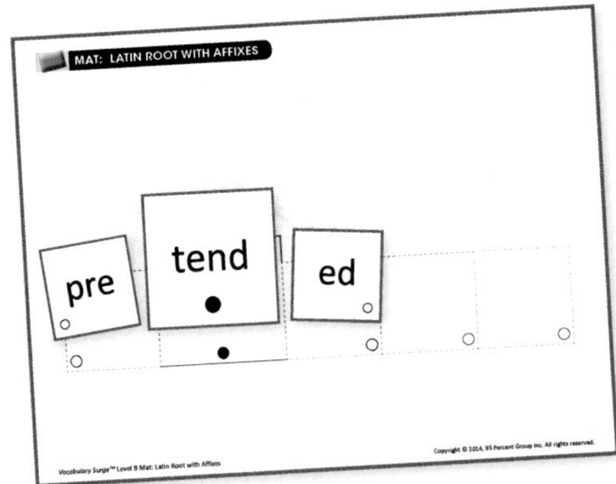


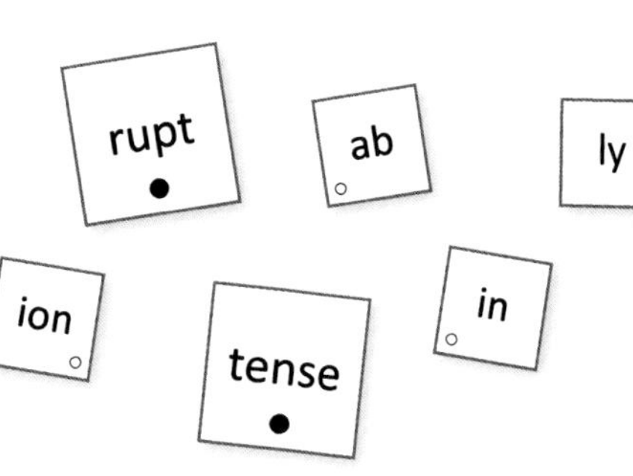


**WE DO** Let's combine **Cards** to build a word.

- I select cards ***pre, tend,*** and ***ed***.
- Where shall I place the prefix ***pre-***? On the left side of the mat
- Where do I place the Latin root ***tend***? In the large center box, matching the solid circles
- Finally, where shall I place the inflected ending ***-ed***? To the right of ***tend***, matching the circle on the mat to the one on the card
- What word have we built? Pretended
- What is the definition of ***pretended***? Acted like someone or something else
- What part of speech is the word ***pretended*** and how do you know? Verb, action word

**WORD MULTIPLIER**

**DIRECTIONS** Record the words and complete the chart. Record additional words on notebook paper.

| SET 1 | Word Parts | Words | Part of Speech |
|---|---|---|---|
| 1. | ab+rupt+ly | abruptly | adverb |
| | Write the Meaning: | suddenly | |
| 2. | cor+rupt+ion | corruption | noun |
| | Write the Meaning: | something that is dishonest or immoral | |

| SET 2 | Word Parts | Words | Part of Speech |
|---|---|---|---|
| 1. | in+tend+ed | intended | verb |
| | Write the Meaning: | had a purpose in mind | |
| 2. | ex+tend+ed | extended | verb |
| | Write the Meaning: | to have stretched out | |
| 3. | pre+tent+ious | pretentious | adverb |
| | Write the Meaning: | trying to appear to be more than you really are | |

**YOU DO** Use your **Cards** and **Mats** to build more words. Complete the **Day 7 Recording Sheet** with your partner. Write additional words on notebook paper.

**Possible Words:**

**rupt:** abrupt, abruptly, corrupt, corruption, corruptly

**tend/tense/tens~~e~~/tent:** extend, extended, intend, intended, intense, pretend, pretended, pretense, pretentious, tend, tended, tense

**rupt, tend/tense/tens~~e~~/tent**
**per-**

## DAY 8 • Demonstrate Meaning

### BUILD MEANING

MATERIALS
• Whiteboards
• Markers

**DIRECTIONS** Complete the I Do and We Do sections with the whole class, and pair students to work on the You Do activity. Students can record their ideas on small whiteboards. Ask a few pairs to share their work with the class.

**I DO** Listen to me demonstrate understanding of the meaning of the Latin root ***rupt***.

- The first word is ***abruptly***. We learned yesterday that ***abruptly*** means suddenly. I'm going to think of examples of times when things happened ***abruptly***.
  - It ***abruptly*** began pouring at the ball game.
  - The school bus stopped ***abruptly***, throwing students against their seats.
- The second word is ***disrupted***, which means to have broken in or disturbed something. I'm going to think of examples of things that were ***disrupted***.
  - Today's reading lesson was ***disrupted*** by the fire drill.
  - Traffic was ***disrupted*** by the heavy snowfall.

**WE DO** Let's try the next one together with the Latin root ***tens***.

- The first word is ***tensed***. The Latin root ***tens*** means to stretch or strain, and the inflected ending ***-ed*** means it happened in the past. ***Tensed*** means nervous or stretched tight. I felt ***tense*** while a teacher handed back test papers.
  - Name a time when you felt ***tense***.
- The second word is ***pretense***. The prefix ***pre-*** means before, and the Latin root ***tens*** means to stretch or strain. ***Pretense*** means stretching the truth.
  - Name a time when you acted with ***pretense***.

**PROMPT IDEAS** ***tensed***
- getting a shot
- taking a test
- performing a play

**PROMPT IDEAS** ***pretense***
- acting calm when nervous
- seeming to like something when you don't
- pretending to be brave when scared

**YOU DO** Now it's your turn. Work with a partner, and record your ideas on a whiteboard so you're ready to share with the class. You'll have five minutes to think of examples for two words that contain the Latin root ***tend***.

- The two words are ***pretend*** and ***extend***.
  - What does the prefix ***pre-*** mean? Before What does the root ***tend*** mean? To stretch or strain What does ***pretend*** mean? To stretch the truth, make believe
  - What does the prefix ***ex-*** mean? Out What does the root ***tend*** mean? To stretch or strain What does ***extend*** mean? To stretch out far
  - Think of an example of when you ***pretended*** or might ***pretend***.
  - Think of an example of something you can ***extend***.

**PROMPT IDEAS** ***pretend***
- acting in a play
- playing a joke
- imitating someone else

**PROMPT IDEAS** ***extend***
- your arms
- video game
- tape measure

 

# claim/clam, dic/dict, rupt, tend/tense/tens~~e~~/tent, voc/voke/vok~~e~~ per-, -ship

## DAY 9 • Review What You Learned

### STEP 1 REVIEW THE MEANING

MATERIALS
- Word parts projected on document camera, overhead projector, or PowerPoint™

**Review *claim/clam, dic/dict, rupt, tend/tense/tens~~e~~/tent,* and *voc/voke/vok~~e~~*/ Affixes *per-* and *-ship***

**DIRECTIONS** Display the morphemes so students can see them, and ask for the Certified Definition of each one.

**When I show you the word parts, think about the Certified Definitions we discussed as you prepare to answer.**

| Latin Root | Certified Definition | Affix | Certified Definition |
|---|---|---|---|
| *claim/clam* | to declare, call out, or cry out | *-ship* | office, state, dignity, skill, quality, or profession |
| *dic/dict* | to say or tell | | |
| *voc/voke/vok~~e~~* | to call or voice | | |
| **Latin Root** | **Certified Definition** | | **Certified Definition** |
| *rupt* | to break or burst | *per-* | thorough or completely |
| *tend/tense/tens~~e~~/tent* | to stretch or strain | | |

### STEP 2 CHECK MEANING

MATERIALS
- Day 9 Recording Sheet

**DIRECTIONS** Read the following sentences to check that students understand the meanings of ***claim/clam, dic/dict, rupt, tend/tens/tens~~e~~/tent,*** and ***voc/voke/vok~~e~~***. Model the first sentence for students using the We Do step, below.

**WE DO** As I read this sentence, think about the Certified Definitions of the Latin root that fits the blank.

1. Juan re__________ed his video game from his brother.

- Which Latin root do you think fits on the line? Claim
- What is the new word? Reclaimed
- What do you think the word ***reclaimed*** means? Called back

**YOU DO** With your partner, complete the rest of the sentences on the **Day 9 Recording Sheet** by finding the Latin root that best fits on the line. Record the new words and their meanings.

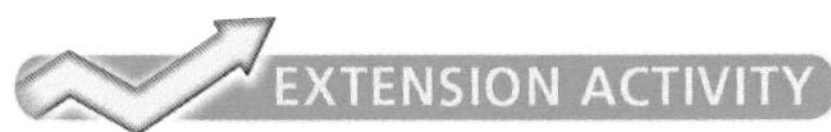

EXTENSION ACTIVITY

Students write two sentences with missing Latin roots to challenge the class.

CHECK MEANING

1. Juan **re** claim **ed** his video game from his brother. reclaimed
   Meaning: to get back something lost or taken away
2. My dad likes to dict **ate** every hour of my weekend activities. dictate
   Meaning: to tell someone what to do
3. The class president voc **alized** a speech at graduation. vocalized
   Meaning: voiced words or sounds
4. Jeff tend **ed** his hold on the kite in the strong wind. tended
   Meaning: paid attention to
5. The fire alarm's **inter** rupt **ion** of the game caused the students to leave. interruption
   Meaning: causing something to stop from continuing in the normal way
6. The bullfrog's throat will **dis** tend each time he croaks. distend
   Meaning: to stretch or bulge

claim/clam, dic/dict, rupt, tend/tense/tensé/tent, voc/voke/voké per-, -ship

# DAY 10 • 2nd Review Day

## STEP 1 MAKE CONNECTIONS

MATERIALS
- Day 10 Recording Sheet

**DIRECTIONS** Students pair up to write sentences with either one or two of the words that are provided.

**I am going to model how to use one word containing this week's Latin roots in a meaningful sentence. The word is *disruptive*.**

- The noise in the hall was ***disruptive***.
- It is your turn to write five more sentences using the words on the top of the recording sheet.
- Sentences with two words get two points and sentences with one word get one point.

MAKE CONNECTIONS

| Words | | |
|---|---|---|
| abruptly | disruptive | proclaim |
| abdicate | extensive | rupture |
| clamor | interruption | rupturing |
| corruptly | prediction | tense |
| dictator | predictor | vocalist |
| dictatorship | pretentious | vocalize |

1. The noise in the hall was disruptive.
2. Tom's cat stopped abruptly.
3. Last year the volcano's lava was rupturing from the ground.
4. The child's temperature was a predictor she was sick.
5. The vocalist's behavior was pretentious.

## STEP 2 CHALLENGE: MORPHEME MADNESS

MATERIALS
- Notebook paper
- Latin Mat
- Cards listed in the table below

**DIRECTIONS** Students pair up to use **Cards** and **Mats** to build words. They also record all of the words they build and the words' definitions.

| Word Parts | Cards |
|---|---|
| **Latin Roots** | claim, clam, dic, dict, rupt, tend, tense, tensé, tent, voc, voke, voké |
| **Inflected Endings** | ed, ing |
| **Prefixes** | contra, cor, dis, ex, in, inter, pre, re |
| **Suffixes** | al, até, ion |

**Now it's your turn to build words.**

- First, find a partner.
- Use the **Cards** and **Mats** to build words.
- Record the words and their definitions on a separate sheet of paper.

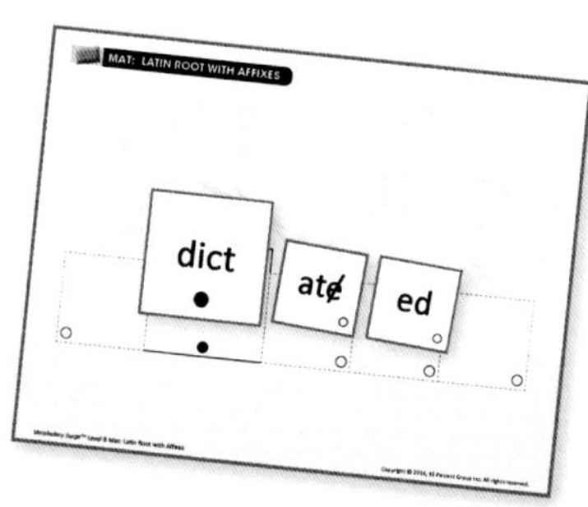


 

# cline/clin~~e~~, flu/fluc/flux, jac/ject, rect/recti/reg, verse/vers~~e~~/vert di-

## DAY 1 • Introduce Latin Roots

### UNCOVER THE MEANING

**MATERIALS**
- Days 1 & 2 Recording Sheet

#### Introduce *flu/fluc/flux* and *jac/ject*

**DIRECTIONS** Pair students and distribute the **Days 1 & 2 Recording Sheet**. Model the first completed example. After students have completed the first two columns, ask them to share what they wrote. Then provide the Certified Definition. Explain that understanding parts of words, such as Latin roots, can help students uncover the meaning of many words.

**I'm going to model using my detective skills to figure out what the underlined word parts mean.**

- I'll use the other words in the sentences to develop a Working Definition of a word part.
- Listen as I read the first set of three sentences.
  1. There has been a huge ***influx*** of jellyfish coming in to shore and washing up on the beach.
  2. The force of the water changes and ***fluctuates*** depending on whether the dam's gates are open or closed.
  3. People show their ***affluence*** by continuing to buy expensive things.
- In **Column 1**, I record the clue words coming in, washing up, force, changes, and continuing that help me understand the meaning of ***flu/fluc/flux***.
- I think that ***flu/fluc/flux*** means change or move. This is my Working Definition, which I record in **Column 2**.
- In **Column 3**, I write the Certified Definition of ***flu/fluc/flux***: to flow.

**Now it's your turn.**

- With your partner, read the next set of sentences on the **Days 1 & 2 Recording Sheet**.
- Use your detective skills to figure out what the underlined word parts mean.
- Consider which words or phrases in the sentences provide clues about meaning. Record them in **Column 1**.
- Write a Working Definition in **Column 2**.
- Only complete **Columns 1** and **2** and then wait for the discussion. You will fill in **Column 3** after I provide a Certified Definition.

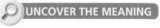

UNCOVER THE MEANING

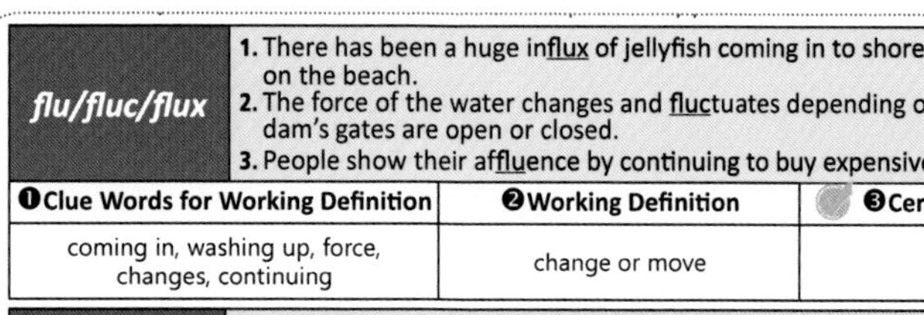

| *flu/fluc/flux* | 1. There has been a huge influx of jellyfish coming in to shore and washing up on the beach. 2. The force of the water changes and fluctuates depending on whether the dam's gates are open or closed. 3. People show their affluence by continuing to buy expensive things. | |
|---|---|---|
| ❶ Clue Words for Working Definition | ❷ Working Definition | ❸ Certified Definition |
| coming in, washing up, force, changes, continuing | change or move | to flow |

| *jac/ject* | 1. The machine projects light across the room and onto a screen. 2. When the nurse injected Kim with the needle, the medicine thrust into her arm. 3. Chris rejected the moldy orange, refusing to accept it on his lunch tray. | |
|---|---|---|
| ❶ Clue Words for Working Definition | ❷ Working Definition | ❸ Certified Definition |
| across, onto, thrust, refusing to accept | expel, push | to throw; lie |

# DAY 2 • Deepen the Meaning

## CHECK MEANING

**DIRECTIONS** Using the **Cards** and **Mat**, confirm that students understand how the meaning of the word evolves as more parts are added.

**MATERIALS**
- Pocket chart, document camera, or PowerPoint™
- Days 1 & 2 Recording Sheet
- Cards:
  Teacher: ent, flu, ly
  Student: Roots: flux, ject
  Prefixes: in, re
  Suffixes: ion

**I DO**

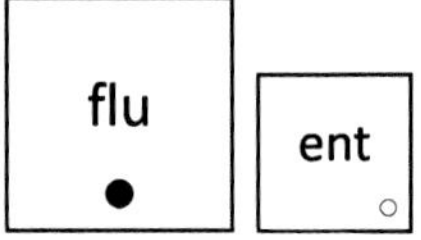


- The suffix ***-ent*** means action.
- Adding ***-ent*** to ***flu*** changes the meaning of the root. The combination of word parts means to do something in a smooth, flowing way.
- Now I'm going to use my knowledge of the word to answer the question.

1. What does it mean when we say that Ingrid is ***fluent*** in German? She speaks German well.

**WE DO**

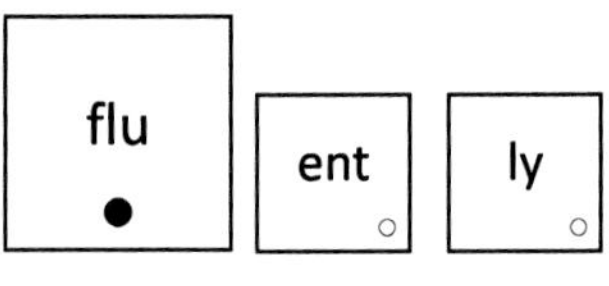


- The suffix ***-ly*** (bold, italics) means like or manner of.
- How does adding the ***-ly*** to ***fluent*** change the meaning? Doing something in a smooth, flowing way
- Listen to me use the word ***fluently*** in a question and we will use our knowledge of its parts to figure out the answer.

2. What does it mean when Jamal reads the passage ***fluently***. He reads it in a smooth, flowing way.

**YOU DO** Use your **Cards** and **Mats** to complete the chart on the **Days 1 & 2 Recording Sheet**.

| Latin Roots | Certified Definition |
|---|---|
| flu/fluc/flux | to flow |
| jac/ject | to throw or lie |
| **Prefixes** | **Certified Definition** |
| ad- | towards, near |
| in- | in or not |
| pro- | earlier, to support |
| re- | again, back |
| **Suffixes** | **Certified Definition** |
| -ence | action, state, or quality |
| -ent | action, state, or quality |
| -ion | state or being, quality, or action |
| -ly | like |
| **Inflected Endings** | **Certified Definition** |
| -ed | past tense |
| -ing | present |

**DIRECTIONS** Build the words with the Cards and Mats. Describe how adding new parts changes the meaning of the words.

| Word | Prefix | Latin Root | Suffix |
|---|---|---|---|
| inject | in: in, on, or towards | ject: to throw | |
| Meaning: | to insert one thing into another | | |
| injection | in: in, on, or towards | ject: to throw | ion: action |
| Meaning: | a fluid forced into someone or something | | |
| influx | in: in | flux: to flow | |
| Meaning: | an inflow | | |
| reflux | re: back | flux: to flow | |
| Meaning: | a flowing back | | |

# flu/fluc/flux, jac/ject

## DAY 3 • Word Multiplier

### WORD MULTIPLIER

MATERIALS
- Day 3 Recording Sheet
- Notebook paper
- Latin Mat
- Cards:
  Latin Roots: flu, fluc, flux, jac, ject
  Inflected Endings: ed, ing
  Prefixes: ad, in, pro, re
  Suffixes: ence, ent, ion, ly

**Build words with *flu/fluc/flux* and *jac/ject***

**DIRECTIONS** Students work together to build words using their Cards and Mats.

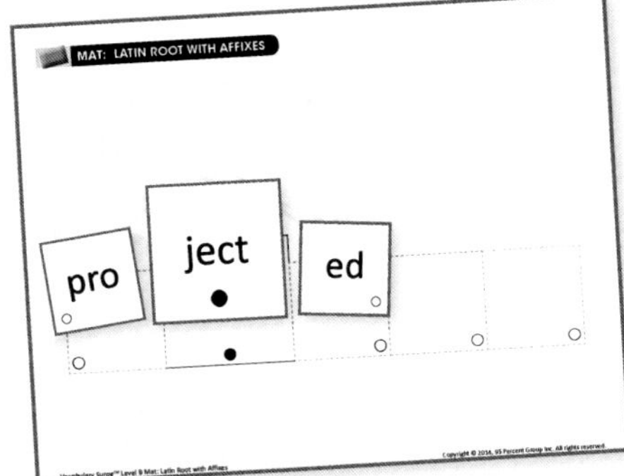


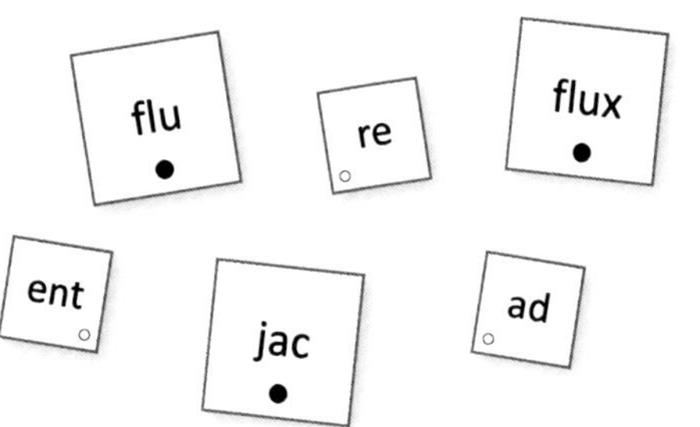


**I DO** Watch me combine Cards to build a word.

- I select cards ***pro, ject,*** and ***ed***.
- I place the prefix ***pro-*** on the left side of the mat, matching the circle on the mat to the one on the card.
- I place the Latin root ***ject*** in the large center box, matching the solid circles.
- Finally, I place the inflected ending ***-ed*** to the right of ***ject***, matching the circle on the mat to the one on the card.
- I have built the word ***projected***.

**WE DO** Let me try another.

- I choose the cards ***flu, ent,*** and ***ly***.
- Where should I place the card ***flu***? In the middle box
- Why do we place it here? Because it is the Latin root and has a solid circle like the mat
- Where shall I place suffix ***-ent***? In the box to the right of ***flu***
- Where shall I place suffix ***-ly***? In the box to the right of ***ent***
- Look at the example on your **Day 3 Recording Sheet** to see how to write the parts of ***fluently*** and the whole word. ***Flu*** means to flow, ***-ent*** means action, and ***-ly*** means characterized by.
- When we put these word parts together, ***fluently*** means doing something in a smooth, flowing way.
- What part of speech is ***fluently*** and how do you know? Adverb, describes or modifies a verb

**WORD MULTIPLIER**

| SET 1 | Word Parts | Word | Part of Speech |
|---|---|---|---|
| 1. | flu+ent+ly | fluently | adverb |
| | Write the Meaning: | doing something in a smooth, flowing way | |
| 2. | in+flu+ence | influence | noun, verb |
| | Write the Meaning: | N: power over something or someone else<br>V: to have power over something | |
| 3. | re+flux+ing | refluxing | verb |
| | Write the Meaning: | flowing back | |

| SET 2 | Word Parts | Word | Part of Speech |
|---|---|---|---|
| 1. | ad+jac+ent | adjacent | adjective |
| | Write the Meaning: | lies next to or near | |
| 2. | pro+ject+ed | projected | verb |
| | Write the Meaning: | threw forward or planned ahead | |

**YOU DO** Use your **Cards** and **Mats** to build more words. Complete the **Day 3 Recording Sheet** with your partner. Write additional words on notebook paper. We will review the words when you have finished.

**Possible Words**:

**flu/fluc/flux:** fluent, fluently, flux, fluxing, influence, influx, influxing, reflux, refluxing

**jac/ject:** adjacent, project, projected, projection

## DAY 4 • Demonstrate Meaning

### BUILD MEANING

MATERIALS
- Whiteboards
- Markers

**DIRECTIONS** Complete the I Do and We Do sections with the whole class, and pair students to work on the You Do activity. Students can record their ideas on small whiteboards. Ask a few pairs to share their work with the class.

**I DO** Listen to me demonstrate understanding of the meaning of the Latin root *flu*.

- The first word is ***fluently***. We learned yesterday that ***fluently*** means doing something in a smooth, flowing way. I'm going to think of examples of times when something happened ***fluently***.
  - Melissa ***fluently*** read a chapter book to the class.
  - I don't ***fluently*** speak Spanish.
- The second word is ***influence***, which means power over someone or something. I'm going to think of an example of something that has ***influenced*** me.
  - My friend's ***influence*** led me to go to the movies.
  - Jason's bike accident ***influences*** me to wear my helmet.

**WE DO** Let's try the next one together with the Latin root *ject*.

- The first word is ***project***. The prefix ***pro-*** means forward, and the Latin root ***ject*** means to throw. ***Project*** means to throw something forward.
  I ***project*** my voice so you can hear me.
  - What things might we ***project***?
- The second word is ***inject***. The prefix ***in-*** means in, and the Latin root ***ject*** means to throw. ***Inject*** means to insert one thing into another.
  - Name something you can ***inject***.

**PROMPT IDEAS** ***project***
- your voice
- cannonball
- rocket

**PROMPT IDEAS** ***inject***
- a shot of medicine into your arm
- cream into a doughnut
- fluids through a syringe

**YOU DO** Now it's your turn. Work with a partner, and record your ideas on a whiteboard so you're ready to share with the class. You'll have five minutes to think of examples for two words that contain the Latin root *flu*.

- The two words are ***influence*** and ***fluctuate***.
  - What does the Latin root ***flu*** mean? Flow What does ***influence*** mean? To persuade or have power over something
  - What does the Latin root ***flu*** mean? Flow What does ***fluctuate*** mean? To change constantly
  - Think of an example of something that you can ***influence***. It can be something you do ***influence*** or something that is possible to ***influence***.
  - Think of an example of something that ***fluctuates***. It can be something you have observed or something you might observe.

**PROMPT IDEAS** ***influence***
- choice for dinner
- birthday party plans
- group project

**PROMPT IDEAS** ***fluctuate***
- outside temperature
- price of gasoline
- population of birds

cline/clin~~e~~, rect/recti/reg,
verse/vers~~e~~/vert di-

# DAY 5 • Introduce Latin Roots

## UNCOVER THE MEANING

MATERIALS
• Days 5 & 6 Recording Sheet

### Introduce *cline/clin~~e~~, rect/recti/reg,* and *verse/vers~~e~~/vert; di-*

**DIRECTIONS** Pair students and distribute the Days 5 & 6 Recording Sheet. Model the first completed example. After students have completed the first two columns, ask them to share what they wrote. Then provide the Certified Definition. Explain that understanding parts of words, such as Latin roots, can help students uncover the meaning of many words.

**I'm going to model using my detective skills to figure out what the underlined word parts mean.**

- I'll use the other words in the sentences to develop a Working Definition of a word part.
- Listen as I read the first set of two sentences.
  1. The ball easily rolled down the steep ***decline***.
  2. Dad tipped back in his ***recliner*** until he was leaning way back.
- In **Column 1**, I record the clue words down, steep, tipped, and leaning that help me understand the meaning of ***cline***.
- I think that ***cline*** means slant or angle. This is my Working Definition, which I record in **Column 2**.
- In **Column 3**, I will write the Certified Definition of ***cline***: to lean.

**Now it's your turn.**

- With your partner, read the next set of sentences on the Days 5 & 6 Recording Sheet.
- Use your detective skills to figure out what the underlined word parts mean.
- Consider which words or phrases in the sentences provide clues about meaning. Record them in **Column 1**.
- Write a Working Definition in **Column 2**.
- Only complete **Columns 1** and **2** and then wait for the discussion. You will fill in **Column 3** after I provide a Certified Definition.

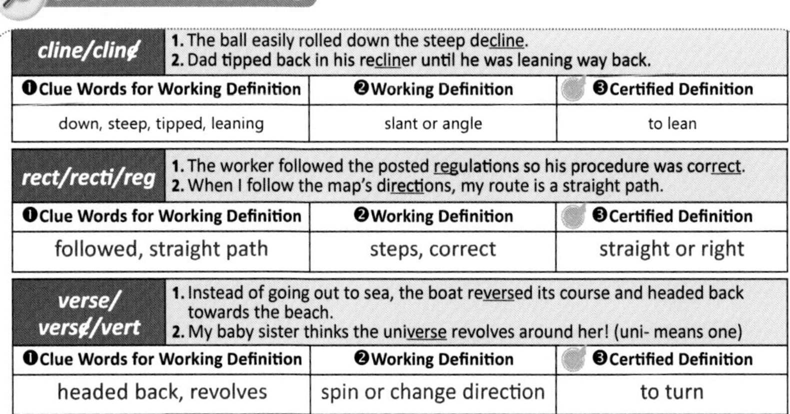

UNCOVER THE MEANING

| cline/clin~~e~~ | 1. The ball easily rolled down the steep decline.<br>2. Dad tipped back in his recliner until he was leaning way back. | |
|---|---|---|
| ❶ Clue Words for Working Definition | ❷ Working Definition | ❸ Certified Definition |
| down, steep, tipped, leaning | slant or angle | to lean |

| rect/recti/reg | 1. The worker followed the posted regulations so his procedure was correct.<br>2. When I follow the map's directions, my route is a straight path. | |
|---|---|---|
| ❶ Clue Words for Working Definition | ❷ Working Definition | ❸ Certified Definition |
| followed, straight path | steps, correct | straight or right |

| verse/vers~~e~~/vert | 1. Instead of going out to sea, the boat reversed its course and headed back towards the beach.<br>2. My baby sister thinks the universe revolves around her! (uni- means one) | |
|---|---|---|
| ❶ Clue Words for Working Definition | ❷ Working Definition | ❸ Certified Definition |
| headed back, revolves | spin or change direction | to turn |

# cline/clin~~e~~, rect/recti/reg, verse/vers~~e~~/vert di-

## DAY 6 • Deepen the Meaning

### CHECK MEANING

**MATERIALS**
- Pocket chart, document camera, or PowerPoint™
- Days 5 & 6 Recording Sheet
- Cards:
  Teachers: con, re, vert
  Students: Roots: cline, rect
  Prefixes: de, di, in
  Suffixes: ion

**DIRECTIONS** Using the **Cards** and **Mat**, confirm that students understand how the meaning of the word evolves as more parts are added.

**I DO**

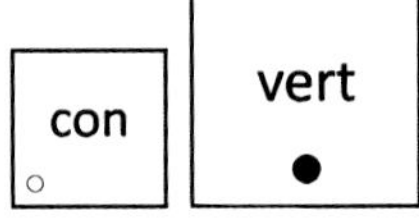

- The prefix ***con-*** means with.
- Adding ***con-*** to ***vert*** changes the meaning of the root. The combination of word parts means to change something to a different form.
- Now, I'm going to use my knowledge of the word to answer the question.

1. What does it mean when we say that Vern might ***convert*** the class to be recyclers? I think Vern will make them, like himself, a recycler.

**WE DO**

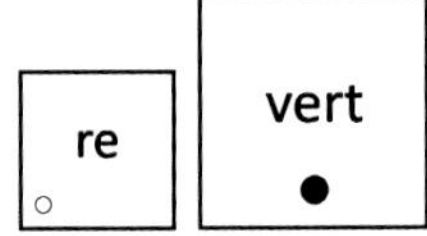

- The prefix ***re-*** means again.
- How does adding ***re-*** to ***vert*** change the meaning? To change something back to the way it was
- Listen to me use the word ***revert*** in a question and we will use our knowledge of its parts to figure out the answer.

2. What does it mean when the toddler ***reverts*** to using a bottle? He goes back to using a bottle.

**YOU DO** Use your **Cards** and **Mats** to complete the chart on the **Days 5 & 6 Recording Sheet**.

| Latin Roots | Certified Definition |
|---|---|
| cline/clin~~e~~ | lean |
| rect/recti/reg | straight or right |
| verse/vers~~e~~/vert | to turn |
| **Prefixes** | **Certified Definition** |
| de- | away from, down |
| di- | two |
| in- | in or not |
| re- | again, back |
| **Suffixes** | **Certified Definition** |
| -al | related to, like |
| -ion | action |
| -ness | state of |
| **Inflected Endings** | **Certified Definition** |
| -ed | past tense |
| -ing | present |

**DIRECTIONS** Build the words with your Cards and Mats. Describe how adding new parts changes the meaning of the words.

| Word | Prefix | Latin Root | Suffix |
|---|---|---|---|
| incline | in: in | cline: to lean | |
| Meaning: | to lean towards doing something | | |
| decline | de: away from | cline: to lean | |
| Meaning: | to lean away from doing something; to slope downward | | |
| direct | di: two | rect: straight | |
| Meaning: | to guide someone or to move in a straight route between two points | | |
| direction | di: two | rect: straight | ion: action |
| Meaning: | the course or region to which something travels | | |

# cline/clin~~e~~, rect/recti/reg, verse/vers~~e~~/vert di-

## DAY 7 • Word Multiplier

### WORD MULTIPLIER

**Build words with *cline/clin~~e~~, rect/recti/reg,* and *verse/vers~~e~~/vert; di-***

**DIRECTIONS** Students work together to build words using their **Cards** and **Mats**.

MATERIALS
- Day 7 Recording Sheet
- Notebook paper
- Latin Mat
- Cards:
  Latin Roots: clin~~e~~, rect, recti, reg, verse, vers~~e~~, vert
  Inflected Endings: ed, ing
  Prefixes: de, di, in, re
  Suffixes: al, ion, ness

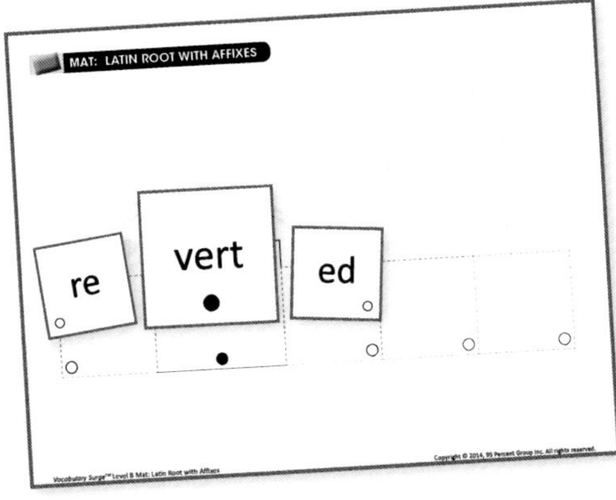


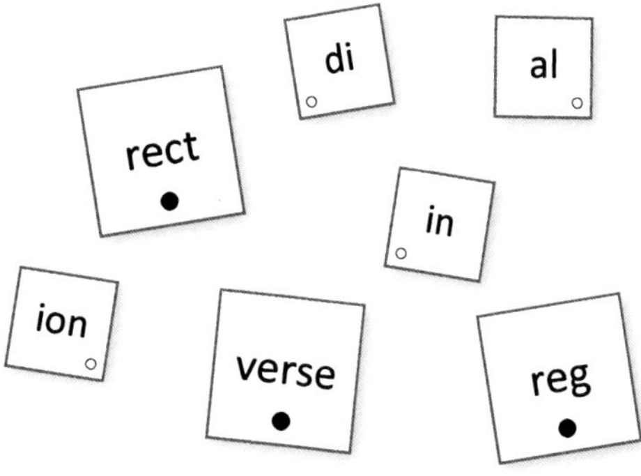


**WE DO** Let's combine **Cards** to build a word.

- I select cards ***re, vert,*** and ***ed***.
- Where shall I place the prefix ***re-***? On the left side of the mat
- Where do I place the Latin root ***vert***? In the large center box, matching the solid circles
- Where shall I place the inflected ending ***-ed***? In the box to the right of ***vert***, matching the circle on the mat to the one on the card
- What word have we built? Reverted What is the definition of ***reverted***? To have gone back to the way it was
- What is the part of speech is ***reverted*** and how do you know? Verb, words ending in *-ed* are usually verbs

**WORD MULTIPLIER**

| SET 1 | Word Parts | Word | Part of Speech |
|---|---|---|---|
| 1. | de+clin~~e~~+ed | declined | verb |
| | Write the Meaning: | sloped downward or turned something down | |
| 2. | re+clin~~e~~+ing | reclining | verb |
| | Write the Meaning: | leaning backwards | |
| **SET 2** | **Word Parts** | **Word** | **Part of Speech** |
| 1. | di+rect+ness | directness | noun |
| | Write the Meaning: | being accurate or on course | |
| 2. | reg+ion | region | noun |
| | Write the Meaning: | a geographical area or part of the world | |
| **SET 3** | **Word Parts** | **Word** | **Part of Speech** |
| 1. | in+vert+ed | inverted | verb |
| | Write the Meaning: | to have turned upside down or to have reversed position | |
| 2. | re+vers~~e~~+al | reversal | noun |
| | Write the Meaning: | the act of turning in the opposite direction | |

**YOU DO** Use your **Cards** and **Mats** to build more words. Complete the **Day 7 Recording Sheet** with your partner. Write additional words on notebook paper.

**Possible Words:**

**cline/clin~~e~~:** declined, declining, reclined, reclining
**rect/recti/reg:** direct, direction, directness, region
**vers/verse/vers~~e~~/vert:** inverse, invert, inverted, inverting, reversal, reverse, reversed, reversing

cline/cline̸, rect/recti/reg, verse/verse̸/vert di-

# DAY 8 • Demonstrate Meaning

## BUILD MEANING

MATERIALS
- Whiteboards
- Markers

**DIRECTIONS** Complete the I Do and We Do sections with the whole class, and pair students to work on the You Do activity. Students can record their ideas on small whiteboards. Ask a few pairs to share their work with the class.

**I DO** Listen to me demonstrate understanding of the meaning of the Latin root ***cline***.

- The first word is ***recline***. We learned yesterday that ***recline*** means lean backwards. I'm going to think of examples of things that can ***recline***.
  - My grandfather ***reclines*** the back of his chair.
  - The woman ***reclines*** on the couch.
- The second word is ***decline***, which means to slope downward or turn something down. I'm going to think of examples of things that ***decline***.
  - I ***decline*** my friend's invitation to go skating.
  - The cost of gas will ***decline*** this month.

**WE DO** Let's try the next one together with the Latin root ***vers***.

- The first word is ***reverse***. The prefix ***re*** means again or back, and the Latin root ***vers*** means to turn. ***Reverse*** means to turn in the opposite direction. My car backs up when it's in ***reverse***.
  - Name something that can ***reverse***.
- The second word is ***diverse***. The prefix ***di-*** means two or twice, and the Latin root ***vers*** means to turn. ***Diverse*** means to be different from another.
  - Name something that might be ***diverse***.

**PROMPT IDEAS** ***reverse***
- car
- decision
- tape recorder

**PROMPT IDEAS** ***diverse***
- types of doughnuts
- species of ocean fish
- students

**YOU DO** Now it's your turn. Work with a partner, and record your ideas on a whiteboard so you're ready to share with the class. You'll have five minutes to think of examples for two words that contain the Latin root ***rect***.

- The two words are ***direct*** and ***correct***.
  - What does the prefix ***di-*** mean? Two What does the root ***rect*** mean? Straight or right What does ***direct*** mean? To guide someone or to move in a straight route between two points
  - What does the prefix ***cor-*** mean? Together or with What does the root ***rect*** mean? Straight or right What does ***correct*** mean? Right
  - Think of an example of something that can be ***direct*** or can be ***directed***.
  - Think of an example of something that can be ***correct***.

**PROMPT IDEAS** ***direct***
- route between two locations
- airplane flight
- shortest route from home to school

**PROMPT IDEAS** ***correct***
- test answer
- math problem
- spelling

 

cline/cline, flu/fluc/flux, jac/ject, rect/recti/reg, verse/verse/vert di-

## DAY 9 • Review What You Learned

### STEP 1 REVIEW THE MEANING

MATERIALS
- Word parts projected on document camera, overhead projector, or PowerPoint™

**Review *cline/cline, flu/fluc/flux, jac/ject, rect/recti/reg,* and *verse/verse/vert***

**Affixes *di-***

**DIRECTIONS** Display the morphemes so students can see them, and ask for the certified definition of each one.

**When I show you the word parts, think about the Certified Definitions we discussed as you prepare to answer.**

| Latin Root | Certified Definition | Prefix | Certified Definition |
|---|---|---|---|
| *flu/fluc/flux* | to flow | ---- | ---- |
| *jac/ject* | to throw | | |
| **Latin Root** | **Certified Definition** | | **Certified Definition** |
| *cline/cline* | lean | *di-* | Two |
| *rect/recti/reg* | straight or right | | |
| *verse/verse/vert* | to turn | *uni-* | One |

### STEP 2 CHECK MEANING

MATERIALS
- Day 9 Recording Sheet

**DIRECTIONS** Read the following sentences to check that students understand the meanings of ***cline/cline, flu/fluc/flux, jac/ject, rect/recti/reg, verse/verse/vert,* and *di-*.** Model the first sentence for students using the We Do Step, below.

**WE DO** As I read this sentence, think about the Certified Definitions of the Latin root that fits the blank.

1. She de__________s the new job offer.

- Which Latin root do you think fits on the line? Cline
- What is the new word? Declines
- What do you think the word ***declines*** means? Turns down

**YOU DO** Complete the rest of the sentences on the **Day 9 Recording Sheet** with your partner to find the Latin root that best fits on the line. Record the new words and their meanings.

CHECK MEANING

1. She **de** cline **s** the new job offer. declines
   Meaning: turns down
2. The **di** rect **or** was in charge of the orchestra. director
   Meaning: the person who guides others by telling them what to do
3. The slide had a very steep **in** cline from the bottom to the top. incline
   Meaning: to lean forward or a forward-leaning slope
4. The nurse put the **in** ject **ion** into my arm. injection
   Meaning: a fluid forced into someone or something
5. The politician's **in** flu **ence** led the senators to pass the bill. influence
   Meaning: power over something or someone
6. There was a large **in** flux of tourists in the spring. influx
   Meaning: an inflow

Students write two sentences with missing Latin roots to challenge the class.

## cline/clin~~e~~, flu/fluc/flux, jac/ject, rect/recti/reg, verse/vers~~e~~/vert di-

# DAY 10 • 2nd Review Day

## STEP 1 MAKE CONNECTIONS

**MATERIALS**
- Day 10 Recording Sheet

**DIRECTIONS** Students pair up to write sentences with either one or two of the words that are provided.

**I am going to model how to use one word containing this week's Latin roots in a meaningful sentence. The** word is ***convert***.

- Jason wanted to ***convert*** his project from a poster to a paper.
- It is your turn to create five more sentences using the words on the top of the recording sheet.
- Sentences with two words get two points and sentences with one word get one point.

MAKE CONNECTIONS

| Words | | |
|---|---|---|
| adjacent | fluently | projection |
| affluence | incline | reclined |
| convert | influenced | rectify |
| directed | influx | regionally |
| director | injection | rejected |
| diversity | inversion | reverted |

1. Jason wanted to convert his project from a poster to a paper.
2. The quarterback threw the pass fluently.
3. In our science experiment we made a projection.
4. Our teacher rejected our idea of no homework tonight.
5. The director wanted to rectify the bad dress rehearsal.

## STEP 2 CHALLENGE: MORPHEME MADNESS

**MATERIALS**
- Notebook paper
- Latin Mat
- Cards listed in the table below

**DIRECTIONS** Students pair up to use **Cards** and **Mats** to build real words. They also record all of the words they build and the words' definitions.

| Word Parts | Cards |
|---|---|
| **Latin Roots** | cline, clin~~e~~, flu, fluc, flux, jac, ject, rect, recti, reg, verse, vers~~e~~, vert |
| **Inflected Endings** | ed, ing, s |
| **Prefixes** | de, di, in, re |
| **Suffixes** | ence, ent, er, ion, ly |

**Now it's your turn to build words.**

- First, find a partner.
- Use the **Cards** and **Mats** to build words.
- Record the words and their definitions on a separate sheet of paper.

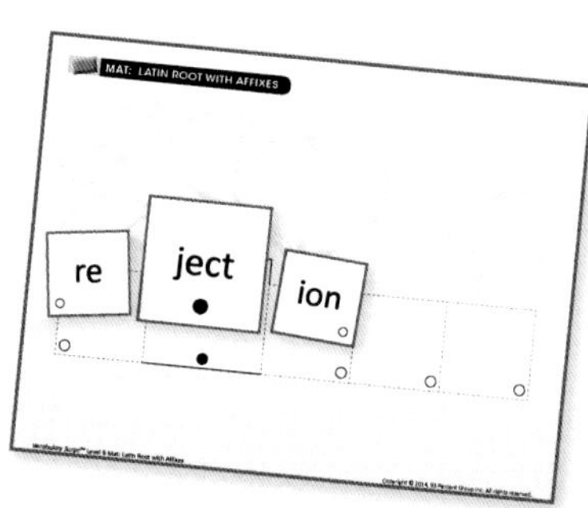

# art, fac/fact/fect/fic, fix, flect/flex, form, pict, scribe/scrib~~e~~/script

## DAY 1 • Introduce Latin Roots

### UNCOVER THE MEANING

MATERIALS
- Days 1 & 2 Recording Sheet

#### Introduce *fac/fact/fect/fic, fix,* and *form*

**DIRECTIONS** Pair students and distribute the **Days 1 & 2 Recording Sheet**. Model the first completed example. After students have completed the first two columns, ask them to share what they wrote. Then provide the Certified Definition. Explain that understanding parts of words, such as Latin roots, can help students uncover the meaning of many words.

**I'm going to model using my detective skills to figure out what the underlined word parts mean.**

- I'll use the other words in the sentences to develop a Working Definition of a word part.
- Listen as I read the first set of two sentences.
    1. *The Wind in the Willows* is a ***fic**tional* book because in the made-up story, all of the animals speak.
    2. The ***fact**ory* workers build tables and desks from recycled wood.
- In **Column 1**, I record the clue words made-up and build that help me understand the meaning of ***fac/fact/fect/fic***.
- I think that ***fac/fact/fect/fic*** means to make or build. This is my Working Definition, which I record in **Column 2**.
- In **Column 3**, I write the Certified Definition of ***fac/fact/fect/fic***: to make or do.

**Now it's your turn.**

- With your partner, read the next set of sentences on the **Days 1 & 2 Recording Sheet**.
- Use your detective skills to figure out what the underlined word parts mean.
- Consider which words or phrases in the sentences provide clues about meaning. Record them in **Column 1**.
- Write a Working Definition in **Column 2**.
- Only complete **Columns 1** and **2** and then wait for the discussion. You will fill in **Column 3** after I provide a Certified Definition.

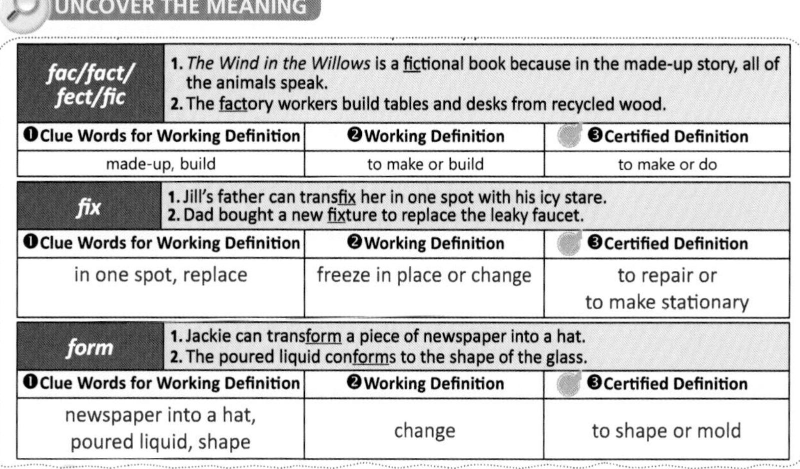

UNCOVER THE MEANING

| *fac/fact/ fect/fic* | 1. *The Wind in the Willows* is a fictional book because in the made-up story, all of the animals speak. 2. The factory workers build tables and desks from recycled wood. | |
|---|---|---|
| ❶ Clue Words for Working Definition | ❷ Working Definition | ❸ Certified Definition |
| made-up, build | to make or build | to make or do |

| *fix* | 1. Jill's father can transfix her in one spot with his icy stare. 2. Dad bought a new fixture to replace the leaky faucet. | |
|---|---|---|
| ❶ Clue Words for Working Definition | ❷ Working Definition | ❸ Certified Definition |
| in one spot, replace | freeze in place or change | to repair or to make stationary |

| *form* | 1. Jackie can transform a piece of newspaper into a hat. 2. The poured liquid conforms to the shape of the glass. | |
|---|---|---|
| ❶ Clue Words for Working Definition | ❷ Working Definition | ❸ Certified Definition |
| newspaper into a hat, poured liquid, shape | change | to shape or mold |

# fac/fact/fect/fic, fix, form

## DAY 2 • Deepen the Meaning

### CHECK MEANING

**MATERIALS**
- Pocket chart, document camera, or PowerPoint™
- Days 1 & 2 Recording Sheet
- Cards:
  Teacher: fect, ion, per
  Student: Roots: fix, form
  Prefixes: re, trans
  Inflected Endings: ing

**DIRECTIONS** Using the **Cards** and **Mat**, confirm that students understand how the meaning of the word evolves as more parts are added.

**I DO**

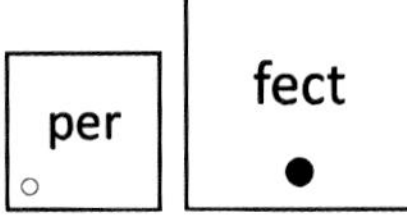


- The prefix ***per-*** means thorough or completely.
- Adding ***per-*** to ***fect*** spells the word ***perfect***. The combination of word parts means to make completely right.
- Now, I'm going to use my knowledge of the word to answer the question.

1. What does it mean when we say the test is ***perfect?*** It is completely right.

**WE DO**

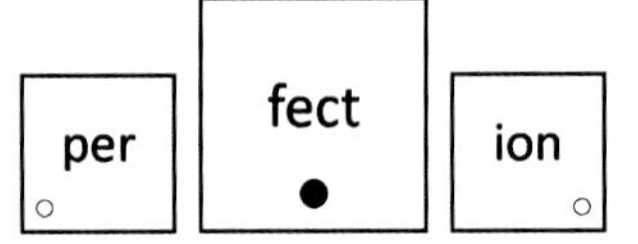


- The prefix ***per-*** means thorough or completely.
- After adding ***per-*** to ***fect***, what's the meaning? To make completely right
- The suffix ***-ion*** means quality.
- After adding ***-ion*** to ***perfect***, what is the meaning? The quality of being perfect or right
- Listen to me use the word ***perfection*** in a question and we will use our knowledge of its parts to figure out the answer.

2. What does it mean when the pie is baked to ***perfection?*** It was flawlessly and perfectly cooked.

**YOU DO** Use your **Cards** and **Mats** to complete the chart on the **Days 1 & 2 Recording Sheet**.

| Latin Roots | Certified Definition |
|---|---|
| fac/fact/fect/fic | to make or do |
| fix | to repair or make stationary |
| form | to shape or mold |
| **Prefixes** | **Certified Definition** |
| non- | not |
| per- | through, completely |
| re- | again, back |
| trans- | across, beyond |
| **Suffixes** | **Certified Definition** |
| -al | like |
| -at~~e~~ | to make |
| -ion/tion | action |
| -ize | to make |
| -ly | like |
| -tion | action |
| **Inflected Endings** | **Certified Definition** |
| -ed | past tense |
| -ing | present participle |
| **Connecting Letters** | |
| -t- | |

**CHECK MEANING**

| Word | Prefix | Latin Root | Inflected Ending |
|---|---|---|---|
| fixing | | fix: to repair or make stationary | ing: present |
| Meaning: | repairing | | |
| transfix | trans: beyond | fix: to repair or make stationary | |
| Meaning: | to hold motionless because of surprise or shock | | |
| reform | re: again | form: to shape or mold | |
| Meaning: | to make changes | | |
| transforming | trans: across, beyond | form: to shape or mold | ing: present |
| Meaning: | changing form, structure, or appearance | | |

# fac/fact/fect/fic, fix, form

## DAY 3 • Word Multiplier

### WORD MULTIPLIER

**Build words with *fac/fact/fect/fic, fix,* and *form***

MATERIALS
- Day 3 Recording Sheet
- Notebook paper
- Latin Mat
- Cards:
  Latin Roots: fac, fact, fect, fic, fix, form
  Inflected Endings: ed, ing
  Prefixes: non, per, trans
  Suffixes: al, ate, ion, ize, ly, ion, tion

**DIRECTIONS** Students work together to build words using their **Cards** and **Mats**.

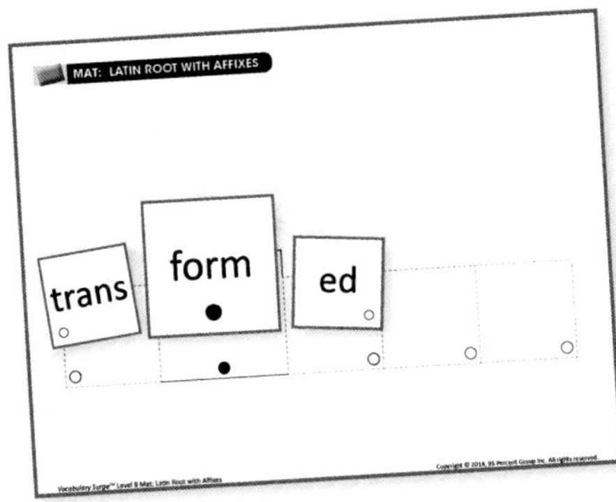


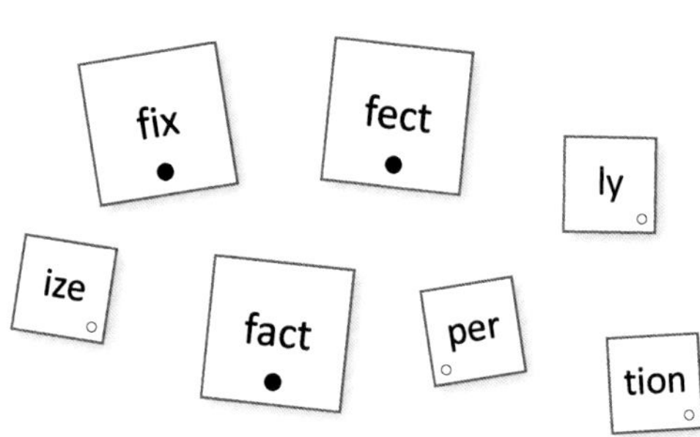


**I DO** Watch me combine **Cards** to build a word.
- I select cards ***trans, form,*** and ***ed***.
- I place the prefix ***trans-*** on the left side of the mat, matching the circle on the mat to the one on the card.
- I place the Latin root ***form*** in the large center box, matching the solid circles.
- Finally, I place the inflected ending *-**ed*** on the right side of ***form***, matching the circle on the mat to the one on the card.
- I have built the word ***transformed***.

**WE DO** Let me try another.
- I choose the cards ***non, fic,*** and ***tion***.
- Where should I place the card ***non***? In the box on the left
- Why do we place it here? Because it is a prefix
- Where shall I place ***fic***? In the middle box
- Why do we place it here? Because it is the Latin root and has a solid circle like the mat
- Where shall I place suffix ***-tion***? In the box to the right of ***fic***
- Look at the example on your **Day 3 Recording Sheet** to see how to write the parts of ***nonfiction*** and the whole word. ***Non-*** means not, ***fic*** means to make or do, and ***-tion*** means action.
- When we put these word parts together, ***nonfiction*** means a text that provides information about a topic.
- What part of speech is ***nonfiction*** and how do you know? Noun, a kind of writing

**WORD MULTIPLIER**

| SET 1 | Word Parts | Word | Part of Speech |
|---|---|---|---|
| 1. | non+fic+tion | nonfiction | noun |
| | Write the Meaning: | a text that provides information about a topic | |
| 2. | per+fect+ion | perfection | noun |
| | Write the Meaning: | the quality of being perfect or right | |

| SET 2 | Word Parts | Word | Part of Speech |
|---|---|---|---|
| 1. | fix+ed+ly | fixedly | adjective |
| | Write the Meaning: | firmly fastened in place | |
| 2. | trans+fix+ing | transfixing | verb |
| | Write the Meaning: | holding motionless because of surprise or shock | |

| SET 3 | Word Parts | Word | Part of Speech |
|---|---|---|---|
| 1. | form+al+ize | formalize | verb |
| | Write the Meaning: | to give something shape or structure | |
| 2. | trans+form+ate+ion | transformation | noun |
| | Write the Meaning: | the state of something that was changed | |

**YOU DO** Use your **Cards** and **Mats** to build more words. Complete the **Day 3 Recording Sheet** with your partner. Write additional words on notebook paper. We will review the words when you have finished.

**Possible Words**:
**fac/fact/fect/fic:** faction, fiction, perfect
**fix:** fixed, fixing, transfix, transfixed, transfixedly
**form:** formal, formation, formational, transform, transformational

## DAY 4 • Demonstrate Meaning

### BUILD MEANING

*MATERIALS*
- *Whiteboards*
- *Markers*

**DIRECTIONS** Complete the I Do and We Do sections with the whole class, and pair students to work on the You Do activity. Students can record their ideas on small whiteboards. Ask a few pairs to share their work with the class.

**I DO** Listen to me demonstrate understanding of the meaning of the Latin root ***form***.

- The first word is ***transformed***. The word ***transformed*** means changed form, structure, or appearance. I'm going to think of times when something was ***transformed***.
  - The artist ***transformed*** a stump into a carved bear.
  - The actor's makeup ***transformed*** his face into that of an old man.
- The second word is ***formal***, which means something that follows customs that are not casual. I'm going to think of an example of things that are ***formal***.
  - Many guests wore fancy dresses and tuxedos to the ***formal*** party.
  - Students often send ***formal*** invitations to attend their graduation.

**WE DO** Let's try the next one together with the Latin root ***fect***.

- The first word is ***defect***. The prefix ***de-*** means away from or down, and the Latin root ***fect*** means to make or do. A ***defect*** means a manufacturing imperfection or mistake. The ***defect*** in the milk carton caused it to leak.
  - What things might have a ***defect***?
- The second word is ***perfect***. The prefix ***per-*** means completely, and the Latin root ***fect*** means make or do. ***Perfect*** means to make completely right.
  - Name something that could be ***perfect.***

**PROMPT IDEAS** ***defect***
- dented tool
- bent bike
- leaky pen

**PROMPT IDEAS** ***perfect***
- spelling test
- birthday party
- puzzle

**YOU DO** Now it's your turn. Work with a partner, and record your ideas on a whiteboard so you're ready to share with the class. You'll have five minutes to think of examples for two words that contain the Latin root ***fix***.

- The two words are ***fixed*** and ***fixture***.
  - What does the Latin root ***fix*** mean? To repair or to make stationary What does the inflected ending ***-ed*** mean? Past What does ***fixed*** mean? To have repaired
  - What does the Latin root ***fix*** mean? To repair What does the suffix ***-ure*** mean? Use or function What does ***fixture*** mean? Something that has been in the same place or is stationary.
  - Think of an example of something that might need to be ***fixed.***
  - Think of an example of a ***fixture*** in a house.

**PROMPT IDEAS** ***fixed***
- broken toy
- broken bike
- broken zipper

**PROMPT IDEAS** ***fixture***
- sink
- tub
- doorknob

 

# art, flect/flex, pict, scribe/ scrib~~e~~/script

## DAY 5 • Introduce Latin Roots

### UNCOVER THE MEANING

**Introduce *art, flect/flex, pict,* and *scribe/scrib~~e~~/script***

MATERIALS
- Days 5 & 6 Recording Sheet

**DIRECTIONS** Pair students and distribute the Days 5 & 6 Recording Sheet. Model the first completed example. After students have completed the first two columns, ask them to share what they wrote. Then provide the Certified Definition. Explain that understanding parts of words, such as Latin roots, can help students uncover the meaning of many words.

**I'm going to model using my detective skills to figure out what the underlined word parts mean.**

- I'll use the other words in the sentences to develop a Working Definition of a word part.
- Listen as I read the first set of two sentences.

    1. The ***art**ist* carved the sculpture from marble.
    2. The collector found a native ***art**ifact* shaped like a bull.

- In **Column 1**, I record the clue words carved, sculpture, and shaped that help me understand the meaning of ***art***.
- I think that ***art*** means shaped by hand. This is my Working Definition, which I record in **Column 2**.
- In **Column 3**, I will write the Certified Definition of ***art***: something skillful or beautiful.

**Now it's your turn.**

- With your partner, read the next set of sentences on the Days 5 & 6 Recording Sheet.
- Use your detective skills to figure out what the underlined word parts mean.
- Consider which words or phrases in the sentences provide clues about meaning. Record them in **Column 1**.
- Write a Working Definition in **Column 2**.
- Only complete **Columns 1** and **2** and then wait for the discussion. You will fill in **Column 3** after I provide a Certified Definition.

UNCOVER THE MEANING

| *art* | 1. The artist carved the sculpture from marble.<br>2. The collector found a native artifact shaped like a bull. | |
|---|---|---|
| ❶ Clue Words for Working Definition | ❷ Working Definition | ❸ Certified Definition |
| carved, sculpture, shaped | shaped by hand | something skillful or beautiful |
| *flect/flex* | 1. The flexible pipe conformed to the shape of the wall.<br>2. The catcher deflected the baseball away from his face. | |
| ❶ Clue Words for Working Definition | ❷ Working Definition | ❸ Certified Definition |
| conformed, shape, away | shaped or move away | to bend or curve |
| *pict* | 1. The artist used her brushes to create a picture.<br>2. In *Jack and the Beanstalk*, the evil giant was depicted as a villain. | |
| ❶ Clue Words for Working Definition | ❷ Working Definition | ❸ Certified Definition |
| brushes, create, evil | image, describe | to paint |
| *scribe/scrib~~e~~/ script* | 1. Michael described the sights and sounds when he reported on his vacation.<br>2. The doctor penned a prescription for the patient. | |
| ❶ Clue Words for Working Definition | ❷ Working Definition | ❸ Certified Definition |
| reported, penned | to tell or write | to write |

# DAY 6 • Deepen the Meaning

## CHECK MEANING

MATERIALS
- Pocket chart, document camera, or PowerPoint™
- Days 5 & 6 Recording Sheet
- Cards:
  Teacher: de, pict, ure
  Student:
  Roots: art, script
  Prefixes: in, trans
  Suffixes: ic, ion, ist

**DIRECTIONS** Using the **Cards** and **Mat**, confirm that students understand how the meaning of the word evolves as more parts are added.

**I DO**

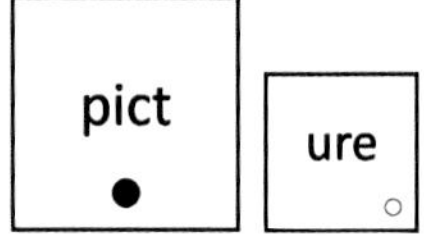

- The suffix ***-ure*** means function.
- Adding ***-ure*** to ***pict*** spells the word ***picture***. The combination of word parts means a visual image of a person, scene, or object.
- Now, I'm going to use my knowledge of the word to answer the question.

1. What does it mean when Tyree creates a ***picture*** of a robin? He makes an image of a robin.

**WE DO**

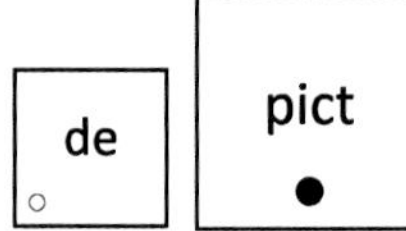

- The prefix ***de-*** means down.
- After adding ***de-*** to ***pict***, what's the meaning? To portray something through an image or in words
- Listen to me use the word ***depict*** in a question and we will use our knowledge of its parts to figure out the answer.

2. What does it mean when the teacher can ***depict*** the cells using colored pencils? She draws the cells on paper.

**YOU DO** Use your **Cards** and **Mats** to complete the chart on the **Days 5 & 6 Recording Sheet**.

| Latin Roots | Certified Definition |
|---|---|
| art | something skillful or beautiful |
| flect/flex | to bend or curve |
| pict | to paint |
| scribe/ scrib~~e~~/script | to write |
| **Prefixes** | **Certified Definition** |
| de- | away from, down |
| in- | in, on, or toward |
| pre- | before, earlier |
| sub- | under, beneath, or below |
| trans- | across, beyond |
| **Suffixes** | **Certified Definition** |
| -ible | able |
| -ic | having the characteristic |
| -ion | action |
| -ist | one who performs a specific action |
| **Inflected Endings** | **Certified Definition** |
| -ing | present |

CHECK MEANING

| Word | Latin Root | Suffix | Suffix |
|---|---|---|---|
| artist | art: something skillful or beautiful | ist: one who performs a specific action | |
| Meaning: | a person who creates something skillful or beautiful | | |
| artistic | art: something skillful or beautiful | ist: one with a skill | ic: having the characteristic of |
| Meaning: | showing skill in creating something beautiful | | |
| **Word** | **Prefix** | **Latin Root** | **Suffix** |
| transcript | trans: across, beyond | script: to write | |
| Meaning: | a written report that is an official document | | |
| inscription | in: in, on, or toward | script: to write | ion: state of being, quality, or action |
| Meaning: | something written, often in a note or book | | |

 

# art, flect/flex, pict, scribe/scrib~~e~~/script

## DAY 7 • Word Multiplier

### WORD MULTIPLIER

**Build words with *art, flect/flex, pict,* and *scribe/scrib~~e~~/script***

**DIRECTIONS** Students work together to build words using their **Cards** and **Mats**.

MATERIALS
- Day 7 Recording Sheet
- Notebook paper
- Latin Mat
- Cards:
  - Latin Roots: art, flect, flex, pict, scribe, scrib~~e~~, script
  - Inflected Endings: ing
  - Prefixes: de, pre, sub
  - Suffixes: ible, ic, ion, ist

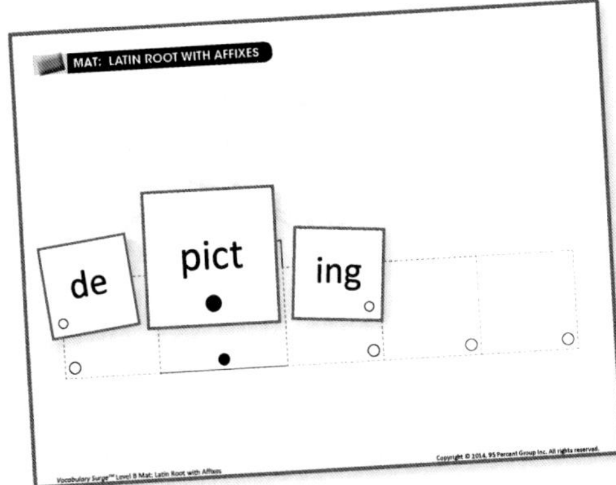


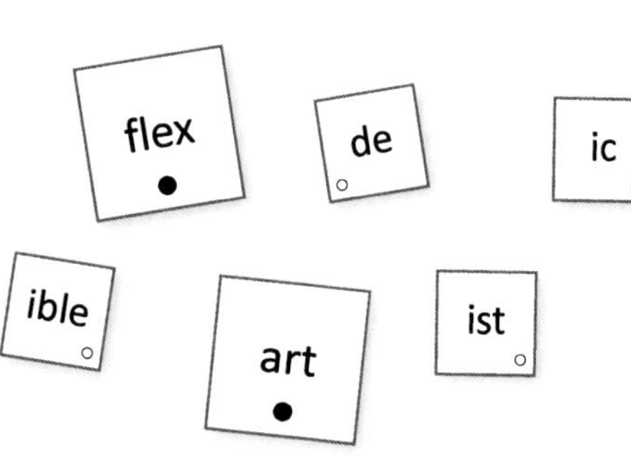


**WE DO** Let's combine cards to build a word.

- I select cards ***de, pict,*** and ***ing***.
- Where shall I place the prefix ***de-***? On the left side of the mat
- Where do I place the Latin root ***pict***? In the large center box, matching the solid circles.
- Finally, where shall I place the inflected ending ***-ing***? On the right side of the mat, matching the circle on the mat to the one on the card
- What word have we built? Depicting What is the definition of ***depicting***? Portraying something through a picture or with words
- What is the part of speech of the word ***depicting*** and how do you know? Verb, describes an action

**WORD MULTIPLIER**

| | Word Parts | Word | Part of Speech |
|---|---|---|---|
| **SET 1** | | | |
| 1. | art+ist+ic | artistic | adjective |
| Write the Meaning: | showing skill in creating something beautiful | | |
| **SET 2** | | | |
| 1. | de+flect+ing | deflecting | verb |
| Write the Meaning: | causing to bend or turn to a different course | | |
| 2. | flex+ible | flexible | adjective |
| Write the Meaning: | able to bend or curve | | |
| **SET 3** | | | |
| 1. | de+pict+ion | depiction | noun |
| Write the Meaning: | a portrayal of an idea through a picture or with words | | |
| **SET 4** | | | |
| 1. | pre+scribe | prescribe | verb |
| Write the Meaning: | to specify actions to be followed usually in writing | | |
| 2. | sub+script+ion | subscription | noun |
| Write the Meaning: | an arrangement to receive a magazine or attend concerts over a period of time | | |

**YOU DO** Use your **Cards** and **Mats** to build more words. Complete the **Day 7 Recording Sheet** with your partner. Write additional words on notebook paper.

**Possible Words:**

**art:** artist, artistic
**flect/flex:** deflect, deflecting, flexible, flexing
**pict:** depict, depiction
**scribe:** prescribe, subscribe, subscription

art, flect/flex, pict, scribe/scrib~~e~~/script

## DAY 8 • Demonstrate Meaning

### BUILD MEANING

MATERIALS
- Whiteboards
- Markers

**DIRECTIONS** Complete the I Do and We Do sections with the whole class, and pair students to work on the You Do activity. Students can record their ideas on small whiteboards. Ask a few pairs to share their work with the class.

**I DO** Listen to me demonstrate understanding of the meaning of the Latin root ***flex***.

- The first word is ***flexible***. We learned that ***flexible*** means able to bend or curve. I'm going to think of examples of things that are ***flexible***.
  - The gymnast's body was ***flexible*** when she did a backbend.
  - Straws that are ***flexible*** are easy to bend.
- The second word is ***flexing***, which means bending or tensing muscles. I'm going to think of examples of things that are ***flexing***.
  - Juan is ***flexing*** his muscles to show how strong he is.
  - Betsy is ***flexing*** a ball to strengthen her fingers.

**WE DO** Let's try the next one together with the Latin root ***art***.

- The first word is ***artist***. The Latin root ***art*** means something skillful or beautiful, and the suffix ***-ist*** means one who performs a specific action. An ***artist*** is a person who creates something skillful or beautiful. The ***artist*** paints sunflowers with watercolors.
  - Name an ***artist*** or a time when you were an ***artist***.
- The second word is ***artifact***. The Latin root ***art*** means something skillful or beautiful, and the Latin root ***fact*** means something that is the truth or is known. ***Artifact*** means an object, often handmade, from an earlier time.
  - Name something that is an ***artifact***.

**PROMPT IDEAS** ***artist***
- art teacher
- used paints
- made a pot

**PROMPT IDEAS** ***artifact***
- arrowhead
- covered wagon
- pyramids

**YOU DO** Now it's your turn. Work with a partner, and record your ideas on a whiteboard so you're ready to share with the class. You'll have five minutes to think of examples for two words that contain the Latin root ***scrib***.

- The two words are ***prescribe*** and ***scribe***.
  - What does the Latin root ***scrib*** mean? To write What does ***scribe*** mean? A person who serves in the role of copying or taking notes
  - What does the prefix ***pre-*** mean? Before or earlier What does ***prescribe*** mean? To specify actions to be followed usually in writing
  - Think of an example of something that someone might ***prescribe***.
  - Think of an example of a time you were a ***scribe*** or might be one.

**PROMPT IDEAS** ***prescribe***
- game rules
- a recipe
- test directions

**PROMPT IDEAS** ***scribe***
- recording notes
- outlining a group's ideas
- copying information from the board

# art, fac/fact/fect/fic, fix, flect/flex, form, pict, scribe/scrib~~e~~/script

## DAY 9 • Review What You Learned

### STEP 1 REVIEW THE MEANING

MATERIALS
- Word parts projected on document camera, overhead projector, or PowerPoint™

**Review *art, fac/fact/fect/fic, fix, flect/flex, form, pict,* and *scribe/scrib~~e~~/script***

**DIRECTIONS** Display the morphemes so students can see them, and ask for the Certified Definition of each one.

**When I show you the word parts, think about the Certified Definitions we discussed as you prepare to answer.**

| Latin Root | Certified Definition | Latin Root | Certified Definition |
|---|---|---|---|
| fac/fact/fect/fic | to make or do | art | something skillful or beautiful |
| fix | to fix or make stationary | flect/flex | to bend or curve |
| form | to shape or mold | pict | to paint |
| | | scribe/ scrib~~e~~/script | to write |

### STEP 2 CHECK MEANING

MATERIALS
- Day 9 Recording Sheet

**DIRECTIONS** Read the following sentences to check that students understand the meanings of ***art, fac/fact/fect/fic, fix, flect/flex, form, pict,*** and ***scribe/scrib~~e~~/script***. Model the first sentence for students using the We Do Step, below.

**WE DO** As I read this sentence, think about the Certified Definitions of the Latin root that fits the blank.

1. The workers in the __________ory took a lunch break.

- Which Latin root do you think fits on the line? Fact
- What is the new word? Factory
- What do you think the word ***factory*** means? A place where things are made or assembled

**YOU DO** Complete the rest of the sentences on the **Day 9 Recording Sheet** with your partner to find the Latin root that best fits on the line. Record the new words and their meanings.

CHECK MEANING

1. The workers in the _fact_ **ory** took a lunch break. _factory_
   Meaning: _a place where things are made or assembled_
2. Mom's favorite plastic cup was **de** _form_ **ed** by the dishwasher's heat. _deformed_
   Meaning: _something that has changed shape_
3. Use an umbrella to **de** _flect_ the rain. _deflect_
   Meaning: _to cause to bend or turn to a different course_
4. The actors **per** _form_ **ed** on stage in *The Wizard of Oz*. _performed_
   Meaning: _to have done something like acting or playing music_
5. The pharmacist filled the **pre** _script_ **ion**. _prescription_
   Meaning: _a directive, usually written by a doctor for a medicine_
6. The beautiful vase was _art_ **fully** made. _artfully_
   Meaning: _created with skill and imagination_

Students write two sentences with missing Latin roots to challenge the class.

art, fac/fact/fect/fic, fix, flect/flex, form, pict, scribe/scrib~~e~~/script

# DAY 10 • 2nd Review Day

## STEP 1 MAKE CONNECTIONS

MATERIALS
- Day 10 Recording Sheet

**DIRECTIONS** Students pair up to write sentences with either one or two of the words that are provided.

**I am going to model how to use a word containing this week's Latin roots in a meaningful sentence. The word is *factored*.**

- Jen's love of warm weather ***factored*** into her decision to move to Florida.
- It is your turn to write five more sentences using the words on the top of the recording sheet.
- Sentences with two words get two points and sentences with one word get one point.

MAKE CONNECTIONS

| Words | | |
|---|---|---|
| artist | fixture | picture |
| conforming | flexible | prescription |
| deflect | formation | reflected |
| depicted | inscribed | subscribing |
| factored | perfected | transfixed |
| fictional | perform | transformed |

1. Jen's love of warm weather factored into her decision to move to Florida.
2. The crossing guard is a fixture at the busy intersection.
3. At the air show the pilots flew their jets in formation.
4. The defender tried to deflect the quarterback's pass.
5. Our class perfected the song so we were asked to perform at the concert.

## STEP 2 CHALLENGE: MORPHEME MADNESS

MATERIALS
- Notebook paper
- Latin Mat
- Cards listed in the table below

**DIRECTIONS** Students pair up to use **Cards** and **Mats** to build words. They also record all of the words they build and the words' definitions.

| Word Parts | Cards |
|---|---|
| **Latin Roots** | art, fac, fact, fect, fic, fix, flect, flex, form, pict, scribe, scrib~~e~~, script |
| **Inflected Endings** | ed, ing |
| **Prefixes** | de, con, in, per, pre, trans |
| **Suffixes** | ate, at~~e~~, ion, ist, or |

**Now it's your turn to build words.**
- First, find a partner.
- Use the **Cards** and **Mats** to build real words.
- Record the words and their definitions on a separate sheet of paper.

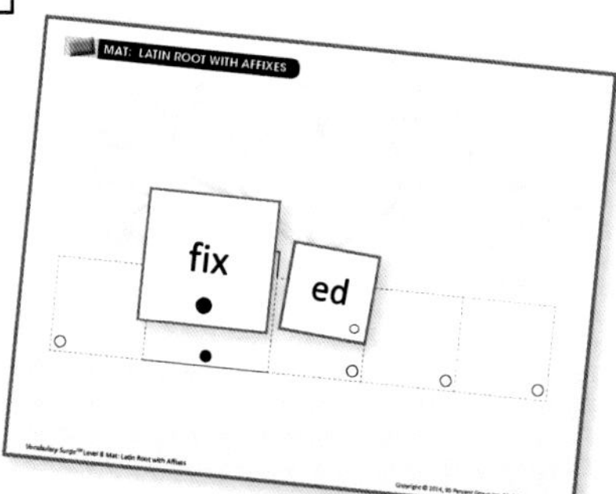

# cogn, grad/grade/gradɇ/gress, mot/mote/motɇ/move/movɇ, pend/pense/pensɇ, put/pute/putɇ, spec/spect, vent -age

## DAY 1 • Introduce Latin Roots

### UNCOVER THE MEANING

MATERIALS
- Days 1 & 2 Recording Sheet

**Introduce *cogn, pend/pense/pensɇ, put/pute/putɇ,* and *spec/spect*; *-age***

**DIRECTIONS** Pair students and distribute the Days 1 & 2 Recording Sheet. Model the first completed example. After students have completed the first two columns, ask them to share what they wrote. Then provide the Certified Definition. Explain that understanding parts of words such as Latin roots can help students uncover the meaning of many words.

**I'm going to model using my detective skills to figure out what the underlined word parts mean.**

- I'll use the other words in the sentences to develop a Working Definition of a word part.
- Listen as I read the first set of two sentences.
    1. When the crowd ***recognized*** the car, they decided it must belong to someone famous.
    2. Nia thought Cal's costume was great because he was completely ***unrecognizable***.
- In **Column 1**, I record the clue words decided and thought that help me understand the meaning of ***cogn***.
- I think that ***cogn*** means to think. This is my Working Definition, which I record in **Column 2**.
- In **Column 3**, I write the Certified Definition of ***cogn***: to know.

**Now it's your turn.**

- With your partner, read the next set of sentences on the Days 1 & 2 Recording Sheet.
- Use your detective skills to figure out what the underlined word parts mean.
- Consider which words or phrases in the sentences provide clues about meaning. Record them in **Column 1**.
- Write a Working Definition in **Column 2**.
- Only complete **Columns 1** and **2** and then wait for the discussion. You will fill in **Column 3** after I provide a Certified Definition.

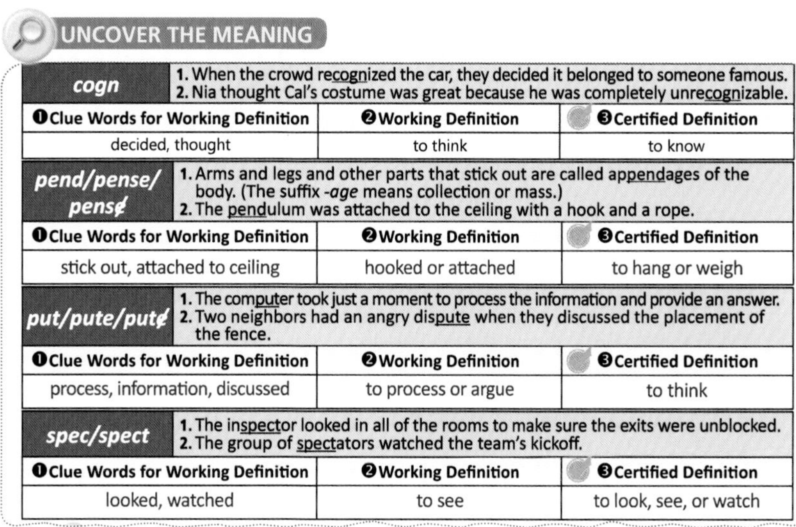

UNCOVER THE MEANING

| cogn | 1. When the crowd recognized the car, they decided it belonged to someone famous. 2. Nia thought Cal's costume was great because he was completely unrecognizable. | |
|---|---|---|
| ❶ Clue Words for Working Definition | ❷ Working Definition | ❸ Certified Definition |
| decided, thought | to think | to know |
| **pend/pense/pensɇ** | 1. Arms and legs and other parts that stick out are called appendages of the body. (The suffix *-age* means collection or mass.) 2. The pendulum was attached to the ceiling with a hook and a rope. | |
| ❶ Clue Words for Working Definition | ❷ Working Definition | ❸ Certified Definition |
| stick out, attached to ceiling | hooked or attached | to hang or weigh |
| **put/pute/putɇ** | 1. The computer took just a moment to process the information and provide an answer. 2. Two neighbors had an angry dispute when they discussed the placement of the fence. | |
| ❶ Clue Words for Working Definition | ❷ Working Definition | ❸ Certified Definition |
| process, information, discussed | to process or argue | to think |
| **spec/spect** | 1. The inspector looked in all of the rooms to make sure the exits were unblocked. 2. The group of spectators watched the team's kickoff. | |
| ❶ Clue Words for Working Definition | ❷ Working Definition | ❸ Certified Definition |
| looked, watched | to see | to look, see, or watch |

**cogn, pend/pense/pensé, put/pute/puté, spec/spect -age**

## DAY 2 • Deepen the Meaning

### CHECK MEANING

**MATERIALS**
- Pocket chart, document camera, or PowerPoint™
- Days 1 & 2 Recording Sheet
- Cards:
  Teacher: cogn, ion, itế, ize, re
  Student: Latin Roots: pend, spect
  Prefixes: in, sus
  Suffixes: ion
  Inflected Ending: ing

**DIRECTIONS** Using the **Cards** and **Mat**, confirm that students understand how the meaning of the word evolves as more parts are added.

**I DO**

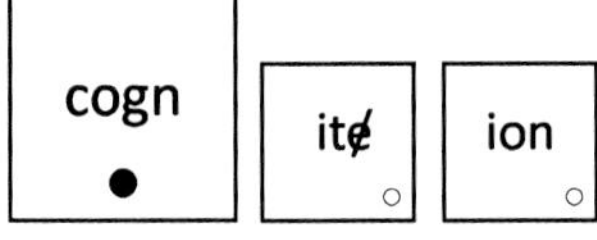


- The suffix ***-ite*** means quality of.
- The suffix ***-ion*** means action.
- Adding ***-ite*** and ***-ion*** to ***cogn*** spells the word ***cognition***. The combination of word parts means the act or process of knowing.
- Now, I'm going to use my knowledge of the word to answer the question.

1. What does it mean when the test checks the student's math ***cognition***? It checks what he knows.

**WE DO**

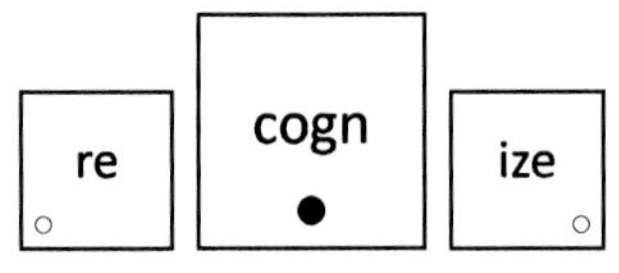


- The prefix ***re-*** means again.
- The suffix ***-ize*** means make.
- After adding ***re-*** and ***-ize*** to the Latin root ***cogn***, what is the meaning? To identify someone or something seen previously
- Listen to me use the word ***recognize*** in a question and we will use our knowledge of its parts to figure out the answer.

2. What does it mean if Emily can ***recognize*** her friend? Emily knows and remembers her when she sees her again.

**YOU DO** Use your **Cards** and **Mats** to complete the chart on the **Days 1 & 2 Recording Sheet**.

| Latin Roots | Certified Definition |
|---|---|
| cogn | to know |
| pend/pense/pensé | to hang or weigh |
| put/pute/puté | to think |
| spec/spect | to look, see, watch |
| **Prefixes** | **Certified Definition** |
| ap- | toward, near |
| de- | away from, down |
| in- | in |
| pro- | forward or earlier |
| re- | again, back |
| sus- | below |
| **Suffixes** | **Certified Definition** |
| -age | collection |
| -er/-or | has a special characteristic |
| -ial | relating to or characterized by |
| -ion | action |
| -ist | one who performs a special action |
| -ize | become, change |
| -y | inclined to |
| **Inflected Endings** | **Certified Definition** |
| -ing | present |

**CHECK MEANING**

| Word | Prefix | Latin Root | Suffix |
|---|---|---|---|
| inspect | in: in | spect: to look | |
| Meaning: | to examine closely and critically | | |
| inspection | in: in | spect: to look | ion: action |
| Meaning: | the act of carefully and critically looking at something | | |
| **Word** | **Prefix** | **Latin Root** | **Inflected Ending** |
| suspend | sus: below | pend: to hang or weigh | |
| Meaning: | to hang an object by attaching it to something above | | |
| pending | | pend: to hang or weigh | ing: now |
| Meaning: | awaiting a decision or settlement | | |

# cogn, pend/pense/pens~~e~~, put/pute/put~~e~~, spec/spect -age

## DAY 3 • Word Multiplier

### WORD MULTIPLIER

**Build words with *cogn, pend/pense/ pens~~e~~, put/pute/put~~e~~,* and *spec/spect***

MATERIALS
- Day 3 Recording Sheet
- Notebook paper
- Latin Mat
- Cards:
  Latin Roots: cogn, pend, put, spec, spect
  Prefixes: ap, de, pro, re
  Suffixes: age, ial, ist, ize, or, y

**DIRECTIONS** Students work together to build words using their **Cards** and **Mats**.

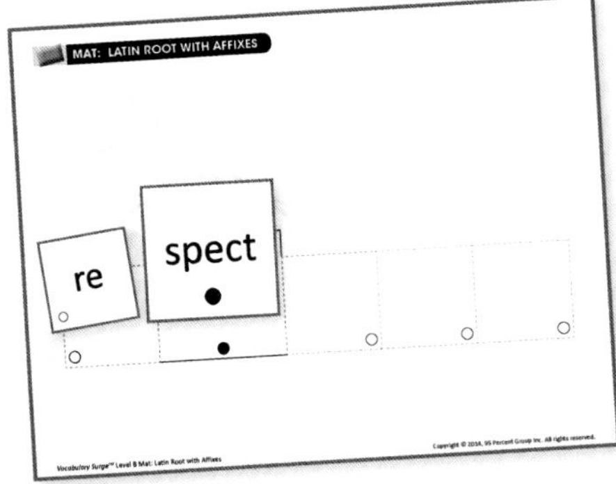


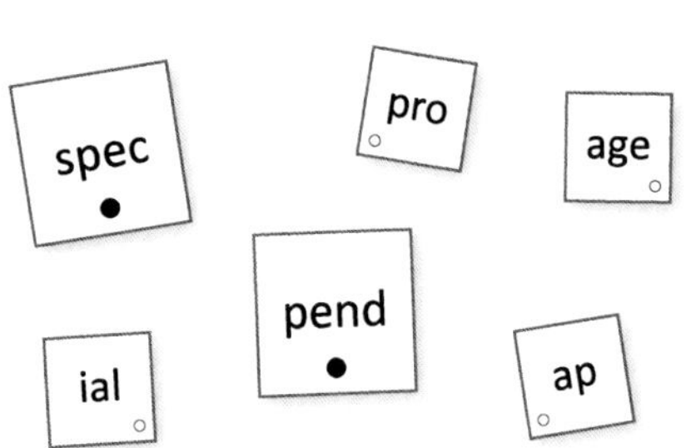


**I DO** Watch me combine **Cards** to build a word.
- I select cards ***re*** and ***spect***.
- I place the prefix ***re-*** on the left side of the mat, matching the circle on the mat to the one on the card.
- I place the Latin root ***spect*** in the large center box, matching the solid circles.
- I have built the word ***respect***.

**WE DO** Let me try another.
- I choose the cards ***re, cogn,*** and ***ize***.
- Where should I place the card ***re***? In the box on the left
- Why do we place it here? Because it is the prefix
- Where should I place the card ***cogn***? In the middle box
- Why do we place it here? Because it is the Latin root and has a solid circle like the mat
- Where shall I place the suffix ***-ize***? In the box to the right of *cogn*
- Look at the example on your **Day 3 Recording Sheet** to see how to write the parts of ***recognize*** and the whole word. ***Re-*** means again, ***cogn*** means to think, and ***-ize*** means become, change, or make.
- When we put these word parts together, ***recognize*** means to identify someone or something previously seen.
- What part of speech is ***recognize*** and how do you know? Verb, action word

**WORD MULTIPLIER**

| SET 1 | Word Parts | Word | Part of Speech |
|---|---|---|---|
| 1. | re+cogn+ize | recognize | verb |
| | Write the Meaning: | to identify someone or something seen previously | |
| 2. | de+put+y | deputy | noun |
| | Write the Meaning: | an assistant who helps the leader | |

| SET 2 | Word Parts | Word | Part of Speech |
|---|---|---|---|
| 1. | ap+pend+age | appendage | noun |
| | Write the Meaning: | a projecting part, such as an arm or leg | |
| 2. | de+pend | depend | verb |
| | Write the Meaning: | to rely on, or place trust in, someone or something | |

| SET 3 | Word Parts | Word | Part of Speech |
|---|---|---|---|
| 1. | pro+spect+or | prospector | noun |
| | Write the Meaning: | a person who looks for valuable minerals | |
| 2. | spec+ial+ist | specialist | noun |
| | Write the Meaning: | a person who is qualified with a certain skill | |

**YOU DO** Use your **Cards** and **Mats** to build more words. Complete the **Day 3 Recording Sheet** with your partner. Write additional words on notebook paper. We will review the words when you have finished

**Possible Words:**

**cogn/put:** deputy, recognize
**pend/pense/pens~~e~~:** append, appendage, depend
**spec/spect:** prospect, prospector, special, specialist

cogn, pend/pense/pens~~e~~, put/pute/put~~e~~, spec/spect -age

## DAY 4 • Demonstrate Meaning

### BUILD MEANING

MATERIALS
- Whiteboards
- Markers

**DIRECTIONS** Complete the I Do and We Do sections with the whole class, and pair students to work on the You Do activity. Students can record their ideas on small whiteboards. Ask a few pairs to share their work with the class.

**I DO** Listen to me demonstrate understanding of the meaning of the Latin root ***pend***.

- The first word is ***depend***. We learned that ***depend*** means to rely on, or place trust in, someone or something. I'm going to think of examples of times when I ***depend*** on something.
    - Students ***depend*** on the bus to drive them to school.
    - People ***depend*** on seatbelts to keep them safe.
- The second word is ***pending***, which means awaiting a decision or settlement. I'm going to think of examples of things that are ***pending***.
    - Jason is coming over to my house, ***pending*** approval from his mom.
    - My grandmother's application to adopt a dog is still ***pending***.

**WE DO** Let's try the next one together with the Latin root ***spect***.

- The first word is ***spectator***. The Latin root ***spect*** means to see, the suffix ***-ate*** means to cause or make, and the suffix ***or-*** means one who does. A ***spectator*** is a person who watches. There is a single ***spectator*** watching the game.
    - When were you were a ***spectator*** or when might you be one?
- The second word is ***inspect***. The prefix ***in-*** means in, and the Latin root ***spect*** means to see. ***Inspect*** means to examine closely and critically.
    - Name something that you ***inspected*** or might ***inspect*** in the future.

**PROMPT IDEAS** ***spectator***
- watch a race
- watch a match
- watch TV

**PROMPT IDEAS** ***inspect***
- a map, for directions
- a mound, for dirt
- a radio, to repair it

**YOU DO** Now it's your turn. Work with a partner, and record your ideas on a whiteboard so you're ready to share with the class. You'll have five minutes to think of examples for two words that contain the Latin root ***pute***.

- The two words are ***input*** and ***compute***.
    - What does the prefix ***in-*** mean? In What does the Latin root ***pute*** mean? To think What does ***input*** mean? To put in information
    - What does the prefix ***com-*** mean? Together What does the Latin root ***pute*** mean? To think What does ***compute*** mean? To calculate
- Think of an example of something that you can ***input***. It can be something you have ***inputted*** or something possible.
- Think of an example of a time you ***computed*** something. Again, it can be something that you did or something that you could possibly do.

**PROMPT IDEAS** ***input***
- address into the computer
- information on a test
- phone number into your cell phone

**PROMPT IDEAS** ***computed***
- math problem
- cost of something
- time to get home

# grad/grade/grad~~e~~/gress, mot/mote/mot~~e~~/move/mov~~e~~, vent

## DAY 5 • Introduce Latin Roots

### UNCOVER THE MEANING

**Introduce *grad/grade/grad~~e~~/gress, mot/mote/mot~~e~~/move/mov~~e~~,* and *vent***

MATERIALS
- Days 5 & 6 Recording Sheet

**DIRECTIONS** Pair students and distribute the **Days 5 & 6 Recording Sheet**. Model the first completed example. After students have completed the first two columns, ask them to share what they wrote. Then provide the Certified Definition. Explain that understanding parts of words, such as Latin roots, can help students uncover the meaning of many words.

**I'm going to model using my detective skills to figure out what the underlined word parts mean.**

- I'll use the other words in the sentences to develop a Working Definition of a word part.
- Listen as I read the first set of two sentences.

    1. The turtle's ***progress*** was extremely slow compared to the rabbit's speed.
    2. The slow and ***gradual*** release of the lake's water left the boats on the sand.

- In **Column 1**, I record the clue words slow and speed that help me understand the meaning of ***grad/grade/gress***.
- I think that ***grad/grade/gress*** means slow movement. This is my Working Definition, which I record in **Column 2**.
- In **Column 3**, I will write the Certified Definition of ***grad/grade/gress***: step, degree, walk.

**Now it's your turn.**

- With your partner, read the next set of sentences on the **Days 5 & 6 Recording Sheet**.
- Use your detective skills to figure out what the underlined word parts mean.
- Consider which words or phrases in the sentences provide clues about meaning. Record them in **Column 1**.
- Write a Working Definition in **Column 2**.
- Only complete **Columns 1** and **2** and then wait for the discussion. You will fill in **Column 3** after I provide a Certified Definition.

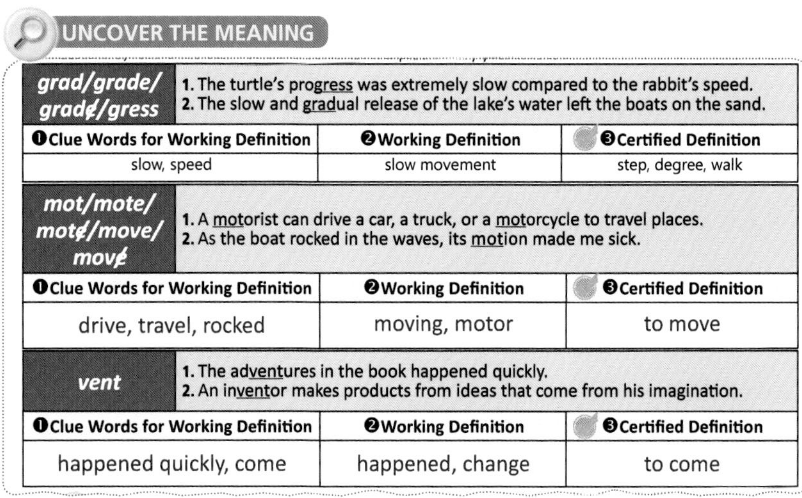

UNCOVER THE MEANING

| grad/grade/grad~~e~~/gress | 1. The turtle's progress was extremely slow compared to the rabbit's speed. 2. The slow and gradual release of the lake's water left the boats on the sand. | |
|---|---|---|
| ❶Clue Words for Working Definition | ❷Working Definition | ❸Certified Definition |
| slow, speed | slow movement | step, degree, walk |

| mot/mote/mot~~e~~/move/mov~~e~~ | 1. A motorist can drive a car, a truck, or a motorcycle to travel places. 2. As the boat rocked in the waves, its motion made me sick. | |
|---|---|---|
| ❶Clue Words for Working Definition | ❷Working Definition | ❸Certified Definition |
| drive, travel, rocked | moving, motor | to move |

| vent | 1. The adventures in the book happened quickly. 2. An inventor makes products from ideas that come from his imagination. | |
|---|---|---|
| ❶Clue Words for Working Definition | ❷Working Definition | ❸Certified Definition |
| happened quickly, come | happened, change | to come |

**grad/grade/grad~~e~~/gress,**
**mot/mote/mot~~e~~/move/mov~~e~~, vent**

## DAY 6 • Deepen the Meaning

### CHECK MEANING

*MATERIALS*
- *Pocket chart, document camera, or PowerPoint™*
- *Days 5 & 6 Recording Sheet*
- *Cards:*
  *Teacher: in, ion, or, vent*
  *Student: Latin Roots: gress, mot, mote, mot~~e~~, move, mov~~e~~*
  *Prefixes: pro, re*

**DIRECTIONS** Using the **Cards** and **Mats**, confirm that students understand how the meaning of the word evolves as more parts are added.

**I DO**

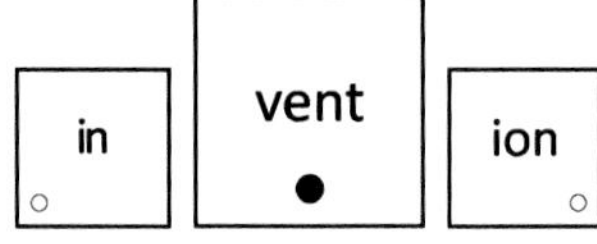


- The prefix ***in-*** means in.
- Adding ***in-*** to ***vent*** spells the word ***invent***. The combination of word parts means to create something from the imagination.
- The suffix ***-ion*** means action.
- Adding ***-ion*** to ***invent*** changes the meaning of the word. The combination of word parts means a newly created device or machine.
- Now, I'm going to use my knowledge of the word to answer the question.
  1. What does it mean if Lyle creates an ***invention*** for catching solar energy? He creates a new way to capture the sun's energy.

**WE DO**

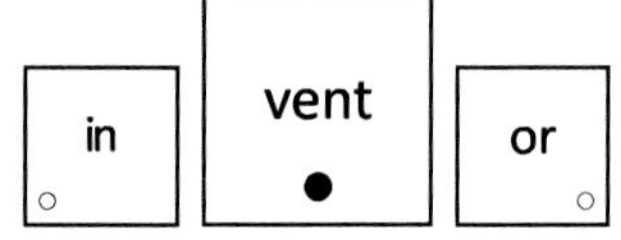


- The prefix ***in-*** means in.
- How does adding ***in-*** to ***vent*** change the meaning? To create something from the imagination
- The suffix ***-or*** means one who does.
- How does adding ***-or*** to ***invent*** change the meaning? The combination of word parts means one who creates something new or useful.
- Listen to me use the word ***inventor*** in a question and we will use our knowledge of its parts to figure out the answer.
  1. What does it mean if someone is an ***inventor***? A person who creates a new device or machine

**YOU DO** Use your **Cards** and **Mats** to complete the chart on the **Days 5 & 6 Recording Sheet**.

| Latin Roots | Certified Definition |
|---|---|
| grad/grade/grad~~e~~/gress | step, degree, to walk |
| mot/mote/mot~~e~~/move/mov~~e~~ | to move |
| vent | to come |
| **Prefixes** | **Certified Definition** |
| ad- | toward, near |
| in- | in or not |
| pro- | forward |
| re- | back or again |
| un- | not |
| **Suffixes** | **Certified Definition** |
| -able | able, can do |
| -ion | action |
| -ous | full of or having |
| -ure/-ur~~e~~ | state of |

| Word | Prefix | Latin Root | Suffix |
|---|---|---|---|
| move | | move: to move | |
| Meaning: | to pass from one place to another | | |
| remove | re: again | move: to move | |
| Meaning: | to take back or take away | | |
| progress | pro: forward | gress: step, degree | |
| Meaning: | to move forward toward a goal | | |
| regress | re: back | gress: step, degree | |
| Meaning: | to move backward | | |

# grad/grade/grad~~e~~/gress, mot/mote/mot~~e~~/move/mov~~e~~, vent

## DAY 7 • Word Multiplier

### WORD MULTIPLIER

**Build words with *grad/grade/grad~~e~~/gress, mot/mote/mot~~e~~/move/mov~~e~~*, and *vent***

**DIRECTIONS** Students work together to build words using their **Cards** and **Mats**.

MATERIALS
- Day 7 Recording Sheet
- Notebook paper
- Latin Mat
- Cards:
  Latin Roots: grad~~e~~, gress, mot, move, mov~~e~~, vent
  Inflected Endings: ed, ing
  Prefixes: ad, in, pro, re, un
  Suffixes: able, ion, ous, ur~~e~~

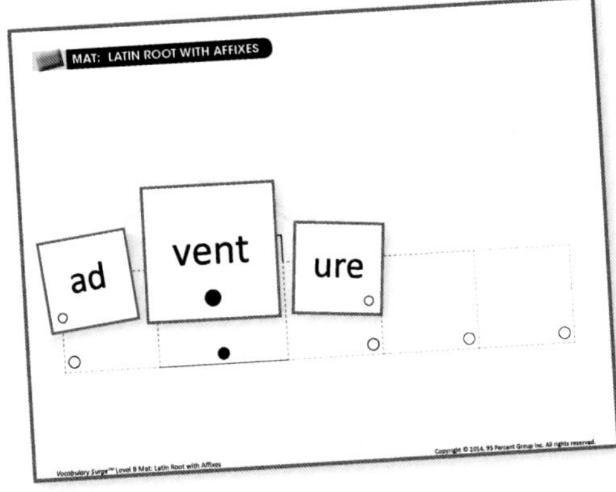


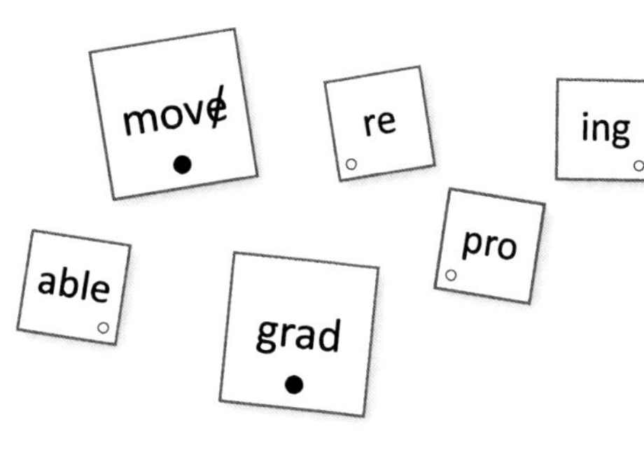


**WE DO** Let's combine cards to build a word.

- I select cards ***ad, vent,*** and ***ure***.
- Where shall I place the prefix ***ad-***? On the left side of the mat
- Where do I place the Latin root ***vent***? In the large center box, matching the solid circles
- Finally, where shall I place the suffix ***-ure***? To the right of ***vent***, matching the circle on the mat to the one on the card
- What word have we built? Adventure What is the definition of ***adventure***? An exciting and sometimes risky activity
- What part of speech is the word ***adventure*** and how do you know? Noun; it is a thing

WORD MULTIPLIER

| SET 1 | Word Parts | Word | Part of Speech |
|---|---|---|---|
| 1. | pro+gress+ion | progression | noun |
| | Write the Meaning: | the action of moving forward toward a goal | |
| 2. | un+grad~~e~~+ed | ungraded | adjective |
| | Write the Meaning: | not yet evaluated; made level or sloping | |
| **SET 2** | **Word Parts** | **Word** | **Part of Speech** |
| 1. | mot+ion+ing | motioning | verb |
| | Write the Meaning: | gesturing with hands or other parts of the body | |
| 2. | re+mov~~e~~+able | removable | adjective |
| | Write the Meaning: | possible to move or take away | |
| **SET 3** | **Word Parts** | **Word** | **Part of Speech** |
| 1. | ad+vent+ur~~e~~+ous | adventurous | adjective |
| | Write the Meaning: | ready to do something exciting or risky | |
| 2. | in+vent+ion | invention | noun |
| | Write the Meaning: | a newly created device or machine | |

**YOU DO** Use your **Cards** and **Mats** to build more words. Complete the **Day 7 Recording Sheet** with your partner. Write additional words on notebook paper.

**Possible Words:**

**grad/grade/grad~~e~~/gress:** grade, graded, progress, progressed, progression, ungraded

**mot/mote/mot~~e~~/move/mov~~e~~:** motion, motioning, moveable, removable, remote, remove, removing

**vent:** advent, adventurous, invent, invention

grad/grade/grad~~e~~/gress,
mot/mote/mot~~e~~/move/mov~~e~~, vent

## DAY 8 • Demonstrate Meaning

### BUILD MEANING

MATERIALS
- Whiteboards
- Markers

**DIRECTIONS** Complete the I Do and We Do sections with the whole class, and pair students to work on the You Do activity. Students can record their ideas on small whiteboards. Ask a few pairs to share their work with the class.

**I DO** Listen to me demonstrate understanding of the meaning of the Latin root ***grad***.

- The first word is ***gradual***. We learned that ***gradual*** means taking place little by little. I'm going to think of examples of things that are ***gradual***.
  - The choir stands are built in ***gradual*** steps.
  - Water is released from the dam in ***gradual*** stages to stop flooding.
- The second word is ***gradation***, which means a process or change taking place gradually in stages or steps. I'm going to think of examples of things that can be a ***gradation***.
  - The color on this drawing shows a ***gradation*** of blues.
  - The student's projects showed a ***gradation*** in completion.

**WE DO** Let's try the next one together with the Latin root ***mot***.

- The first word is ***motion***. The Latin root ***mot*** means to move, and the suffix ***-ion*** means a quality or action. ***Motion*** means movement. The boat's ***motion*** made me feel sick.
  - Name a ***motion*** you can make or have felt.
- The second word is ***motor***. The Latin root ***mot*** means to move, and the suffix ***-or*** means one who does. ***Motor*** means a machine that moves something.
  - Name something that has a ***motor***.

**PROMPT IDEAS** ***motion***
- swinging a bat
- throwing a ball
- moving vehicle

**PROMPT IDEAS** ***motor***
- car
- air conditioner
- hair dryer

**YOU DO** Now it's your turn. Work with a partner, and record your ideas on a whiteboard so you're ready to share with the class. You'll have five minutes to think of examples for two words that contain the Latin root ***vent***.

- The two words are ***event*** and ***prevent***.
  - What does the Latin root ***vent*** mean? To come What does ***event*** mean? Something that happens
  - What does the prefix ***pre-*** mean? Before What does the Latin root ***vent*** mean? To come What does ***prevent*** mean? To stop something before it happens
  - Think of an example of something that is an ***event***.
  - Think of an example of something you can ***prevent***.

**PROMPT IDEAS** ***event***
- birthday party
- show
- wedding
- concert

**PROMPT IDEAS** ***prevent***
- sunburn by using sunscreen
- hunger by eating
- thirst by drinking

cogn, grad/grade/gradȩ/gress, mot/mote/motȩ/move/movȩ, pend/pense/pensȩ, put/pute/putȩ, spec/spect, vent -age

## DAY 9 • Review What You Learned

### STEP 1 REVIEW THE MEANING

**Review *cogn, grad/grade/gradȩ/gress, mot/mote/motȩ/move/movȩ, pend/pense/pensȩ, put/pute/putȩ, spec/spect,* and *vent* Suffix *-age***

MATERIALS
- Word parts projected on document camera, overhead projector, or PowerPoint™

**DIRECTIONS** Display the morphemes so students can see them, and ask for the Certified Definition of each one.

**When I show you the word parts, think about the Certified Definitions we discussed as you prepare to answer.**

| Latin Root | Certified Definition | Latin Root | Certified Definition |
|---|---|---|---|
| cogn | to know | grad/grade/gradȩ/gress | step, degree, walk |
| pend/pense/pensȩ | to hang or weigh | mot/mote/motȩ/move/movȩ | to move |
| put/pute/putȩ | to think | vent | to come |
| | | **Suffix** | **Certified Definition** |
| spec/spect | to look, see, or watch | -age | collection, mass, relationship |

### STEP 2 CHECK MEANING

MATERIALS
- Day 9 Recording Sheet

**DIRECTIONS** Read the following sentence to check that students understand the meanings of ***cogn, grad/grade/gradȩ/gress, mot/mote/motȩ/move/movȩ, pend/pense/pensȩ, put/pute/putȩ, spec/spect,*** and ***vent***. Model the first sentence for students using the We Do step, below.

**WE DO** As I read this sentence, think about the Certified Definitions of the Latin root that fits the blank.

1. Com__________ers were once so large, they took up entire rooms!

- Which Latin root do you think fits on the line? Put
- What is the new word? Computers
- What do you think the word ***computers*** means? Machines that can store and process information

**YOU DO** Complete the rest of the sentences on the **Day 9 Recording Sheet** with your partner to find the Latin root that best fits on the line. Record the new words and their meanings.

CHECK MEANING

1. **Com** put **ers** were once so large, they took up entire rooms! computers
   Meaning: machines that can store and process information
2. The **pro** spect **or** was hunting for a lost silver mine. prospector
   Meaning: person who looks for valuable minerals
3. *The* ***Ad*** vent ***ures*** *of Tintin* is one of my favorite movies. Adventures
   Meaning: exciting and sometimes risky activities
4. The soccer game held us in **sus** pense because the two teams were equally skilled. suspense
   Meaning: a condition of uncertainty or excitement
5. The fawn stood mot **ionless** in the middle of the meadow. motionless
   Meaning: without movement
6. The grad **uates** stood proudly in their caps and gowns for the pictures. graduates
   Meaning: people who have moved from one level to the next

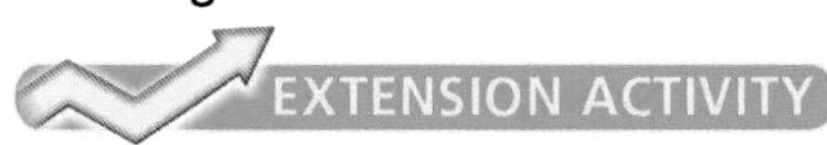


Students write two sentences with missing Latin roots to challenge the class.

**cogn, grad/grade/grad~~e~~/gress, mot/mote/mot~~e~~/move/mov~~e~~, pend/pense/pens~~e~~, put/pute/put~~e~~, spec/spect, vent -age**

# DAY 10 • 2nd Review Day

## STEP 1 MAKE CONNECTIONS

*MATERIALS*
- *Day 10 Recording Sheet*

**DIRECTIONS** Students pair up to write sentences with either one or two of the words that are provided.

**I am going to model how to use one word containing this week's Latin roots in a meaningful sentence. The word is *recognize*.**

- I always ***recognize*** my favorite singer's voice!
- It is your turn to create five more sentences using the words on the top of the recording sheet.
- Sentences with two words get two points and sentences with one word get one point.

**MAKE CONNECTIONS**

yourself to write sentences with two of the words from the list.

| Words | | |
|---|---|---|
| adventurous | immobile | removable |
| convention | inspection | recognize |
| depend | invention | respected |
| disputed | preventive | specialist |
| event | progress | spectator |
| gradual | prospect | suspenseful |

1. I always recognize my favorite singer's voice!
2. The novel our class read had a suspenseful ending.
3. The players disputed the referee's call.
4. We depend on the school bus to take us home.
5. The traffic made gradual progress on the busy highway.

## STEP 2 CHALLENGE: MORPHEME MADNESS

*MATERIALS*
- *Notebook paper*
- *Latin Mat*
- *Cards listed in the table below*

**DIRECTIONS** Students pair up to use **Cards** and **Mats** to build words. They also record all of the words they build and the words' definitions.

| Word Parts | Cards |
|---|---|
| **Latin Roots** | cogn, grad, grade, grad~~e~~, gress, mot, mote, mot~~e~~, move, mov~~e~~, pend, pense, pens~~e~~, put, pute, put~~e~~, spec, spect, vent |
| **Inflected Endings** | ed, ing |
| **Prefixes** | com, dis, in, re, pro, sus |
| **Suffixes** | ion, ize, iz~~e~~ |

**Now it's your turn to build words.**

- First, find a partner.
- Use the **Cards** and **Mats** to build words.
- Record the words and their definitions on a separate sheet of paper.

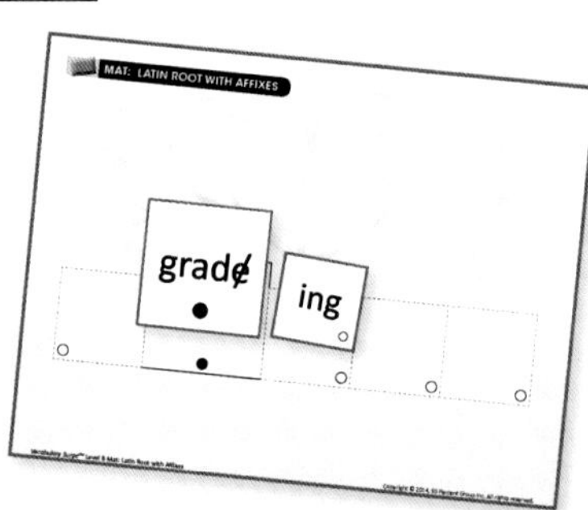

# spir/spire/spir~~e~~, sist/stat, tact/tang, tain/ten/tinu/tinue, vis/vise/vis~~e~~

## DAY 1 • Introduce Latin Roots

### UNCOVER THE MEANING

MATERIALS
- Days 1 & 2 Recording Sheet

#### Introduce *spir/spire/spir~~e~~, tact/tang,* and *vis/vise/vis~~e~~*

**DIRECTIONS** Pair students and distribute the **Days 1 & 2 Recording Sheet**. Model the first completed example. After students have completed the first two columns, ask them to share what they wrote. Then provide the Certified Definition. Explain that understanding parts of words, such as Latin roots, can help students uncover the meaning of many words.

**I'm going to model using my detective skills to figure out what the underlined word parts mean.**

- I'll use the other words in the sentences to develop a Working Definition of a word part.
- Listen as I read the first set of two sentences.

  1. Viewing the pictures in the science book helped the students ***vis*ualize** a volcano.
  2. The eye doctor checked Kye's ***vis*ion** because he was having trouble seeing.

- In **Column 1**, I record the clue words viewed, eye, and seeing that help me understand the meaning of ***vis***.
- I think that ***vis*** means to view or see. This is my Working Definition, which I record in **Column 2**.
- In **Column 3**, I write the Certified Definition of ***vis***: to see.

**Now it's your turn.**

- With your partner, read the next set of sentences on the **Days 1 & 2 Recording Sheet**.
- Use your detective skills to figure out what the underlined word parts mean.
- Consider which words or phrases in the sentences provide clues about meaning. Record them in **Column 1**.
- Write a Working Definition in **Column 2**.
- Only complete **Columns 1** and **2** and then wait for the discussion. You will fill in **Column 3** after I provide a Certified Definition.

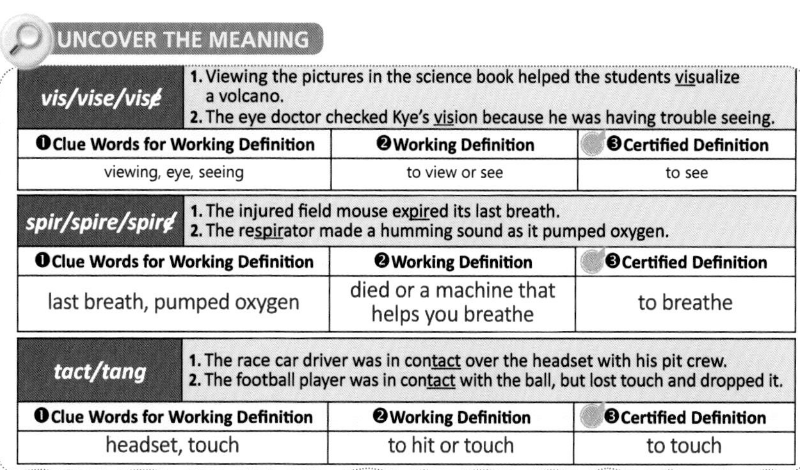

UNCOVER THE MEANING

| vis/vise/vis~~e~~ | 1. Viewing the pictures in the science book helped the students visualize a volcano. 2. The eye doctor checked Kye's vision because he was having trouble seeing. | |
|---|---|---|
| ❶ Clue Words for Working Definition | ❷ Working Definition | ❸ Certified Definition |
| viewing, eye, seeing | to view or see | to see |

| spir/spire/spir~~e~~ | 1. The injured field mouse expired its last breath. 2. The respirator made a humming sound as it pumped oxygen. | |
|---|---|---|
| ❶ Clue Words for Working Definition | ❷ Working Definition | ❸ Certified Definition |
| last breath, pumped oxygen | died or a machine that helps you breathe | to breathe |

| tact/tang | 1. The race car driver was in contact over the headset with his pit crew. 2. The football player was in contact with the ball, but lost touch and dropped it. | |
|---|---|---|
| ❶ Clue Words for Working Definition | ❷ Working Definition | ❸ Certified Definition |
| headset, touch | to hit or touch | to touch |

# DAY 2 • Deepen the Meaning

## CHECK MEANING

**DIRECTIONS** Using the **Cards** and **Mat**, confirm that students understand how the meaning of the word evolves as more parts are added.

**I DO**

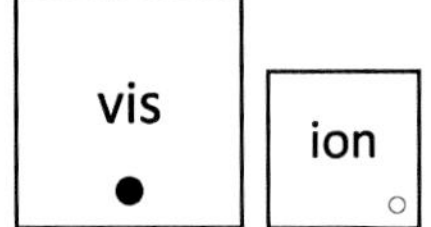


- The suffix ***-ion*** means action.
- Adding ***-ion*** to ***vis*** spells the word ***vision***. The combination of word parts means sight or a thought that is like seeing a future idea in the mind.
- Now, I'm going to use my knowledge of the word to answer the question.
  1. What does it mean when we say the runner has a ***vision*** of winning? She sees the future in her head.

**MATERIALS**
- Pocket chart, document camera, or PowerPoint™
- Days 1 & 2 Recording Sheet
- Cards:
  Teacher: ary, ion, vis
  Student: Roots: spire, spir~~e~~, tact
  Prefixes: con, in
  Inflected Endings: ed

**WE DO**

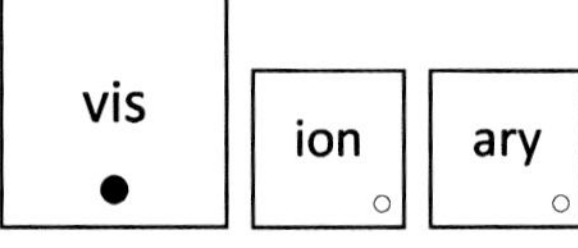


- The suffix ***-ion*** means action.
- After adding ***-ion*** to ***vis***, what's the meaning? A thought that is like seeing a future idea in the mind
- The suffix ***-ary*** means relating to.
- After adding ***-ary*** to ***vision***, what's the meaning? A person who is able to see a future idea in his or her mind
- Listen to me use the word ***visionary*** in a question and we will use our knowledge of its parts to figure out the answer.
  2. What does it mean when we say the scientist is a ***visionary***? She is a person who is able to see a future idea in her mind.

**YOU DO** Use your **Cards** and **Mat** to complete the chart on the **Days 1 & 2 Recording Sheet.**

| Latin Roots | Certified Definition |
|---|---|
| spir/spire/spir~~e~~ | to breathe |
| tact/tang | to touch |
| vis/vise/vis~~e~~ | to see |
| **Prefixes** | **Certified Definition** |
| ad- | to, toward |
| con- | together, with |
| in- | in, on, or toward |
| re- | again, back |
| super- | of superior quality or size |
| **Suffixes** | **Certified Definition** |
| -ate/-at~~e~~ | cause, make |
| -ent | action, state, or quality |
| -ible | able |
| -ic | having the characteristic of |

**CHECK MEANING**

**DIRECTIONS** **Build the words with the Cards and Mat. Describe how adding new parts changes the meaning of the words.**

| Word | Prefix | Latin Root | Inflected Ending |
|---|---|---|---|
| inspire | in: in | spire: to breathe | |
| Meaning: | to energize like breathing life into something | | |
| inspired | in: in | spir~~e~~: to breathe | ed |
| Meaning: | to have filled with energy, like breathing life into something | | |
| intact | in: not | tact: to touch | |
| Meaning: | untouched or remaining complete | | |
| contact | con: together, with | tact: to touch | |
| Meaning: | to be in touch with someone | | |

| Suffixes | Certified Definition |
|---|---|
| -ion | state of being, quality, or action |
| -or | has a special characteristic |
| **Inflected Endings** | **Certified Definition** |
| -ed | past tense |

# spir/spire/spir~~e~~, tact/tang, vis/vise/vis~~e~~

## DAY 3 • Word Multiplier

### WORD MULTIPLIER

**Build words with *spir/spire/spir~~e~~, tact/tang* and *vis/vise/vis~~e~~***

MATERIALS
- Day 3 Recording Sheet
- Notebook paper
- Latin Mat
- Cards:
  Latin Roots: spir, spire, spir~~e~~, tact, vis~~e~~
  Inflected Endings: ed, ing
  Prefixes: ad, con, in, re, super
  Suffixes: at~~e~~, ent, ible, ic, ion, or

**DIRECTIONS** Students work together to build words using their **Cards** and **Mats**.

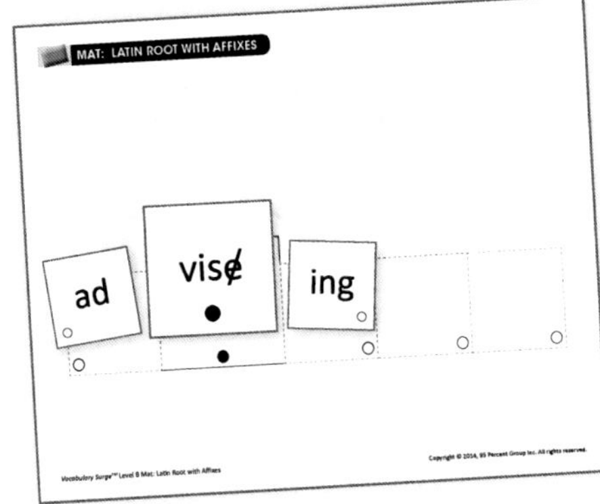


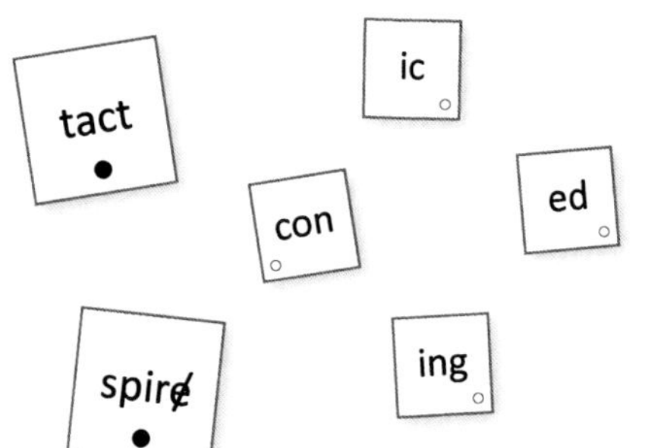


**I DO** Watch me combine **Cards** to build a word.

- I select cards ***ad, vis~~e~~,*** and ***ing***.
- I place the prefix ***ad-*** on the left side of the mat, matching the circle on the mat to the one on the card.
- I place the Latin root ***vis~~e~~*** in the large center box, matching the solid circles.
- Finally, I place the inflected ending ***-ing*** to the right of ***vis~~e~~***, matching the circle on the mat to the one on the card.
- I have built the word ***advising***.

**WE DO** Let me try another.

- I choose the cards ***in, spir~~e~~, at~~e~~,*** and ***ion***.
- Where should I place the card ***in-***? In the box on the left of the mat
- Why do we place it here? Because it is a prefix and has a circle like the mat
- Where should I place the card ***spir~~e~~***? In the large, middle box
- Why do we place it here? Because it is the Latin root and has a solid circle like the mat
- Where shall I place the suffixes ***at~~e~~*** and ***ion***? In the boxes to the right of *spir*
- Look at the example on your **Day 3 Recording Sheet** to see how to write the parts of ***inspiration*** and the whole word. ***In-*** means in, ***spir~~e~~*** means to breathe, ***ate*** means cause, and ***ion*** means state of being, quality or action.
- When we put these word parts together, ***inspiration*** means an inspiring or motivating action.
- What part of speech is ***inspiration*** and how do you know? Noun, thing

**WORD MULTIPLIER**

| | Word Parts | Word | Part of Speech |
|---|---|---|---|
| **SET 1** | | | |
| 1. | in+spir+at~~e~~+ion | inspiration | noun |
| Write the Meaning: | an inspiring, or energizing, action or influence | | |
| 2. | re+spir+at~~e~~+ion | respiration | noun |
| Write the Meaning: | the act of breathing; inhaling and exhaling | | |
| **SET 2** | | | |
| 1. | con+tact | contact | verb |
| Write the Meaning: | to be in touch with someone | | |
| 2. | tact+ic | tactic | noun |
| Write the Meaning: | a plan of action | | |
| **SET 3** | | | |
| 1. | ad+vis~~e~~+or | advisor | noun |
| Write the Meaning: | someone who provides advice or guidance | | |
| 2. | super+vis~~e~~+ing | supervising | verb |
| Write the Meaning: | watching over people's work | | |

**YOU DO** Use your **Cards** and **Mats** to build more words. Complete the **Day 3 Recording Sheet** with your partner. Write additional words on notebook paper. We will review the words when you have finished.

**Possible Words:**
**spir/spire/spir~~e~~:** inspire, inspired, inspiration, respire, respired, respiration
**tact/tang:** contact, intact, tactic
**vis/vise/vis~~e~~:** advise, advisor, advising, supervising, visor

## DAY 4 • Demonstrate Meaning

### BUILD MEANING

*MATERIALS*
- *Whiteboards*
- *Markers*

**DIRECTIONS** Complete the I Do and We Do sections with the whole class, and pair students to work on the You Do activity. Students can record their ideas on small whiteboards. Ask a few pairs to share their work with the class.

**I DO** Listen to me demonstrate understanding of the meaning of the Latin root ***spire***.

- The first word is ***expired***. ***Expired*** means to have breathed one's last breath or ended. I'm going to think of examples of times when something ***expired***.
  - My favorite magazine subscription ***expired*** last month.
  - When my goldfish died, my grandfather said it had ***expired***.
- The second word is ***inspired***, which means to energize by breathing life into something. I'm going to think of an example of things that were ***inspired***.
  - When I was young, I was ***inspired*** by my favorite tennis player.
  - My sketch of our dog was ***inspired*** by a photograph I saw in a book.

**WE DO** Let's try the next one together with the Latin root ***vis***.

- The first word is ***vision***. The Latin root ***vis*** means to see, and the suffix ***-ion*** means action. ***Vision*** is sight or a thought that is like seeing a future idea in your mind. My ***vision*** of a perfect vacation includes sunbathing on a white, sandy beach.
  - Name a ***vision*** you have or might have in the future.
- The second word is ***revised***. The prefix ***re-*** means again or back, the Latin root ***vis*** means to see, and inflected ending ***-ed*** means in the past. ***Revised*** means to look at something again to improve it.
  - Name some things you ***revised*** or might ***revise*** in the future.

**PROMPT IDEAS** ***vision***
- perfect birthday cake
- scoring a goal
- winning the spelling bee

**PROMPT IDEAS** ***revised***
- book report
- homework answer
- opinion of someone

**YOU DO** Now it's your turn. Work with a partner, and record your ideas on a whiteboard so you're ready to share with the class. You'll have five minutes to think of examples for two words that contain the Latin root ***tact***.

- The two words are ***intact*** and ***contact***.
  - What does the prefix ***in-*** mean? Not What does the Latin root ***tact*** mean? To touch What does ***intact*** mean? Untouched or remaining complete
  - What does the prefix ***con-*** mean? Together What does the Latin root ***tact*** mean? To touch What does ***contact*** mean? To meet or touch
- Think of an example of something that you can keep ***intact***.
- Think of an example of ***contact*** you've made or can make.

**PROMPT IDEAS** ***intact***
- completed puzzle
- baseball card collection
- group of friends

**PROMPT IDEAS** ***contact***
- bat to a baseball
- two magnets together
- foot to a soccer ball

 

sist/stat, tain/ten/tinu/tinue

## DAY 5 • Introduce Latin Roots

### UNCOVER THE MEANING

**Introduce *sist/stat* and *tain/ten/tinu/tinue***

MATERIALS
- Days 5 & 6 Recording Sheet

**DIRECTIONS** Pair students and distribute the **Days 5 & 6 Recording Sheet**. Model the first completed example. After students have completed the first two columns, ask them to share what they wrote. Then provide the Certified Definition. Explain that understanding parts of words, such as Latin roots, can help students uncover the meaning of many words.

**I'm going to model using my detective skills to figure out what the underlined word parts mean.**

- I'll use the other words in the sentences to develop a Working Definition of a word part.
- Listen as I read the first set of three sentences.
  1. The ***stat**ionary* exercise bike remains in one spot in the gym.
  2. My grandmother firmly *in**sist**ed* that I take the cookies home.
  3. Jess can't get the paint off the floor because it is *re**sist**ant* to the cleaner.
- In **Column 1**, I record the clue words remains in one spot, firmly, and can't get the paint off that help me understand the meaning of ***sist/stat***.
- I think that ***sist/stat*** means stays or holds. This is my Working Definition, which I record in **Column 2**.
- In **Column 3**, I will write the Certified Definition of ***sist/stat***: to stand.

**Now it's your turn.**

- With your partner, read the next set of sentences on the **Days 5 & 6 Recording Sheet**.
- Use your detective skills to figure out what the underlined word parts mean.
- Consider which words or phrases in the sentences provide clues about meaning. Record them in **Column 1**.
- Write a Working Definition in **Column 2**.
- Only complete **Columns 1** and **2** and then wait for the discussion. You will fill in **Column 3** after I provide a Certified Definition.

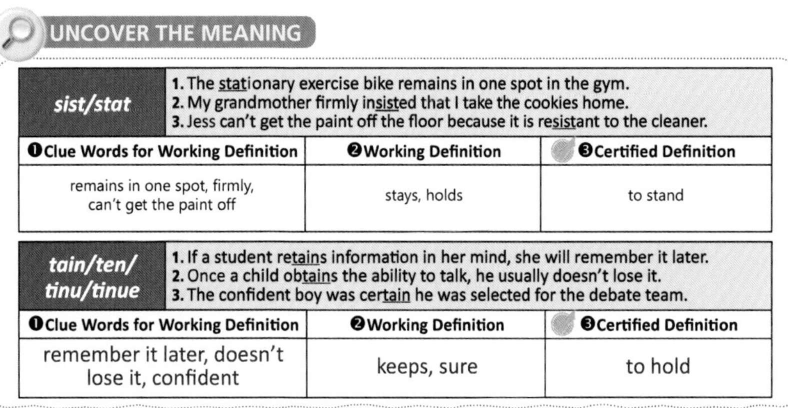

UNCOVER THE MEANING

| sist/stat | 1. The stationary exercise bike remains in one spot in the gym.<br>2. My grandmother firmly insisted that I take the cookies home.<br>3. Jess can't get the paint off the floor because it is resistant to the cleaner. | |
|---|---|---|
| ❶ Clue Words for Working Definition | ❷ Working Definition | ❸ Certified Definition |
| remains in one spot, firmly, can't get the paint off | stays, holds | to stand |

| tain/ten/tinu/tinue | 1. If a student retains information in her mind, she will remember it later.<br>2. Once a child obtains the ability to talk, he usually doesn't lose it.<br>3. The confident boy was certain he was selected for the debate team. | |
|---|---|---|
| ❶ Clue Words for Working Definition | ❷ Working Definition | ❸ Certified Definition |
| remember it later, doesn't lose it, confident | keeps, sure | to hold |

# DAY 6 • Deepen the Meaning

## CHECK MEANING

MATERIALS
- Pocket chart, document camera, or PowerPoint™
- Days 5 & 6 Recording Sheet
- Cards:
  Teacher: con, de, tain
  Student: Roots: sist, tain, tinue
  Prefixes: con, re
  Suffix: ent

**DIRECTIONS** Using the **Cards** and **Mat**, confirm that students understand how the meaning of the word evolves as more parts are added.

**I DO**

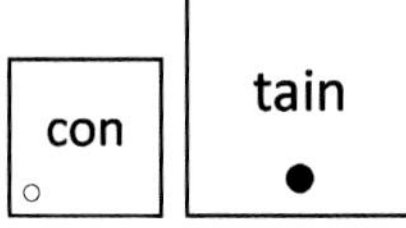


- The prefix ***con-*** means together or with.
- Adding ***con-*** to ***tain*** spells the word ***contain***. The combination of word parts means to hold something within an area.
- Now I'm going to use my knowledge of the word to answer the question.
  1. What does it mean when we say we were able to ***contain*** the spill? We were able to hold it within an area.

**WE DO**

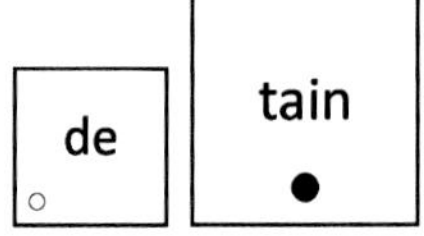


- The prefix ***de-*** means away from or down.
- After adding ***de-*** to ***tain***, what's the meaning? Hold back
- Listen to me use the word ***detain*** in a question and we will use our knowledge of its parts to figure out the answer.
  2. What does it mean when we ***detain*** the school bus until everyone gets on? We hold it.

**YOU DO** Use your **Cards** and **Mat** to complete the chart on the **Days 5 & 6 Recording Sheet**.

| Latin Roots | Certified Definition |
|---|---|
| sist/stat | to stand |
| tain/ten/ tinu/tinue | to hold |
| **Prefixes** | **Certified Definition** |
| con- | together, with |
| in- | in |
| re- | again, back |
| sub- | under, beneath, or below |
| **Suffixes** | **Certified Definition** |
| -ence | action, state, or quality |
| -ent | action, state, or quality |
| -ive | showing a quality |
| -ment | act of, state of, or result of an action |
| -ous | like |

**DIRECTIONS** Build the words with the Cards and Mat. Describe how adding new parts changes the meaning of the words.

| Word | Prefix | Latin Root | Suffix |
|---|---|---|---|
| consistent | con: with | sist: to stand | ent: action, state, or quality |
| Meaning: | always happening the same way | | |
| resistant | re: again, back | sist: to stand | ent: action, state, or quality |
| Meaning: | standing against or opposing an idea | | |
| continue | con: with | tinue: to hold | |
| Meaning: | to keep doing something | | |
| contain | con: with | tain: to hold | |
| Meaning: | to hold something within an area | | |

# sist/stat, tain/ten/tin/tinu/tinue

## DAY 7 • Word Multiplier

### WORD MULTIPLIER

**Build words with *stat/sist* and *tain/ten/tinu/tinue***

**DIRECTIONS** Students work together to build words using their **Cards** and **Mats**.

MATERIALS
- Day 7 Recording Sheet
- Notebook paper
- Latin Mat
- Cards:
  Latin Roots: sist, stat, tain, tinu, tinue
  Prefixes: con, in, re, sub
  Suffixes: ence, ive, ment, ous

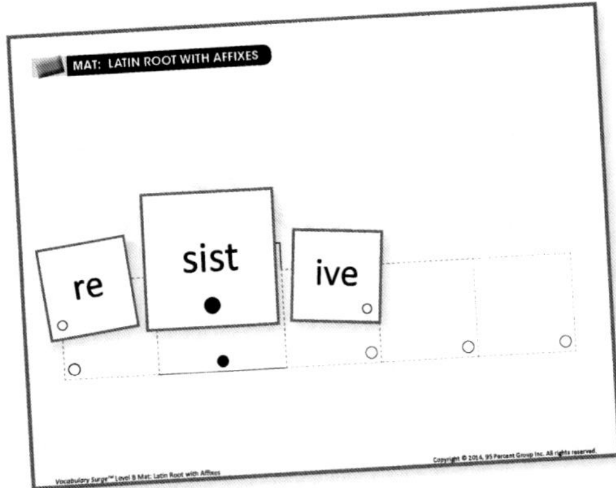


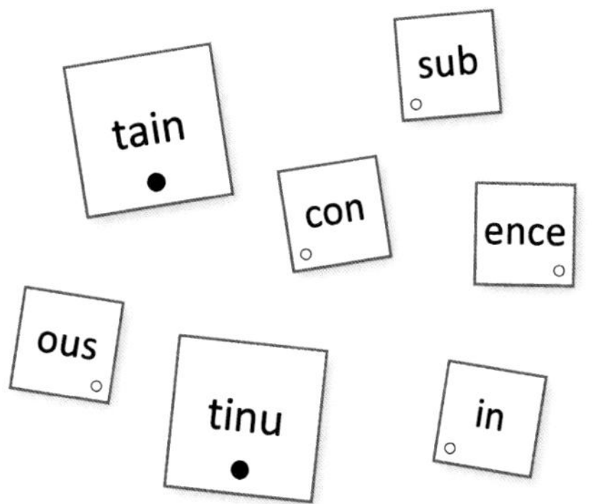


**WE DO** Let's combine **Cards** to build a word.

- I select cards ***re, sist,*** and ***ive***.
- Where should I place the prefix ***re-***? On the left side of the mat
- Where shall I place the Latin root ***sist***? In the large center box, matching the solid circles
- Finally, where shall I place the suffix ***-ive***? To the right of ***sist***, matching the circle on the mat to the one on the card
- What word have we built? Resistive What is the definition of ***resistive***? Holding firm standing against something

**YOU DO** Use your **Cards** and **Mats** to build more words. Complete the **Day 7 Recording Sheet** with your partner. Write additional words on notebook paper.

**WORD MULTIPLIER**

| SET 1 | Word Parts | Word | Part of Speech |
|---|---|---|---|
| 1. | in+sist+ence | insistence | noun |
| | Write the Meaning: | standing firm with a demand | |
| 2. | re+sist | resist | verb |
| | Write the Meaning: | to stand against or oppose an idea | |
| 3. | con+sist | consist | verb |
| | Write the Meaning: | to be made up of | |

| SET 2 | Word Parts | Word | Part of Speech |
|---|---|---|---|
| 1. | con+tain+ment | containment | noun |
| | Write the Meaning: | the act or process of holding something within limits | |
| 2. | con+tinu+ous | continuous | adjective |
| | Write the Meaning: | to keep doing something without stopping | |
| 3. | re+tain | retain | verb |
| | Write the Meaning: | to continue to hold someone or something | |

**Possible Words:**

**sist/stat/stit:** consist, consistence, insist, insistence, resist, subsistence

**tain/ten/tinu/tinue:** contain, containment, continue, continuous, retain

## DAY 8 • Demonstrate Meaning

### BUILD MEANING

MATERIALS
- Whiteboards
- Markers

**DIRECTIONS** Complete the I Do and We Do whole class, and pair students to work on the You Do. Students can record their ideas on small whiteboards. Ask a few pairs to share their work with the class.

**I DO** Listen to me demonstrate understanding of the meaning of the Latin root ***stat***.

- The first word is ***stationary***. We learned yesterday that ***stationary*** means to stay in one place. I'm going to think of examples of things that are ***stationary***.
  - The man walks on a ***stationary*** treadmill for exercise.
  - The car was ***stationary*** when the teen climbed into it.
- The second word is ***statue***, which means a likeness of something in marble or clay. I'm going to think of examples of ***statues***.
  - The pigeons perched along the back of the marble ***statue***.
  - The artist made a clay ***statue*** of Rip Van Winkle.

**WE DO** Let's try the next one together with the Latin root ***tain***.

- The first word is ***retain***. The prefix ***re-*** means again or back, and the Latin root ***tain*** means to hold. ***Retain*** means to hold someone or something. Small rocks in the bottom of the pot helps a plant ***retain*** moisture.
  - Name something you have ***retained*** or might ***retain*** in the future.
- The second word is ***obtain***. The prefix ***ob-*** means to, and the Latin root ***tain*** means to hold. ***Obtain*** means to gain or get something.
  - Name something that you have been able to ***obtain*** or can ***obtain***.

**PROMPT IDEAS** ***retain***
- someone's respect
- information for a test
- food retains freshness

**PROMPT IDEAS** ***obtain***
- good grade
- new bike
- dessert

**YOU DO** Now it's your turn. Work with a partner, and record your ideas on a whiteboard so you're ready to share with the class. You'll have five minutes to think of examples for two words that contain the Latin root ***sist***.

- The two words are ***insist*** and ***resist***.
  - What does the prefix ***in-*** mean? In or towards What does the Latin root ***sist*** mean? To stand What does ***insist*** mean? To stand firm about what you want
  - What does the prefix ***re-*** mean? Again or back What does the Latin root ***sist*** mean? To stand What does ***resist*** mean? To stand against or oppose an idea
- Think of an example of something you can ***insist*** on.
- Think of an example of something you can ***resist***.

**PROMPT IDEAS** ***insist***
- ice cream on your pie
- no vegetables
- wearing favorite shoes

**PROMPT IDEAS** ***resist***
- eating foods you don't like
- going to bed
- being like everyone else

 

# sist/stat, spir/spire/spir~~e~~, tact/tang, tain/ten/tinu/tinue, vis/vise/vis~~e~~

## DAY 9 • Review What You Learned

### STEP 1 REVIEW THE MEANING

**Review *spir/spire/spir~~e~~, sist/stat, tact/tang, tain/ten/tinu/tinue,* and *vis/vise/vis~~e~~***

MATERIALS
- Word parts projected on document camera, overhead projector, or PowerPoint™

DIRECTIONS Display the morphemes so students can see them, and ask for the Certified Definition of each one.

**When I show you the word parts, think about the Certified Definitions we discussed as you prepare to answer.**

| Latin Root | Certified Definition |
|---|---|
| *spir/spire/spir~~e~~* | to breathe |
| *tact/tang* | to touch |
| *vis/vise/vis~~e~~* | to see |
| **Latin Root** | **Certified Definition** |
| *sist/stat* | to stand |
| *tain/ten/tinu/tinue* | to hold |

### STEP 2 CHECK MEANING

MATERIALS
- Day 9 Recording Sheet

DIRECTIONS Read the following sentences to check that students understand the meanings of ***spir/spire/spir~~e~~, sist/stat, tact/tang, tain/ten/tinu/tinue,*** and ***vis/vise/vis~~e~~***. Model the first sentence for students using the We Do Step, below.

WE DO As I read this sentence, think about the Certified Definition of the Latin root that fits the blank.

1. Air is in__________ible to our eyes.

- Which Latin root do you think fits on the line? Vis
- What is the new word? Invisible
- What do you think the word ***invisible*** means? Something that cannot be seen

YOU DO Complete the rest of the sentences on the **Day 9 Recording Sheet** with your partner to find the Latin root that best fits on the line. Record the new words and their meanings.

CHECK MEANING

1. Air is **in** vis **ible** to our eyes. invisible
   Meaning: something that cannot be seen
2. The vase is **in** tact even though it fell to the floor. intact
   Meaning: untouched or remaining complete
3. The sponge can **re** tain all of the water from the spill. retain
   Meaning: to continue to hold someone or something
4. The fortuneteller claimed to have a vis **ion** about what was going to happen. vision
   Meaning: sight, or a thought that is like seeing a future idea in the mind
5. The teacher's comment about my work will **in** spire me to work harder. inspire
   Meaning: to energize, like breathing life into something
6. The children were **re** sist **ant** when Dad wanted to leave the park. resistant
   Meaning: standing against or opposing an idea

Students write two sentences with missing Latin roots to challenge the class.

sist/stat, spir/spire/spir~~e~~, tact/tang, tain/ten/tinu/tinue, vis/vise/vis~~e~~

# DAY 10 • 2nd Review Day

## STEP 1 MAKE CONNECTIONS

MATERIALS
- Day 10 Recording Sheet

**DIRECTIONS** Students pair up to write sentences with either one or two of the words that are provided.

**I am going to model how to use one word containing this week's Latin roots in a meaningful sentence. The word is *expiration*.**

- I check the ***expiration*** date on food packages.
- It is your turn to write five more sentences using the words on the top of the recording sheet.
- Sentences with two words get two points and sentences with one word get one point.

MAKE CONNECTIONS

| Words | | |
|---|---|---|
| advised<br>advisor<br>consistent<br>contact<br>contacting<br>contain | continue<br>continuous<br>detained<br>expiration<br>insisting<br>inspired | invisible<br>resistant<br>revise<br>stationary<br>visor<br>visualize |

1. I check the expiration date on food packages.
2. The ink was so light on the copy that it was almost invisible.
3. I was detained because of the flat tire.
4. The boy was resistant to jump into the cold lake!
5. The athlete inspired us with her consistent performance.

## STEP 2 CHALLENGE: MORPHEME MADNESS

MATERIALS
- Notebook paper
- Latin Mat
- Cards listed in the table below

**DIRECTIONS** Students pair up to use **Cards** and **Mats** to build words. They also record all of the words they build and the words' definitions.

| Word Parts | Cards |
|---|---|
| **Latin Roots** | spir, spire, spir~~e~~, sist, stat, tact, tang, tain, ten, tinu, tinue, vis, vise, vis~~e~~ |
| **Inflected Endings** | ed, ing |
| **Prefixes** | in, re, con, super |
| **Suffixes** | tion, ment |

**Now it's your turn to build words.**

- First, find a partner.
- Use the **Cards** and **Mats** to build words.
- Record the words and their definitions on a separate sheet of paper.

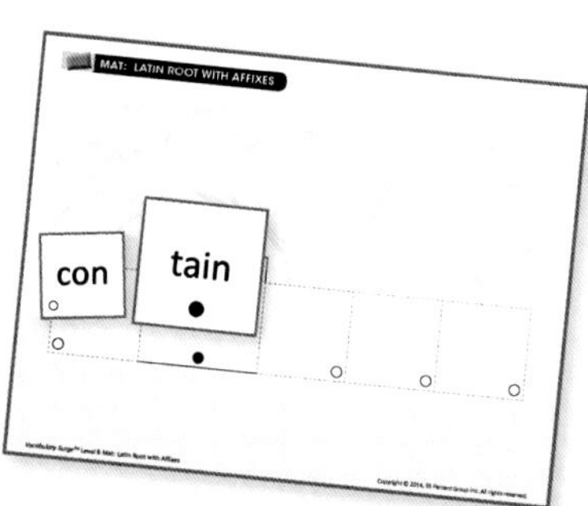


 

# cas/cid/cide/cid¢, cause/caus¢/cuse/cus¢, cern, cis/cise/cis¢, sec/sect/seg

# bi-, multi-

## DAY 1 • Introduce Latin Roots

### UNCOVER THE MEANING

MATERIALS
- Days 1 & 2 Recording Sheet

#### Introduce *cern, cis/cise/cis¢,* and *sec/sect/seg; bi-*

**DIRECTIONS** Pair students and distribute the **Days 1 & 2 Recording Sheet**. Model the first completed example. After students have completed the first two columns, ask them to share what they wrote. Then provide the Certified Definition. Explain that understanding parts of words, such as Latin roots, can help students uncover the meaning of many words.

**I'm going to model using my detective skills to figure out what the underlined word parts mean.**

- I'll use the other words in the sentences to develop a Working Definition of a word part.
- Listen as I read the first set of two sentences.

  1. Theo used the ***scissors*** to separate the fabric into two pieces.
  2. To remove the nail, Dad used a razor to make an ***incision*** in my bike tire.

- In **Column 1**, I record the clue words separate, remove, and razor that help me understand the meaning of ***cis***.
- I think that ***cis*** means separate or slice. This is my Working Definition, which I record in **Column 2**.
- In **Column 3**, I write the Certified Definition of ***cis***: to cut.

**Now it's your turn.**

- With your partner, read the next set of sentences on the **Days 1 & 2 Recording Sheet**.
- Use your detective skills to figure out what the underlined word parts mean.
- Consider which words or phrases in the sentences provide clues about meaning. Record them in **Column 1**.
- Write a Working Definition in **Column 2**.
- Only complete **Columns 1** and **2** and then wait for the discussion. You will fill in **Column 3** after I provide a Certified Definition.

UNCOVER THE MEANING

| *cis/cise/cis¢* | 1. They used the scissors to separate the fabric into two pieces.<br>2. To remove the nail, Dad used a razor to make an incision in my bike tire. | |
|---|---|---|
| ❶ Clue Words for Working Definition | ❷ Working Definition | ❸ Certified Definition |
| separate, remove, razor | separate, slice | to cut |

| *cern* | 1. The chef can discern the difference in the flavors of two types of cinnamon.<br>2. Keith found the slight variation in color of the uniforms indiscernible. | |
|---|---|---|
| ❶ Clue Words for Working Definition | ❷ Working Definition | ❸ Certified Definition |
| difference, slight variation | identify | to separate |

| *sec/sect/seg* | 1. During the science lab, students dissected a worm into its main parts.<br>2. At the intersection of the roads, we could choose separate directions. | |
|---|---|---|
| ❶ Clue Words for Working Definition | ❷ Working Definition | ❸ Certified Definition |
| main parts, separate directions | pull apart, separate | to cut |

cern, cis/cise/cis⊄, sec/sect/seg
bi-

# DAY 2 • Deepen the Meaning

## CHECK MEANING

MATERIALS
- Pocket chart, document camera, or PowerPoint™
- Days 1 & 2 Recording Sheet
- Cards:
  Teacher: bi, ion, sect
  Student: Latin Roots: cern, cis, cise
  Prefixes: con, de, dis, pre
  Suffixes: ion

**DIRECTIONS** Using the **Cards** and **Mat**, confirm that students understand how the meaning of the word evolves as more parts are added.

**I DO**

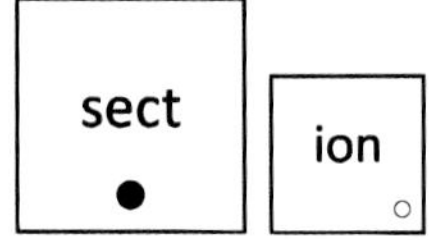

- The suffix ***-ion*** means action.
- Adding ***-ion*** to ***sect*** spells the word ***section***. The combination of word parts means a part that is cutoff or separated.
- Now, I'm going to use my knowledge of the word to answer the question.
  1. What does it mean when I say that I'll ***section*** my orange? I'll separate it into parts.

**WE DO**

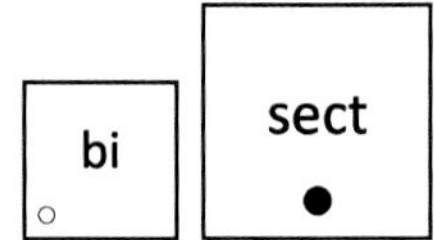

- The prefix ***bi-*** means two.
- How does adding ***bi-*** to ***sect*** change the meaning? Divide into two parts
- Listen to me use the word ***bisect*** in a question and we will use our knowledge of its parts to figure out the answer.
  2. What does it mean when we ***bisect*** an apple? We divide it into two parts.

**YOU DO** Use your **Cards** and **Mats** to complete the chart on the **Days 1 & 2 Recording Sheet**.

| Latin Roots | Certified Definition |
|---|---|
| cern | to separate |
| cis/cise/cis⊄ | to cut |
| sec/sect/seg | to cut |
| **Prefixes** | **Certified Definition** |
| bi- | two |
| con- | together, with |
| de- | away from, down |
| dis- | not, apart |
| in- | in |
| pre- | before, earlier |
| trans- | across or beyond |
| **Suffixes** | **Certified Definition** |
| -ible | able, can do |
| -ion | state of being, quality, or action |
| -or | one who does |
| **Inflected Endings** | **Certified Definition** |
| -ed | past |
| -ing | present participle |

**CHECK MEANING**

**DIRECTIONS** Build the words with the Cards and Mat. Describe how adding new parts changes the meaning of the words.

| Word | Prefix | Latin Root | Suffix |
|---|---|---|---|
| concern | con: together, with | cern: to separate | |
| Meaning: | to worry or show interest | | |
| discern | dis: apart | cern: to separate | |
| Meaning: | to recognize or perceive clearly | | |
| precise | pre: before, earlier | cise: to cut | |
| Meaning: | exactly or carefully defined or stated | | |
| decision | de: away from, down | cis: to cut | ion: state of being, quality, or action |
| Meaning: | a judgment often made from several choices | | |

 

# cern, cis/cise/cis~~e~~, sec/sect/seg
# bi-

## DAY 3 • Word Multiplier

### WORD MULTIPLIER

**Build words with *cern, cis/cise/cis~~e~~,* and *sec/sect/seg; bi-***

MATERIALS
- Day 3 Recording Sheet
- Notebook paper
- Latin Mat
- Cards:
  Latin Roots: cern, cis, cise, sec, sect, seg
  Prefixes: dis, in, pre, trans
  Suffixes: ible, ion, or
  Inflected Endings: ed, ing

**DIRECTIONS** Students work together to build words using their **Cards** and **Mats**.

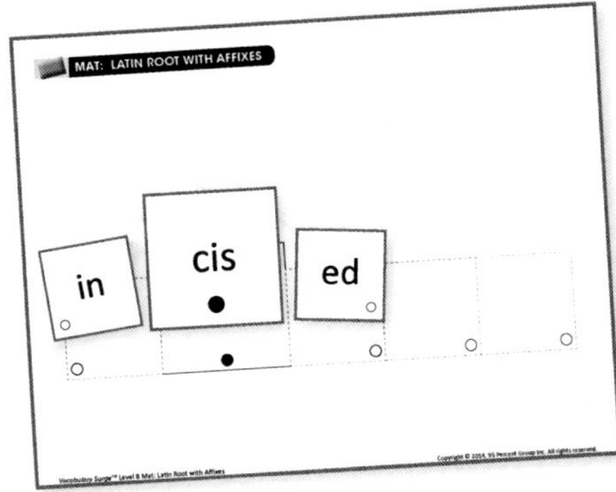


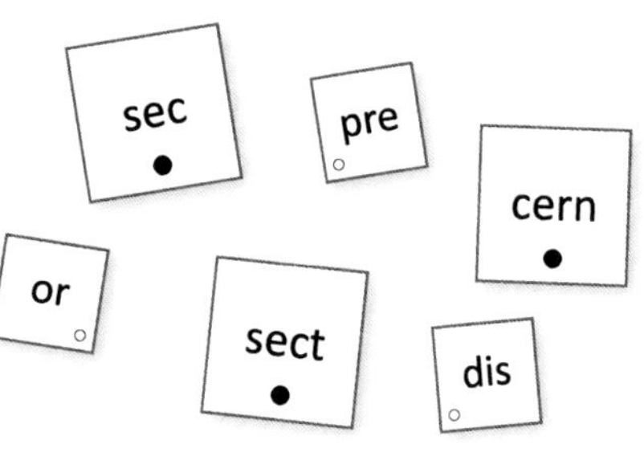


**I DO** Watch me combine **Cards** to build a word.

- I select cards ***in***, ***cis,*** and ***ed***.
- I place the prefix ***in-*** on the left side of the mat, matching the circle on the mat to the one on the card.
- I place the Latin root ***cis*** in the large center box, matching the solid circles.
- Finally, I place the inflected ending ***-ed*** to the right of ***cis***, matching the circle on the mat to the one on the card.
- I have built the word ***incised***.

**WE DO** Let me try another.

- I choose the cards ***dis***, ***cern***, and ***ible***.
- Where should I place the card ***dis***? In the box on the left
- Why do we place it here? Because it is the prefix
- Where should I place the card ***cern***? In the middle box
- Why do we place it here? Because it is the Latin root and has a solid circle like the mat
- Where shall I place ***-ible***? In the box to the right of ***cern***
- Look at the example on your **Day 3 Recording Sheet** to see how to write the parts of ***discernible*** and the whole word. ***Dis-*** means not or apart, ***cern*** means to separate, and ***-ible*** means able or can do.
- When we put these word parts together, ***discernible*** means able to recognize or perceive clearly.
- What part of speech is ***discernible*** and how do you know? Adjective, because it describes something

**WORD MULTIPLIER**

| SET 1 | Word Parts | Word | Part of Speech |
|---|---|---|---|
| 1. | dis+cern+ible | discernible | adjective |
| | Write the Meaning: | able to recognize or perceive clearly | |
| 2. | dis+cern+ing | discerning | verb; adjective |
| | Write the Meaning: | V: Recognizing things that are distinctly different<br>ADJ: showing good judgment | |

| SET 2 | Word Parts | Word | Part of Speech |
|---|---|---|---|
| 1. | in+cis+ion | incision | noun |
| | Write the Meaning: | a cut, usually made in surgery | |
| 2. | pre+cise | precise | adjective |
| | Write the Meaning: | exactly and carefully defined or stated | |

| SET 3 | Word Parts | Word | Part of Speech |
|---|---|---|---|
| 1. | sect+or | sector | noun |
| | Write the Meaning: | a section of something larger | |
| 2. | tran+sect+ed | transected | verb; adjective |
| | Write the Meaning: | V: to cut something the long side<br>ADJ: having been cut along the long side | |

**YOU DO** Use your **Cards** and **Mats** to build more words. Complete the **Day 3 Recording Sheet** with your partner. Write additional words on notebook paper. We will review the words when you have finished.

**Possible Words:**
**cern:** discern, discernible, discerning **cis/cise/cis~~e~~:** incise, incision, precise, precision
**sec/sect/seg:** sect, sector, sectored, transect, transected

cern, cis/cise/cis¢, sec/sect/seg
bi-

## DAY 4 • Demonstrate Meaning

### BUILD MEANING

MATERIALS
- Whiteboards
- Markers

**DIRECTIONS** Complete the I Do and We Do sections with the whole class, and pair students to work on the You Do activity. Students can record their ideas on small whiteboards. Ask a few pairs to share their work with the class.

**I DO** Listen to me demonstrate understanding of the meaning of the Latin root ***cern***.

- The first word is ***discern***. We learned that ***discern*** means to recognize or perceive clearly. I'm going to think of examples of times when someone can ***discern*** something.
  - My brother can ***discern*** between cinnamon and pumpkin candles by their smells.
  - When walking into a dark house, it is hard to ***discern*** the carpet colors.
- The second word is ***concern***, which means a worry about something. I'm going to think of examples of times when someone had a ***concern***.
  - The teacher had a ***concern*** when her class didn't do well on a test.
  - The painter had a ***concern*** that that he didn't have enough paint to finish the kitchen.

**WE DO** Let's try the next one together with the Latin root ***sect***.

- The first word is ***section***. The Latin root ***sect*** means to cut, and the suffix ***-ion*** means a state of being, quality, or action. ***Section*** means a part that is cut off or separated. My favorite ***section*** of the newspaper is the comics.
  - Name things that are divided into ***sections*** or might appear in ***sections***.

**PROMPT IDEAS** ***section***
- pizza
- chapters in a book
- orange

- The second word is ***sector***. The Latin root ***sect*** means to cut, and the suffix ***-or*** means one who does. ***Sector*** means a section of something larger.
  - Name something that is divided into ***sectors***.

**PROMPT IDEAS** ***sector***
- the states
- counties
- countries in Europe

**YOU DO** Now it's your turn. Work with a partner, and record your ideas on a whiteboard so you're ready to share with the class. You'll have five minutes to think of examples for two words that contain the Latin root ***cis***.

- The two words are ***decisive*** and ***incision***.
  - What does the Latin root ***cis*** mean? To cut What does the prefix ***de-*** mean? Away from or down What does the suffix ***-ive*** mean? Showing a quality or tendency What is ***decisive***? Showing little hesitation in making decisions
  - What does the prefix ***in-*** mean? In What does the Latin root ***cis*** mean? To cut What does the suffix ***-ion*** mean? Action What does the ***incision*** mean? A cut, usually made in surgery
  - Think of an example of when someone was ***decisive***.
  - Think of an example of an ***incision***.

**PROMPT IDEAS** ***decisive***
- declaring indoor recess in a storm
- referee making a call
- selecting a piece of candy

**PROMPT IDEAS** ***incision***
- cut during surgery
- cut into the back of a piñata
- cut into a pumpkin

cas/cid/cide/cid~~e~~, cause/caus~~e~~/cuse/cus~~e~~
multi-

## DAY 5 • Introduce Latin Roots

### UNCOVER THE MEANING

**Introduce *cas/cid/cide/cid~~e~~* and *cause/caus~~e~~/cuse/cus~~e~~*; *multi-***

MATERIALS
- Days 5 & 6 Recording Sheet

**DIRECTIONS** Pair students and distribute the **Days 5 & 6 Recording Sheet**. Model the first completed example. After students have completed the first two columns, ask them to share what they wrote. Then provide the Certified Definition. Explain that understanding parts of words, such as Latin roots, can help students uncover the meaning of many words.

**I'm going to model using my detective skills to figure out what the underlined word parts mean.**

- I'll use the other words in the sentences to develop a Working Definition of a word part.
- Listen as I read the first set of three sentences.

    1. On this special day the guests arrive to celebrate the happy ***occasion.***
    2. The ***accident*** happened when the tire hit the curb.
    3. The ***cascade*** of water tumbled down the hillside.

- In **Column 1**, I record the clue words special day, celebrate, happened, and tumbled that help me understand the meaning of ***cas/cid/cide***.
- I think that ***cas/cid/cide*** means event or fall. This is my Working Definition, which I record in **Column 2**.
- In **Column 3**, I will write the Certified Definition of ***cas/cid/cide***: to fall or befall.

**Now it's your turn.**

- With your partner, read the next set of sentences on the **Days 5 & 6 Recording Sheet**.
- Use your detective skills to figure out what the underlined word parts mean.
- Consider which words or phrases in the sentences provide clues about meaning. Record them in **Column 1**.
- Write a Working Definition in **Column 2**.
- Only complete **Columns 1** and **2** and then wait for the discussion. You will fill in **Column 3** after I provide a Certified Definition.

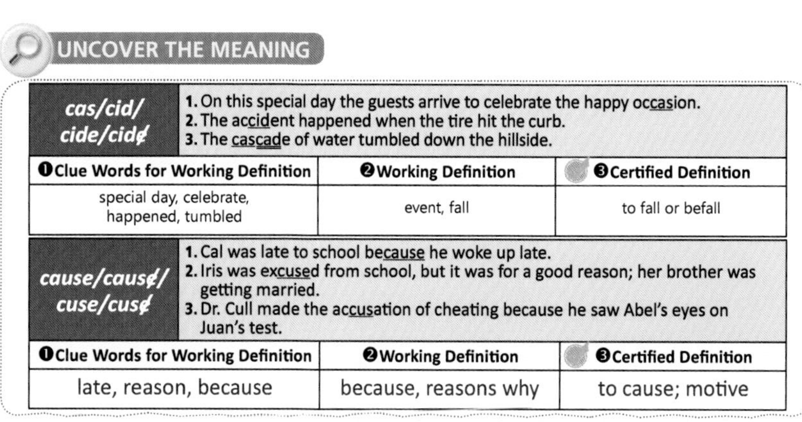

UNCOVER THE MEANING

| cas/cid/cide/cid~~e~~ | 1. On this special day the guests arrive to celebrate the happy occasion.<br>2. The accident happened when the tire hit the curb.<br>3. The cascade of water tumbled down the hillside. | |
|---|---|---|
| ❶ Clue Words for Working Definition | ❷ Working Definition | ❸ Certified Definition |
| special day, celebrate, happened, tumbled | event, fall | to fall or befall |

| cause/caus~~e~~/cuse/cus~~e~~ | 1. Cal was late to school because he woke up late.<br>2. Iris was excused from school, but it was for a good reason; her brother was getting married.<br>3. Dr. Cull made the accusation of cheating because he saw Abel's eyes on Juan's test. | |
|---|---|---|
| ❶ Clue Words for Working Definition | ❷ Working Definition | ❸ Certified Definition |
| late, reason, because | because, reasons why | to cause; motive |

cas/cid/cide/cid¢, cause/caus¢/cus/cuse/cus¢ multi-

# DAY 6 • Deepen the Meaning

## CHECK MEANING

**MATERIALS**
- Pocket chart, document camera, or PowerPoint™
- Days 5 & 6 Recording Sheet
- Cards:
  Teacher: al, cas, ion, oc
  Student: Latin Roots: cause, cus
  Prefixes: ac, be, ex
  Inflected Ending: ing

**DIRECTIONS** Using the **Cards** and **Mat**, confirm that students understand how the meaning of the word evolves as more parts are added.

**I DO**

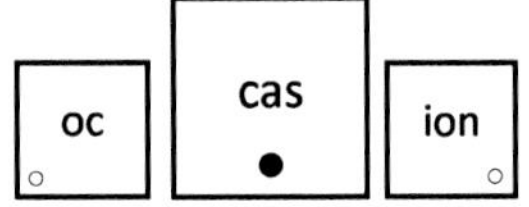


- The Latin root ***cas*** means to fall.
- Adding ***oc-*** and ***-ion*** spells the word ***occasion***. The combination of word parts means a special or important time or event.
- Now, I'm going to use my knowledge of the word to answer the question.

  1. What does it mean when we celebrate the ***occasion*** of your birth? We are celebrating your birthday, which is a special event.

**WE DO**

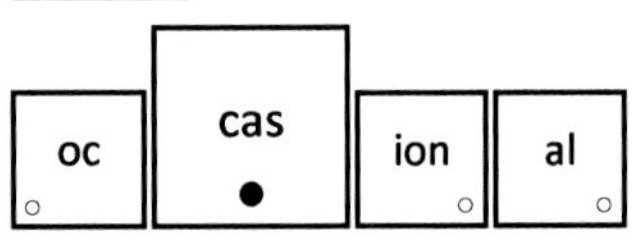


- The prefix ***oc-*** means down, against, or facing. The suffix ***-ion*** means action, and the suffix ***-al*** means related to or like.
- After adding ***-al***, what's the meaning? Happening from time to time
- Listen to me use the word ***occasional*** in a question and we will use our knowledge of its parts to figure out the answer.

  2. What does it mean when there is an ***occasional*** evening of staying up late? We do it from time to time.

**YOU DO** Use your **Cards** and **Mats** to complete the chart on the **Days 5 & 6 Recording Sheet**.

| Latin Roots | Certified Definition |
|---|---|
| cas/cid/cide/cid¢ | to fall or befall |
| cause/caus¢/cus/cuse/cus¢ | to cause, motive |
| **Prefixes** | **Certified Definition** |
| ac- | toward, in, or near |
| be- | with |
| ex- | out |
| in- | in |
| oc- | down, against, or facing |
| multi- | many |
| **Suffixes** | **Certified Definition** |
| -able | able, can do |
| -al | related to, like |
| -ent | action, state, or quality |
| -er | one who does, is from, or has a special characteristic |
| -ion | action |
| -ity | state of being, quality, action |
| -ly | like |
| **Inflected Endings** | **Certified Definition** |
| -ed | past tense |
| -ing | present participle |

| Word | Prefix | Latin Root | Suffix |
|---|---|---|---|
| excuse | ex: out | cuse: to cause; motive | |
| Meaning: | to apologize or judge as forgiven | | |
| accuse | ac: in, toward, or near | cuse: to cause; motive | |
| Meaning: | to assign with fault or blame | | |
| because | be: with | cause: to cause; motive | |
| Meaning: | a reason, or motive, for something | | |
| causing | | cause: to cause, motive | ing: present participle |
| Meaning: | making something happen | | |

# cas/cid/cide/cid~~e~~, cause/caus~~e~~/cuse/cus~~e~~ multi-

## DAY 7 • Word Multiplier

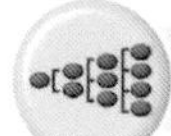

### WORD MULTIPLIER

**Build words with *cas/cid/cide/cid~~e~~* and *cause/caus~~e~~/cuse/cus~~e~~; multi-***

*MATERIALS*
- *Day 7 Recording Sheet*
- *Notebook paper*
- *Latin Mat*
- *Cards:*
  *Latin Roots: cas, cid, cus~~e~~, sect*
  *Prefixes: ac, ex, in, multi, oc*
  *Suffixes: able, al ent, er, ion, ity, ly*
  *Inflected Ending: ed*

**DIRECTIONS** Students work together to build words using their **Cards** and **Mats**.

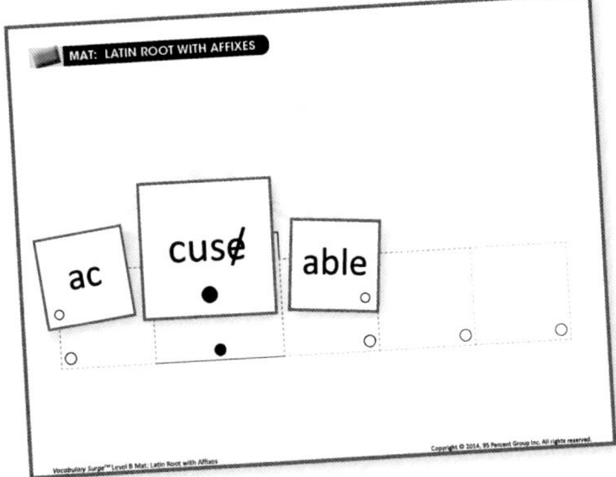


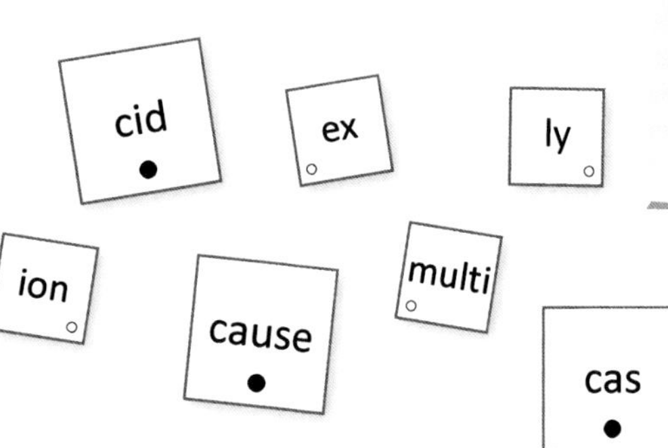

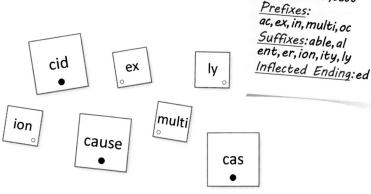

**WE DO** Let's combine cards to build a word.

- I select cards ***ac, cus~~e~~,*** and ***able***.
- Where shall I place the prefix ***ac-***? In the box on the left side of the mat
- Where do I place the Latin root ***cus~~e~~***? In the large center box, matching the solid circles
- Finally, where shall I place the suffix ***-able***? To the right of ***cus***, matching the circle on the mat to the one on the card
- What word have we built? Accusable What is the definition of ***accusable***? Able to be blamed
- What is the part of speech of the word ***accusable*** and how do you know? Adjective; it describes something

**WORD MULTIPLIER**

| SET 1 | Word Parts | Word | Part of Speech |
|---|---|---|---|
| 1. | ac+cid+ent | accident | noun |
| Write the Meaning: | an unfortunate happening usually resulting in harm | | |
| 2. | in+cid+ent+al | incidental | adjective |
| Write the Meaning: | happens by chance | | |
| 3. | oc+cas+ion+al+ly | occasionally | adverb |
| Write the Meaning: | happening from time to time | | |
| **SET 2** | **Word Parts** | **Word** | **Part of Speech** |
| 1. | ac+cus~~e~~+er | accuser | noun |
| Write the Meaning: | one who blames someone else for an event | | |
| 2. | ex+cus~~e~~+able | excusable | adjective |
| Write the Meaning: | to judge as forgiven | | |
| 3. | multi+sect+ion+al | multisectional | adjective |
| Write the Meaning: | having many sections or parts | | |

**YOU DO** Use your **Cards** and **Mats** to build more words. Complete the **Day 7 Recording Sheet** with your partner. Write additional words on notebook paper.

**Possible Words:**

**cause/cus/cuse/sect:** accuser, excusable, excuse, excuser, multisectional

**cas/cid/cide/cid~~e~~:** incident, incidentally, occasion, occasional, occasioned

## DAY 8 • Demonstrate Meaning

### BUILD MEANING

MATERIALS
- Whiteboards
- Markers

**DIRECTIONS** Complete the I Do and We Do sections with the whole class, and pair students to work on the You Do activity. Students can record their ideas on small whiteboards. Ask a few pairs to share their work with the class.

**I DO** Listen to me demonstrate understanding of the meaning of the Latin root ***cas***.

- The first word is ***occasion***. We learned that ***occasion*** means a special or important time or event. I'm going to think of examples of times when something is a special ***occasion***.
  - My birthday is a special ***occasion,*** and I always celebrate with a party.
  - On the ***occasion*** of my parent's 25th wedding anniversary, they took a cruise.
- The second word is ***cascade***, which means a chain of steps like a waterfall. I'm going to think of examples of a ***cascade***.
  - The mermaid fountain in the park has a ***cascade*** of water.
  - When the hairdresser cut the girl's long hair, a ***cascade*** of hair fell to the ground.

**WE DO** Let's try the next one together with the Latin root ***cause***.

- The first word is ***cause***. The Latin root ***cause*** means to cause or a motive. The flat tire was the ***cause*** of the bike crash.
  - Name a time when you ***caused*** something
- The second word is ***because***. The prefix ***be-*** means completely or thoroughly, and the Latin root ***cause*** means to cause; motive. ***Because*** means a reason, or motive, for an action.
  - Name a time when something happened ***because*** of something you did.

**PROMPT IDEAS** ***cause***
- a spill in the kitchen
- an injury
- a poor grade

**PROMPT IDEAS** ***because***
- mother is happy/cleaned room
- stayed safe/wore bike helmet
- stayed dry/carried umbrella

**YOU DO** Now it's your turn. Work with a partner, and record your ideas on a whiteboard so you're ready to share with the class. You'll have five minutes to think of examples for two words that contain the Latin root ***cuse***.

- The two words are ***accuse*** and ***excuse***.
  - What does the prefix ***ac-*** mean? In or towards What does the Latin root ***cuse*** mean? To cause or a motive What does ***accuse*** mean? To assign blame or fault
  - What does the prefix ***ex-*** mean? Out What does the Latin root ***cuse*** mean? To cause or a motive What does ***excuse*** mean? To apologize or judge as forgiven
  - Think of an example of a time when you ***accused*** someone of doing something or might ***accuse*** someone.
  - Think of an example of something for which you might make an ***excuse***.

**PROMPT IDEAS** ***accuse***
- eating your snack
- cheating at a game
- saying something unkind

**PROMPT IDEAS** ***excuse***
- arrived late for school
- wore wrong clothes
- forgot to do homework

# cas/cid/cide/cid~~e~~, cause/caus~~e~~/cuse/cus~~e~~, cern, cis/cise/cis~~e~~, sec/sect/seg bi-, multi-

## DAY 9 • Review What You Learned

### STEP 1 REVIEW THE MEANING

**Review *cas/cid/cide/cid~~e~~, cause/caus~~e~~/cuse/cus~~e~~, cern, cis/cise/cis~~e~~, sec/sect/seg* Prefixes *bi-, multi-***

*MATERIALS*
- Word parts projected on document camera, overhead projector, or PowerPoint™

**DIRECTIONS** Display the morphemes so students can see them, and ask for the Certified Definition of each one.

**When I show you the word parts, think about the Certified Definitions we discussed as you prepare to answer.**

| Latin Root | Certified Definition | Prefix | Certified Definition |
|---|---|---|---|
| *cern* | to separate | *bi-* | two |
| *cis/cise/cis~~e~~* | to cut | | |
| *sec/sect/seg* | to cut | | |
| **Latin Root** | **Certified Definition** | **Prefix** | **Certified Definition** |
| *cas/cid/cide/cid~~e~~* | to fall or befall | *multi-* | many |
| *cause/caus~~e~~/cuse/cus~~e~~* | to cause; motive | | |

### STEP 2 CHECK MEANING

*MATERIALS*
- Day 9 Recording Sheet

**DIRECTIONS** Read the following sentences to check that students understand the meanings of ***cas/cid/cide/cid~~e~~, cause/caus~~e~~/cuse/cus~~e~~, cern, cis/cise/cis~~e~~,*** and ***sec/sect/seg; prefixes: bi-*** and ***multi-***.
Model the first sentence for students using the We Do Step, below.

**WE DO** As I read this sentence, think about the Certified Definitions of the Latin root that fits the blank.

1. The students dis____________ worms in science lab.

- Which Latin root do you think fits on the line? Sect
- What is the new word? Dissect
- What do you think the word ***dis<u>sect</u>*** means? To cut apart to examine the structure

**YOU DO** Complete the rest of the sentences on the **Day 9 Recording Sheet** with your partner to find the Latin root that best fits on the line. Record the new words and their meanings.

**EXTENSION ACTIVITY**

Students write two sentences with missing Latin roots to challenge the class.

**CHECK MEANING**

1. The students **dis** sect worms in science lab. dissect
   Meaning: to cut apart to examine the structure
2. Gage was able to **dis** cern between the smell of the two flowers. discern
   Meaning: to recognize or perceive clearly
3. Jules performed in the drum sect **ion** of the band. section
   Meaning: a part that is cut off or separated
4. The mess is **ex** cus **able** because Spot is just a puppy. excusable
   Meaning: to judge as forgiven
5. The **in** cid **ent** involving the car and the truck was serious. incident
   Meaning: an event or something that is caused by something else
6. Candy was happy **be** cause her birthday was on Saturday. because
   Meaning: a reason, or motive, for something

cas/cid/cide/cid¢, cause/caus¢/cuse/cus¢, cern, cis/cise/cis¢, sec/sect/seg bi-, multi-

# DAY 10 • 2nd Review Day

## STEP 1 MAKE CONNECTIONS

*MATERIALS*
- *Day 10 Recording Sheet*

**DIRECTIONS** Students pair up to write sentences with either one or two of the words that are provided.

**I am going to model how to use two words containing this week's Latin roots in a meaningful sentence. The words are *discern* and *insect*.**

- Mrs. Lee is able to ***discern*** the type of ***insect*** by its antenna.
- It is your turn to write five more sentences using the words on the top of the recording sheet.
- Sentences with two words get two points and sentences with one word get one point.

MAKE CONNECTIONS

| Words | | |
|---|---|---|
| accident | causing | insect |
| accuse | concerned | occasion |
| accusing | decided | occasionally |
| because | decision | precise |
| cascaded | excuse | section |
| cause | incident | segment |

1. Rapunzel's hair cascaded down her back.
2. My family occasionally eats in a restaurant.
3. I am concerned that my favorite team will not make the playoffs.
4. We saw only a segment of the show.
5. Texting while driving was the cause of the accident.

## STEP 2 CHALLENGE: MORPHEME MADNESS

*MATERIALS*
- *Notebook paper*
- *Latin Mat*
- *Cards listed in the table below*

**DIRECTIONS** Students pair up to use **Cards** and **Mats** to build words. They also record all of the words they build and the words' definitions.

| Word Parts | Cards |
|---|---|
| **Latin Roots** | cas, cause, caus¢, cern, cid, cide, cid¢, cis, cise, cis¢ cuse, cus¢, sec, sect, seg |
| **Inflected Endings** | ed, ing |
| **Prefixes** | ac, con, de, dis, in, oc, pre |
| **Suffixes** | al, ed, ent, ing, ion, ly |

**Now it's your turn to build words.**

- First, find a partner.
- Use the **Cards** and **Mats** to build words.
- Record the words and their definitions on a separate sheet of paper.

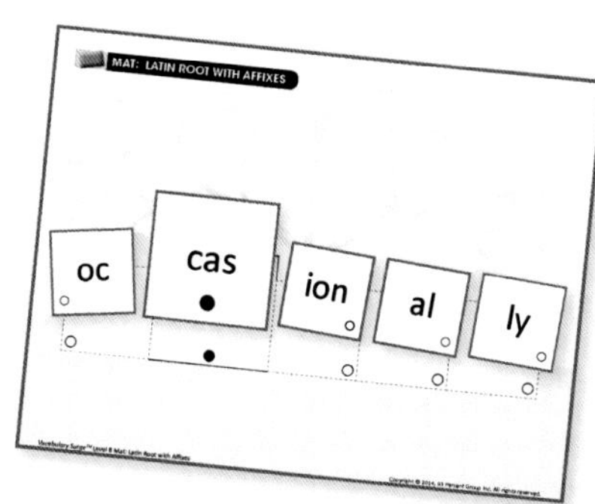

# aud, cede/ced~~e~~/ceed/cess, fer, grate/grat~~e~~, magna/magni    semi-, -tude

## DAY 1 • Introduce Latin Roots

### UNCOVER THE MEANING

**MATERIALS**
- Days 1 & 2 Recording Sheet

#### Introduce *aud, cede/ced~~e~~/ceed/cess,* and *fer; semi-*

**DIRECTIONS** Pair students and distribute the Days 1 & 2 Recording Sheet. Model the first completed example. After students have completed the first two columns, ask them to share what they wrote. Then provide the Certified Definition. Explain that understanding parts of words, such as Latin roots, can help students uncover the meaning of many words

**I'm going to model using my detective skills to figure out what the underlined word parts mean.**

- I'll use the other words in the sentences to develop a Working Definition of a word part.
- Listen as I read the first set of two sentences.
    - The music on the radio was ***semiaudible*** to Chandra. (The prefix semi- means half or part.)
    - The static on the ***audio*** clip made it difficult to hear the voices.
- In **Column 1**, I record the clue words music, hear, and voices that help me understand the meaning of ***aud***.
- I think that ***aud*** means sound or hear. This is my Working Definition, which I record in **Column 2**.
- In **Column 3**, I write the Certified Definition of ***aud***: to hear, listen.

**Now it's your turn.**

- With your partner, read the next set of sentences on the Days 1 & 2 Recording Sheet.
- Use your detective skills to figure out what the underlined word parts mean.
- Consider which words or phrases in the sentences provide clues about meaning. Record them in **Column 1**.
- Write a Working Definition in **Column 2**.
- Only complete **Columns 1** and **2** and then wait for the discussion. You will fill in **Column 3** after I provide a Certified Definition.

**UNCOVER THE MEANING**

| *aud* | 1. The music on the radio was semiaudible to Chandra. (The prefix semi- means half or part.) 2. The static on the audio clip made it difficult to hear the voices. | |
|---|---|---|
| ❶ Clue Words for Working Definition | ❷ Working Definition | ❸ Certified Definition |
| music, hear, voices | sound, hear | to hear, listen |
| *cede/ced~~e~~/ceed/cess* | 1. After they conceded the game, the team went home. 2. The procession of clowns marched in the parade. | |
| ❶ Clue Words for Working Definition | ❷ Working Definition | ❸ Certified Definition |
| went home, marched | gave up, group in motion | to go, yield, or surrender |
| *fer* | 1. Rather than attend college this year, Leela deferred entrance until next year. 2. When Sanjay sold his car, he transferred the title to the new owner. | |
| ❶ Clue Words for Working Definition | ❷ Working Definition | ❸ Certified Definition |
| next year, to the new owner | give up | to bear or yield |

**aud, cede/ced⊄/ceed/cess, fer**
**semi-**

# DAY 2 • Deepen the Meaning

## CHECK MEANING

MATERIALS
- Pocket chart, document camera, or PowerPoint™
- Days 1 & 2 Recording Sheet
- Cards:
  Teacher: aud, i, ence, ible, in
  Student:
  Latin Roots: cede, ceed, fer
  Prefixes: de, pro, re

**DIRECTIONS** Using the **Cards** and **Mat**, confirm that students understand how the meaning of the word evolves as more parts are added.

**I DO**

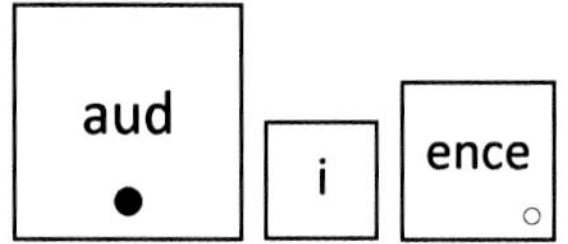


- The suffix ***-ence*** means action, state, or quality.
- Adding ***-i-*** and ***-ence*** to ***aud*** spells the word ***audience***. The combination of word parts means a group that listens or watches.
- Now, I'm going to use my knowledge of the word to answer the question.
  1. What does it mean when I say that the musician plays before a live ***audience***? Plays for a group

**WE DO**

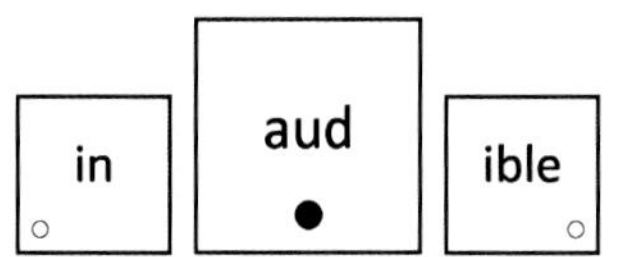


- The prefix ***in-*** means not.
- The suffix ***-ible*** means able or can do.
- After adding ***in-*** and ***-ible*** to ***aud*** what's the meaning? Not able to hear
- Listen to me use the word ***inaudible*** in a question and we will use our knowledge of its parts to figure out the answer.
  2. What does it mean when a song is ***inaudible***? It can't be heard

**YOU DO** Use your **Cards** and **Mat** to complete the chart on the **Days 1 & 2 Recording Sheet**.

| Latin Roots | Certified Definition |
|---|---|
| aud | to hear, listen |
| cede/ced⊄/ceed/cess | to go, yield, or surrender |
| fer | to bear or yield |
| **Prefixes** | **Certified Definition** |
| de- | away from, down |
| pro- | forward, earlier, to support |
| re- | again, back |
| semi- | half |
| suc- | under, beneath, or below |
| trans- | across, beyond |
| **Suffixes** | **Certified Definition** |
| -able | able, can do |
| -ence | action, state, or quality |
| -ible | able, can do |
| -ion | state of being, action, quality |
| -ive | showing a quality |
| **Connecting Letters** | |
| -i- | |

**CHECK MEANING**

| Word | Prefix | Latin Root |
|---|---|---|
| proceed | pro: forward, earlier, to support | ceed: to go, yield, or surrender |
| Meaning: | to continue | |
| recede | re: again, back | cede: to go, yield, or surrender |
| Meaning: | to move backwards | |
| defer | de: away from, down | fer: to bear or yield |
| Meaning: | to put something off | |
| refer | re: again, back | fer: to bear or yield |
| Meaning: | to send someone to another for help or advice | |

# aud, cede/ced¢/ceed/cess, fer
# semi-

## DAY 3 • Word Multiplier

### WORD MULTIPLIER

**Build words with *aud, cede/ced¢/ceed/cess,* and *fer; semi-***

**DIRECTIONS** Students work together to build words using their **Cards** and **Mats**.

*MATERIALS*
- Day 3 Recording Sheet
- Notebook paper
- Latin Mat
- Cards:
  Latin Roots: aud, cede, ced¢, ceed, cess, fer
  Prefixes: de, re, semi, suc, trans
  Suffixes: able, ence, ible, ive
  Connecting Letter: i

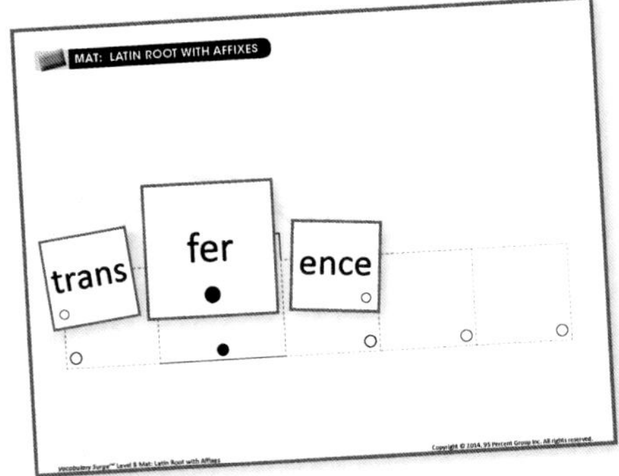


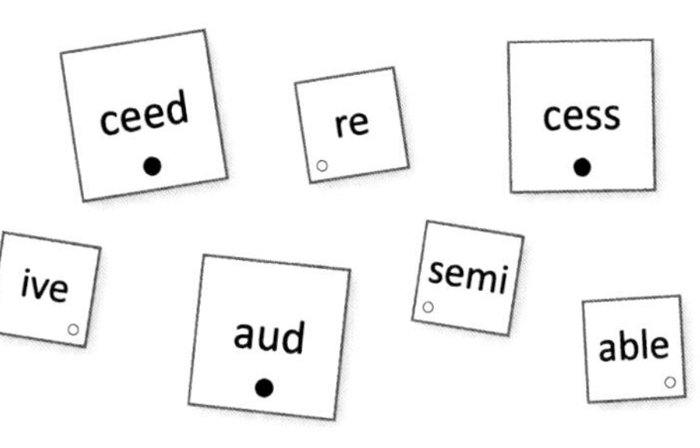


**I DO** Watch me combine **Cards** to build a word.

- I select cards ***trans***, ***fer***, and ***ence***.
- I place the prefix ***trans-*** on the left side of the mat, matching the circle on the mat to the one on the card.
- I place the Latin root ***fer*** in the large center box, matching the solid circles.
- Finally, I place the suffix ***-ence*** to the right of ***fer***, matching the circle on the mat to the one on the card.
- I have built the word ***transference***.

**WE DO** Let me try another.

- I choose the cards ***aud***, ***i***, and ***ence***.
- Where shall I place the card ***aud***? In the large, middle box
- Why do we place it here? Because it is the Latin root and has a solid circle like the mat
- Where shall I place the connecting letter ***-i-***? In the box to the right of ***aud***
- Where shall I place the suffix ***-ence***? In the box to the right of ***i***
- Look at the example on your **Day 3 Recording Sheet** to see how to write the parts of ***audience*** and the whole word. ***Aud*** means to hear or listen, and ***-ence*** means action, state, or quality.
- When we put these word parts together, ***audience*** means a group that listens or watches.
- What part of speech is ***audience*** and how do you know? Noun, it refers to a group

**WORD MULTIPLIER**

| SET 1 | Word Parts | Word | Part of Speech |
|---|---|---|---|
| 1. | aud+i+ence | audience | noun |
| | Write the Meaning: | a group that listens or watches | |
| 2. | semi+aud+ible | semiaudible | adjective |
| | Write the Meaning: | partially heard | |
| **SET 2** | **Word Parts** | **Word** | **Part of Speech** |
| 1. | re+cess+ive | recessive | adjective |
| | Write the Meaning: | tending to go back | |
| 2. | suc+ceed | succeed | verb |
| | Write the Meaning: | to attain a goal; to follow another in office | |
| **SET 3** | **Word Parts** | **Word** | **Part of Speech** |
| 1. | de+fer+ence | deference | noun |
| | Write the Meaning: | a readiness to yield to others | |
| 2. | trans+fer+able | transferable | adjective |
| | Write the Meaning: | able to yield ownership | |

**YOU DO** Use your **Cards** and **Mat** to build more words. Complete the **Day 3 Recording Sheet** with your partner. Write additional words on notebook paper. We will review the words when you have finished.

**Possible Words:**
**aud:** audible, audience, semiaudible
**cede/ced¢/ceed/cess: receed,** recess, recessive, succeed, success, successive
**fer:** defer, deferrable transfer, transferable, transference

aud, cede/ced¢/ceed/cess, fer
semi-

## DAY 4 • Demonstrate Meaning

### BUILD MEANING

**MATERIALS**
- Whiteboards
- Markers

**DIRECTIONS** Complete the I Do and We Do sections with the whole class, and pair students to work on the You Do activity. Students can record their ideas on small whiteboards. Ask a few pairs to share their work with the class.

**I DO** Listen to me demonstrate understanding of the meaning of the Latin root ***aud***.

- The first word is ***audible***. We learned that ***audible*** means able to be heard. I'm going to think of examples of times when something was ***audible***.
    - The speaker on my laptop is barely ***audible***.
    - The band's music was so loud that it was ***audible*** over the shouting of the crowd.
- The second word is ***audio***, which relates to something that can be listened to or heard. I'm going to think of examples of times from my life when I encountered ***audio***.
    - While driving over the mountains, the radio's ***audio*** sounds scratchy.
    - My grandmother listens to ***audio*** books while cooking.

**WE DO** Let's try the next one together with the Latin root ***cess***.

- The first word is ***recess***. The prefix ***re-*** means again or back, and the Latin root ***cess*** means to go, yield, or surrender. ***Recess*** means a time to stop working. Between math and social studies, the students go out for ***recess*** to refresh their minds.
    - When have you taken a ***recess*** or wanted one?
- The second word is ***process***. The prefix ***pro-*** means forward or earlier, and the Latin root ***cess*** means to go, yield, or surrender. ***Process*** means a series of steps to complete a task.
    - Name some activities where you use a ***process*** to complete them.

**PROMPT IDEAS** ***recess***
- after a test
- while cleaning my room
- in the middle of doing homework

**PROMPT IDEAS** ***process***
- making a sandwich
- solving a math problem
- getting ready for school

**YOU DO** Now it's your turn. Work with a partner, and record your ideas on a whiteboard so you're ready to share with the class. You'll have five minutes to think of examples for two words that contain the Latin root ***fer***.

- The two words are ***defer*** and ***refer***.
    - What does the prefix ***de-*** mean? Down What does the Latin root ***fer*** mean? To bear or yield What does ***defer*** mean? To put something off
    - What does the prefix ***re-*** mean? Again or back What does the Latin root ***fer*** mean? To bear or yield What does ***refer*** mean? To send someone to another for help or advice
    - Think of an example of how you might ***defer*** to someone else's decision.
    - Think of an example for ***refer***. It can be something that you did or something that you could possibly do.

**PROMPT IDEAS** ***defer***
- defer to parent's rules
- defer to friend's need
- defer doing homework

**PROMPT IDEAS** ***refer***
- send friend to another for advice
- send parent to teacher
- refer to an internet source

 

# grate/grat~~e~~, magna/magni -tude

## DAY 5 • Introduce Latin Roots

### UNCOVER THE MEANING

**Introduce *grate/grat~~e~~*, and *magna/magni*; *bene-* and *-tude***

MATERIALS
- Days 5 & 6 Recording Sheet

**DIRECTIONS** Pair students and distribute the Days 5 & 6 Recording Sheet. Model the first completed example. After students have completed the first two columns, ask them to share what they wrote. Then provide the Certified Definition. Explain that understanding parts of words, such as Latin roots, can help students uncover the meaning of many words.

**I'm going to model using my detective skills to figure out what the underlined word parts mean.**

- I'll use the other words in the sentences to develop a Working Definition of a word part.
- Listen as I read the first set of two sentences.

  1. Enzo was thirsty, so he was ***grateful*** for the water break.
  2. The waiter responded ***gratefully*** for the tip.

- In **Column 1**, I record the clue words thirsty and happy that help me understand the meaning of ***grate***.
- I think that ***grate*** means thankful, happy. This is my Working Definition, which I record in **Column 2**.
- In **Column 3**, I will write the Certified Definition of ***grate***: thanks, pleasing.

**Now it's your turn.**

- With your partner, read the next set of sentences on the **Days 5 & 6 Recording Sheet**.
- Use your detective skills to figure out what the underlined word parts mean.
- Consider which words or phrases in the sentences provide clues about meaning. Record them in **Column 1**.
- Write a Working Definition in **Column 2**.
- Only complete **Columns 1** and **2** and then wait for the discussion. You will fill in **Column 3** after I provide a Certified Definition.

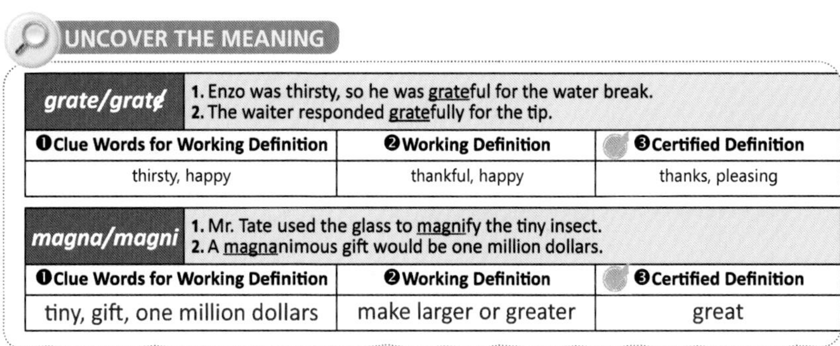

UNCOVER THE MEANING

| grate/grat~~e~~ | 1. Enzo was thirsty, so he was grateful for the water break. 2. The waiter responded gratefully for the tip. | |
|---|---|---|
| ❶ Clue Words for Working Definition | ❷ Working Definition | ❸ Certified Definition |
| thirsty, happy | thankful, happy | thanks, pleasing |

| magna/magni | 1. Mr. Tate used the glass to magnify the tiny insect. 2. A magnanimous gift would be one million dollars. | |
|---|---|---|
| ❶ Clue Words for Working Definition | ❷ Working Definition | ❸ Certified Definition |
| tiny, gift, one million dollars | make larger or greater | great |

**grate/grat~~e~~, magna/magni**
**bene-, -tude**

# DAY 6 • Deepen the Meaning

## CHECK MEANING

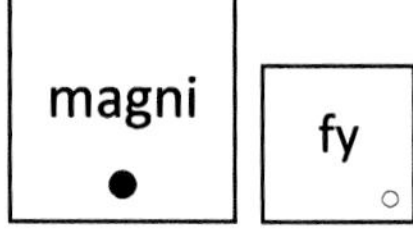

**DIRECTIONS** Using the **Cards** and **Mat**, confirm that students understand how the meaning of the word evolves as more parts are added.

MATERIALS
- Pocket chart, document camera, or PowerPoint™
- Days 5 & 6 Recording Sheet
- Cards:
  Teacher: ate, ify, magna
  Student:
  Latin Roots: grate, magni
  Prefixes: un
  Suffixes: ful, fy, tude

**I DO**

magni ● | fy ○

- The suffix ***-fy*** means make or become.
- Adding ***-fy*** to ***magni*** spells the ***magnify***. The combination of word parts means to make something appear larger.
- Now, I'm going to use my knowledge of the word to answer the question.
  1. What does it mean when you ***magnify*** cells with a microscope? Make them appear larger

**WE DO**

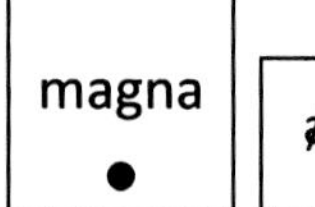

magna ● | ~~a~~te ○

- The suffix ***-~~a~~te*** means rank or office.
- How does adding ***-~~a~~te*** to ***magna*** change the meaning? A person of great power in an organization or government
- Listen to me use the word ***magnate*** in a question and we will use our knowledge of its parts to figure out the answer.
  2. What does it mean when you call someone a ***magnate***? Person of great power within an organization or government

**YOU DO** Use your **Cards** and **Mat** to complete the chart on the **Days 5 & 6 Recording Sheet**.

| Latin Roots | Certified Definition |
|---|---|
| fact/fic/fit | make or do |
| grate/grat~~e~~ | thanks |
| magna/magni | great |
| **Prefixes** | **Certified Definition** |
| dis- | not |
| un- | not |
| **Suffixes** | **Certified Definition** |
| -er | one who does, is from, or has a special characteristic |
| -ful | full |
| -fy | make or become |
| -ly | like |
| -tude | condition, quality |
| **Inflected Endings** | **Certified Definition** |
| -ing | present participle |

CHECK MEANING

| Word | Prefix | Latin Root | Suffix |
|---|---|---|---|
| grateful | | grate: thanks, pleasing | ful: full of |
| Meaning: | to feel thankful or pleased | | |
| ungrateful | un: not | grate: thanks, pleasing | ful: full of |
| Meaning: | to fail to show appreciation | | |
| magnify | | magni: great | fy: make or become |
| Meaning: | to increase to a greater size | | |
| magnitude | | magni: great | tude: condition, state, quality |
| Meaning: | great size or importance | | |

# grate/gratɇ, magna/magni -tude

## DAY 7 • Word Multiplier

### WORD MULTIPLIER

**Build words with *grate/gratɇ* and *magna/magni*; *-tude***

**DIRECTIONS** Students work together to build words using their **Cards** and **Mats**.

MATERIALS
- Day 7 Recording Sheet
- Notebook paper
- Latin Mat
- Cards:
  Latin Roots: grate, gratɇ magna, magni
  Prefixes: un
  Suffixes: er, ful, fy, ly, tude

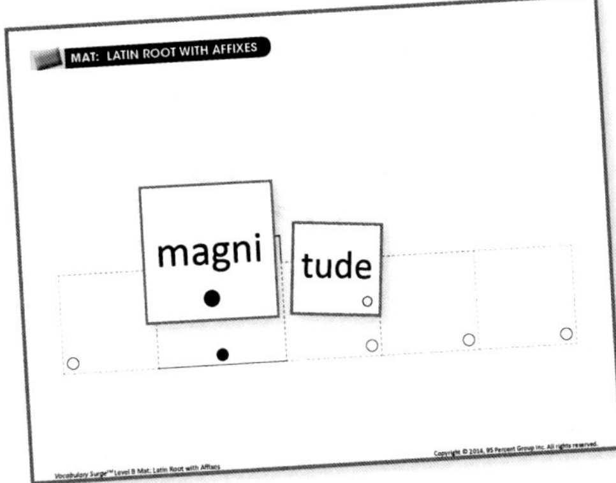


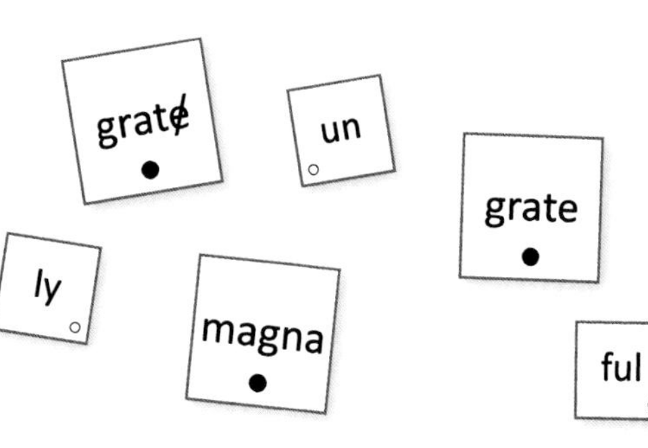


**WE DO** Let's combine **Cards** to build a word.

- I select cards ***magni*** and ***tude***.
- Where shall I place the Latin root ***magni***? In the large, center box, matching the solid circles
- Finally, where shall I place the suffix ***-tude***? To the right of ***magni***, matching the circle on the mat to the one on the card
- What word have we built? Magnitude
  What is the definition of ***magnitude***? Great size or importance

**YOU DO** Use your **Cards** and **Mats** to build more words. Complete the **Day 7 Recording Sheet** with your partner. Write additional words on notebook paper.

**WORD MULTIPLIER**

| SET 1 | Word Parts | Words | Part of Speech |
|---|---|---|---|
| 1. | grate+ful | grateful | adjective |
| | Write the Meaning: | to feel thankful or pleased | |
| 2. | grate+ful+ly | gratefully | adverb |
| | Write the Meaning: | a way of doing something that shows thankfulness | |
| 3. | un+grate+ful | ungrateful | adjective |
| | Write the Meaning: | failing to show appreciation | |

| SET 2 | Word Parts | Words | Part of Speech |
|---|---|---|---|
| 1. | magni+tude | magnitude | noun |
| | Write the Meaning: | great size or importance | |
| 2. | magni+fy+ing | magnifying | verb |
| | Write the Meaning: | to make a greater size or importance | |
| 3. | magni+fi+er | magnifier | noun |
| | Write the Meaning: | a device to make objects appear larger | |

**Possible Words:**

**grate/gratɇ:** grateful, gratefully, ungrateful

**magna/magni:** magnify, magnifier, magnifying magnitude

grate/grat~~e~~, magna/magni
-tude

## DAY 8 • Demonstrate Meaning

### BUILD MEANING

MATERIALS
• Whiteboards
• Markers

**DIRECTIONS** Complete the I Do and We Do sections with the whole class, and pair students to work on the You Do activity. Students can record their ideas on small whiteboards. Ask a few pairs to share their work with the class.

**I DO** Listen to me demonstrate understanding of the meaning of the Latin prefix ***grate***.

- The first word is ***grateful***. Amy was ***grateful*** for the compliment from her teacher. I'm going to think of examples of things to be ***grateful*** for.
  - My mother was ***grateful*** that everyone got home safely for Thanksgiving
  - When Jorge got an A on his class project, he was ***grateful*** for doing well.
- The second word is ***ungrateful,*** which means failing to show appreciation.
  - It felt like Jeremy was ***ungrateful*** that his brother had offered to help.
  - When I saw the way that Marilyn talked to the school bus driver, her attitude seems ***ungrateful***.

**WE DO** Let's try the next one together with the Latin root ***magni***.

- The first word is ***magnify***. The Latin root ***magni*** means great, and the suffix ***-fy*** means make or become. ***Magnify*** means to increase to a greater size. The scientist will ***magnify*** the onion skin to see the cells.
  - Name a time when you ***magnified*** something or might ***magnify*** something in the future.
- The second word is ***magnificent***. The Latin root ***magni*** means great, the Latin root ***fic*** means to make or do, and the suffix ***-ent*** means a quality. ***Magnificent*** means impressive or great.
  - Name something that is ***magnificent***.

**PROMPT IDEAS** ***magnify***
- a leaf under a microscope
- sounds with a microphone
- a point in a story

**PROMPT IDEAS** ***magnificent***
- pyramids
- Great Wall of China
- Grand Canyon

**YOU DO** Now it's your turn. Work with a partner, and record your ideas on a whiteboard so you're ready to share with the class. You'll have five minutes to think of examples for two words that contain the Latin root ***grate***.

- The two words are ***grateful*** and ***disgrace***.
  - What does the Latin root ***grate*** mean? Thanks, pleasing What does the suffix ***-ful*** mean? Full of What does ***grateful*** mean? To feel thankful or pleased
  - What does the prefix ***dis-*** mean? Not, apart What does the Latin root ***grac*** mean? Thanks What does ***disgrace*** mean? To fall out of grace or to be shameful
  - Think of an example of when you were ***grateful*** or might be ***grateful*** for something.
  - Think of an example of when you were in ***disgrace***.

**PROMPT IDEAS** ***grateful***
- good weather
- money for ice cream
- loving family

**PROMPT IDEAS** ***disgrace***
- got in trouble at school
- caught telling a lie
- made fun of an elder person

 

# aud, cede/ced~~e~~/ceed/cess, fer grate/grat~~e~~, magna/magni; semi-, -tude

## DAY 9 • Review What You Learned

### STEP 1 REVIEW THE MEANING

**Review *aud, cede/ced~~e~~/ceed/cess, fer, grate/grat~~e~~,* and *magna/magni***

**Prefix *semi-* Suffix *-tude***

MATERIALS
- Word parts projected on document camera, overhead projector, or PowerPoint™

**DIRECTIONS** Display the morphemes so students can see them, and ask for the certified definition of each one.

**When I show you the word parts, think about the Certified Definitions we discussed as you prepare to answer.**

| Latin Root | Certified Definition | Prefix | Certified Definition |
|---|---|---|---|
| aud | to hear, listen | semi- | half, partial |
| cede/ced~~e~~/ceed/cess | to go, yield, or surrender | | |
| fer | to bear or yield | | |
| **Latin Root** | **Certified Definition** | **Suffix** | **Certified Definition** |
| grate/grat~~e~~ | thanks, pleasing | -tude | condition, state, quality |
| magna/magni | great | | |

### STEP 2 CHECK MEANING

MATERIALS
- Day 9 Recording Sheet

**DIRECTIONS** Read the following sentences to check that students understand the meanings of ***aud, ced/ced~~e~~/ceed/cess, fer, grate/grat~~e~~,*** and ***magna/magni;*** **prefix: *semi-*; suffix: *-tude*.** Model the first sentence for students using the We Do Step, below.

**WE DO** As I read this sentence, think about the certified definitions of the Latin root that fits the blank.

1. Josh was trans______ring the plant from the pot to the garden.

- Which Latin root do you think fits on the line? Fer
- What is the new word? Transferring
- What do you think the word ***transferring*** means? Giving ownership to another

**YOU DO** Complete the rest of the sentences on the **Day 9 Recording Sheet** with your partner to find the Latin root that best fits on the line. Record the new words and their meanings.

Students write two sentences with missing Latin roots to challenge the class.

CHECK MEANING

1. Josh was **trans** fer **ing** the plant to the garden. transferring
   Meaning: to move from one place to another
2. The grass is **re** ced~~e~~ **ing** from the edge of the road. receding
   Meaning: pulling back or away from
3. Mrs. George checked the report's **re** fer **ences**. references
   Meaning: something which points to another source for information
4. The microscope's magni **fication** allows the class to see the onion cells. magnification
   Meaning: enlargement of a view
5. The ticket to the game was **trans** fer **able** to my friend. transferable
   Meaning: able to yield ownership
6. My mom was **suc** cess **ful** in finding a new shirt at the store. successful
   Meaning: having accomplished goals

aud, cede/ced̸e/ceed/cess, fer, grate/grat̸e, magna/magni; semi-, -tude

## DAY 10 • 2nd Review Day

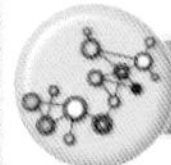

### STEP 1 MAKE CONNECTIONS

MATERIALS
- Day 10 Recording Sheet

**DIRECTIONS** Students pair up to write sentences with either one or two of the words that are provided.

**I am going to model how to use a word containing this week's Latin root in a meaningful sentence. The word is *re<u>cede</u>*.**

- When the rain stopped the flood waters began to ***re<u>cede</u>***.
- It is your turn to create five more sentences using the words on the top of the recording sheet.
- Sentences with two words get two points and sentences with one word get one point.

MAKE CONNECTIONS

| Words | | |
|---|---|---|
| agree | disagree | proceeded |
| audible | disagreement | recede |
| audience | grateful | recess |
| auditorium | inferred | succeeding |
| beneficial | magnificent | successfully |
| benefit | prefer | transfer |

1. When the rain stopped the flood waters began to recede.
2. Our class quietly proceeded down the hall.
3. Regular exercise is beneficial to your health.
4. We had a disagreement about the best flavor of ice cream.
5. Because of the weather we inferred our recess would be indoors.

### STEP 2 CHALLENGE: MORPHEME MADNESS

MATERIALS
- Notebook paper
- Latin Mat
- Cards listed in the table below

**DIRECTIONS** Students pair up to use **Cards** and **Mats** to build words. They also record all of the words they build and the words' definitions.

| Word Parts | Cards |
|---|---|
| **Latin Roots** | aud, ceed, cede, ced̸e, cess, fer, grate, grat̸e, magna, magni |
| **Inflected Endings** | ed, ing |
| **Prefixes** | dis, pre, pro, suc, trans |
| **Suffixes** | ence, ful, ly |
| **Connecting Letter** | i |

**Now it's your turn to build words.**

- First, find a partner.
- Use the **Cards** and **Mats** to build words.
- Record the words and their definitions on a separate sheet of paper.

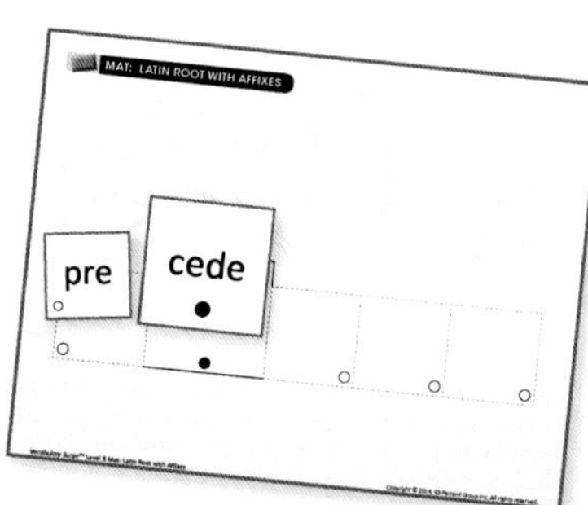


 

# cred, feder/fid/fide/fid~~e~~, judge/judg~~e~~/judic, jur/jus, leg, sense/sens~~e~~/sent -ice, -ism

## DAY 1 • Introduce Latin Roots

### UNCOVER THE MEANING

**Introduce *judge/judg~~e~~/judic, jur/jus,* and *leg***

MATERIALS
• Days 1 & 2 Recording Sheet

**DIRECTIONS** Pair students and distribute the Days 1 & 2 Recording Sheet. Model the first completed example. After students have completed the first two columns, ask them to share what they wrote. Then provide the Certified Definition. Explain that understanding parts of words, such as Latin roots, can help students uncover the meaning of many words.

**I'm going to model using my detective skills to figure out what the underlined word parts mean.**

- I'll use the other words in the sentences to develop a Working Definition of a word part.
- Listen as I read the first set of two sentences.
  1. The ***judge*** chose the poodle as the winner of the dog show.
  2. Annie used her ***judgment*** to decide between milk and soda.
- In **Column 1**, I record the clue words chose and decide that help me understand the meaning of ***judge/judic***.
- I think that ***judge/judic*** means choosing between. This is my Working Definition, which I record in **Column 2**.
- In **Column 3**, I write the Certified Definition of ***judge/judic***: to rule or decide.

**Now it's your turn.**

- With your partner, read the next set of sentences on the Days 1 & 2 Recording Sheet.
- Use your detective skills to figure out what the underlined word parts mean.
- Consider which words or phrases in the sentences provide clues about meaning. Record them in **Column 1**.
- Write a Working Definition in **Column 2**.
- Only complete **Columns 1** and **2** and then wait for the discussion. You will fill in **Column 3** after I provide a Certified Definition.

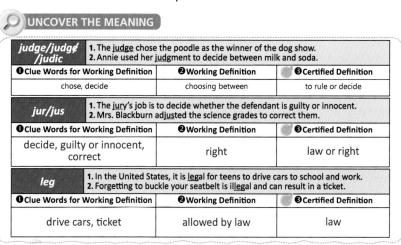

**UNCOVER THE MEANING**

| judge/judg~~e~~/judic | 1. The judge chose the poodle as the winner of the dog show.<br>2. Annie used her judgment to decide between milk and soda. | |
|---|---|---|
| ❶Clue Words for Working Definition | ❷Working Definition | ❸Certified Definition |
| chose, decide | choosing between | to rule or decide |

| jur/jus | 1. The jury's job is to decide whether the defendant is guilty or innocent.<br>2. Mrs. Blackburn adjusted the science grades to correct them. | |
|---|---|---|
| ❶Clue Words for Working Definition | ❷Working Definition | ❸Certified Definition |
| decide, guilty or innocent, correct | right | law or right |

| leg | 1. In the United States, it is legal for teens to drive cars to school and work.<br>2. Forgetting to buckle your seatbelt is illegal and can result in a ticket. | |
|---|---|---|
| ❶Clue Words for Working Definition | ❷Working Definition | ❸Certified Definition |
| drive cars, ticket | allowed by law | law |

judge/judg~~e~~/judic, jur/jus, leg
-ice

# DAY 2 • Deepen the Meaning

## CHECK MEANING

MATERIALS
- Pocket chart, document camera, or PowerPoint™
- Days 1 & 2 Recording Sheet
- Cards:
  Teacher: al, il, leg
  Student: Latin Roots: judge, judg~~e~~, jur
  Suffixes: ment, or, y

**DIRECTIONS** Using the **Cards** and **Mat**, confirm that students understand how the meaning of the word evolves as more parts are added.

**I DO**

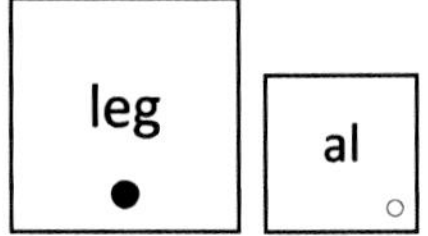

- The prefix ***-al*** means related to or like.
- Adding ***-al*** to ***leg*** spells the word ***legal***. The combination of word parts means that based on law.
- Now, I'm going to use my knowledge of the word to answer the question.

1. What does it mean when I say that it is ***legal*** for a teenager to babysit? It is allowed by law.

**WE DO**

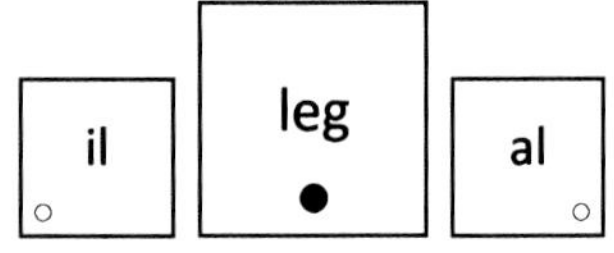

- The prefix ***il-*** means not.
- The suffix ***-al*** means related to or like.
- How does adding ***il-*** and ***-al*** to ***leg*** change the meaning? Against the law
- Listen to me use the word ***illegal*** in a question and we will use our knowledge of its parts to figure out the answer.

2. What does it mean when it is stated that it is ***illegal*** to ride a bike without a helmet? It is against the law.

**YOU DO** Use your **Cards** and **Mat** to complete the chart on the **Days 1 & 2 Recording Sheet**.

| Latin Roots | Certified Definition |
|---|---|
| judge/judg~~e~~/judic | to rule or decide |
| jur/jus | law or right |
| leg | law |
| **Prefixes** | **Certified Definition** |
| il- | not |
| **Suffixes** | **Certified Definition** |
| -al | related to or like |
| -ary | relating to |
| -ize | become, change, or make |
| -ment | act of, state of, or result of an action |
| -or | one who does |
| -y | characterized by |

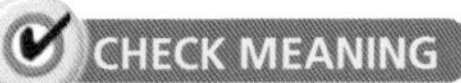

CHECK MEANING

**DIRECTIONS** Build the words with the Cards and Mat. Describe how adding new parts changes the meaning of the words.

| Word | Latin Root | Suffix |
|---|---|---|
| juror | jur: law, right | or: one who does |
| Meaning: | a member of a jury who makes decisions based on the law | |
| jury | jur: law, right | y: characterized by |
| Meaning: | a group of citizens who decide on a verdict based on the law | |
| judge | judge: to rule or decide | |
| Meaning: | a person who hears and decides on court cases | |
| judgment | judg~~e~~: to rule or decide | ment: result of an action |
| Meaning: | a ruling or decision based on careful thought | |

 

# judge/judg~~e~~/judic, jur/jus, leg -ice

## DAY 3 • Word Multiplier

### WORD MULTIPLIER

**Build words with *judge/judg~~e~~/judic, jur/jus* and *leg***

MATERIALS
- Day 3 Recording Sheet
- Notebook paper
- Latin Mat
- Cards: Latin Roots: judge, judg~~e~~, judic, jur, leg
Prefixes: il
Suffixes: al, ary, ize, ment, or, y
Connecting Letter: i

**DIRECTIONS** Students work together to build words using their **Cards** and **Mats**.

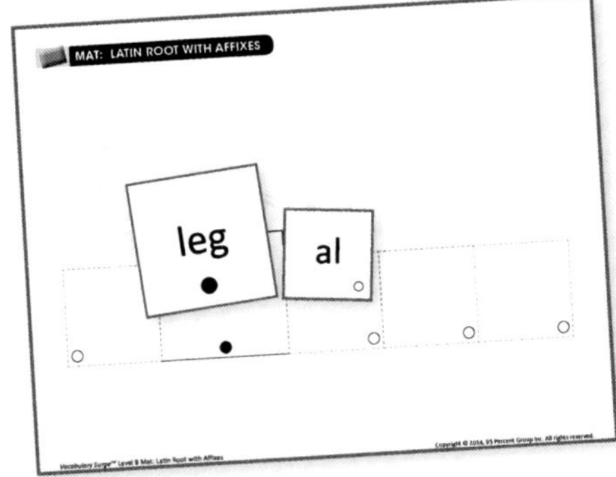


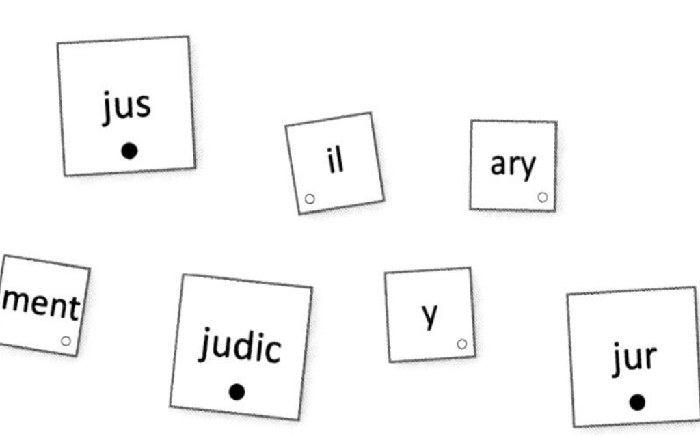


**I DO** Watch me combine **Cards** to build a word.

- I select cards ***leg*** and ***al***.
- I place Latin root ***leg*** in the large center box, matching the solid circles.
- I place the suffix ***-al*** to the right of ***leg***, matching the circle on the mat to the one on the card.
- I have built the word ***legal***.

**WE DO** Let me try another.

- I choose the cards ***judg~~e~~*** and ***ment***.
- Where shall I place the card ***judg~~e~~***? In the large, middle box
- Why do we place it here? Because it is the Latin root and has a solid circle like the mat
- Where shall I place the suffix ***-ment***? In the box to the right of ***judge***

**WORD MULTIPLIER**

| SET 1 | Word Parts | Word | Part of Speech |
|---|---|---|---|
| 1. | judg~~e~~+ment | judgment | noun |
| | Write the Meaning: | a ruling or decision based on careful thought | |
| 2. | judic+i+ary | judiciary | noun |
| | Write the Meaning: | a system of courts of justice in a country | |
| **SET 2** | **Word Parts** | **Word** | **Part of Speech** |
| 1. | jur+or | juror | noun |
| | Write the Meaning: | a member of a jury who makes decisions based on the law | |
| 2. | jur+y | jury | noun |
| | Write the Meaning: | a group of citizens who decide on a verdict based on the law | |
| **SET 3** | **Word Parts** | **Word** | **Part of Speech** |
| 1. | il+leg+al | illegal | adjective |
| | Write the Meaning: | against the law | |
| 2. | leg+al+ize | legalize | verb |
| | Write the Meaning: | to make something allowable by law | |

- Look at the example on your **Day 3 Recording Sheet** to see how to write the parts of ***judgment*** and the whole word. ***Judg~~e~~*** means to rule or decide, and ***-ment*** means result of an action.
- When we put these word parts together, ***judgment*** means a ruling or decision based on careful thought.
- What part of speech is ***judgment*** and how do you know? Noun; it is a ruling

**YOU DO** Use your **Cards** and **Mats** to build more words. Complete the **Day 3 Recording Sheet** with your partner. Write additional words on notebook paper. We will review the words when you have finished.

**Possible Words:**

**judge/judg~~e~~/judic:** judge, judgment, judgmental, judicial, judiciary

**jur/jus:** jury, juror

## judge/judg~~e~~/judic, jur/jus, leg -ice

# DAY 4 • Demonstrate Meaning

## BUILD MEANING

**MATERIALS**
- Whiteboards
- Markers

**DIRECTIONS** Complete the I Do and We Do sections with the whole class, and pair students to work on the You Do activity. Students can record their ideas on small whiteboards. Ask a few pairs to share their work with the class.

**I DO** Listen to me demonstrate understanding of the meaning of the Latin root ***jus***.

- The first word is ***adjust***. We learned that ***adjust*** means to change something so that it fits or works better. I'm going to think of examples of times when someone had to ***adjust*** something.
    - My grandfather had to ***adjust*** the speaker on his TV.
    - After losing weight, my uncle needed to ***adjust*** his belt.
- The second word is ***justice***, which means the quality of something being right or moral. I'm going to think of examples of things that received ***justice***.
    - When the team challenged the win, the referee ruled with ***justice***.
    - The victim sought ***justice*** when the thief was brought to court.

**WE DO** Let's try the next one together with the Latin root ***leg***.

- The first word is ***legally***. The Latin root ***leg*** means law, the suffix ***-al*** means related to or like, and the suffix ***-ly*** means characterized by. ***Legally*** means allowable by law. Teachers are ***legally*** allowed to take students on fieldtrips.
    - When have you done something ***legally*** or might do something ***legally***?
- The second word is ***legalize***. The Latin root ***leg*** means law, the suffix ***-al*** means related to or like, and the suffix ***-ize*** means become or change.
- ***Legalize*** means to make something allowable by law.
- Name something that you might like to ***legalize***.

**PROMPT IDEAS** ***legally***
- babysit at age 12
- wear a seatbelt
- cross the street in the crosswalk

**PROMPT IDEAS** ***legalize***
- riding a bike without a helmet
- driving a car under age 16
- free ice cream every day

**YOU DO** Now it's your turn. Work with a partner, and record your ideas on a whiteboard so you're ready to share with the class. You'll have five minutes to think of examples for two words that contain the Latin root ***judge***.

- The two words are ***judged*** and ***judgelike***.
    - What does the Latin root ***judge*** mean? To rule or decide What does the inflected ending ***-ed*** mean? Past What does ***judged*** mean? To have reached a decision
    - What does the Latin root ***judge*** mean? To rule or decide What does the suffix ***-like*** mean? Like What does ***judgelike*** mean? Like a judge
    - Think of an example of something that might be ***judged***.
    - Think of an example of someone who might be ***judgelike***.

**PROMPT IDEAS** ***judged***
- art contest
- race
- science fair

**PROMPT IDEAS** ***judgelike***
- parent
- teacher
- principal

cred, feder/fid/fide/fid~~e~~, sense/sens~~e~~/sent
-ism

## DAY 5 • Introduce Latin Roots

### UNCOVER THE MEANING

**Introduce *cred, feder/fid/fide/fid~~e~~,* and *sense/sens~~e~~/sent***

**Suffix *-ism***

MATERIALS
- Days 5 & 6 Recording Sheet

**DIRECTIONS** Pair students and distribute the **Days 5 & 6 Recording Sheet**. Model the first completed example. After students have completed the first two columns, ask them to share what they wrote. Then provide the Certified Definition. Explain that understanding parts of words, such as Latin roots, can help students uncover the meaning of many words.

**I'm going to model using my detective skills to figure out what the underlined word parts mean.**

- I'll use the other words in the sentences to develop a Working Definition of a word part.
- Listen as I read the first set of two sentences.
    1. The lawyer asked the ***credible*** witness to tell the truth about what happened.
    2. Sanjay tried to ***discredit*** the company by telling lies about their product.
- In **Column 1**, I record the clue words tell the truth and telling lies that help me understand the meaning of ***cred***.
- I think that ***cred*** means truthful. This is my Working Definition which I record in **Column 2**.
- In **Column 3**, I will write the Certified Definition of ***cred***: to believe.

**Now it's your turn.**

- With your partner, read the next set of sentences on the **Days 5 & 6 Recording Sheet**.
- Use your detective skills to figure out what the underlined word parts mean.
- Consider which words or phrases in the sentences provide clues about meaning. Record them in **Column 1**.
- Write a Working Definition in **Column 2**.
- Only complete **Columns 1** and **2** and then wait for the discussion. You will fill in **Column 3** after I provide a Certified Definition.

UNCOVER THE MEANING

| *cred* | 1. The lawyer asked the credible witness to tell the truth about what happened.<br>2. Sanjay tried to discredit the company by telling lies about their product. | |
|---|---|---|
| ❶ Clue Words for Working Definition | ❷ Working Definition | ❸ Certified Definition |
| tell the truth, telling lies | truthful | to believe |
| *feder/fid/fide/fid~~e~~* | 1. Jorge believed that Beth would keep his secret confidential.<br>2. The bakers promised to follow the recipe with fidelity. | |
| ❶ Clue Words for Working Definition | ❷ Working Definition | ❸ Certified Definition |
| believed, pledged | believe | trust or faith |
| *sense/sens~~e~~/sent* | 1. Sonya could sense the plane's loss of altitude because her ears popped.<br>2. A haunted house is a sensory experience because of the frightening things seen and heard. | |
| ❶ Clue Words for Working Definition | ❷ Working Definition | ❸ Certified Definition |
| her ears popped, seen, heard | to tell or feel | to feel, perceive, or know |

## cred, feder/fid/fide/fid¢, sense/sens¢/sent -ism

# DAY 6 • Deepen the Meaning

## CHECK MEANING

MATERIALS
- Pocket chart, document camera, or PowerPoint™
- Days 5 & 6 Recording Sheet
- Cards:
  Teacher: ible, or, sens¢
  Student: Latin Roots: cred, fid, fide
  Prefixes: con, in
  Suffixes: ent, ible

**DIRECTIONS** Using the **Cards** and **Mat**, confirm that students understand how the meaning of the word evolves as more parts are added.

**I DO**

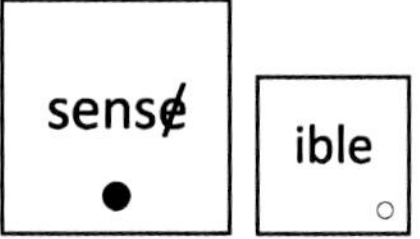

- The suffix ***-ible*** means able.
- Adding ***-ible*** to ***sens¢*** spells ***sensible***. The combination of word parts means having or showing good judgment.
- Now, I'm going to use my knowledge of the word to answer the question.
  1. What does it mean when you take a ***sensible*** bike route to school? You show good judgment by picking a safe route.

**WE DO**

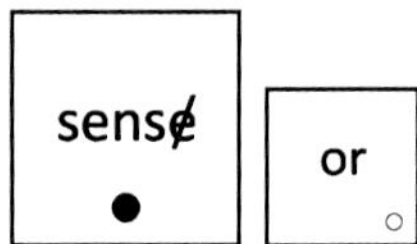

- The suffix ***-or*** means one who does.
- Adding ***-or*** to ***sens¢*** changes the meaning of the word. The combination of word parts means a mechanical device sensitive to light, temperature, or other measures.
- Listen to me use the word ***sensor*** in a question and we will use our knowledge of its parts to figure out the answer.
  2. What does it mean when you say you'll use a ***sensor***? It means you'll use a mechanical device to measure something.

**YOU DO** Use your **Cards** and **Mat** to complete the chart on the **Days 5 & 6 Recording Sheet**.

| Latin Roots | Certified Definition |
|---|---|
| cred | to believe |
| feder/fid/fide/fid¢ | trust or faith |
| sense/sens¢/sent | to feel, perceive, know |
| **Prefixes** | **Certified Definition** |
| con- | with |
| dis- | not |
| in- | not |
| **Suffixes** | **Certified Definition** |
| -al | related to |
| -ent | quality |
| -ible | able |
| -ion | state of being, quality, action |
| -ism | doctrine, belief |
| -or | one who does |
| -y | characterized by |
| **Connecting Letters** | |
| -e- | |

| Word | Prefix | Latin Root | Suffix |
|---|---|---|---|
| credible | | cred: to believe | ible: able, can do |
| Meaning: | believable | | |
| incredible | in: not | cred: to believe | ible: able, can do |
| Meaning: | too unusual to be believed | | |
| confide | con: with | fide: trust or faith | |
| Meaning: | to trust another person with a secret | | |
| confident | con: with | fid: trust or faith | ent: quality |
| Meaning: | to be sure of oneself or a belief | | |

 

# cred, feder/fid/fide/fid¢, sense/sens¢/sent -ism

## DAY 7 • Word Multiplier

### WORD MULTIPLIER

**Build words with *cred, feder/fid/fide/fid¢,* and *sense/sens¢/sent; -ism***

MATERIALS
- Day 7 Recording Sheet
- Notebook paper
- Latin Mat
- Cards:
  Latin Roots: cred, feder, fid, fide, sent
  Inflected Ending: ed
  Prefixes: con, dis, in
  Suffixes: al, ent, ible, ion, ism, or, y

**DIRECTIONS** Students work together to build words using their **Cards** and **Mats**.

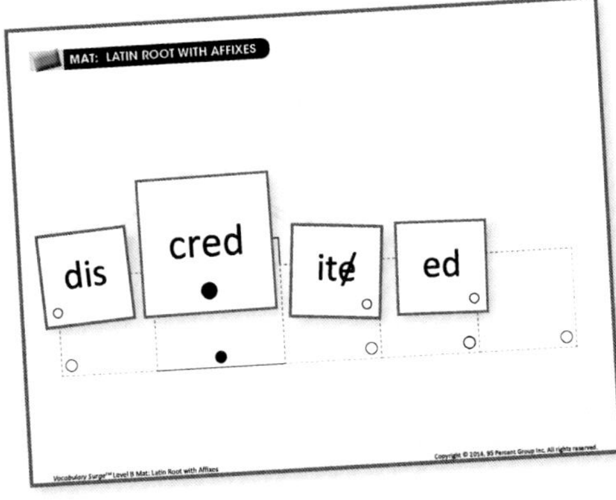


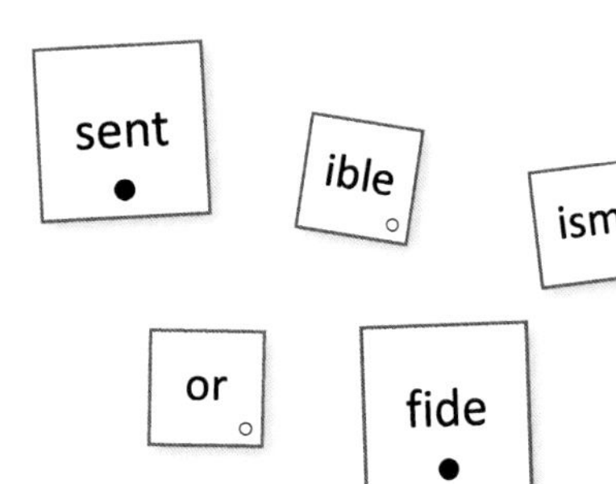


**WE DO** Let's combine **Cards** to build a word.

- I select cards ***dis***, ***cred***, ***it¢***, and ***ed***.
- Where shall I place the prefix ***dis-***? On the left side of the mat
- Where shall I place the Latin root ***cred***? In the large, center box, matching the solid circles
- Where shall I place the suffix ***-it¢***? In the box to the right of ***cred***
- Finally, where shall I place the inflected ending ***-ed***? To the right of ***-it¢***, matching the circle on the mat to the one on the card
- What word have we built? Discredited What is the definition of ***discredited***? To have injured the credit or reputation of a person or idea

**WORD MULTIPLIER**

| SET 1 | Word Parts | Word | Part of Speech |
|---|---|---|---|
| 1. | cred+ible | credible | adjective |
| | Write the Meaning: | believable | |
| 2. | in+cred+ible | incredible | adjective |
| | Write the Meaning: | too unusual to be believed | |
| **SET 2** | **Word Parts** | **Word** | **Part of Speech** |
| 1. | feder+al+ism | federalism | noun |
| | Write the Meaning: | a government where there is a central government and parts | |
| 2. | con+fid+ent | confident | noun |
| | Write the Meaning: | to be sure of oneself or a belief | |
| **SET 3** | **Word Parts** | **Word** | **Part of Speech** |
| 1. | dis+sent+ion | dissention | noun |
| | Write the Meaning: | disagreement | |
| 2. | sens+or+y | sensory | adjective |
| | Write the Meaning: | relating to the senses (hearing, sight, smell, taste, or touch) | |

**YOU DO** Use your **Cards** and **Mats** to build more words. Complete the **Day 7 Recording Sheet** with your partner. Write additional words on notebook paper.

**Possible Words**:

**cred:** credible, credibly, credited, discredited, incredible

**feder/fid/fide/fid¢:** confide, confided, confident, federal, federalism

**sens/sent:** dissent, dissention, sensor, sensory

cred, feder/fid/fide/fid~~e~~, sense/sens~~e~~/sent
-ism

## DAY 8 • Demonstrate Meaning

### BUILD MEANING

MATERIALS
- Whiteboards
- Markers

**DIRECTIONS** Complete the I Do and We Do sections with the whole class, and pair students to work on the You Do activity. Students can record their ideas on small whiteboards. Ask a few pairs to share their work with the class.

**I DO** Listen to me demonstrate understanding of the meaning of the Latin root ***fid***.

- The first word is ***confidence***. The tutor has ***confidence*** that the student is prepared for the math test. I'm going to think of examples of things that people have ***confidence*** in.
  - The rider has ***confidence*** that his horse can jump the fence.
  - Coach has ***confidence*** that the team will win the next game.
- The second word is ***confidential***, which means intended to be kept secret. I'm going to think of examples of things that might be ***confidential***.
  - The president locks his ***confidential*** papers in the safe.
  - Bethany keeps Jane's secret ***confidential***.

**WE DO** Let's try the next one together with the Latin root ***sens~~e~~***.

- The first word is ***sensory***. The Latin root ***sens~~e~~*** means to feel, perceive, or know, the suffix ***-or*** means having a special characteristic, and the suffix ***-y*** mean characterized by. ***Sensory*** means relating to the senses. The haunted house was a ***sensory*** experience with scary sights and sounds.
- Name a time when you had a ***sensory*** experience or a place where you might have one.
- The second word is ***senses***. The Latin root ***sens~~e~~*** means to feel, perceive, or know, and the inflected ending ***-es*** means more than one. ***Senses*** are the five abilities that people have including sight, sound, smell, taste, and touch.
- Name something that affects your ***senses***.

**PROMPT IDEAS** ***sensory***
- beach
- bakery
- school cafeteria

**PROMPT IDEAS** ***senses***
- salt
- burnt food
- soft blanket

**YOU DO** Now it's your turn. Work with a partner, and record your ideas on a whiteboard so you're ready to share with the class. You'll have five minutes to think of examples for two words that contain the Latin root ***cred***.

- The two words are ***credible*** and ***incredible***.
  - What does the Latin root ***cred*** mean? To believe What does the suffix ***-ible*** mean? Able What does ***credible*** mean? Believable
  - What does the prefix ***in-*** mean? Not What does the Latin root ***cred*** mean? To believe What does ***incredible*** mean? Too unusual to be believed
  - Think of an example of something ***credible*** you might see or do.
  - Think of an example of something that is ***incredible***.

**PROMPT IDEAS** ***credible***
- scoring a soccer goal
- arriving home on time
- scoring an A on a test

**PROMPT IDEAS** ***incredible***
- walking through walls
- completing a book report in 5 minutes
- scoring every point in a basketball game

# cred, feder/fid/fide/fid~~e~~, judge/judg~~e~~/judic, jur/jus, leg, sense/sens~~e~~/sent -ice, -ism

## DAY 9 • Review What You Learned

### STEP 1 REVIEW THE MEANING

**Review *cred, feder/fid/fide/fid~~e~~, judge/judg~~e~~/judic, jur/jus, leg, sense/sens~~e~~/sent***
**Suffixes *-ice* and *-ism***

MATERIALS
- Word parts projected on document camera, overhead projector, or PowerPoint™

**DIRECTIONS** Display the morphemes so students can see them, and ask for the certified definition of each one.

**When I show you the word parts, think about the Certified Definitions we discussed as you prepare to answer.**

| Latin Root | Certified Definition | Suffix | Certified Definition |
|---|---|---|---|
| *cred* | to believe | *-ice* | forms a noun |
| *feder/fid/fide/fid~~e~~* | trust or faith | *-ism* | doctrine or belief |
| *sense/sens~~e~~/sent* | to feel, perceive, know | | |

### STEP 2 CHECK MEANING

MATERIALS
- Day 9 Recording Sheet

**DIRECTIONS** Read the following sentences to check that students understand the meanings of ***cred, feder/fid/fide/fid~~e~~, judge/judg~~e~~/judic, jur/jus, leg,*** and ***sense/sens~~e~~/sent; -ism***. Model the first sentence for students using the We Do Step, below.

**WE DO** As I read this sentence, think about the certified definition of the Latin root that fits the blank.

1. The soldiers of the Con______acy Army were led by General Robert E. Lee.

- Which Latin root do you think fits on the line? Feder
- What is the new word? Confederacy
- What do you think the word Confederacy means? A group that bands together with the same beliefs

**YOU DO** Complete the rest of the sentences on the **Day 9 Recording Sheet** with your partner to find the Latin root that best fits on the line. Record the new words and their meanings.

CHECK MEANING

1. The soldiers of the **Con** feder **acy** Army were led by General Robert E. Lee. Confederacy
   Meaning: a group that bands together with the same beliefs
2. Danielle said she wanted to **con** fide that she was scared to get into the pool. confide
   Meaning: to trust another person with a secret
3. It is **il** leg **al** to let your dog off its leash on New York City streets. illegal
   Meaning: against the law
4. The team made its **as** sent clear when they agreed to play in the rain. assent
   Meaning: to agree or give in
5. The inspector's jur **isdiction** was limited to the city. jurisdiction
   Meaning: a territory over which an organization can rule
6. Because of Liam's poor handwriting, the note looked like all **non** sense words. nonsense
   Meaning: spoken or written words that have no meaning

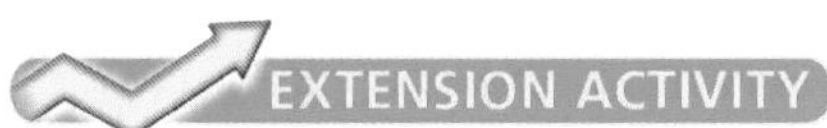


Students write two sentences with missing Latin roots to challenge the class.

cred, feder/fid/fide/fid~~e~~, judge/judg~~e~~/judic, jur/jus, leg, sense/sens~~e~~/sent -ice, -ism

## DAY 10 • 2nd Review Day

### STEP 1 MAKE CONNECTIONS

MATERIALS
- Day 10 Recording Sheet

**DIRECTIONS** Students pair up to write sentences with either one or two of the words that are provided.

**I am going to model how to use a word containing this week's Latin root in a meaningful sentence. The word is *incredibly*.**

- The musician's performance was ***incredibly*** good.
- It is your turn to create five more sentences using the words on the top of the recording sheet.
- Sentences with two words get two points and sentences with one word get one point.

MAKE CONNECTIONS

yourself to write sentences with two of the words from the list.

| Words | | |
|---|---|---|
| credit | federal | illegal |
| incredible | judge | legal |
| incredibly | judgement | legalize |
| confided | jury | nonsense |
| confidence | adjust | sensible |
| confident | justice | sensor |

1. The musician's performance was incredibly good.
2. We had to adjust the volume so everyone could hear.
3. It is illegal to drive faster than the speed limit.
4. At sunset the sensor turns on the outdoor lights.
5. We were confident that the jury would make a fair decision.

### STEP 2 CHALLENGE: MORPHEME MADNESS

MATERIALS
- Notebook paper
- Latin Mat
- Cards listed in the table below

**DIRECTIONS** Students pair up to use **Cards** and **Mats** to build words. They also record all of the words they build and the words' definitions.

| Word Parts | Cards |
|---|---|
| **Latin Roots** | cred, feder, fid, fide, fid~~e~~, judge, judg~~e~~, judic, jur, jus, leg, sense, sens~~e~~, sent |
| **Inflected Endings** | ed, ing |
| **Prefixes** | con, dis, il, in, non |
| **Suffixes** | acy, al, ary, as, ate, ible, ibly, ice, ism, ment |

**Now it's your turn to build words.**

- First, find a partner.
- Use the **Cards** and **Mats** to build real words.
- Record the words and their definitions on a separate sheet of paper.

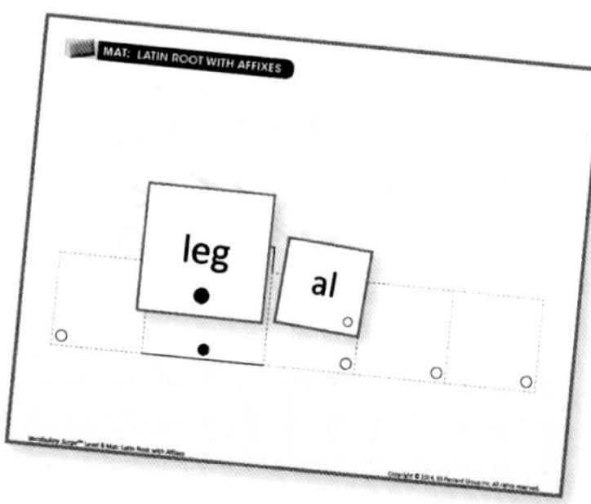


 

# anni/annu, close/clos~~e~~/clude/clud~~e~~/clus, corp, dorm, fine/fin~~e~~/fin/finis, vit/vita/viv

## DAY 1 • Introduce Latin Roots

### UNCOVER THE MEANING

**Introduce *anni/annu, close/clos~~e~~/clude/clud~~e~~/clus,* and *fine/fin~~e~~/fin/finis***

MATERIALS
- Days 1 & 2 Recording Sheet

**DIRECTIONS** Pair students and distribute the **Days 1 & 2 Recording Sheet**. Model the first completed example. After students have completed the first two columns, ask them to share what they wrote. Then provide the Certified Definition. Explain that understanding parts of words, such as Latin roots, can help students uncover the meaning of many words.

**I'm going to model using my detective skills to figure out what the underlined word parts mean.**

- I'll use the other words in the sentences to develop a Working Definition of a word part.
- Listen as I read the first set of two sentences.
  1. The ***annu**al* Fourth of July Parade only occurs once every twelve months.
  2. Jose's parents celebrate their ***anni**versary* with a party every May 12.
- In **Column 1**, I record the clue words once, twelve months, and every May 12 that help me understand the meaning of ***anni/annu***.
- I think that ***anni/annu*** means yearly. This is my Working Definition, which I record in **Column 2**.
- In **Column 3**, I write the Certified Definition of ***anni/annu***: year.

**Now it's your turn.**

- With your partner, read the next set of sentences on the **Days 1 & 2 Recording Sheet**.
- Use your detective skills to figure out what the underlined word parts mean.
- Consider which words or phrases in the sentences provide clues about meaning. Record them in **Column 1**.
- Write a Working Definition in **Column 2**.
- Only complete **Columns 1** and **2** and then wait for the discussion. You will fill in **Column 3** after I provide a Certified Definition.

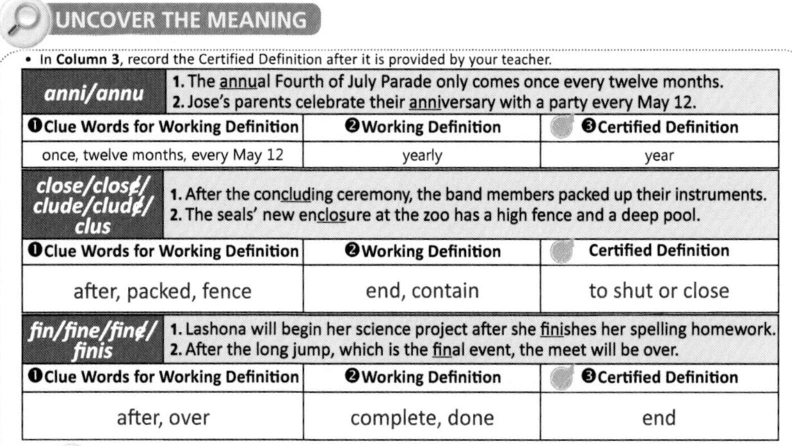

UNCOVER THE MEANING

- In **Column 3**, record the Certified Definition after it is provided by your teacher.

| anni/annu | 1. The annual Fourth of July Parade only comes once every twelve months. 2. Jose's parents celebrate their anniversary with a party every May 12. | |
|---|---|---|
| ❶ Clue Words for Working Definition | ❷ Working Definition | ❸ Certified Definition |
| once, twelve months, every May 12 | yearly | year |
| **close/clos~~e~~/clude/clud~~e~~/clus** | 1. After the concluding ceremony, the band members packed up their instruments. 2. The seals' new enclosure at the zoo has a high fence and a deep pool. | |
| ❶ Clue Words for Working Definition | ❷ Working Definition | Certified Definition |
| after, packed, fence | end, contain | to shut or close |
| **fin/fine/fin~~e~~/finis** | 1. Lashona will begin her science project after she finishes her spelling homework. 2. After the long jump, which is the final event, the meet will be over. | |
| ❶ Clue Words for Working Definition | ❷ Working Definition | ❸ Certified Definition |
| after, over | complete, done | end |

## anni/annu, close/closé/clude/cludé/clus, fine/finé/finis

# DAY 2 • Deepen the Meaning

## CHECK MEANING

**MATERIALS**
- Pocket chart, document camera, or PowerPoint™
- Days 1 & 2 Recording Sheet
- Cards:
  Teacher: al, annu, ly
  Student:
  Latin Roots: closé, clus, finé
  Prefixes: con
  Suffixes: al, ion, ize, ure

**DIRECTIONS** Using the **Cards** and **Mat**, confirm that students understand how the meaning of the word evolves as more parts are added.

**I DO**

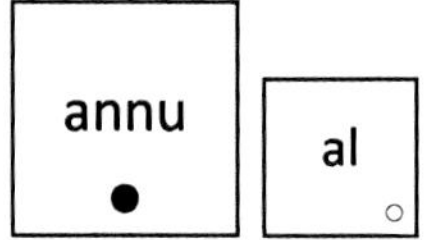


- The suffix ***-al*** means in or near.
- Adding ***-al*** to ***annu*** spells the word ***annual***. The combination of word parts means occurs once a year.
- Now, I'm going to use my knowledge of the word to answer the question.

1. What does it mean when I say that Thanksgiving is an ***annual*** event? It occurs once a year.

**WE DO**

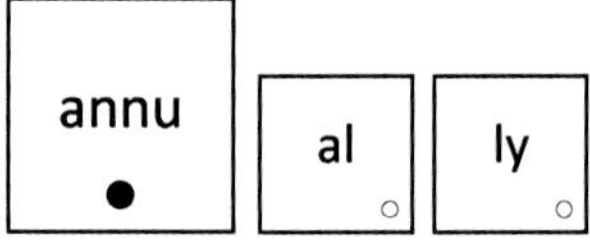


- The suffix ***-al*** means in or near.
- Adding ***-al*** to ***annu*** spells the word ***annual***. The combination of word parts means occurs once a year.
- The suffix ***-ly*** means characterized by.
- Adding ***-ly*** to ***annual*** spells ***annually***, which changes the meaning from occurs once a year to describing something occurring once a year.
- Listen to me use the word ***annually*** in a question and we will use our knowledge of its parts to figure out the answer.

2. What does it mean when Valentine's Day comes ***annually*** in February? It's occurring once a year.

**YOU DO** Use your **Cards** and **Mat** to complete the chart on the **Days 1 & 2 Recording Sheet**.

| Latin Roots | Certified Definition |
|---|---|
| anni/annu | year |
| close/closé/clude/cludé/clus | to shut or close |
| fin/fine/finé/finis | end |
| **Prefixes** | **Certified Definition** |
| con- | with |
| in- | in |
| pre- | before, earlier |
| semi- | half |
| un- | not |
| **Suffixes** | **Certified Definition** |
| -al | related to, like |
| -ion | state of being, action |
| -ish | origin, nature, or resembling |
| -ist | one who performs a specific action |
| -ize | become, change, or make |
| -ly/y | characterized by |
| -ure | process, function |

### CHECK MEANING

**DIRECTIONS** Build the words with the Cards and Mat. Describe how adding new parts changes the meaning of the words.

| Word | Prefix | Latin Root | Suffix |
|---|---|---|---|
| conclusion | con: together, with | clus: to shut or close | ion: state of being |
| Meaning: | something that has reached an end | | |

| Word | Latin Root | Suffix | Suffix |
|---|---|---|---|
| closure | closé: to shut, close | ure: process, function | |
| Meaning: | to have something end or close | | |
| final | finé: end | al: related to, like | |
| Meaning: | end, last | | |
| finalize | finé: end | al: related to, like | ize: become, change, or make |
| Meaning: | to put in finished form | | |

| Inflected Endings | Certified Definition |
|---|---|
| -ed | past |
| -ing | present |

 

# anni/annu, close/clos~~e~~/clude/clud~~e~~/ clus, fine/fin~~e~~/finis

## DAY 3 • Word Multiplier

### WORD MULTIPLIER

**Build words with *anni/annu, close/clos~~e~~/clude/clud~~e~~/clus,* and *fine/fin~~e~~/finis***

**DIRECTIONS** Students work together to build words using their **Cards** and **Mats**.

MATERIALS
- Day 3 Recording Sheet
- Notebook paper
- Latin Mat
- Cards:
  Latin Roots: anni, annu, close, clos~~e~~, clude, clud~~e~~, clus, fin, fine, fin~~e~~, finis
  Inflected Endings: ed, ing
  Prefixes: in, pre, semi, un
  Suffixes: al, ion, ish, ist

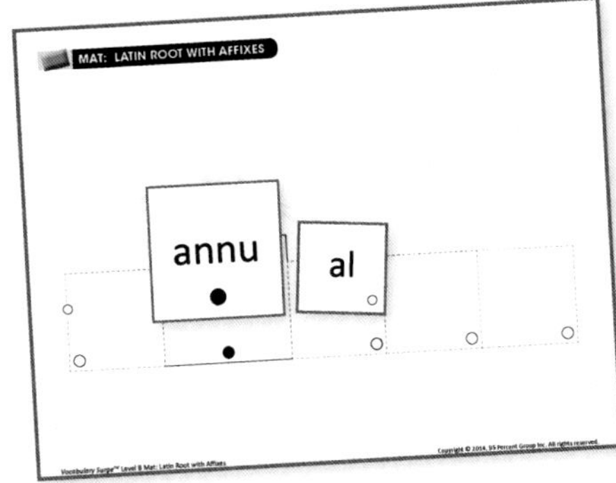


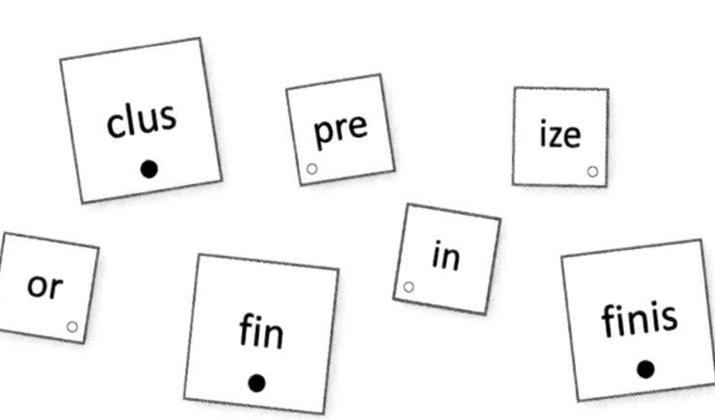


**I DO** Watch me combine **Cards** to build a word.

- I select cards ***annu*** and ***al***.
- I place the Latin root ***annu*** in the large center box, matching the solid circles.
- Finally, I place the suffix ***-al*** to the right of ***annu***, matching the circle on the mat to the one on the card.
- I have built the word ***annual***.

**WE DO** Let me try another.

- I choose the cards ***annu***, ***al***, and ***ly***.
- Where shall I place the card ***annu***? In the large, middle box
- Why do we place it here? Because it is the Latin root and has a solid circle like the mat
- Where shall I place the suffixes ***-al*** and ***-ly***? In the boxes to the right of ***annu***

**WORD MULTIPLIER**

| SET 1 | Word Parts | Word | Part of Speech |
|---|---|---|---|
| 1. | annu+al+ly | annually | adverb |
| | Write the Meaning: | occuring once a year | |
| 2. | semi+annu+al | semiannual | adjective |
| | Write the Meaning: | occurring twice a year | |
| **SET 2** | **Word Parts** | **Word** | **Part of Speech** |
| 1. | in+clus+ion | inclusion | noun |
| | Write the Meaning: | closed or contained within a group | |
| 2. | pre+clud~~e~~+ing | precluding | verb |
| | Write the Meaning: | ruling out in advance | |
| **SET 3** | **Word Parts** | **Word** | **Part of Speech** |
| 1. | fin~~e~~+al+ist | finalist | noun |
| | Write the Meaning: | a contestant in the finals of a competition | |
| 2. | un+fin+ish+ed | unfinished | adjective |
| | Write the Meaning: | not ended or done | |

- Look at the example on your **Day 3 Recording Sheet** to see how to write the parts of ***annually*** and the whole word. ***Annu*** means year, ***-al*** means related to, and ***-ly*** means like.
- When we put these word parts together, ***annually*** means occurring once a year.
- What part of speech is ***annually*** and how do you know? Adverb; it describes an action

**YOU DO** Use your **Cards** and **Mats** to build more words. Complete the **Day 3 Recording Sheet** with your partner. Write additional words on notebook paper. We will review the words when you have finished.

**Possible Words:**

**anni/annu:** annual, annually, semiannual, semiannually

**clus/clud~~e~~:** including, inclusion, precluding, preclusion

**fin/fin~~e~~:** final, finish

anni/annu, close/clos¢/clude/clud¢/clus, fine/fin¢/finis

## DAY 4 • Demonstrate Meaning

### BUILD MEANING

MATERIALS
- Whiteboards
- Markers

**DIRECTIONS** Complete the I Do and We Do sections with the whole class, and pair students to work on the You Do activity. Students can record their ideas on small whiteboards. Ask a few pairs to share their work with the class.

**I DO** Listen to me demonstrate understanding of the meaning of the Latin root ***anni***.

- The first word is ***anniversary***. We learned that ***anniversary*** means a yearly date of an event. I'm going to think of examples of things with an ***anniversary***.
  - We celebrate my parent's wedding ***anniversary***.
  - The school staff and students celebrated the tenth ***anniversary*** of the school.
- The second word is ***semiannual***, which means occurs twice a year. I'm going to think of examples of things that might be ***semiannual***.
  - A car gets a ***semiannual*** check-up to keep it running well.
  - Many people schedule a ***semiannual*** visit to their doctor to check their vision.

**WE DO** Let's try the next one together with the Latin root ***clude***.

- The first word is ***include***. The prefix ***in-*** means in, and the Latin root ***clude*** means to shut or close.
- To ***include*** means to enclose or take into a group. The math lessons ***include*** multiplication and division.
  - When have you ***included*** someone or something?
- The second word is ***conclude***. The prefix ***con-*** means with, and the Latin root ***clude*** means to shut or close. ***Conclude*** means with closure.
  - Name some activities you have ***concluded***.

**PROMPT IDEAS** ***includes***
- invited a friend
- went with my parents
- added an apple to lunch

**PROMPT IDEAS** ***conclude***
- a project
- eating dinner
- a chore

**YOU DO** Now it's your turn. Work with a partner, and record your ideas on a whiteboard so you're ready to share with the class. You'll have five minutes to think of examples for two words that contain the Latin root ***fin***.

- The two words are ***finally*** and ***finish***.
  - What does the Latin root ***fin*** mean? End What does the suffix ***-al*** mean? Towards, near What does the suffix ***-ly*** mean? Characterized by What does ***finally*** mean? Near the end
  - What does the Latin root ***fin*** mean? End What does the suffix ***-ish*** mean? Resembling What does ***finish*** mean? To come to an end
  - Think of an example of something you ***finally*** completed.
  - Think of an example of something you might ***finish***. It can be something that you did or something that you could possibly do.

**PROMPT IDEAS** ***finally***
- cleaning your room
- novel for English class
- raking the yard

**PROMPT IDEAS** ***finish***
- dessert
- watching a video
- playing a game

 

corp, dorm, vit/vita/viv

## DAY 5 • Introduce Latin Roots

### UNCOVER THE MEANING

**Introduce *corp, dorm,* and *vit/vita/viv***

MATERIALS
- Days 5 & 6 Recording Sheet

**DIRECTIONS** Pair students and distribute the Days 5 & 6 Recording Sheet. Model the first completed example. After students have completed the first two columns, ask them to share what they wrote. Then provide the Certified Definition. Explain that understanding parts of words, such as Latin roots, can help students uncover the meaning of many words.

**I'm going to model using my detective skills to figure out what the underlined word parts mean.**

- I'll use the other words in the sentences to develop a Working Definition of a word part.
- Listen as I read the first set of two sentences.
    1. The ***viv***id colors of the painting made the scene almost come alive.
    2. Eating foods rich in ***vitamins*** each day will improve one's health and energy level.
- In **Column 1**, I record the clue words come alive, health, and energy that help me understand the meaning of ***vit/vita/viv***.
- I think that ***vit/vita/viv*** means alive or life. This is my Working Definition, which I record in **Column 2**.
- In **Column 3**, I will write the Certified Definition of ***vit/vita/viv***: to live.

**Now it's your turn.**

- With your partner, read the next set of sentences on the Days 5 & 6 Recording Sheet.
- Use your detective skills to figure out what the underlined word parts mean.
- Consider which words or phrases in the sentences provide clues about meaning. Record them in **Column 1**.
- Write a Working Definition in **Column 2**.
- Only complete **Columns 1** and **2** and then wait for the discussion. You will fill in **Column 3** after I provide a Certified Definition.

UNCOVER THE MEANING

| ***vit/vita/viv*** | 1. The vivid colors of the painting made the scene almost come alive. 2. Eating foods rich in vitamins each day will improve one's health and energy level. | |
|---|---|---|
| **❶ Clue Words for Working Definition** | **❷ Working Definition** | **❸ Certified Definition** |
| come alive, health, energy | alive, life | to live |

| ***corp*** | 1. The corpse of the dried worm lay on the sidewalk. 2. Ms. Parker works in the main office of a large corporation that has many branches. | |
|---|---|---|
| **❶ Clue Words for Working Definition** | **❷ Working Definition** | **❸ Certified Definition** |
| dried, main, many branches | dead body, business group | body |

| ***dorm*** | 1. During summer camp, Sara bunked in the girl's dormitory. 2. The dormer windows in the bedrooms extended out from the second story of the roof. | |
|---|---|---|
| **❶ Clue Words for Working Definition** | **❷ Working Definition** | **❸ Certified Definition** |
| bunked, extended out | slept, bedroom | to sleep |

# DAY 6 • Deepen the Meaning

## CHECK MEANING

**MATERIALS**
- Pocket chart, document camera, or PowerPoint™
- Days 5 & 6 Recording Sheet
- Cards:
  - Teacher: al, ly, vit
  - Student:
  - Latin Roots: corp, dorm
  - Suffixes: al, ant, ate, er, or

**DIRECTIONS** Using the **Cards** and **Mat**, confirm that students understand how the meaning of the word evolves as more parts are added.

**I DO**

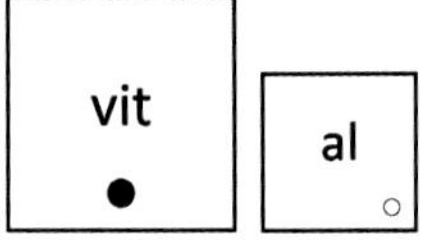


- The suffix ***-al*** means related to or like.
- Adding ***-al*** to ***vit*** spells the word ***vital***. The combination of word parts means full of life or important.
- Now, I'm going to use my knowledge of the word to answer the question.

1. What does it mean when you say water is ***vital*** to plant life? Water is important.

**WE DO**

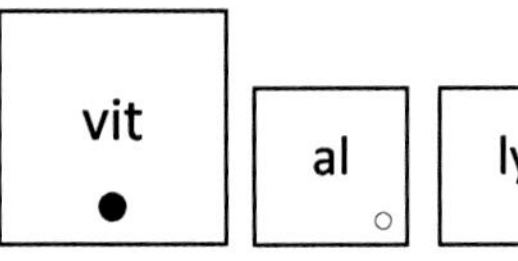


- The suffix ***-al*** means related to or like.
- Adding ***-al*** to ***vit*** spells the word ***vital***. The combination of word parts means full of life or important.
- The suffix ***-ly*** means characterized by.
- Adding ***-ly*** to ***vital*** spells ***vitally***, which changes the meaning from full of life or important to of great importance.
- Listen to me use the word ***vitally*** in a question and we will use our knowledge of its parts to figure out the answer.

2. What does it mean when it is ***vitally*** critical to turn on a heater in the winter? It is very important.

**YOU DO** Use your **Cards** and **Mat** to complete the chart on the **Days 5 & 6 Recording Sheet.**

| Latin Roots | Certified Definition |
|---|---|
| corp | body |
| dorm | to sleep |
| vit/vita/viv | to live |
| **Suffixes** | **Certified Definition** |
| -al | towards, near |
| -ant | action, state, or quality |
| -ate/-até | rank, office |
| -er | has a special characteristic |
| -ion | state of being or quality |
| -ize | become, change, or make |
| -or | has a special characteristic |

**CHECK MEANING**

Build the words with the Cards and Mat. Describe how adding new parts changes the meaning of the words.

| Word | Latin Root | Suffix | Suffix |
|---|---|---|---|
| dormer | dorm: to sleep | er: has a special characteristic | |
| Meaning: | a window that juts out from the roof, often in a second-story bedroom | | |
| dormant | dorm: to sleep | ant: state, quality | |
| Meaning: | sleeplike state | | |
| corporate | corp: body | or: to believe | ate: quality of |
| Meaning: | related to an organized body of people | | |
| corporal | corp: body | or: to believe | al: related to, like |
| Meaning: | relating to the body | | |

## corp, dorm, vit/vita/viv

# DAY 7 • Word Multiplier

## WORD MULTIPLIER

MATERIALS
- Day 7 Recording Sheet
- Notebook paper
- Latin Mat
- Cards:
  Latin Roots: corp, dorm, vit
  Suffixes: al, ant, ate, atė, er, ion, ize, or

**Build words with *corp, dorm,* and *vit/vita/viv***

**DIRECTIONS** Students work together to build words using their **Cards** and **Mats**.

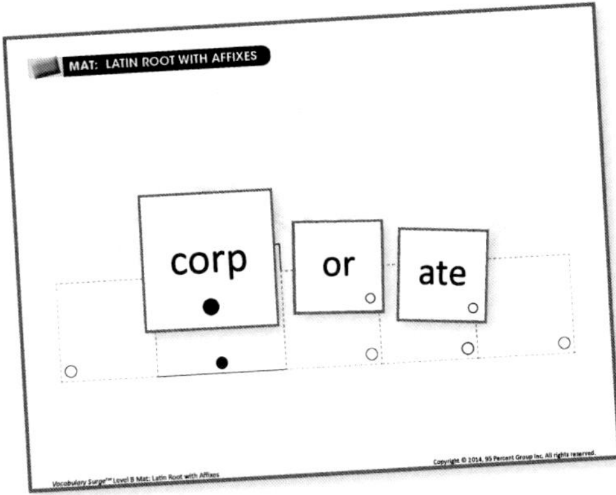


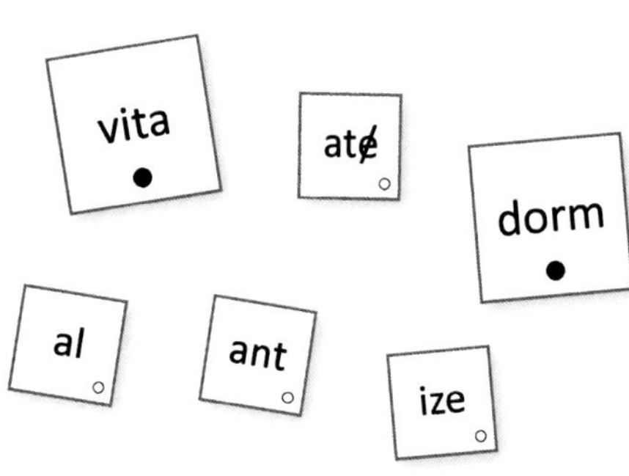


**WE DO** Let's combine **Cards** to build a word.

- I select cards ***corp***, ***or***, and ***ate***.
- Where shall I place the Latin root ***corp***? In the large, center box, matching the solid circles
- Where shall I place the suffix ***-or***? To the right of ***corp***, matching the circle on the mat to the one on the card
- Finally, where shall I place the suffix ***-ate***? To the right of ***or***, matching the circle on the mat to the one on the card
- What word have we built? Corporate What is the definition of ***corporate***? Related to an organized body of people

**WORD MULTIPLIER**

| SET 1 | Word Parts | Words | Part of Speech |
|---|---|---|---|
| 1. | corp+or+ate | corporate | adjective |
| | Write the Meaning: | related to an organized body of people | |
| 2. | corp+or+atė+ion | corporation | noun |
| | Write the Meaning: | a business organization | |

| SET 2 | Word Parts | Words | Part of Speech |
|---|---|---|---|
| 1. | dorm+ant | dormant | adjective |
| | Write the Meaning: | a sleeplike state | |
| 2. | dorm+er | dormer | noun |
| | Write the Meaning: | a window that juts out from the roof, usually in a bedroom | |

| SET 3 | Word Parts | Words | Part of Speech |
|---|---|---|---|
| 1. | vit+al | vital | adjective |
| | Write the Meaning: | full of life, important | |
| 2. | vit+al+ize | vitalize | verb |
| | Write the Meaning: | to fill with energy or life | |

**YOU DO** Use your **Cards** and **Mats** to build more words. Complete the **Day 7 Recording Sheet** with your partner. Write additional words on notebook paper.

**Possible Words:**

**corp:** corporal, corporate, corporation
**dorm:** dorm, dormant, dormer
**vit:** vital, vitalize

## DAY 8 • Demonstrate Meaning

### BUILD MEANING

MATERIALS
- Whiteboards
- Markers

**DIRECTIONS** Complete the I Do and We Do sections with the whole class, and pair students to work on the You Do activity. Students can record their ideas on small whiteboards. Ask a few pairs to share their work with the class.

**I DO** Listen to me demonstrate understanding of the meaning of the Latin root ***corp***.

- The first word is ***corpse***. I found the ***corpse*** of a spider on the floor. I'm going to think of examples of things that might be a ***corpse***.
  - The ***corpse*** of the beetle was shiny and green.
  - On the sand lay the ***corpse*** of a jellyfish.
- The second word is ***corpulent,*** which means having a large and bulky body. I'm going to think of examples of things that are ***corpulent***.
  - The cat was lean, not ***corpulent*** at all.
  - The frog overate until it could barely move its ***corpulent*** belly.

**WE DO** Let's try the next one together with the Latin root ***dorm***.

- The first word is ***dormant***. The Latin root ***dorm*** means sleep, and the suffix ***-ant*** means state. ***Dormant*** means in a sleeplike state.
- The snake was ***dormant*** under the woodpile all winter.
  - Name something that is ***dormant***.
- The second word is ***dormitory***. The Latin root ***dorm*** means sleep, the suffix ***-ite*** means quality of, the suffix ***-or*** means having a special characteristic, and the suffix ***-y*** means characterized by. ***Dormitory*** means a large room or building for sleeping many people.
  - Name a place that might have a ***dormitory***.

**PROMPT IDEAS** ***dormant***
- bears during winter
- squirrels during winter
- pupa in a cocoon

**PROMPT IDEAS** ***dormitory***
- camp
- college
- boarding school

**YOU DO** Now it's your turn. Work with a partner, and record your ideas on a whiteboard so you're ready to share with the class. You'll have five minutes to think of examples for two words that contain the Latin root ***viv***.

- The two words are ***vivid*** and ***vividly***.
  - What does the Latin root ***viv*** mean? To live What does ***vivid*** mean? Full of life or color
  - What does the suffix ***-ly*** mean? Characterized by What does the Latin root ***viv*** mean? To live What does ***vividly*** mean? Lively, brightly
  - Think of an example of something that might have ***vivid*** colors.
  - Think of an example of when someone did something ***vividly***.

**PROMPT IDEAS** ***vivid***
- painting
- parrot
- sunset

**PROMPT IDEAS** ***vividly***
- artist painting
- author's writing in a book
- actor playing a character

 

# anni/annu, close/clos~~e~~/clude/clud~~e~~/clus, fine/fin~~e~~/finis, vit/vita/viv

## DAY 9 • Review What You Learned

### STEP 1 REVIEW THE MEANING

**Review *anni/annu, close/clos~~e~~/clude/clud~~e~~/clus, corp, dorm, fin/fine/fin~~e~~/finis,* and *vit/vita/viv***

*MATERIALS*
- Word parts projected on document camera, overhead projector, or PowerPoint™

**DIRECTIONS** Display the morphemes so students can see them, and ask for the certified definition of each one.

**When I show you the word parts, think about the Certified Definitions we discussed as you prepare to answer.**

| Latin Root | Certified Definition | Latin Root | Certified Definition |
|---|---|---|---|
| **anni/annu** | year | **corp** | body |
| **close/clos~~e~~/clude/clud~~e~~/clus** | to shut or close | **dorm** | to sleep |
| **fin/fine/fin~~e~~/finis** | end | **vit/vita/viv** | to live |

### STEP 2 CHECK MEANING

*MATERIALS*
- Day 9 Recording Sheet

**DIRECTIONS** Read the following sentences to check that students understand the meanings of ***anni/annu, close/clos~~e~~/clude/clud~~e~~/clus, corp, dorm, fin/fine/fin~~e~~/finis,*** and ***vit/vita/viv***. Model the first sentence for students using the We Do Step, below.

**WE DO** As I read this sentence, think about the certified definition of the Latin root that fits the blank.

1. The lawyer was not anxious to dis______ the information to the jury.

- Which Latin root do you think fits on the line? Clos
- What is the new word? Enclosure
- What do you think the word ***enclosure*** means? Something that closes something else, like a fence

**YOU DO** Complete the rest of the sentences on the **Day 9 Recording Sheet** with your partner to find the Latin root that best fits on the line. Record the new words and their meanings.

**EXTENSION ACTIVITY**

Students write two sentences with missing Latin roots to challenge the class.

**CHECK MEANING**

1. The lawyer was not anxious to **dis** close the information to the jury. disclose
   Meaning: to make known
2. Jelly fish look like a corp **ulent** blob of jelly. corpulent
   Meaning: having a large or bulky body
3. The **semi** annu **al** picnic is held on Memorial Day and Halloween. semiannual
   Meaning: occurring twice a year
4. Sadly, the rental time for the movie was fin **ite**. finite
   Meaning: having an end
5. The class observed that the pupa was dorm **ant** for three weeks. dormant
   Meaning: in a sleeplike state
6. The neon sign's viv **idness** hurt Britney's eyes. vividness
   Meaning: having the appearance of liveliness

anni/annu, close/closé/clude/cludé/clus, corp, dorm, fin/fine/finé/finis, vit/vita/viv

# DAY 10 • 2nd Review Day

## STEP 1 MAKE CONNECTIONS

MATERIALS
- Day 10 Recording Sheet

**DIRECTIONS** Students pair up to write sentences with either one or two of the words that are provided.

**I am going to model how to use a word containing this week's Latin root in a meaningful sentence. The word is *confined*.**

- At night the new puppy was ***confined*** to the kitchen.
- It is your turn to create five more sentences using the words on the top of the recording sheet.
- Sentences with two words get two points and sentences with one word get one point.

MAKE CONNECTIONS

yourself to write sentences with two of the words from the list.

| Words | | |
|---|---|---|
| anniversary | dormant | finish |
| annual | dormitory | include |
| closing | enclosing | infinity |
| conclusion | exclude | revitalize |
| confined | finally | semiannual |
| defined | finalist | vital |

1. At night the new puppy was confined to the kitchen.
2. The store advertises semiannual sales in January and July.
3. Many plants are dormant in cold weather.
4. A balanced diet is vital for good health.
5. We came to the conclusion that enclosing our patio was a good idea.

## STEP 2 CHALLENGE: MORPHEME MADNESS

MATERIALS
- Notebook paper
- Latin Mat
- Cards listed in the table below

**DIRECTIONS** Students pair up to use **Cards** and **Mats** to build real words. They also record all of the words they build and the words' definitions.

| Word Parts | Cards |
|---|---|
| **Latin Roots** | anni, annu, close, closé, clude, cludé, clus, corp, dorm, fin, fine, finé, vit, vita, viv |
| **Inflected Endings** | ed, ing |
| **Prefixes** | bi, con, dis, in |
| **Suffixes** | al, ion, ish, ive, ize, or, ure |

**Now it's your turn to build words.**

- First, find a partner.
- Use the **Cards** and **Mats** to build real words.
- Record the words and their definitions on a separate sheet of paper.

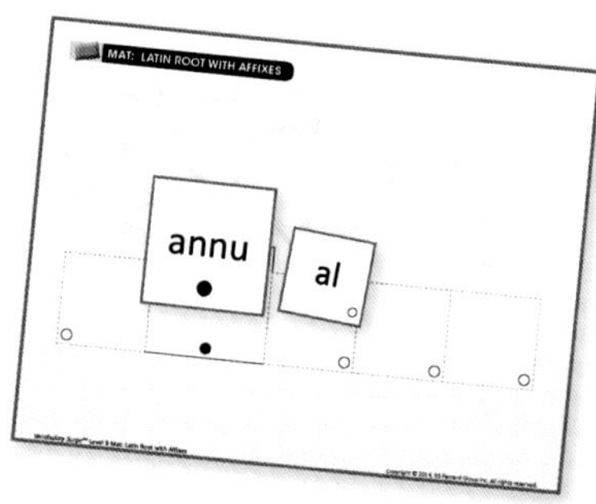


 

# Greek Mat

## Introduction

- Whiteboards and markers
- Greek Mat
- Cards:

Teacher:
graph, phone, photo, tele

Student:
Greek Combining Forms: auto, graph
Inflected Endings: ed, ing

### Introduce the Greek Combining Forms Mat

**We've been working with Latin words in the past lessons. Now we're moving to the Greek layer of language.**

**First let's talk about the way words are constructed in the Greek layer of language.**

- The Latin layer was the second layer of language, which was added to the Anglo-Saxon layer long ago when the people who spoke a Latin-based language moved into the regions of English-speaking people. Latin words are constructed with a Root that must be in the center and then at least one or more prefixes and suffixes surrounding the Root. The Latin Root doesn't make a word by itself.
- Greek words are constructed differently than Latin words. There are no central Roots, and there don't have to be prefixes and affixes. Greek words are constructed by attaching separate and unique pieces called Greek Combining Forms. They can be combined in any order; the same part can appear at the beginning or the end of the word. An example is the Greek Combining Form ***photo***. It can be found in the words ***photograph*** or ***telephoto***.

**Now let's talk about the mat and word cards we'll use.**

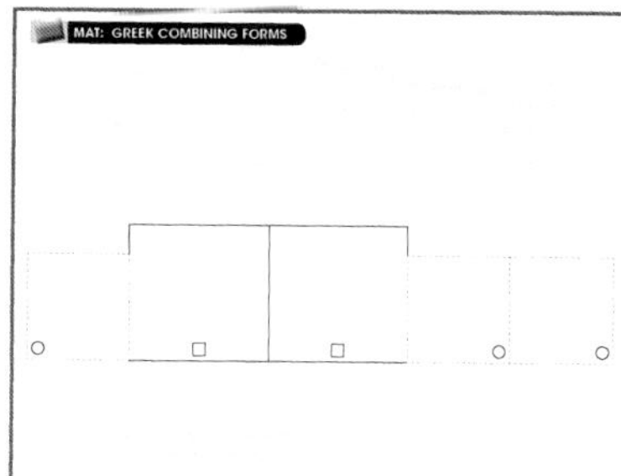


- Look at this mat. There is an image in the background. What does it look like? Columns on a Greek building That's to remind us that this is the Greek layer. Now look at the boxes on the mat. Are they all the same size? No, there are two sizes How many large boxes are there? Two
- Look inside the boxes at the squares. What shape was in the boxes of the Latin roots? Circles or dots Is the square on the large boxes filled in, or solid? No Are there any smaller boxes? Yes there are two boxes after the large box This is where suffixes go. What shape is in these boxes? Circles like on the Latin mats Greek words can have Latin prefixes and suffixes, so these shapes are like the Latin mat. Notice that there can be more than one suffix in the words we'll be building.

**Now let's use the mat and word cards to build some words.**

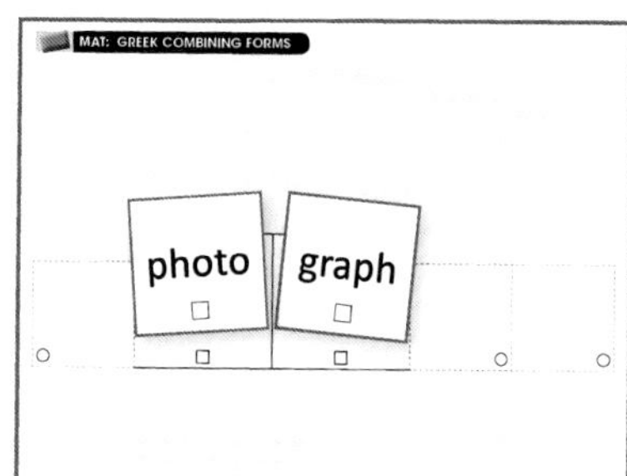


I DO • Watch me build the word ***photograph***.

- The first Greek Combining Form is ***photo***. It goes in the large box to the left of the Greek Mat. Next, I place the second Greek Combining Form, ***graph***, to the right of ***photo***, matching the size of the large box and the open square to the one on the mat. The new word is ***photograph***. The word means an image created using light.

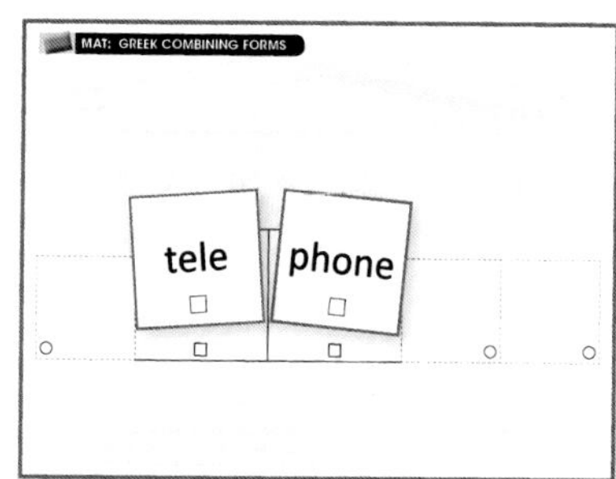


WE DO Help me build the word ***telephone*** on the Greek Mat.

- Where shall I place the word card ***tele***? In the left large box
- Why do I place it there? Because it is the first Greek Combining Form
- Where shall I place the word card ***phone***? In the second large box to the right of ***tele***
- Why do I place it there? Because it is a Greek Combining Form and the square on the card matches the square on the mat
- What word have I built? Telephone

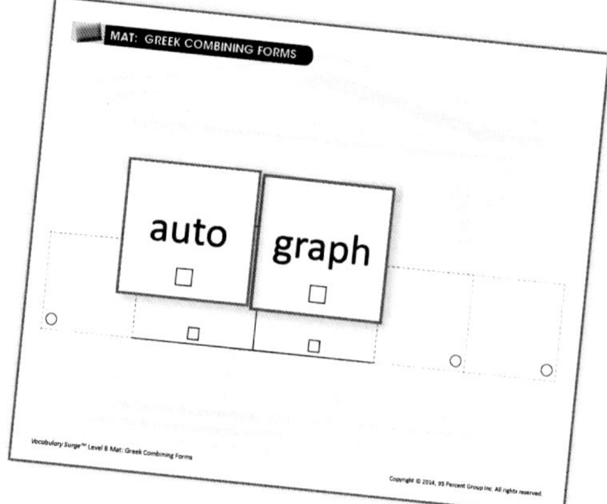


**YOU DO** With a partner, collect the following word cards:

Greek Combining Form: ***auto, graph***

Inflected Endings: ***ed, ing***

- What's the definition of the Greek combining form ***auto***? Self, same
- What's the definition of the Greek combining form ***graph***? Written or drawn
- With your partner build the word ***autograph*** on your Greek Mat.

---

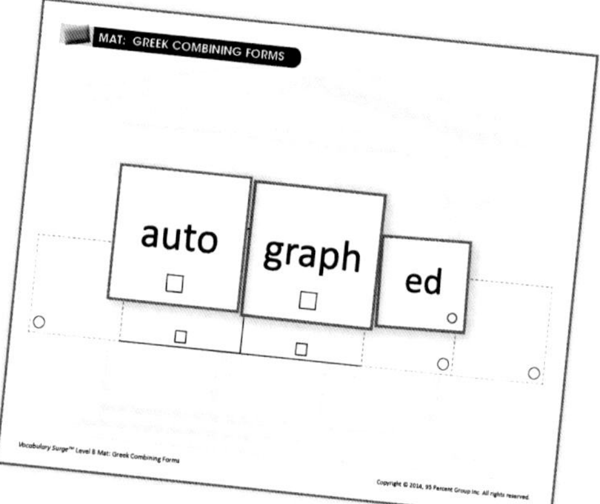


- Let's review your word.
- Where did you place the word card ***auto***? On the left large box
- Why did you place it there? Because it is the first Greek Combining Form
- Where is the Greek Combining Form ***graph***? On the second large box to the right of ***auto***
- Why is it placed there? Because it is the second Greek Combining Form
- What word have you built so far? Autograph
- How could you change the word ***autograph*** to ***autographed***? By adding the inflected ending *-**ed***
- Where would you place the card ***-ed***? In the box on the right side of the mat, next to ***graph***
- Why would you place it there? Because it is a inflected ending and the circle on the card matches the circle on the mat
- What word have you built so far? Autographed
- Now change it to build the word ***autographing.***

---

- You will be using this Greek mat and Greek Combining Form cards in the next four lessons.

 

# auto, chron/chrono, gram, graph, mono phon/phone/phono, photo, tele

## DAY 1 • Introduce Greek Combining Forms

### UNCOVER THE MEANING

MATERIALS
- Days 1 & 2 Recording Sheet

**Introduce *graph, phon/phone/phono,* and *photo; tele***

**DIRECTIONS** Pair students and distribute the Days 1 & 2 Recording Sheet. Model the first completed example. After students have completed the first two columns, ask them to share what they wrote. Then provide the Certified Definition. Explain that understanding parts of words, such as Greek combining forms, can help students uncover the meaning of many words.

**I'm going to model using my detective skills to figure out what the underlined word parts mean.**

- I'll use the other words in the sentences to develop a Working Definition of a word part.
- Listen as I read the first set of two sentences.
  1. The ***photograph*** of the sunset glowed with bright colors.
  2. The ***photographer*** used extra lamps at night to take the best pictures.
- In **Column 1**, I record the clue words glowed, bright, and lamps that help me understand the meaning of ***photo***.
- I think that ***photo*** means sunlight or lamp light. This is my Working Definition, which I record in **Column 2**.
- In **Column 3**, I write the Certified Definition of ***photo***: light.

**Now it's your turn.**

- With your partner, fill in the remaining spaces on the Days 1 & 2 Recording Sheet.
- Use your detective skills to figure out what the underlined word parts mean.
- Consider which words or phrases in the sentences provide clues about meaning. Record them in **Column 1**.
- Write a Working Definition in **Column 2**.
- Only complete **Columns 1** and **2** and then wait for the discussion. You will fill in **Column 3** after I provide a Certified Definition.

UNCOVER THE MEANING

| ***photo & graph*** | 1. The photograph of the sunset glowed with bright colors.<br>2. The photographer used extra lamps at night to take the best pictures.<br>3. The graphic image showed a drawing of the International Space Station. | |
|---|---|---|
| **❶ Clue Words for Working Definition** | **❷ Working Definition** | **❸ Certified Definition** |
| ***photo:*** glowed, bright, lamps | sunlight or lamp light | light |
| ***graph:*** picture, drawing | drawing, image | written or drawn |

| ***phon/phono / phone & tele*** | 1. The phonograph plays music using a disc with special grooves etched into it.<br>2. Telephones are used to speak to people who are not nearby.<br>3. In the old days, people sent messages far across the country using a telegraph. | |
|---|---|---|
| **❶ Clue Words for Working Definition** | **❷ Working Definition** | **❸ Certified Definition** |
| ***phon/phono/phone:*** plays music, speak | noise | sound |
| ***tele:*** not nearby, messages, far | away | far, distant |

# DAY 2 • Deepen the Meaning

## CHECK MEANING

MATERIALS
- Pocket chart, document camera, or PowerPoint™
- Days 1 & 2 Recording Sheet
- Cards:
  Teacher: graph, photo, tele, y
  Student: Greek Combining Forms: graph, phono, phone, photo, tele
  Suffix: er

**DIRECTIONS** Using the **Cards** and **Mat**, confirm that students understand how the meaning of the word evolves as more parts are added.

**I DO**

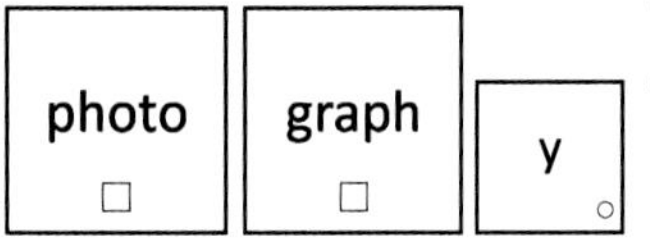


- The Greek combining form ***graph*** means written or drawn.
- The suffix **-*y*** means characterized by.
- Adding **-*y*** to ***photo*** and ***graph*** spells the word ***photography***. The combination of word parts means the process of recording images using light.
- Now, I'm going to use my knowledge of the word to answer the question.

1. What does it mean when I say that the college offers ***photography*** classes? It has classes to teach the process of recording images using light.

**WE DO**

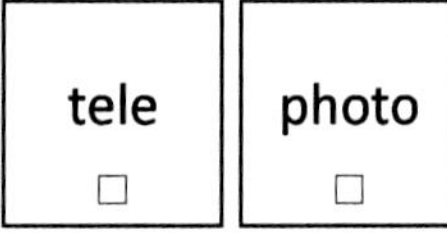


- The Greek combining form ***tele*** means far or distant.
- Adding ***tele*** to ***photo*** spells the word ***telephoto***. The combination of word parts means a lens to take photographs of objects far away.
- Listen to me use the word ***telephoto*** in a question and we will use our knowledge of its parts to figure out the answer.

2. What does it mean when Clayton uses a ***telephoto*** lens to film the moon? He's taking a picture of something far away.

**YOU DO** Use your **Cards** and **Mats** to complete the chart on the **Days 1 & 2 Recording Sheet**.

| Greek Combining Forms | Certified Definition |
|---|---|
| graph | written, drawn |
| phon/phone/phono | sound |
| photo | light |
| tele | far, distant |
| **Suffixes** | **Certified Definition** |
| -er | one who does |
| -ic | having the characteristic of |
| -y | inclined to |
| **Inflected Ending** | **Certified Definition** |
| -ed | past |
| -ing | present |

CHECK MEANING

**DIRECTIONS** Build the words with the Cards and Mat. Describe how adding new parts changes the meaning of the words.

| Word | Greek Combining Form | Greek Combining Form | Suffix |
|---|---|---|---|
| phonograph | phono: sound | graph: written or drawn | |
| Meaning: | a machine that plays music using discs with etched grooves | | |
| photographer | photo: light | graph: written or drawn | er: one who does |
| Meaning: | a person who uses a camera to take pictures | | |
| telegraph | tele: far, distant | graph: written or drawn | |
| Meaning: | a device that sends messages in code over long distances | | |
| telephone | tele: far, distant | phone: sound | |
| Meaning: | a device for speaking with someone who is not nearby | | |

# graph, phon/phone/phono, photo, tele

## DAY 3 • Word Multiplier

### WORD MULTIPLIER

**Build words with *graph, phon/phone/phono, photo,* and *tele***

**DIRECTIONS** Students work together to build words using their **Cards** and **Mats**.

MATERIALS
- Day 3 Recording Sheet
- Notebook paper
- Greek Mat
- Cards:
  Greek Combining Forms: graph, gram, phon, phono, phone, photo, tele
  Inflected Endings: ing
  Suffixes: er, ic, y
  Connecting Letter: o

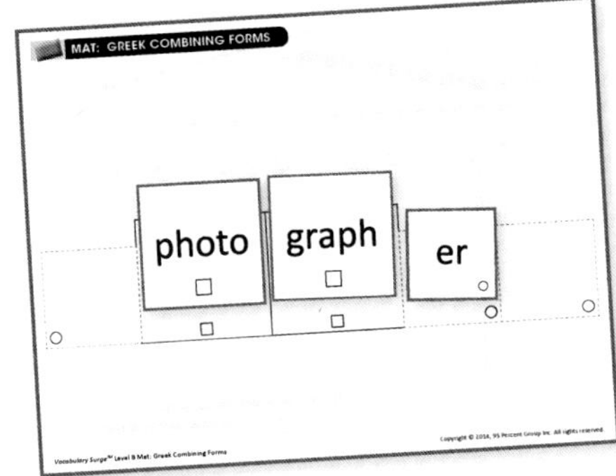


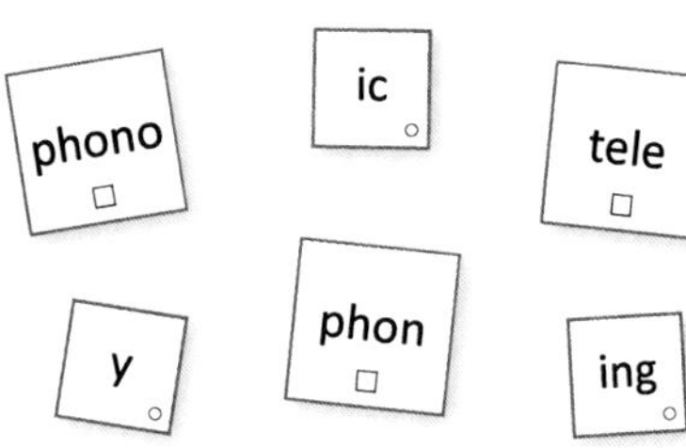


**I DO** Watch me combine **Cards** to build a word.

- I select cards ***photo, graph,*** and ***er***.
- I place the Greek combining form ***photo*** in the large box on the left side of the mat, matching the square on the mat to the one on the card.
- I place the Greek combining form ***graph*** in the large box to the right of ***photo***, matching the square on the mat to the one on the card.
- I place the suffix ***-er*** in the box to the right of ***graph***.
- I have built the word ***photographer***.

**WE DO** Let me try another.

- I choose the cards ***phono, graph,*** and ***ic***.
- Where should I place the Greek combining form ***phono***? In the box on the left side of the mat
- Why do we place it here? Because it is a Greek combining form
- Where shall I place the Greek combining form ***graph***? In the box to the right of ***phono***
- Why do we place it here? Because it is a Greek combining form
- Where shall I place suffix ***-ic***? In the box to the right of ***graph***
- Look at the example on your **Day 3 Recording Sheet** to see how to write the parts of ***phonographic*** and the whole word. ***Phono*** means sound, ***graph*** means written or drawn, and ***-ic*** means having the characteristic of.
- When we put these word parts together, ***phonographic*** means a way of writing based on sound.
- What part of speech is ***phonographic*** and how do you know? Adjective; it describes a way of writing

**WORD MULTIPLIER**

| | Word Parts | Word | Part of Speech |
|---|---|---|---|
| 1. | phono+graph+ic | phonographic | adjective |
| | Write the Meaning: | a way of writing based on sound | |
| 2. | graph+o+phone | graphophone | noun |
| | Write the Meaning: | a device for playing sounds from records | |
| 3. | photo+graph+y | photography | noun |
| | Write the Meaning: | the process of recording images using light | |
| 4. | tele+graph+ic | telegraphic | adjective |
| | Write the Meaning: | a type of coded message sent over long distances using a telegraph | |
| 5. | tele+gram | telegram | noun |
| | Write the Meaning: | a message sent by telegraph | |
| 6. | tele+photo | telephoto | adjective |
| | Write the Meaning: | a type of lens to take photographs of objects far away | |

**YOU DO** Use your **Cards** and **Mats** to build more words. Complete the **Day 3 Recording Sheet** with your partner. Write additional words on notebook paper. We will review the words when you have finished.

**Possible Words:**
graph, graphing, graphic, phonograph, photo, photograph, photographer, photographic, photographing, telegraph, telegraphing

## DAY 4 • Demonstrate Meaning

### BUILD MEANING

MATERIALS
• Whiteboards
• Markers

**DIRECTIONS** Complete the I Do and We Do whole class, and pair students to work on the You Do. Students can record their ideas on small whiteboards. Ask a few pairs to share their work with the class.

**I DO** Listen to me demonstrate understanding of the meaning of the Greek combining form ***graph***.

- The first word is ***graphic***. We learned that ***graphic*** means something that is written or drawn. I'm going to think of examples of things that are a ***graphic***.
  - The ***graphic*** on the map shows the location of lakes.
  - Eliza draws a ***graphic*** of the school's hallways for the new girl.
- The second word is ***photograph***, which means an image created using light. I'm going to think of examples of things that might be recorded by a ***photograph***.
  - When Yolanda blows out the candles on her cake, her grandma takes a ***photograph***.
  - Mom often looks at the ***photograph*** of her parents.

**WE DO** Let's try the next one together with the Greek combining form ***phono***.

- The first word is ***phonograph***. The Greek combining form ***phono*** means sound, and the Greek combining form ***graph*** means written or drawn. ***Phonograph*** means a device that plays music using etched discs. Grandpa's ***phonograph*** played old records that made the songs sound scratchy.
  - Who might own a ***phonograph***?
- The second word is ***telephone***. The Greek combining form ***tele*** means far or distant, and the Greek combining form ***phone*** means sound. ***Telephone*** means a device used to speak with someone who is not nearby.
  - Name reasons you have made a call on a ***telephone***.

**PROMPT IDEAS** ***phonograph***
- parents
- grandparents
- museum

**PROMPT IDEAS** ***telephone***
- to call a friend
- to call parents
- to call a movie theatre

**YOU DO** Now it's your turn. Work with a partner, and record your ideas on a whiteboard so you're ready to share with the class. You'll have five minutes to think of examples for two words that contain the Greek combining forms ***photo*** and ***tele***.

- The two words are ***photographer*** and ***telephoto***.
  - What does the Greek combining form ***photo*** mean? Light What does the Greek combining form ***graph*** mean? Written or drawn What does the suffix ***-er*** mean? One who does What does ***photographer*** mean? A person who uses a camera to create images using light
  - What does the Greek combining form ***tele*** mean? Far, distant What does the Greek combining form ***photo*** mean? Light What does ***telephoto*** mean? A lens for taking pictures of objects far away
  - Think of an example of a ***photographer***. It may be someone you know or a time when you were one.
  - Think of an example of a picture you might take with a ***telephoto*** lens.

**PROMPT IDEAS** ***photographer***
- my mom
- our teacher
- school photographer

**PROMPT IDEAS** ***telephoto***
- moon
- airplane in the sky
- bird in tree

 

auto, chron/chrono, gram, mono

# DAY 5 • Introduce Greek Combining Forms

## UNCOVER THE MEANING

### Introduce *auto, chron/chrono, gram,* and *mono*

MATERIALS
- Days 5 & 6 Recording Sheet

**DIRECTIONS** Pair students and distribute the **Days 5 & 6 Recording Sheet**. Model the first completed example. After students have completed the first two columns, ask them to share what they wrote. Then provide the Certified Definition. Explain that understanding parts of words, such as Greek combining forms, can help students uncover the meaning of many words.

**I'm going to model using my detective skills to figure out what the underlined word parts mean.**

- I'll use the other words in the sentences to develop a Working Definition of a word part.
- Listen as I read the first set of two sentences.

    1. The ***chronogram*** for the year 1750 was carved by George Washington on the Natural Bridge.

    2. Keri's aunt was sick for a long time; she had a ***chronic*** illness.

- In **Column 1**, I record the clues 1750 and long time that help me understand the meaning of ***chron/ chrono***.
- I think that ***chron/chrono*** means time or year. This is my Working Definition, which I record in **Column 2**.
- In **Column 3**, I will write the Certified Definition of ***chron/chrono***: time.

**Now it's your turn.**

- With your partner, fill in the remaining spaces on the **Days 5 & 6 Recording Sheet**.
- Use your detective skills to figure out what the underlined word parts mean.
- Consider which words or phrases in the sentences provide clues about meaning. Record them in **Column 1**.
- Write a Working Definition in **Column 2**.
- Only complete **Columns 1** and **2** and then wait for the discussion. You will fill in **Column 3** after I provide a Certified Definition.

UNCOVER THE MEANING

| ***auto & chron/chrono*** | 1. The chronogram for the year 1750 was carved by George Washington on the Natural Bridge.<br>2. Keri's aunt was sick for a long time; she had a chronic illness.<br>3. The author signed an autograph of his name using a red pen. | |
|---|---|---|
| **❶Clue Words for Working Definition** | **❷Working Definition** | **❸Certified Definition** |
| ***chron/chrono:*** 1750, long time | time or year | time |
| ***auto:*** his name | self or owner | self, same |

| ***gram & mono*** | 1. Joshua's initials were sewn on his backpack as a monogram.<br>2. The letters ***s*** and ***h*** work together to make the phonogram sound **/sh/**.<br>3. The monograph about tigers was written in the author's own handwriting. | |
|---|---|---|
| **❶Clue Words for Working Definition** | **❷Working Definition** | **❸Certified Definition** |
| ***gram:*** initials, letters | writing | written or drawn |
| ***mono:*** first, the author's own | single | one |

# DAY 6 • Deepen the Meaning

## CHECK MEANING

**MATERIALS**
- Pocket chart, document camera, or PowerPoint™
- Days 5 & 6 Recording Sheet
- Cards:
  Teacher: auto, graph, ic
  Student: Greek Combining Forms: chrono, gram, mono, phono, tele

**DIRECTIONS** Using the **Cards** and **Mat**, confirm that students understand how the meaning of the word evolves as more parts are added.

**I DO**

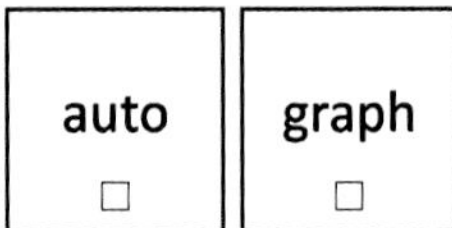


- The combining form ***auto*** means one.
- Adding ***auto*** to ***graph*** spells the word ***autograph***. The combination of word parts means someone's signature or name.
- Now I'm going to use my knowledge of the word to answer the question.
  1. What does it mean when you say the artist signs her ***autograph*** on the painting? She writes her name.

**WE DO**

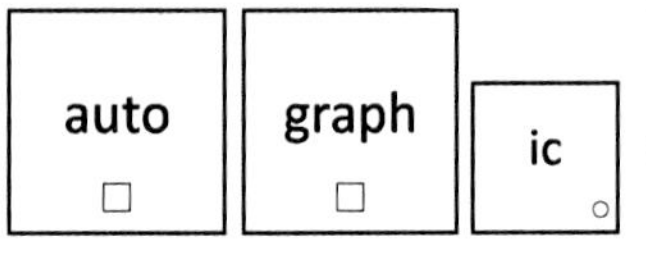


- The suffix ***-ic*** means related to.
- Adding ***-ic*** to ***autograph*** spells the word ***autographic***. The combination of word parts means related to someone's signature or name.
- Listen to me use the word ***autographic*** in a question and we will use our knowledge of its parts to figure out the answer.
  2. What does it mean when the computer prints a name in an ***autographic*** way? It prints in a way that looks like someone's signature.

**YOU DO** Use your **Cards** and **Mats** to complete the chart on the **Days 5 & 6 Recording Sheet**.

| Greek Combining Forms | Certified Definition |
|---|---|
| auto | self, same |
| chron/chrono | time |
| gram/graph | written, drawn |
| mono | one |
| phono | sound |
| tele | far, distant |
| **Suffix** | **Certified Definition** |
| -ar | relating to |
| -ic | having the characteristic of |
| -ile | relating to, suited for, or capable of |

**CHECK MEANING**

**DIRECTIONS** Build the words with the Cards and Mat. Describe how adding new parts changes the meaning of the words.

| Word | Greek Combining Form | Greek Combining Form |
|---|---|---|
| monogram | mono: one | gram: written or drawn |
| Meaning: | the initials of someone's name | |
| phonogram | phono: sound | gram: written or drawn |
| Meaning: | the letter, or letters, that represent a speech sound | |
| telegram | tele: far, distant | gram: written or drawn |
| Meaning: | a message sent by a telegraph | |
| chronogram | chrono: time | gram: written or drawn |
| Meaning: | an inscription representing a date | |

# auto, chron/chrono, gram, mono

## DAY 7 • Word Multiplier

### WORD MULTIPLIER

**Build words with *auto, chron/chrono, gram,* and *mono***

**DIRECTIONS** Students work together to build words using their **Cards** and **Mats**.

MATERIALS
- Day 7 Recording Sheet
- Notebook paper
- Greek Mat
- Cards: Greek Combining Forms: auto, chron, chrono, gram, graph, mono, phono, tele Suffixes: ar, ic, ile Connecting Letters: m

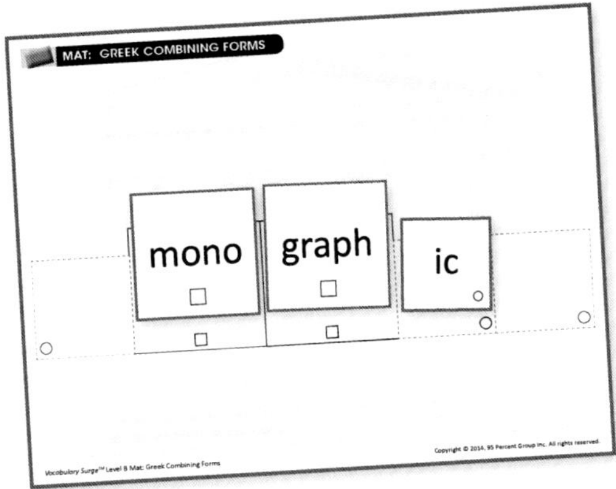


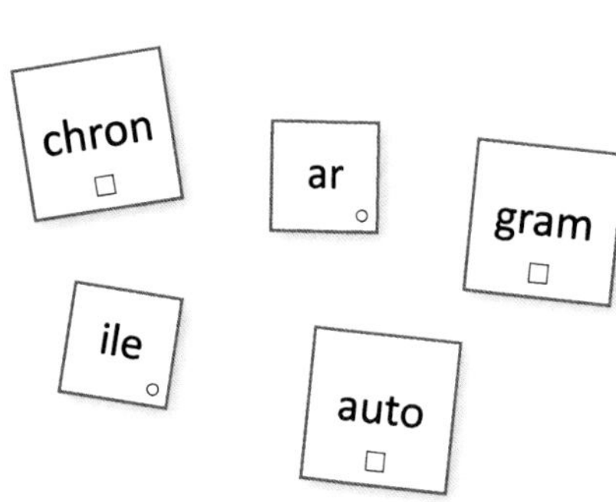


**WE DO** Let's combine **Cards** to build a word.

- I select cards ***mono, graph,*** and ***ic***.
- Where shall I place the Greek combining form ***mono***? On the left side of the mat
- Why do we place it here? Because it is a Greek combining form
- Where shall I place the Greek combining form ***graph***? In the box to the right of ***mono***
- Why do we place it here? Because it is a Greek combining form
- Finally, where shall I place the suffix ***-ic***? To the right of ***graph***, matching the circle on the mat to the one on the card
- What word have we built? Monographic
- What is the definition of ***monographic***? Relating to a written account on a single topic

**WORD MULTIPLIER**

| | Word Parts | Word | Part of Speech |
|---|---|---|---|
| 1. | tele+graph | telegraph | adjective |
| | Write the Meaning: | a device of coded messages sent over long distances using a telegraph | |
| 2. | chrono+graph+ic | chronographic | adjective |
| | Write the Meaning: | relating to writing that describes a date | |
| 3. | chrono+gram | chronogram | noun |
| | Write the Meaning: | a timepiece that measures brief intervals of time | |
| 4. | mono+gram | monogram | noun |
| | Write the Meaning: | the initials of someone's name | |
| 5. | mono+graph | monograph | noun |
| | Write the Meaning: | a written account of a single topic | |
| 6. | tele+gram | telegram | noun |
| | Write the Meaning: | a message sent by a telegraph | |

**YOU DO** Use your **Cards** and **Mats** to build more words. Complete the **Day 7 Recording Sheet** with your partner. Write additional words on notebook paper.

**Possible Words:**
auto, chronic, chronograph, gram, graph, graphic

## DAY 8 • Demonstrate Meaning

### BUILD MEANING

MATERIALS
• Whiteboards
• Markers

**DIRECTIONS** Complete the I Do and We Do whole class, and pair students to work on the You Do. Students can record their ideas on small whiteboards. Ask a few pairs to share their work with the class.

**I DO** Listen to me demonstrate understanding of the meaning of the Greek combining form ***chron***.

- The first word is ***chronic***. The theatre owner was frustrated by the ***chronic*** issue of leaks in the ceiling. I'm going to think of examples of things that might be ***chronic***.
  - Jessie has a ***chronic*** sore throat this winter.
  - My little sister has the ***chronic*** problem of losing her shoes.
- The second word is ***chronograph***, which means writing that describes a date. I'm going to think of examples of ***chronographs***.
  - When we write out the words, "August 1, 2014," we have written a ***chronograph***.
  - The ***chronograph*** for my birth year may be written in Roman numerals.

**WE DO** Let's try the next one together with the Greek combining form ***auto***.

- The first word is ***autograph***. The Greek combining form ***auto*** means self or same, and the Greek combining form ***graph*** means written or drawn. Kacey needed her mom's ***autograph*** on the permission slip.
  - Name something that needs or has an ***autograph***.

**PROMPT IDEAS** ***autograph***
- painting
- sculpture
- book

- The second word is ***automotive***. The Greek combining form ***auto*** means self or same, the Latin root ***mot*** means move, and the suffix ***-ive*** means showing a quality. ***Automotive*** means relating to a vehicle powered by a motor.
  - Name a type of ***automotive*** part.

**PROMPT IDEAS** ***automotive***
- headlights
- windshield wipers
- seatbelts

**YOU DO** Now it's your turn. Work with a partner, and record your ideas on a whiteboard so you're ready to share with the class. You'll have five minutes to think of examples for two words that contain the Greek combining form ***gram***.

- The two words are ***monogram*** and ***telegram***.
  - What does the Greek combining form ***mono*** mean? One What does the Greek combining form ***gram*** mean? Written or drawn What does ***monogram*** mean? The initials of someone's name
  - Think of an example of something that might have a ***monogram***.
  - What does the Greek combining form ***tele*** mean? Distant or far What does the Greek combining form ***gram*** mean? Written or drawn What does ***telegram*** mean? A message sent by a telegraph
  - Think of an example of a message someone might have sent in a ***telegram***.

**PROMPT IDEAS** ***monogram***
- purse
- backpack
- pillow case

**PROMPT IDEAS** ***telegram***
- Help!
- Come quickly!
- Meet me

# auto, chron/chrono, gram, graph, mono, phon/phone/phono, photo, tele

## DAY 9 • Review What You Learned

### STEP 1 REVIEW THE MEANING

**Review *auto, chron/chrono, gram, graph, mono, phon/phone/phono, photo,* and *tele***

MATERIALS
- Word parts projected on document camera, overhead projector, or PowerPoint™

**DIRECTIONS** Display the morphemes so students can see them, and ask for the Certified Definition of each one.

**When I show you the word parts, think about the Certified Definitions we discussed as you prepare to answer.**

| Greek Combining Form | Certified Definition | Greek Combining Form | Certified Definition |
|---|---|---|---|
| **graph** | written or drawn | **auto** | self, same |
| **phon/phone/phono** | sound | **chron/chrono** | time |
| **photo** | light | **gram** | written or drawn |
| **tele** | far, distant | **mono** | one |

### STEP 2 CHECK MEANING

MATERIALS
- Day 9 Recording Sheet

**DIRECTIONS** Read the following sentence to check that students understand the meanings of ***auto, chron/chrono, gram, graph, mono, phon/phone/phono, photo,*** and ***tele***. Model the first sentence for students using the We Do step, below.

**WE DO** As I read this sentence, think about the Certified Definitions of the Greek combining form that fits the blank.

1. I found the records to play on Grandpa's __________graph.

- Which Greek combining form do you think fits on the line? Phono
- What is the new word? Phonograph
- What do you think the word ***phonograph*** means? A device that plays music using etched discs

**YOU DO** Complete the rest of the sentences on the **Day 9 Recording Sheet** with your partner to find the Greek combining form that best fits on the line. Record the new words and their meanings.

CHECK MEANING

1. I found the records to play on Grandpa's phono **graph**. phonograph
   Meaning: a device that plays music using etched discs
2. He used a **tele** photo lens to take pictures of the animals. telephoto
   Meaning: a type of lens to take photographs of objects far away
3. I call my aunt on the tele **phone** each week. telephone
   Meaning: a device for speaking with people who are not nearby
4. The flash on my camera helps my **photo** graph turn out clearly. photograph
   Meaning: an image created using light
5. I asked the famous dancer for her auto **graph**. autograph
   Meaning: a person's own signature
6. Erin had her mono **gram** sewn onto her purse. monogram
   Meaning: the initials of someone's name

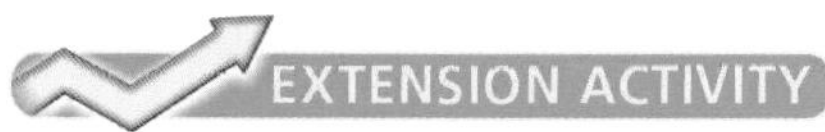

EXTENSION ACTIVITY

Students write two sentences with missing Greek combining forms to challenge the class.

auto, chron/chrono, gram, graph, mono, phon/phone/phono, photo, tele

# DAY 10 • 2nd Review Day

## STEP 1 MAKE CONNECTIONS

*MATERIALS*
- *Notebook paper*

**DIRECTIONS** Students pair up to write sentences with either one or two of the words that are provided.

**I am going to model how to use two words containing this week's Greek combining forms in a meaningful sentence. The words are *photographed* and *monogram*.**

- I ***photographed*** the ***monogram*** on the old flag.
- It is your turn to write five more sentences using the words on the top of the recording sheet.
- Sentences with two words get two points and sentences with one word get one point.

MAKE CONNECTIONS

yourself to write sentences with two of the words from the list.

| Words | | |
|---|---|---|
| autograph | graphic | photographer |
| automobile | graphophone | photography |
| chronic | monogram | telegram |
| chronogram | monograph | telegraphic |
| chronograph | photograph | telephoto |
| chronographer | photographed | televised |

1. The football game was not televised.
2. Mom's towels in the guest bathroom had a monogram with the letter "m."
3. Her description of the sunset was graphic.
4. Since the telephone was invented, there is little need for sending a telegram.
5. The photographer used a telephoto lens to photograph the butterfly.

## STEP 2 CHALLENGE: MORPHEME MADNESS

*MATERIALS*
- *Day 10 Recording Sheet*
- *Notebook paper*
- *Greek Mat*
- *Cards listed in the table below*

**DIRECTIONS** Students pair up to use **Cards** and **Mats** to build words. They also record all of the words they build and the words' definitions.

| Word Parts | Cards |
|---|---|
| **Greek Combining Forms** | auto, chron, chrono, gram, graph, mono, phon, phone, phono, photo, tele |
| **Inflected Endings** | ed, ing |
| **Prefixes** | n/a |
| **Suffixes** | ar, er, ic, ile, ion |
| **Connecting Letter** | o |

**Now it's your turn to build words.**

- First, find a partner.
- Use the **Cards** and **Mats** to build real words.
- Record the words and their definition on a separate sheet of paper.

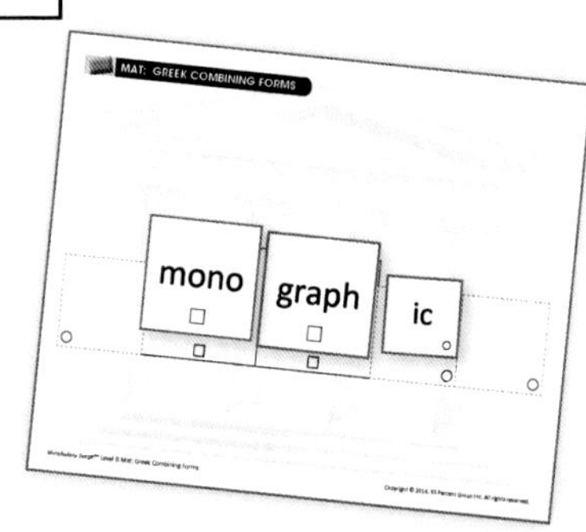


 

# biblio, bio, geo, hydr/hydra/hydro, lith/litho, micro, sphere

## DAY 1 • Introduce Greek Combining Forms

### UNCOVER THE MEANING

MATERIALS
• Days 1 & 2 Recording Sheet

#### Introduce *biblio, lith/litho,* and *micro*

**DIRECTIONS** Pair students and distribute the Days 1 & 2 Recording Sheet. Model the first completed example. After students have completed the first two columns, ask them to share what they wrote. Then provide the Certified Definition. Explain that understanding parts of words, such as Greek combining forms, can help students uncover the meaning of many words.

**I'm going to model using my detective skills to figure out what the underlined word parts mean.**

- I'll use the other words in the sentences to develop a Working Definition of a word part.
- Listen as I read the first set of two sentences.
  1. The list of books used in researching the report was printed in the ***biblio**graphy*.
  2. The ***biblio**grapher* collected all the article's sources.
- In **Column 1**, I record the clue words list of books and sources that help me understand the meaning of ***biblio***.
- I think that ***biblio*** means book. This is my Working Definition, which I record in **Column 2**.
- In **Column 3**, I write the Certified Definition of ***biblio***: book.

**Now it's your turn.**

- With your partner, fill in the remaining spaces on the Days 1 & 2 Recording Sheet.
- Use your detective skills to figure out what the underlined word parts mean.
- Consider which words or phrases in the sentences provide clues about meaning. Record them in **Column 1**.
- Write a Working Definition in **Column 2**.
- Only complete **Columns 1** and **2** and then wait for the discussion. You will fill in **Column 3** after I provide a Certified Definition.

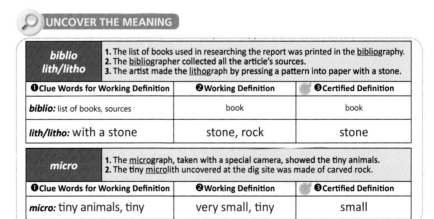

UNCOVER THE MEANING

| *biblio* *lith/litho* | 1. The list of books used in researching the report was printed in the bibliography. 2. The bibliographer collected all the article's sources. 3. The artist made the lithograph by pressing a pattern into paper with a stone. | |
|---|---|---|
| ❶ Clue Words for Working Definition | ❷ Working Definition | ❸ Certified Definition |
| *biblio:* list of books, sources | book | book |
| *lith/litho:* with a stone | stone, rock | stone |

| *micro* | 1. The micrograph, taken with a special camera, showed the tiny animals. 2. The tiny microlith uncovered at the dig site was made of carved rock. | |
|---|---|---|
| ❶ Clue Words for Working Definition | ❷ Working Definition | ❸ Certified Definition |
| *micro:* tiny animals, tiny | very small, tiny | small |

# DAY 2 • Deepen the Meaning

## CHECK MEANING

**DIRECTIONS** Using the **Cards** and **Mat**, confirm that students understand how the meaning of the word evolves as more parts are added.

**MATERIALS**
- Pocket chart, document camera, or PowerPoint™
- Days 1 & 2 Recording Sheet
- Cards: Teacher: graph, lith, litho, mono Student: Greek Combining Forms: biblio, graph, micro, phone, scope Suffixes: er, y

**I DO**

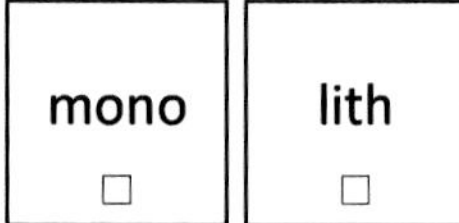


- The Greek combining form ***mono*** means one.
- Adding ***lith*** to ***mono*** spells the word ***monolith***. The combination of word parts means one stone, often in the shape of an obelisk or column.
- Now, I'm going to use my knowledge of the word to answer the question.

1. What does it mean when I say that the huge ***monolith*** stands alone on top of the hill? It is one stone on top of the hill.

**WE DO**

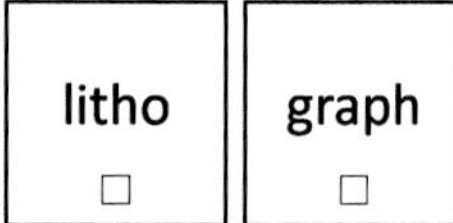


- The Greek combining form ***graph*** means written or drawn.
- Adding ***litho*** to ***graph*** spells the word ***lithograph***. The combination of word parts means an image produced using a design on stone or metal.
- Listen to me use the word ***lithograph*** in a question and we will use our knowledge of its parts to figure out the answer.

2. What does it mean when the art student makes a print with a ***lithograph***? He's making a picture with a design carved on stone or metal.

**YOU DO** Use your **Cards** and **Mats** to complete the chart on the **Days 1 & 2 Recording Sheet**.

| Greek Combining Forms | Certified Definition |
|---|---|
| biblio | book |
| graph | written, drawn |
| lith/litho | stone |
| micro | small |
| mono | one |
| phone | sound |
| scope | to watch or see |
| **Suffixes** | **Certified Definition** |
| -er | one who does |
| -ic | having the characteristic of |
| -y | characterized by |

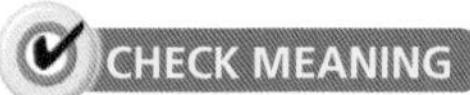


meaning of the words.

| Word | Greek Combining Form | Greek Combining Form | Suffix |
|---|---|---|---|
| bibliography | biblio: book | graph: written or drawn | y: characterized by |
| Meaning: | a list of books or articles, often those used as sources for a report | | |
| bibliographer | biblio: book | graph: written or drawn | er: one who does |
| Meaning: | a person who compiles, or writes, bibliographies | | |
| microphone | micro: small | phone: sound | |
| Meaning: | a device that makes sounds louder | | |
| microscope | micro: small | scope: to watch or see | |
| Meaning: | an instrument for magnifying objects too small to be seen with the eye | | |

# biblio, lith/litho, micro

## DAY 3 • Word Multiplier

### WORD MULTIPLIER

**Build words with *biblio, lith/litho,* and *micro***

MATERIALS
- Day 3 Recording Sheet
- Notebook paper
- Greek Mat
- Cards:
  Greek Combining Forms: biblio, graph, lith, litho, micro, mono, phone
  Suffixes: er, ic, y

**DIRECTIONS** Students work together to build words using their **Cards** and **Mats**.

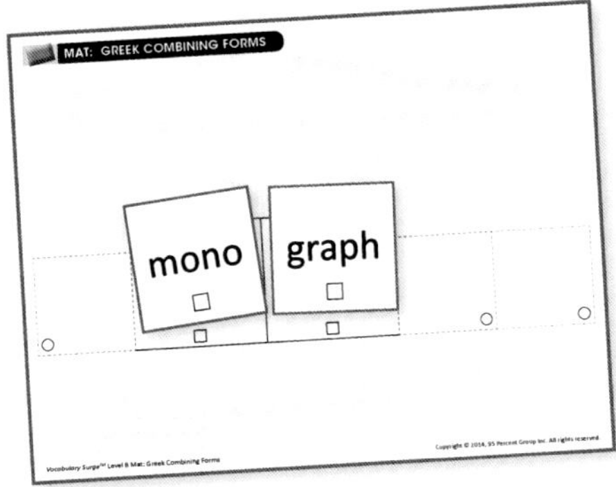


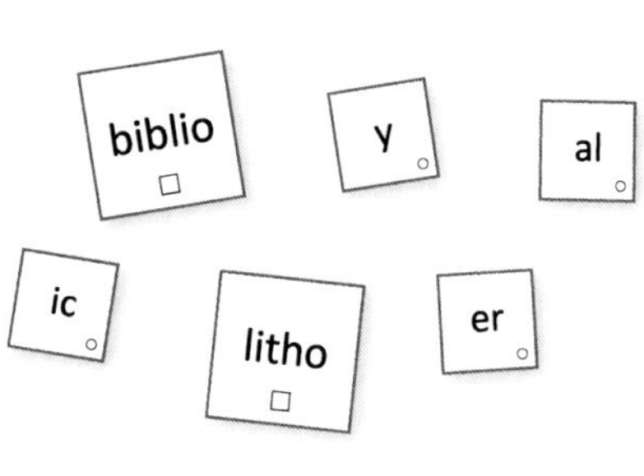


**I DO** Watch me combine **Cards** to build a word.
- I select cards ***mono*** and ***graph***.
- I place the Greek combining form ***mono*** in the large box on the left side of the mat, matching the circle on the mat to the one on the card.
- I place the Greek combining form ***graph*** in the large box to the right of ***mono***, matching the circle on the mat to the one on the card.
- I have built the word ***monograph***.

**WE DO** Let me try another.
- I choose the cards ***biblio, graph,*** and ***er***.
- Where should I place the Greek combining form ***biblio***? In the box on the left side of the mat
- Why do we place it here? Because it is a Greek combining form
- Where shall I place the Greek combining form ***graph***? In the box to the right of ***biblio***
- Why do we place it here? Because it is a Greek combining form
- Where shall I place the suffix ***-er***? In the box to the right of ***graph***
- Look at the example on your **Day 3 Recording Sheet** to see how to write the parts of ***bibliographer*** and the whole word. ***Biblio*** means book, ***graph*** means written or drawn, and ***-er*** means one who does.
- When we put these word parts together, ***bibliographer*** means a person who compiles or writes bibliographies.
- What part of speech is ***bibliographer*** and how do you know? Noun; person

**WORD MULTIPLIER**

| | Word Parts | Word | Part of Speech |
|---|---|---|---|
| 1. | biblio+graph+er | bibliographer | noun |
| | Write the Meaning: | a person who creates bibliographies | |
| 2. | biblio+graph+ic | bibliographic | adjective |
| | Write the Meaning: | relating to a bibliography | |
| 3. | litho+graph+er | lithographer | noun |
| | Write the Meaning: | a person who produces lithographs using ink, paper, and an image on stone or a metal plate | |
| 4. | micro+graph | micrograph | noun |
| | Write the Meaning: | an image from a microscope | |
| 5. | micro+lith+ic | microlithic | adjective |
| | Write the Meaning: | relating to a small stone tool | |
| 6. | mono+lith+ic | monolithic | adjective |
| | Write the Meaning: | related to a monolith | |

**YOU DO** Use your **Cards** and **Mats** to build more words. Complete the **Day 3 Recording Sheet** with your partner. Write additional words on notebook paper. We will review the words when you have finished.

**Possible Words:** lithograph, lithographic, microlith, monograph

# DAY 4 • Demonstrate Meaning

## BUILD MEANING

MATERIALS
- Whiteboards
- Markers

**DIRECTIONS** Complete the I Do and We Do whole class, and pair students to work on the You Do. Students can record their ideas on small whiteboards. Ask a few pairs to share their work with the class.

**I DO** Listen to me demonstrate understanding of the meaning of the Greek combining form ***biblio***.

- The first word is ***biblio**graphy*. We learned that ***biblio**graphy* means a list of books or articles, often those used as sources for a report.
- I'm going to think of places I can find a ***biblio**graphy*.
  - There is a ***biblio**graphy* of funny limericks on the internet.
  - Books often contain a ***biblio**graphy* of resources the author used for research.
- The second word is ***biblio**grapher*. We learned that ***biblio**grapher* means a person who compiles or writes bibliographies. I'm going to think of examples of people who might be a ***biblio**grapher*.
  - The college professor works as a ***biblio**grapher* during holidays.
  - A ***biblio**grapher* puts together a list of personal histories from camp.

**WE DO** Let's try the next one together with the Greek combining form ***lith***.

- The first word is ***litho**graph*. The Greek combining form ***litho*** means stone, and the Greek combining form ***graph*** means written or drawn. ***Litho**graph* means an image produced using a design on stone or metal.
  - Where might you see an image produced by a ***litho**graph*?

**PROMPT IDEAS** ***litho**graph*
- museum
- wall
- school

- The second word is *mono**lith***. The Greek combining form ***mono*** means one, and the Greek combining form ***litho*** means stone. *mono**lith*** means one stone, often in the shape of an obelisk or column.
  - Name a *mono**lith*** or a place you might see one.

**PROMPT IDEAS** *mono**lith***
- in a city park
- in a park
- on a mountain

**YOU DO** Now it's your turn. Work with a partner, and record your ideas on a whiteboard so you're ready to share with the class. You'll have five minutes to think of examples for two words that contain the Greek combining form ***micro***.

- The two words are ***micro**phone* and ***micro**wave*.
  - What does the Greek combining form ***micro*** mean? Small What does the Greek combining form ***phon*** mean? Sound What does ***micro**phone* mean? A device used to make sounds louder
  - What does the Greek combining form ***micro*** mean? Small What does the Anglo-Saxon word ***wave*** mean? Movement like a beam What does ***micro**wave* mean? A device that heats food using small beams of power
  - Think of a time you saw someone use a ***micro**phone*.
  - Think of an example of a time you might use a ***micro**wave* oven.

**PROMPT IDEAS** ***micro**phone*
- assembly
- concert
- on TV

**PROMPT IDEAS** ***micro**wave*
- heat leftovers
- make popcorn
- heat soup

# bio, geo, hydr/hydra/hydro, sphere

## DAY 5 • Introduce Greek Combining Forms

### UNCOVER THE MEANING

**Introduce *bio, geo, hydr/hydra/hydro,* and *sphere***

MATERIALS
• Days 5 & 6 Recording Sheet

**DIRECTIONS** Pair students and distribute the **Days 5 & 6 Recording Sheet**. Model the first completed example. After students have completed the first two columns, ask them to share what they wrote. Then provide the Certified Definition. Explain that understanding parts of words, such as Greek combining forms, can help students uncover the meaning of many words.

**I'm going to model using my detective skills to figure out what the underlined word parts mean.**

- I'll use the other words in the sentences to develop a Working Definition of a word part.
- Listen as I read the first set of two sentences.

    1. The dome of the ***bio**sphere* created a mini, living version of Earth.
    2. The class was expected to read a ***bio**graphy* about a famous person's life.

- In **Column 1**, I record the clue living version and life that help me understand the meaning of ***bio***.
- I think that ***bio*** means live or life. This is my Working Definition, which I record in **Column 2**.
- In **Column 3**, I will write the Certified Definition of ***bio***: life.

**Now it's your turn.**

- With your partner, fill in the remaining spaces on the **Days 5 & 6 Recording Sheet**.
- Use your detective skills to figure out what the underlined word parts mean.
- Consider which words or phrases in the sentences provide clues about meaning. Record them in **Column 1**.
- Write a Working Definition in **Column 2**.
- Only complete **Columns 1** and **2** and then wait for the discussion. You will fill in **Column 3** after I provide a Certified Definition.

UNCOVER THE MEANING

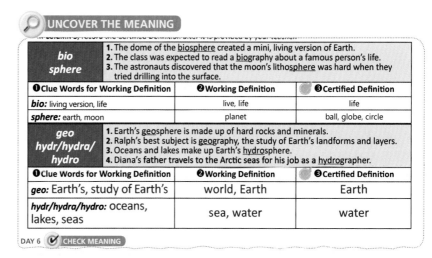

| ***bio sphere*** | 1. The dome of the biosphere created a mini, living version of Earth.<br>2. The class was expected to read a biography about a famous person's life.<br>3. The astronauts discovered that the moon's lithosphere was hard when they tried drilling into the surface. | |
|---|---|---|
| **❶Clue Words for Working Definition** | **❷Working Definition** | **❸Certified Definition** |
| ***bio:*** living version, life | live, life | life |
| ***sphere:*** earth, moon | planet | ball, globe, circle |

| ***geo hydr/hydra/ hydro*** | 1. Earth's geosphere is made up of hard rocks and minerals.<br>2. Ralph's best subject is geography, the study of Earth's landforms and layers.<br>3. Oceans and lakes make up Earth's hydrosphere.<br>4. Diana's father travels to the Arctic seas for his job as a hydrographer. | |
|---|---|---|
| **❶Clue Words for Working Definition** | **❷Working Definition** | **❸Certified Definition** |
| ***geo:*** Earth's, study of Earth's | world, Earth | Earth |
| ***hydr/hydra/hydro:*** oceans, lakes, seas | sea, water | water |

DAY 6 CHECK MEANING

# DAY 6 • Deepen the Meaning

## CHECK MEANING

**MATERIALS**
- Pocket chart, document camera, or PowerPoint™
- Days 5 & 6 Recording Sheet
- Cards:
  Teacher: al, geo, ic, sphere
  Student: Greek Combining Forms: bio, geo, graph, sphere
  Suffixes: er, ic, y

**DIRECTIONS** Using the **Cards** and **Mat**, confirm that students understand how the meaning of the word evolves as more parts are added.

**I DO**

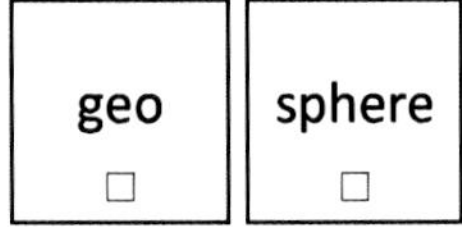


- The combining form ***geo*** means Earth.
- Adding ***geo*** to ***sphere*** spells the word ***geosphere***. The combination of word parts means Earth's circular layers of rock.
- Now I'm going to use my knowledge of the word to answer the question.
  1. What does it mean when you say the ***geosphere*** helps our planet by controlling the mountains, rivers, and minerals? The circular layers of rock help shape the terrain of Earth.

**WE DO**

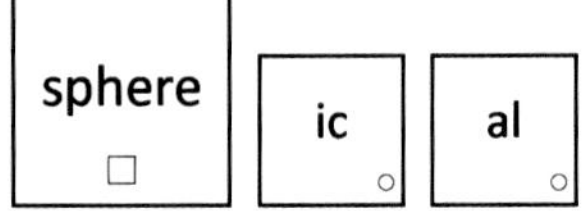


- The suffix ***-ic*** means having the characteristic of, and the suffix ***-al*** means like.
- Adding ***-ic*** and ***-al*** to ***sphere*** spells the word ***spherical***. The combination of word parts means shaped like a ball.
- Listen to me use the word ***spherical*** in a question and we will use our knowledge of its parts to figure out the answer.
  2. What does it mean when we say the melon is ***spherical*** in shape? It is shaped like a ball.

**YOU DO** Use your **Cards** and **Mats** to complete the chart on the **Days 5 & 6 Recording Sheet**.

| Greek Combining Forms | Certified Definition |
|---|---|
| bio | life |
| geo | Earth |
| graph | written, drawn |
| hydr/hydra/hydro | water |
| sphere/spherℯ | ball, globe, circle |
| **Suffixes** | **Certified Definition** |
| -al | like |
| -ate | to make |
| -er | one who does |
| -ic | having the characteristic of |
| -y | characterized by |

**CHECK MEANING**

**DIRECTIONS** Build the words with the Cards and Mat. Describe how adding new parts changes the meaning of the words.

| Word | Greek Combining Form | Greek Combining Form | Suffix |
|---|---|---|---|
| biosphere | bio: life | sphere: ball, globe or circle | |
| Meaning: | an environment with living things | | |
| biographer | bio: life | graph: drawn, written | er: one who does |
| Meaning: | a person who writes about someone else's life | | |
| geography | geo: earth | graph: drawn, written | y: characterized by |
| Meaning: | the study of Earth's landforms | | |
| geospheric | geo: earth | sphere: ball, globe or circle | ic: having the characteristic of |
| Meaning: | related to the geosphere, or rocky, layer surrounding Earth | | |

# bio, geo, hydr/hydra/hydro, sphere

## DAY 7 • Word Multiplier

### WORD MULTIPLIER

**MATERIALS**
- Day 7 Recording Sheet
- Notebook paper
- Greek Mat
- Cards: Greek Combining Forms: bio, geo, graph, hydr, hyrda, hydro, sphere, sphere Suffixes: al, ate, er, ic, y

**Build words with *bio, geo, hydr/hydra/hydro,* and *sphere***

**DIRECTIONS** Students work together to build words using their **Cards** and **Mats**.

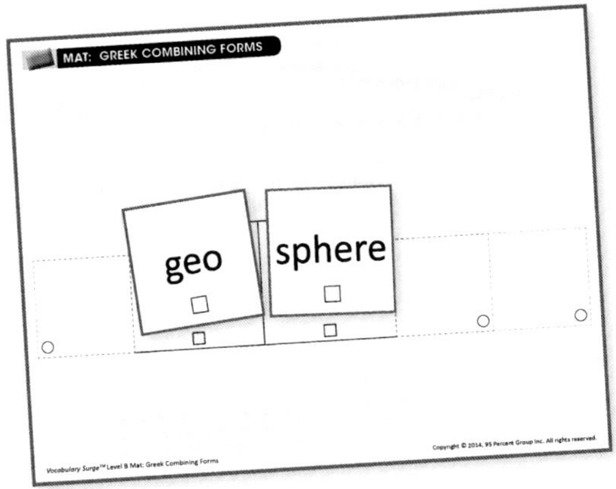


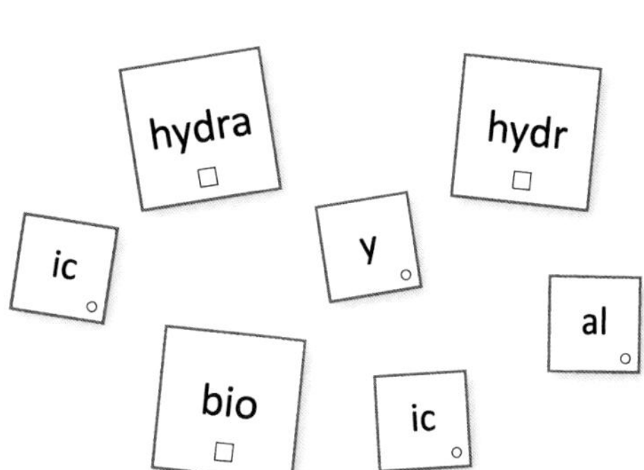


**WE DO** Let's combine **Cards** to build a word.

- I select cards ***geo*** and ***sphere***.
- Where shall I place the Greek combining form ***geo***? On the left side of the mat
- Why do we place it here? Because it is a Greek combining form
- Where shall I place the Greek combining form ***sphere***? In the box to the right of ***geo***
- Why do we place it here? Because it is a Greek combining form
- What word have we built? Geosphere
- What is the definition of ***geosphere***? Earth's circular layers of rock

**YOU DO** Use your **Cards** and **Mats** to build more words. Complete the **Day 7 Recording Sheet** with your partner. Write additional words on notebook paper.

**Possible Words:** hydrate, sphere

**WORD MULTIPLIER**

| | Word Parts | Word | Part of Speech |
|---|---|---|---|
| 1. | bio+graph+y | biography | noun |
| | Write the Meaning: | an account of a person's life | |
| 2. | bio+sphere | biosphere | noun |
| | Write the Meaning: | an environment with living things | |
| 3. | geo+graph+ic | geographic | adjective |
| | Write the Meaning: | relating to the Earth's surface | |
| 4. | geo+sphere | geosphere | noun |
| | Write the Meaning: | the Earth's circular layers of rock | |
| 5. | de+hydr+ate | dehydrate | verb |
| | Write the Meaning: | to cause to lose a lot of water | |
| 6. | spher~~e~~+ic+al | spherical | adjective |
| | Write the Meaning: | having a round form | |

## DAY 8 • Demonstrate Meaning

### BUILD MEANING

MATERIALS
- Whiteboards
- Markers

**DIRECTIONS** Complete the I Do and We Do whole class, and pair students to work on the You Do. Students can record their ideas on small whiteboards. Ask a few pairs to share their work with the class.

**I DO** Listen to me demonstrate understanding of the meaning of the Greek combining form ***hydr***.

- The first word is ***rehydrate***. The runner needs to drink a lot of water to ***rehydrate*** his body. I'm going to think of examples of things that I can ***rehydrate***.
  - I ***rehydrate*** my dying plant with water.
  - The astronauts use water to ***rehydrate*** their food before eating it.
- The second word is ***dehydrates***, which means to cause to lose a lot of water. I'm going to think of examples of something that ***dehydrates***.
  - When a juicy grape ***dehydrates***, it turns into a dried raisin.
  - When making beef jerky, the meat ***dehydrates*** in an oven.

**WE DO** Let's try the next one together with the Greek combining form ***bio***.

- The first word is ***biosphere***. The Greek combining form ***bio*** means life, and the Greek combining form ***sphere*** means ball, globe, or circle. A round aquarium for fish is like a small ***biosphere***.
  - Name something that might live in a ***biosphere***.

**PROMPT IDEAS** ***biosphere***
- butterflies
- plants
- lizards

- The second word is ***biographical***. The Greek combining form ***bio*** means life, the Greek combining form ***graph*** means drawn or written, the suffix ***-ic*** means having the characteristic of, and the suffix ***-al*** means like. ***Biographical*** means related to someone's life story.
  - Name the subject of a ***biographical*** story you've read or might read.

**PROMPT IDEAS** ***biographical***
- Helen Keller
- George Washington
- President Carter

**YOU DO** Now it's your turn. Work with a partner, and record your ideas on a whiteboard so you're ready to share with the class. You'll have five minutes to think of examples for two words that contain the Greek combining form ***sphere***.

- The two words are ***microsphere*** and ***sphere***.
  - What does the Greek combining form ***micro*** mean? Small What does the Greek combining form ***sphere*** mean? Ball, globe, circle What does ***microsphere*** mean? A small ball or globe
  - Think of an example of something that might look like a ***microsphere***.
  - Think of an example of something that might be in the shape of a ***sphere***.

**PROMPT IDEAS** ***microsphere***
- snow globe
- marble
- glass eye

**PROMPT IDEAS** ***sphere***
- globe
- apple
- orange

 

# biblio, bio, geo, hydr/hydra/hydro, lith/litho, micro, sphere

## DAY 9 • Review What You Learned

### STEP 1 REVIEW THE MEANING

**Review *biblio, bio, geo, hydr/hydra/hydro, lith/litho, micro* and *sphere***

MATERIALS
- Word parts projected on document camera, overhead projector, or PowerPoint™

**DIRECTIONS** Display the morphemes so students can see them, and ask for the Certified Definition of each one.

**When I show you the word parts, think about the Certified Definitions we discussed as you prepare to answer.**

| Greek Combining Form | Certified Definition | Greek Combining Form | Certified Definition |
|---|---|---|---|
| **biblio** | book | **bio** | life |
| **lith/litho** | stone | **sphere** | ball, globe, circle |
| **micro** | small | **geo** | Earth |
| **mono** | one | **hydr/hydra/hydro** | water |

### STEP 2 CHECK MEANING

MATERIALS
- Day 9 Recording Sheet

**DIRECTIONS** Read the following sentence to check that students understand the meanings of ***biblio, bio, geo, hydr/hydra/hydro, lith/litho, micro,*** and ***sphere***. Model the first sentence for students using the We Do step, below.

**WE DO** As I read this sentence, think about the Certified Definitions of the Greek combining form that fits the blank.

1. Cass checked the __________**graphy** in the back of the book.

- Which Greek combining form do you think fits on the line? Biblio
- What is the new word? Bibliography
- What do you think the word ***bibliography*** means? A list of books, poems, or articles, often used as sources for a report

**YOU DO** Complete the rest of the sentences on the **Day 9 Recording Sheet** with your partner to find the Greek combining form that best fits on the line. Record the new words and their meanings.

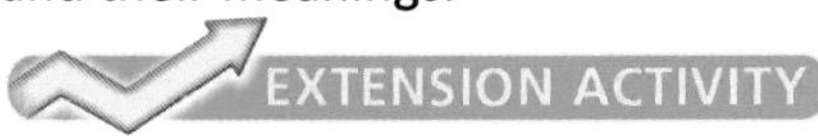

Students write two sentences with missing Greek combining forms to challenge the class.

CHECK MEANING

1. Cass checked the biblio **graphy** in the back of the book. bibliography
   Meaning: a list of books or articles, often those used as sources for a report
2. The **de** hydra **tion** of the apple slices is nearly finished. dehydration
   Meaning: the process of losing a lot of water
3. The granite **mono** lith stood tall in the middle of the hill. monolith
   Meaning: one stone, often in the shape of an obelisk or column
4. Chuck created a clay geo **sphere** representing earth. geosphere
   Meaning: Earth's circular layers of rock
5. The litho **grapher** created art using paper, ink, and a stone pattern. lithographer
   Meaning: a person who produces lithographs using ink, paper, and an image on stone
6. The dome-shaped bio **sphere** was the home of people, plants, and animals. biosphere
   Meaning: part of the Earth's atmosphere that supports life

# biblio, bio, geo, hydr/hydra/hydro, lith/litho, micro, sphere

## DAY 10 • 2nd Review Day

### STEP 1 MAKE CONNECTIONS

MATERIALS
• Notebook paper

**DIRECTIONS** Students pair up to write sentences with either one or two of the words that are provided.

**I am going to model how to use two words containing this week's Greek combining forms in a meaningful sentence. The words are *pictograph* and *monolith*.**

- The ***pictograph*** was carved and painted on the ***monolith***.
- It is your turn to write five more sentences using the words on the top of the recording sheet.
- Sentences with two words get two points and sentences with one word get one point.

MAKE CONNECTIONS

yourself to write sentences with two or more words from the list.

| Words | | |
|---|---|---|
| bibliographer | geosphere | microwave |
| bibliography | hydrosphere | monograph |
| biographer | lithographer | monolith |
| biography | microbus | rehydrate |
| dehydration | microphone | sphere |
| geography | microsphere | spherical |

1. The baseball, soccer ball, and globe all have a spherical shape.
2. When the singer couldn't be heard, she grabbed a microphone.
3. Jessie thought becoming a lithographer would be fun because she loves art.
4. In Rome the tourists rode in a microbus.
5. The hiker had to rehydrate because he was suffering from dehydration.

### STEP 2 CHALLENGE: MORPHEME MADNESS

MATERIALS
• Day 10 Recording Sheet
• Notebook paper
• Greek Mat
• Cards listed in the table below

**DIRECTIONS** Students pair up to use **Cards** and **Mats** to build words. They also record all of the words they build and then record the words' definitions.

| Word Parts | Cards |
|---|---|
| Greek Combining Forms | biblio, bio, geo, gram, graph, hydr, hydra, hydro, lith, litho, micro, mono, phone, scope, spher, sphere, spherø, wave |
| Inflected Endings | ed, ing |
| Prefixes | de, re |
| Suffixes | al, ate, atø, er, ic, ion, y |
| Connecting Letters | n/a |

**Now it's your turn to build words.**

- First, find a partner.
- Use the **Cards** and **Mats** to build real words.
- Record the words and their definition on a separate sheet of paper.

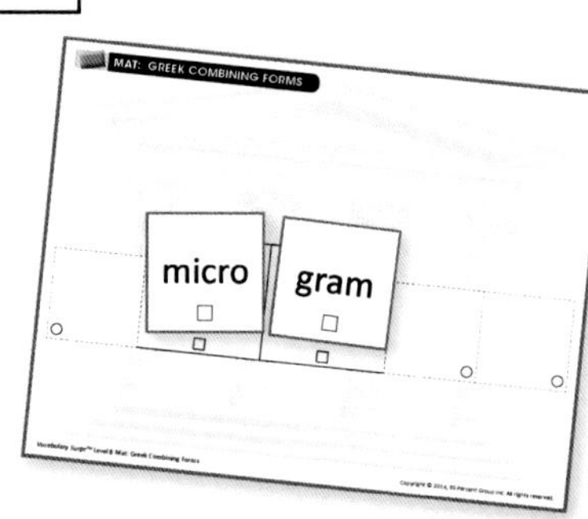


 

# ast/astro, geo, logy/log~~y~~/ology, mechan, morph/morpho, neo, proto, techn/techno poly-, -naut, -nomy

## DAY 1 • Introduce Greek Combining Forms

### UNCOVER THE MEANING

MATERIALS
• Days 1 & 2 Recording Sheet

**Introduce *ast/astro, logy/log~~y~~/ology, morph/morpho,* and *neo; poly-, -naut,* and *-nomy***

**DIRECTIONS** Pair students and distribute the **Days 1 & 2 Recording Sheet**. Model the first completed example. After students have completed the first two columns, ask them to share what they wrote. Then provide the Certified Definition. Explain that understanding parts of words, such as Greek combining forms, can help students uncover the meaning of many words.

**I'm going to model using my detective skills to figure out what the underlined word parts mean.**

- I'll use the other words in the sentences to develop a Working Definition of a word part.
- Listen as I read the first set of two sentences.
    1. Madame Mimi used ***astrology*** to determine Kai's future using the stars' positions.
    2. Hayden studied ***astronomy*** in his training to become an ***astronaut*** in space.
- In **Column 1**, I record the clue words stars and space that help me understand the meaning of ***ast/astro***.
- I think that ***ast/astro*** means stars or space. This is my Working Definition, which I record in **Column 2**.
- In **Column 3**, I write the Certified Definition of ***ast/astro***: star.

**Now it's your turn.**

- With your partner, fill in the remaining spaces on the **Days 1 & 2 Recording Sheet**.
- Use your detective skills to figure out what the underlined word parts mean.
- Consider which words or phrases in the sentences provide clues about meaning. Record them in **Column 1**.
- Write a Working Definition in **Column 2**.
- Only complete **Columns 1** and **2** and then wait for the discussion. You will fill in **Column 3** after I provide a Certified Definition.

UNCOVER THE MEANING

| ast/astro logy/ology | 1. Madame Mimi used astrology to determine Kai's future using the stars' positions. 2. Hayden studied astronomy in his training to become an astronaut in space. 3. The biology lecture was about forest and plains animals. 4. Dr. Hyde teaches hydrology to students learning about the ocean. | |
|---|---|---|
| **❶Clue Words for Working Definition** | **❷Working Definition** | **❸Certified Definition** |
| ***ast/astro:*** stars, space | stars, space | star |
| ***logy/ology:*** stars' positions, studied, lecture, learning | teaching, learning | science, study |
| | ***-naut:*** sailor | ***-nomy:*** law, system of laws |
| **morph/morpho neo** | 1. The bodies of polymorphic starfish can vary in size, color, and number of arms. 2. The polygraph machine's needle charts many points as a person is questioned. 3. The neolithic times were the latest period of the Stone Age. 4. The newborn neomorph had different characteristics than its parents. | |
| **❶Clue Words for Working Definition** | **❷Working Definition** | **❸Certified Definition** |
| ***morph/morpho:*** vary in size, color, number of arms; different characteristics | become different | to change form, shape, structure |
| ***neo:*** latest, parents | new, recent | new, recent |
| | | ***poly:*** many |

## ast/astro, geo, logy/log~~y~~/ology, morph/morpho, neo, poly-, -naut, -nomy

# DAY 2 • Deepen the Meaning

## CHECK MEANING

**MATERIALS**
- Pocket chart, document camera, or PowerPoint™
- Days 1 & 2 Recording Sheet
- Cards: Teacher: logy, morph, neo Student: Greek Combining Forms: astro, geo, hydro, logy, naut, nomy

**DIRECTIONS** Using the **Cards** and **Mat**, confirm that students understand how the meaning of the word evolves as more parts are added.

**I DO**

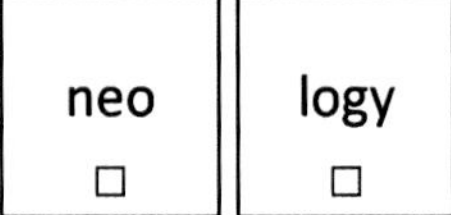


- The Greek combining form ***logy*** means science or study.
- Adding ***neo*** to ***logy*** spells the word ***neology***. The combination of word parts means the study of new words or expressions.
- Now, I'm going to use my knowledge of the word to answer the question.

1. What does it mean when I say that the book *Frindle* is about ***neology***? It is a book about new words or expressions.

**WE DO**

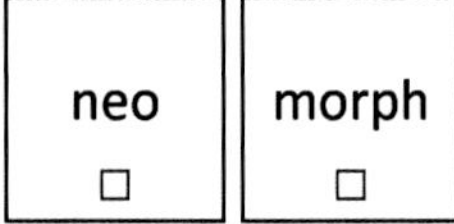


- The Greek combining form ***morph*** means to change form, shape, or structure.
- Adding ***neo*** to ***morph*** spells the word ***neomorph***. The combination of word parts means a new version of something.
- Listen to me use the word ***neomorph*** in a question and we will use our knowledge of its parts to figure out the answer.

2. What does it mean if a ***neomorph*** striped butterfly is born from two plain yellow butterflies? It has changed its color to become a new version of its parents.

**YOU DO** Use your **Cards** and **Mats** to complete the chart on the **Days 1 & 2 Recording Sheet**.

| Greek Combining Forms | Certified Definition |
|---|---|
| **ast/astro** | star |
| **bio** | life |
| **geo** | earth |
| **hydro** | water |
| **logy/log~~y~~** | science, study of |
| **morph/morpho** | to change form, shape, structure |
| **-naut** | sailor |
| **neo** | new, recent |
| **-nomy** | law, system of laws |
| **poly-** | many |

**CHECK MEANING**

**DIRECTIONS** **Build the words with the Cards and Mat. Describe how adding new parts changes the meaning of the words.**

| Word | Greek Combining Form | Greek Combining Form |
|---|---|---|
| **astronaut** | astro: star | naut: sailor |
| **Meaning:** | a person who travels into space among stars and planets | |
| **astronomy** | astro: star | nomy: law, system of laws |
| **Meaning:** | the study of stars and planets | |
| **geology** | geo: Earth | logy: science, study of |
| **Meaning:** | the scientific study of the rock's on the Earth's surface | |
| **hydrology** | hydro: water | logy: science, study of |
| **Meaning:** | the scientific study of the Earth's water | |

**ast/astro, bio, geo, lith, logy/logy̸, morph/morpho, neo poly-, -naut, -nomy**

# DAY 3 • Word Multiplier

## WORD MULTIPLIER

**Build words with *ast/astro, bio, geo, lith, logy/logy̸, morph/morpho, neo; poly-, -naut, and -nomy***

MATERIALS
- Day 3 Recording Sheet
- Notebook paper
- Greek Mat
- Cards:
  Greek Combining Forms: ast, astro, bio, geo, lith, logy, logy̸, morph, morpho, neo
  Prefix: dis, poly
  Suffixes: al, er, ic, ism, naut, nomy

**DIRECTIONS** Students work together to build words using their **Cards** and **Mats**.

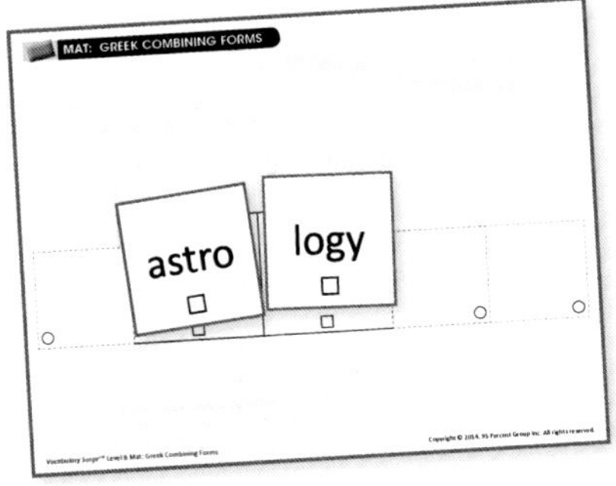


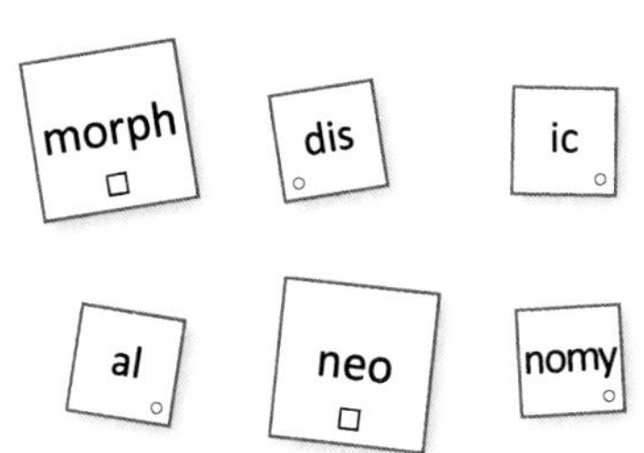


**I DO** Watch me combine **Cards** to build a word.
- I select cards ***astro*** and ***logy***.
- I place the Greek combining form ***astro*** in the large box on the left side of the mat, matching the square on the mat to the one on the card.
- I place the Greek combining form ***logy*** in the large box to the right of ***astro***, matching the square on the mat to the one on the card.
- I have built the word ***astrology***.

**WE DO** Let me try another.
- I choose the cards ***astro, logy̸, ic,*** and ***al***.
- Where should I place the Greek combining form ***astro***? In the box on the left side of the mat
- Why do we place it here? Because it is a Greek combining form
- Where shall I place the Greek combining form ***logy̸***? In the box to the right of ***astro***
- Why do we place it here? Because it is a Greek combining form
- Where shall I place suffix ***-ic***? In the box to the right of ***logy̸***
- Where shall I place suffix ***-al***? In the box to the right of ***ic***
- Look at the example on your **Day 3 Recording Sheet** to see how to write the parts of ***astrological*** and the whole word. ***Astro*** means star, ***logy̸*** means law or system of laws, ***-ic*** means having the characteristic of, and ***-al*** means related to.
- When we put these word parts together, ***astrological*** means related to the study of the stars to predict the future.
- What part of speech is ***astrological*** and how do you know? Adjective; it describes a type of study

WORD MULTIPLIER

| | Word Parts | Word | Part of Speech |
|---|---|---|---|
| 1. | astro+logy̸+ic+al | astrological | adjective |
| | Write the Meaning: | related to the study of the stars to predict the future | |
| 2. | bio+logy | biology | noun |
| | Write the Meaning: | the scientific study of living organisms | |
| 3. | dis+ast+er | disaster | noun |
| | Write the Meaning: | an unfortunate event that causes harm | |
| 4. | geo+morph+ic | geomorphic | adjective |
| | Write the Meaning: | relating to the landforms of Earth | |
| 5. | neo+lith+ic | neolithic | adjective |
| | Write the Meaning: | having the characteristics of the latest period of the Stone Age | |
| 6. | poly+morph+ism | polymorphism | noun |
| | Write the Meaning: | the condition of having more than one adult form | |

**YOU DO** Use your **Cards** and **Mats** to build more words. Complete the **Day 3 Recording Sheet** with your partner. Write additional words on notebook paper. We will review the words when you have finished.

**Possible Words**: logic, logical, morph, neolith, polymorph

## ast/astro, geo, logy/logy/ology, morph, morpho, neo, poly-, -naut, -nomy

# DAY 4 • Demonstrate Meaning

## BUILD MEANING

**MATERIALS**
- Whiteboards
- Markers

**DIRECTIONS** Complete the I Do and We Do whole class, and pair students to work on the You Do. Students can record their ideas on small whiteboards. Ask a few pairs to share their work with the class.

**I DO** Listen to me demonstrate understanding of the meaning of the Greek combining form ***poly-***.

- The first word is ***polygraph***. We learned that ***polygraph*** means a machine that records many pieces of information while someone is questioned.
- I'm going to think of places a ***polygraph*** might be used.
  - Before the suspect is questioned, the police officer connects her to a ***polygraph*** machine.
  - The lawyer speaks in court about the results of the ***polygraph*** test.
- The second word is ***polymorphic***. We learned that ***polymorphic*** means something that varies in appearance. I'm going to think of examples of things that might be ***polymorphic***.
  - A leopard and black panther are considered ***polymorphic*** because, despite differences in color, they are the same species.
  - Lady bugs are ***polymorphic*** because they can have different numbers of black spots.

**WE DO** Let's try the next one together with the Greek combining form ***neo***.

- The first word is ***neolithic***. The Greek combining form ***neo*** means new, the Greek combining form ***lith*** means stone, and the suffix ***-ic*** means having the characteristic of. ***Neolithic*** means having the characteristic of the most recent Stone Age.
  - Where might you see an item from the ***neolithic*** *age*?
- The second word is ***neology***. The Greek combining form ***neo*** means new, and the Greek combining form ***logy*** means the science or study of something. ***Neology*** means the study of new words or expressions.
  - Name several new words or expressions.

**PROMPT IDEAS** ***neolithic***
- museum
- TV
- movie

**PROMPT IDEAS** ***neology***
- tweeting
- friending on Facebook
- iPad or iPhone

**YOU DO** Now it's your turn. Work with a partner, and record your ideas on a whiteboard so you're ready to share with the class. You'll have five minutes to think of examples for two words that contain the Greek combining form ***logy***.

- The two words are ***phonology*** and ***geology***.
  - What does the Greek combining form ***phono*** mean? Sound What does the Greek combining form ***logy*** mean? Science, study What does ***phonology*** mean? The study of sounds in a spoken language
  - What does the Greek combining form ***geo*** mean? Earth What does the Greek combining form ***logy*** mean? Science, study What does ***geology*** mean? The scientific study of the rocks on Earth's surface
  - Name some English speech sounds (called *phonemes*) a linguist might study in the field of ***phonology***.
  - Think of an example of something that a scientist might study in the field of ***geology***.

**PROMPT IDEAS** ***phonology***
- /sh/
- /m/
- /t/

**PROMPT IDEAS** ***geology***
- volcanos
- rocks
- oceans

 

# mechan, proto, techn/techno

## DAY 5 • Introduce Greek Combining Forms

### UNCOVER THE MEANING

MATERIALS
• Days 5 & 6 Recording Sheet

#### Introduce *mechan, proto,* and *techn/techno*

**DIRECTIONS** Pair students and distribute the **Days 5 & 6 Recording Sheet**. Model the first completed example. After students have completed the first two columns, ask them to share what they wrote. Then provide the Certified Definition. Explain that understanding parts of words, such as Greek combining forms, can help students uncover the meaning of many words.

**I'm going to model using my detective skills to figure out what the underlined word parts mean.**

- I'll use the other words in the sentences to develop a Working Definition of a word part.
- Listen as I read the first set of two sentences.

  1. The engineer oiled the ***mechanism*** to keep the fan running smoothly.
  2. The ***mechanic*** was unfamiliar with the new technology and design of the engine.

- In **Column 1**, I record the clue words fan and engine that help me understand the meaning of ***mechan***.
- I think that ***mechan*** means engine or machine. This is my Working Definition, which I record in **Column 2**.
- In **Column 3**, I will write the Certified Definition of ***mechan***: machine.

**Now it's your turn.**

- With your partner, fill in the remaining spaces on the **Days 5 & 6 Recording Sheet**.
- Use your detective skills to figure out what the underlined word parts mean.
- Consider which words or phrases in the sentences provide clues about meaning. Record them in **Column 1**.
- Write a Working Definition in **Column 2**.
- Only complete **Columns 1** and **2** and then wait for the discussion. You will fill in **Column 3** after I provide a Certified Definition.

UNCOVER THE MEANING

| mechan techn/techno | 1. The engineer oiled the mechanism to keep the fan running smoothly. 2. The mechanic was unfamiliar with the new technology and design of the engine. 3. The technical manual shows exactly how to fix the computer. | |
|---|---|---|
| ❶Clue Words for Working Definition | ❷Working Definition | ❸Certified Definition |
| *mechan:* fan, engine | engine, machine | machine |
| *techn/techno:* engine, design, manual, fix | mechanical, design | skill, craft |

| proto | 1. The class built a prototype of a new kind of engine. 2. Space gases and dust combined to form an emergent protostar. | |
|---|---|---|
| ❶Clue Words for Working Definition | ❷Working Definition | ❸Certified Definition |
| *proto:* new, emergent | new | earliest, original |

# DAY 6 • Deepen the Meaning

## CHECK MEANING

MATERIALS
- Pocket chart, document camera, or PowerPoint™
- Days 5 & 6 Recording Sheet
- Cards:
  Teacher: ic, lith, morph, proto
  Student: Greek Combining Forms: logy, mechan, techn, techno
  Inflected Endings: ed
  Suffixes: al, ic, ize

**DIRECTIONS** Using the **Cards** and **Mat**, confirm that students understand how the meaning of the word evolves as more parts are added.

**I DO**

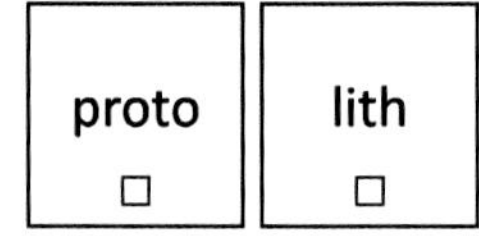

- The combining form ***proto*** means the earliest or original.
- Adding ***proto*** to ***lith*** spells the word ***protolith***. The combination of word parts means the earliest stone tools of the Stone Age.
- Now I'm going to use my knowledge of the word to answer the question.
  1. What does it mean when you say the ***protolith*** looked like an ancient tool? The stone tool looked like it was from a long time ago.

**WE DO**

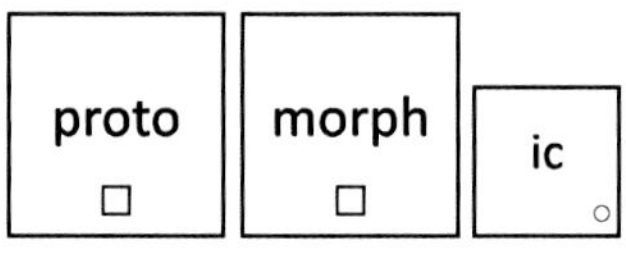

- The combining form ***morph*** means form, shape, or structure. The suffix ***-ic*** means having the characteristic of.
- Adding ***proto*** and ***morph*** and ***ic*** spells the word ***protomorphic***. The combination of word parts means having a primitive structure.
- Listen to me use the word ***protomorphic*** in a question and we will use our knowledge of its parts to figure out the answer.
  2. What does it mean when we say that the worm's body looked ***protomorphic***? The worm's body had structures from a long time ago.

**YOU DO** Use your **Cards** and **Mats** to complete the chart on the **Days 5 & 6 Recording Sheet**.

| Greek Combining Forms | Certified Definition |
|---|---|
| bio | life |
| geo | earth |
| graph | written or drawn |
| lith | with a stone |
| logy/logy | science, study |
| mechan | machine |
| proto | earliest, original |
| techn/techno | skill, craft |
| **Suffixes** | **Certified Definition** |
| -al | related to |
| -ic | having the characteristic of |
| -ism | doctrine, belief |
| -ist | a person who works in a profession or studies a topic |
| -ize | become, change, make |

CHECK MEANING

meaning of the words.

| Word | Greek Combining Form | Suffix | |
|---|---|---|---|
| mechanic | mechan: machine | ic: having the characteristic of | |
| Meaning: | a person who repairs machines | | |
| mechanized | mechan: machine | ize: become, change | ed: past |
| Meaning: | made with mechanical power | | |
| technical | techn: skill, craft | ic: having the characteristic of | al: related to |
| Meaning: | relating to the use of machines | | |
| **Word** | **Greek Combining Form** | | |
| technology | techno: skill, craft | logy: science, study | |
| Meaning: | the study of the mechanical objects that humans use to improve their lives | | |

mechan, proto, techn/techno

# DAY 7 • Word Multiplier

## WORD MULTIPLIER

MATERIALS
- Day 7 Recording Sheet
- Notebook paper
- Greek Mat
- Cards:
Greek Combining Forms: bio, geo, graph, lith, logy, logy, mechan, proto, techn, techno
Anglo-Saxon word: star
Suffixes: al, ic, ism, ist

### Build words with *mechan, proto,* and *techn/techno*

**DIRECTIONS** Students work together to build words using their **Cards** and **Mats**.

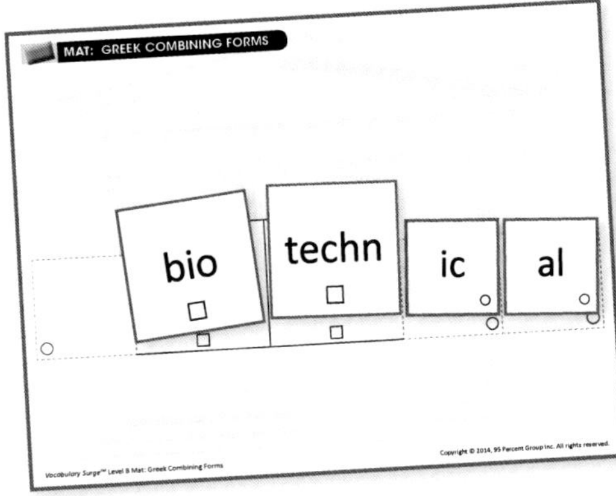


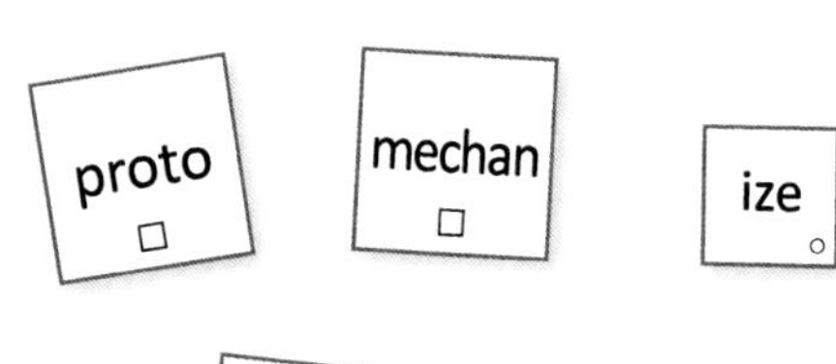


**WE DO** Let's combine **Cards** to build a word.

- I select cards ***bio, techn, ic,*** and ***al***.
- Where shall I place the Greek combining form ***bio***? On the left side of the mat
- Why do we place it here? Because it is a Greek combining form
- Where shall I place the Greek combining form ***techn***? In the box to the right of ***bio***
- Why do we place it here? Because it is a Greek combining form
- Where shall I place the suffix ***-ic***? To the right of ***techn***, matching the circle on the mat to the one on the card
- Finally, where shall I place the suffix ***-al***? To the right of ***ic***, matching the circle on the mat to the one on the card
- What word have we built? Biotechnical
- What is the definition of ***biotechnical***? Relating to the use of living cells to make technology

WORD MULTIPLIER

| | Word Parts | Word | Part of Speech |
|---|---|---|---|
| 1. | bio+techn+ic+al | biotechnical | adjective |
| | Write the Meaning: | related to the use of living cells to make technology | |
| 2. | bio+logy+ist | biologist | noun |
| | Write the Meaning: | a person who studies living organisms | |
| 3. | geo+logy+ist | geologist | noun |
| | Write the Meaning: | a person who studies rocks on Earth's surface | |
| 4. | mechan+ic+al | mechanical | adjective |
| | Write the Meaning: | relating to machinery | |
| 5. | mechan+ism | mechanism | noun |
| | Write the Meaning: | a group of moving parts, often part of a larger machine | |
| 6. | proto+lith+ic | protolithic | adjective |
| | Write the Meaning: | relating to the very beginning of the Stone Age | |

**YOU DO** Use your **Cards** and **Mats** to build more words. Complete the **Day 7 Recording Sheet** with your partner. Write additional words on notebook paper.

**Possible Words**: biotech, mechanic

## DAY 8 • Demonstrate Meaning

### BUILD MEANING

MATERIALS
- Whiteboards
- Markers

**DIRECTIONS** Complete the I Do and We Do whole class, and pair students to work on the You Do. Students can record their ideas on small whiteboards. Ask a few pairs to share their work with the class.

**I DO** Listen to me demonstrate understanding of the meaning of the Greek combining form ***techn***.

- The first word is ***technical***. The ***technical*** manual explains how to use the cell phone. I'm going to think of examples of things that are ***technical***.
  - Sissy studies ***technical*** terms in her biology class.
  - My brother's lack of ***technical*** skills makes it difficult for him to use a computer.
- The second word is ***technology***, which means the use of technical objects to improve life. I'm going to think of examples of people who use ***technology***.
  - An astronaut uses ***technology*** when she lives in the space station.
  - Computer ***technology*** saves us time in math class.

**WE DO** Let's try the next one together with the Greek combining form ***proto***.

- The first word is ***protomorphic***. The Greek combining form ***proto*** means earliest or original, the Greek combining form ***morph*** means to change shape or form or structure, and the suffix ***-ic*** means having the characteristic of. ***Protomorphic*** means having a primitive structure. A jellyfish has a ***protomorphic*** body that is round and simple.
  - Name something that might have a ***protomorphic*** structure.
- The second word is ***prototype***. The Greek combining form ***proto*** means earliest or original, and the Greek combining form ***type*** means stamp or model. ***Prototype*** means the first model created as a trial to explore how the invention might work.
  - Name a ***prototype*** of something you know of or have seen.

**PROMPT IDEAS** ***protomorphic***
- sponge
- balloon
- soap bubble

**PROMPT IDEAS** ***prototype***
- old car
- black and white TV
- log canoe

**YOU DO** Now it's your turn. Work with a partner, and record your ideas on a whiteboard so you're ready to share with the class. You'll have five minutes to think of examples for two words that contain the Greek combining form ***mechan***.

- The two words are ***mechanic*** and ***mechanical***.
  - What does the Greek combining form ***mechan*** mean? Machine What does the suffix ***-ic*** mean? Having the characteristic of What does the suffix ***-al*** mean? Related to What does ***mechanical*** mean? Operated by a machine
  - Think of an example of something a ***mechanic*** might repair.
  - Think of an example of something that might be ***mechanical***.

**PROMPT IDEAS** ***mechanic***
- car
- truck
- train

**PROMPT IDEAS** ***mechanical***
- can opener
- air conditioner
- fan

 

# ast/astro, geo, logy/log~~y~~/ology, mechan, morph/morpho, neo, proto, techn/techno; poly-, -naut, -nomy

## DAY 9 • Review What You Learned

### STEP 1 REVIEW THE MEANING

**Review *ast/astro, geo, logy/log~~y~~/ology, mechan, morph/morpho, neo, proto,* and *techn/techno; poly-, -naut, -nomy***

MATERIALS
- Word parts projected on document camera, overhead projector, or PowerPoint™

**DIRECTIONS** Display the morphemes so students can see them, and ask for the Certified Definition of each one.

**When I show you the word parts, think about the Certified Definitions we discussed as you prepare to answer.**

| Greek Combining Form | Certified Definition | Greek Combining Form | Certified Definition |
|---|---|---|---|
| **ast/astro** | star | **mechan** | machine |
| **logy/log~~y~~/ology** | science, study | **proto** | earliest, original |
| **morph/morpho** | to change form, shape, or structure | **techn/techno** | skill, craft |
| **neo** | new or recent | | |

### STEP 2 CHECK MEANING

MATERIALS
- Day 9 Recording Sheet

**DIRECTIONS** Read the following sentence to check that students understand the meanings of ***ast/astro, geo, logy/log~~y~~/ology, mechan, morph/morpho, neo, proto,*** and ***techn/techno; poly-, -naut, -nomy***. Model the first sentence for students using the We Do step, below.

**WE DO** As I read this sentence, think about the Certified Definitions of the Greek combining form that fits the blank.

1. Because Juan was interested in rocks, he wants to research the profession of a _______**logist**.

- Which Greek combining form do you think fits on the line? Geo
- What is the new word? Geologist
- What do you think the word ***geo**logist* means? A person who studies the rocks on Earth's surface

**YOU DO** Complete the rest of the sentences on the **Day 9 Recording Sheet** with your partner to find the Greek combining form that best fits on the line. Record the new words and their meanings.

Students write two sentences with missing Greek combining forms to challenge the class.

**CHECK MEANING**

1. Because Juan was interested in rocks, he wants to research the profession of a <u>geo</u> **logist**. <u>geologist</u>
   Meaning: <u>a person who studies the rocks on Earth's surface</u>
2. The <u>poly</u> **graph** machine is used to check if someone is telling the truth. <u>polygraph</u>
   Meaning: <u>a lie detector machine, recording lots of information while someone is questioned</u>
3. The <u>mechan</u> **ical** bank grabs the penny and drops it into the treasure chest. <u>mechanical</u>
   Meaning: <u>relating to machinery</u>
4. The <u>astro</u> **nomer** drove to the planetarium at night to watch for shooting stars. <u>astronomer</u>
   Meaning: <u>a person who studies planets and stars</u>
5. When we saw a sign for psychic readings, my dad said he didn't believe in <u>astro</u> **logy**. <u>astrology</u>
   Meaning: <u>a person who attempts to study the stars to predict the future</u>
6. The <u>neo</u> **lithic** knife was discovered in the ruins in the desert. <u>neolithic</u>
   Meaning: <u>having the characteristics of the latest period of the Stone Age</u>

ast/astro, geo, logy/log~~y~~/ology, mechan, morph/morpho, neo, proto, techn/techno; poly-, -naut, -nomy

# DAY 10 • 2nd Review Day

## STEP 1 MAKE CONNECTIONS

MATERIALS
- Day 10 Recording Sheet

**DIRECTIONS** Students pair up to write sentences with either one or two of the words that are provided.

**I am going to model how to use two words containing this week's Greek combining forms in a meaningful sentence. The words are *mechanic* and *technical*.**

- The ***mechanic*** read the ***technical*** manual to learn how to fix the motor.
- It is your turn to create five more sentences using the words on the top of the recording sheet.
- Sentences with two words get two points and sentences with one word get one point.

MAKE CONNECTIONS

| Words | | |
|---|---|---|
| astronaut | disaster | neolith |
| astronomy | geology | neology |
| astrology | geologist | neologism |
| biology | mechanic | polygraph |
| biologist | mechanized | protostar |
| biotechnology | morph | prototype |

1. The mechanic repaired the broken car.
2. When we saw the scientist at the Grand Canyon, we guessed she was a geologist.
3. When someone makes up a new term, it can be called a neologism.
4. While looking at the sky one night last summer we thought about protostars.
5. The astronaut felt like an astronomer while on the space mission.

## STEP 2 CHALLENGE: MORPHEME MADNESS

MATERIALS
- Notebook paper
- Greek Mat
- Cards listed in the table below

**DIRECTIONS** Students pair up to use **Cards** and **Mats** to build real words. Students record all of the words they build and then record the words' definitions.

| Word Parts | Cards |
|---|---|
| **Greek Combining Forms** | ast, astro, geo, logy, log~~y~~, mechan, morph, morpho, naut, neo, nomy, ology, poly, proto, techn, techno |
| **Inflected Endings** | ed |
| **Prefixes** | dis |
| **Suffixes** | al, er, ic, ism, ist, ize, y |
| **Connecting Letters** | n/a |

**Now it's your turn to build words.**
- First, find a partner.
- Use the **Cards** and **Mats** to build real words.
- Record the words and their definition on a separate sheet of paper.

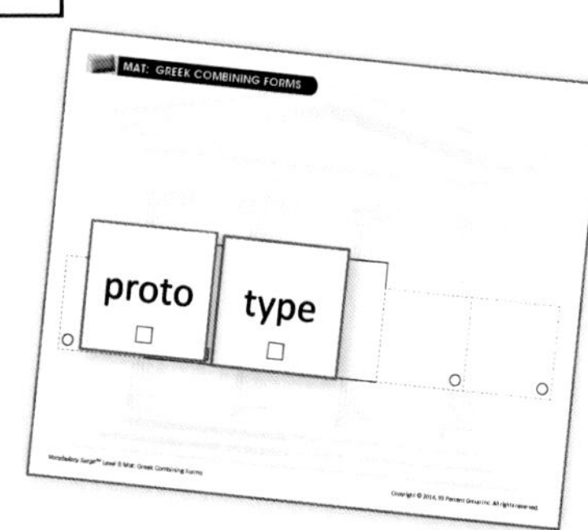

# archaé/arche, cracy/crat, demo, eco, pale/paleo, phob/phobia/phobic, psych/psycho, zoo

## DAY 1 • Introduce Greek Combining Forms

### UNCOVER THE MEANING

MATERIALS
- Days 1 & 2 Recording Sheet

#### Introduce *archaé/arche, eco, pale/paleo,* and *zoo*

**DIRECTIONS** Pair students and distribute the Days 1 & 2 Recording Sheet. Model the first completed example. After students have completed the first two columns, ask them to share what they wrote. Then provide the Certified Definition. Explain that understanding parts of words, such as Greek combining forms, can help students uncover the meaning of many words.

**I'm going to model using my detective skills to figure out what the underlined word parts mean.**

- I'll use the other words in the sentences to develop a Working Definition of a word part.
- Listen as I read the first set of two sentences.
    1. The ***archeologist*** discovered a mummy's tomb.
    2. The ***archeological*** museum was full of King Tut's gold.
- In **Column 1**, I record the clue words mummy's tomb and museum that help me understand the meaning of ***archaé/arche***.
- I think that ***archaé/arche*** means old. This is my Working Definition, which I record in **Column 2**.
- In **Column 3**, I write the Certified Definition of ***archaé/arche***: primitive, ancient.

**Now it's your turn.**

- With your partner, fill in the remaining spaces on the Days 1 & 2 Recording Sheet.
- Use your detective skills to figure out what the underlined word parts mean.
- Consider which words or phrases in the sentences provide clues about meaning. Record them in **Column 1**.
- Write a Working Definition in **Column 2**.
- Only complete **Columns 1** and **2** and then wait for the discussion. You will fill in **Column 3** after I provide a Certified Definition.

UNCOVER THE MEANING

| *archaé/arche* | 1. The archeologist discovered a mummy's tomb. 2. The archeological museum was full of King Tut's gold. | |
|---|---|---|
| ❶ Clue Words for Working Definition | ❷ Working Definition | ❸ Certified Definition |
| mummy's tomb, museum | old | primitive, ancient |

| *pale/paleo* | 1. Stacie loved to collect fossils, so she decided to study paleontology. 2. The paleontologist unearthed the missing dinosaur bones. | |
|---|---|---|
| ❶ Clue Words for Working Definition | ❷ Working Definition | ❸ Certified Definition |
| *pale/paleo:* fossils, dinosaur | fossils, dinosaur | old, ancient |

| *eco* *zoo* | 1. People recycle because they are concerned about the ecology of Earth. 2. The zoologist prepared a report about eagles' habitat and lifespan. | |
|---|---|---|
| ❶ Clue Words for Working Definition | ❷ Working Definition | ❸ Certified Definition |
| *eco:* recycle, earth, habitat | where you live | house, home |
| *zoo:* eagles | animals, birds | animal |

# DAY 2 • Deepen the Meaning

## CHECK MEANING

MATERIALS
- Pocket chart, document camera, or PowerPoint™
- Days 1 & 2 Recording Sheet
- Cards:
  Teacher: al, arche, ic, ology, olog~~y~~
  Student: Greek Combining Forms: eco, logy, log~~y~~, zoo
  Suffix: ist

**DIRECTIONS** Using the **Cards** and **Mat**, confirm that students understand how the meaning of the word evolves as more parts are added.

**I DO**

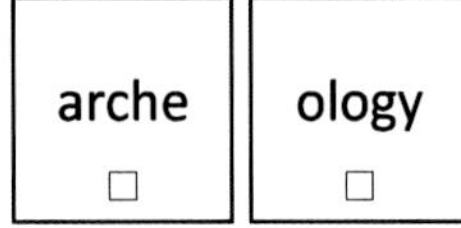


- The Greek combining form ***ology*** means science or study.
- Adding ***arche*** to ***ology*** spells the word ***<u>arche</u>ology***. The combination of word parts means the study of ancient history.
- Now, I'm going to use my knowledge of the word to answer the question.

1. What does it mean when I say that Anna's cousin is studying ***<u>arche</u>ology***? She is studying ancient history.

**WE DO**

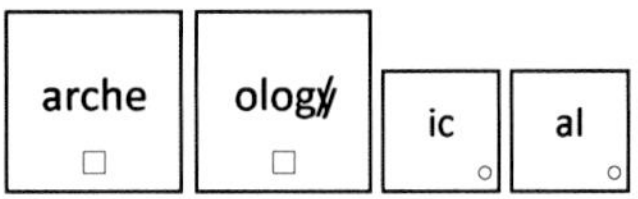


- The Greek combining form ***olog~~y~~*** means science or study. The suffix ***-ic*** means having a characteristic, and the suffix ***-al*** means related to or like.
- Adding ***arche*** to ***olog~~y~~, -ic,*** and ***-al*** spells the word ***<u>arche</u>ological***. The combination of word parts means relating to the study of ancient history.
- Listen to me use the word ***<u>arche</u>ological*** in a question and we will use our knowledge of its parts to figure out the answer.

2. What does it mean if the museum displayed ***<u>arche</u>ological*** objects? The objects were from ancient history.

**YOU DO** Use your **Cards** and **Mats** to complete the chart on the **Days 1 & 2 Recording Sheet**.

| Greek Combining Forms | Certified Definition |
|---|---|
| archa~~e~~/arche | primitive, ancient |
| bio | life |
| eco | house, home |
| graph | written, graph |
| logy/log~~y~~/ ology/olog~~y~~ | science, study |
| pale/paleo | old, ancient |
| zoo | animal |
| **Suffixes** | **Certified Definition** |
| -al | related to, like |
| -ic | having a characteristic |
| -ist | a person who works in a profession or studies a topic |

CHECK MEANING

**DIRECTIONS** Build the words with the Cards and Mat. Describe how adding new parts changes the meaning of the words.

| Word | Greek Combining Form | Greek Combining Form | Suffix |
|---|---|---|---|
| ecology | eco: house, home | logy: science, study | |
| Meaning: | the biological study of how organisms interact with their environments | | |
| ecologist | eco: house, home | log~~y~~: science, study | ist: one who performs a specific action |
| Meaning: | a person who studies how humans affect the environment | | |
| zoology | zoo: animal | logy: science, study | |
| Meaning: | the science or study of animals | | |
| zoologist | zoo: animal | log~~y~~: science, study | ist: one who performs a specific action |

 

# archa~~e~~/arche, eco, pale/paleo, zoo

## DAY 3 • Word Multiplier

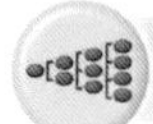

### WORD MULTIPLIER

**Build words with *archa~~e~~/arche, eco, pale/paleo,* and *zoo***

MATERIALS
- Day 3 Recording Sheet
- Notebook paper
- Greek Mat
- Cards: Greek Combining Forms: archa~~e~~, arche, bio, eco, graph, logy, log~~y~~, ology, olog~~y~~ pale, paleo, zoo Suffixes: al, ic, ist

**DIRECTIONS** Students work together to build words using their **Cards** and **Mats**.

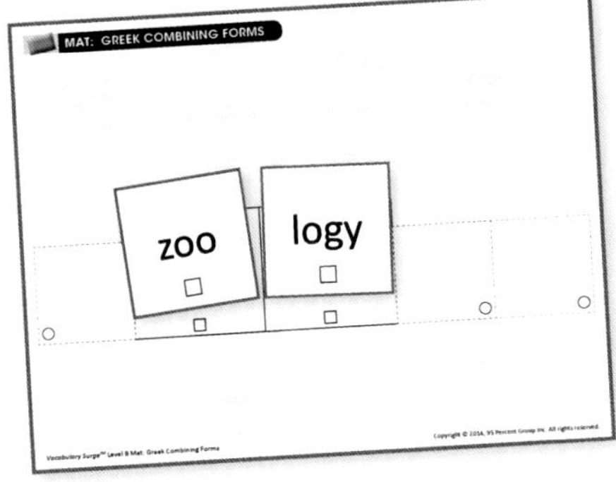


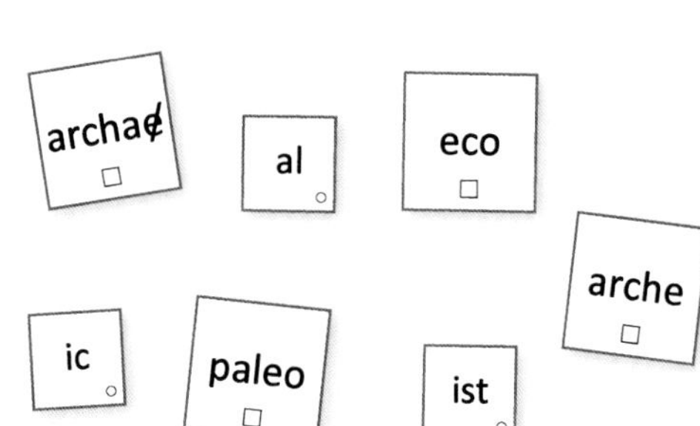


**I DO** Watch me combine **Cards** to build a word.

- I select cards ***zoo*** and ***logy***.
- I place the Greek combining form ***zoo*** in the large box on the left side of the mat, matching the square on the mat to the one on the card.
- I place the Greek combining form ***logy*** in the large box to the right of ***zoo***, matching the square on the mat to the one on the card.
- I have built the word ***zoology***.

**WE DO** Let me try another.

- I choose the cards ***arche, olog~~y~~,*** and ***ist***.
- Where should I place the Greek combining form ***arche***? In the box on the left side of the mat
- Why do we place it here? Because it is a Greek combining form
- Where shall I place the Greek combining form ***olog~~y~~***? In the box to the right of ***arche***
- Why do we place it here? Because it is a Greek combining form
- Where shall I place suffix ***-ist***? In the box to the right of ***olog~~y~~***
- Look at the example on your **Day 3 Recording Sheet** to see how to write the parts of ***archeologist*** and the whole word. ***Arche*** means primitive or ancient, ***ology*** means science or study, and ***-ist*** means a person who works in a profession or studies a topic.
- When we put these word parts together, ***archeologist*** means a person who studies ancient history.
- What part of speech is ***archeologist*** and how do you know? Noun; person

**WORD MULTIPLIER**

| | Word Parts | Word | Part of Speech |
|---|---|---|---|
| 1. | arche+olog~~y~~+ist | archeologist | noun |
| | Write the Meaning: | a person who who studies ancient history | |
| 2. | archa~~e~~+ic | archaic | adjective |
| | Write the Meaning: | very old, or old fashioned | |
| 3. | eco+logy | ecology | noun |
| | Write the Meaning: | the biological study of how organisms interact with their environments | |
| 4. | eco+log~~y~~+ic+al | ecological | adjective |
| | Write the Meaning: | relating to how humans affect the environment | |
| 5. | paleo+graph+ic | paleographic | adjective |
| | Write the Meaning: | relating to ancient writings | |
| 6. | zoo+log~~y~~+ist | zoologist | noun |
| | Write the Meaning: | a person who studies animals | |

**YOU DO** Use your **Cards** and **Mats** to build more words. Complete the **Day 3 Recording Sheet** with your partner. Write additional words on notebook paper. We will review the words when you have finished.

**Possible Words**: archeology, biograph, biographic, biology, ecology, paleology, paleograph

## DAY 4 • Demonstrate Meaning

### BUILD MEANING

MATERIALS
- Whiteboards
- Markers

**DIRECTIONS** Complete the I Do and We Do whole class, and pair students to work on the You Do. Students can record their ideas on small whiteboards. Ask a few pairs to share their work with the class.

**I DO** Listen to me demonstrate understanding of the meaning of the Greek combining form ***paleo***.

- The first word is ***paleontology***. We learned that ***paleontology*** means the science or study of fossils. I'm going to think of how ***paleontology*** might be used.
  - The ***paleontology*** exhibit at the museum is full of dinosaur bones.
  - Dr. Browser studied ***paleontology*** before she visited the fossil dig site in Utah.
- The second word is ***paleographer***. ***Paleographer*** means a person who studies ancient writings. I'm going to think of examples of things that a ***paleographer*** might study.
  - The ***paleographer*** studies the writings on a sheepskin scroll.
  - If a stone tablet is discovered, a ***paleographer*** could be hired to read the markings.

**WE DO** Let's try the next one together with the Greek combining form ***archae/arche***.

- The first word is ***archaic***. The Greek combining form ***archae*** means old or ancient, and the suffix ***-ic*** means having a characteristic. ***Archaic*** means very old or old fashioned.
  - Where might you see an item that is ***archaic***?
- The second word is ***archetype***. The Greek combining form ***arche*** means old or ancient, and the Latin root ***typ*** means stamp or model. ***Archetype*** means similar to the original model of something.
  - Name an ***archetype*** or earlier model of something and its newer version.

**PROMPT IDEAS** ***archaic***
- museum
- antique store
- documentary on TV

**PROMPT IDEAS** ***archetype***
- Model-T car to current car
- rollerskates to rollerblades
- book to e-reader

**YOU DO** Now it's your turn. Work with a partner, and record your ideas on a whiteboard so you're ready to share with the class. You'll have five minutes to think of examples for two words that contain the Greek combining form ***eco***.

- The two words are ***ecologist*** and ***ecology***.
  - What does the Greek combining form ***eco*** mean? House, home What does the Greek combining form ***logy*** mean? Science or study What does the suffix ***-ist*** mean? Person who performs a specific action What does ***ecologist*** mean? A person who studies how humans affect the environment
  - What does the Greek combining form ***eco*** mean? House, home What does the Greek combining form ***logy*** mean? Science or study What does ***ecology*** mean? The biological study of how organisms interact with their environments
  - Name some things an ***ecologist*** might do to protect the environment.
  - Think of an example of something that a scientist might study in the field of ***ecology***.

**PROMPT IDEAS** ***ecologist***
- ride the train instead of drive
- help clean up a national park
- visit a rainforest

**PROMPT IDEAS** ***ecology***
- erosion
- pollution
- recycling

 

# cracy/crat, demo, phob/phobia/phobic, psych/psycho

## DAY 5 • Introduce Greek Combining Forms

### UNCOVER THE MEANING

**Introduce *cracy/crat, demo, phob/phobia/phobic,* and *psych/psycho***

MATERIALS
- Days 5 & 6 Recording Sheet

**DIRECTIONS** Pair students and distribute the **Days 5 & 6 Recording Sheet**. Model the first completed example. After students have completed the first two columns, ask them to share what they wrote. Then provide the Certified Definition. Explain that understanding parts of words, such as Greek combining forms, can help students uncover the meaning of many words.

**I'm going to model using my detective skills to figure out what the underlined word parts mean.**

- I'll use the other words in the sentences to develop a Working Definition of a word part.
- Listen as I read the first set of two sentences.

  1. The ***demographics*** of the U.S. Census show where Americans live.
  2. The ***demographer*** searched records about the Washington family.

- In **Column 1**, I record the clue words American and family that help me understand the meaning of ***demo***.
- I think that ***demo*** means man. This is my Working Definition, which I record in **Column 2**.
- In **Column 3**, I will write the Certified Definition of ***demo***: people.

**Now it's your turn.**

- With your partner, fill in the remaining spaces on the **Days 5 & 6 Recording Sheet**.
- Use your detective skills to figure out what the underlined word parts mean.
- Consider which words or phrases in the sentences provide clues about meaning. Record them in **Column 1**.
- Write a Working Definition in **Column 2**.
- Only complete **Columns 1** and **2** and then wait for the discussion. You will fill in **Column 3** after I provide a Certified Definition.

UNCOVER THE MEANING

| **cracy/crat** | 2. The demographer searched records about the Washington family.<br>3. In a democracy, the citizens are allowed to choose the leaders who rule. | |
|---|---|---|
| **❶ Clue Words for Working Definition** | **❷ Working Definition** | **❸ Certified Definition** |
| ***demo:*** Americans, family | man | people |
| ***cracy/crat:*** citizens, choose, leaders, rule | leaders | rule |
| **phob/phobia/ phobic** | 1. At the party, the guest with demophobia was afraid to be around so many people.<br>2. The photophobic man was compelled to stay indoors with the lights off. | |
| **❶ Clue Words for Working Definition** | **❷ Working Definition** | **❸ Certified Definition** |
| ***phob/phobia:*** afraid, indoors | afraid | irrational fear or hatred |
| **psych/psycho** | 1. Ori visited a psychologist to help him understand his feelings.<br>2. The psychic claimed he could speak to spirits. | |
| **❶ Clue Words for Working Definition** | **❷ Working Definition** | **❸ Certified Definition** |
| ***psych/psycho:*** feelings, spirits | mind | mind or soul |

DAY 6 CHECK MEANING

# cracy/crat, demo, phob/phobia/phobic, psych/psycho

## DAY 6 • Deepen the Meaning

### CHECK MEANING

MATERIALS
- Pocket chart, document camera, or PowerPoint™
- Days 5 & 6 Recording Sheet
- Cards:
  Teacher: al, ic, ist, logy, psych
  Student: Greek Combining Forms: demo, graph, phobia, phono, photo
  Suffixes: er, ic

**DIRECTIONS** Using the **Cards** and **Mat**, confirm that students understand how the meaning of the word evolves as more parts are added.

**I DO**

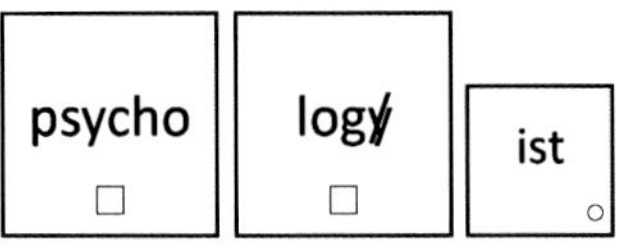


- The Greek combining form ***logy*** means science or study.
- The suffix ***-ist*** means a person who works in a profession or studies a topic.
- Adding ***psycho*** to ***logy*** and ***-ist*** spells the word ***psychologist***. The combination of word parts means a person who studies the human mind and behavior.
- Now I'm going to use my knowledge of the word to answer the question.
  1. What does it mean when you say the ***psychologist*** studies children? She examines how they behave.

**WE DO**

psycho | logy | ic | al

- The Greek combining form ***logy*** means science or study.
- The suffix ***-ic*** means having a characteristic.
- The suffix ***-al*** means act or process.
- How does adding ***psycho*** to ***logy, ic,*** and ***al*** change the meaning? Relating to the study of the human mind and behavior
- Listen to me use the word ***psychological*** in a question and we will use our knowledge of its parts to figure out the answer.
  2. What does it mean when we say that there is a question about the ***psychological*** reason for the man's actions? The question is related to his mind.

**YOU DO** Use your **Cards** and **Mats** to complete the chart on the **Days 5 & 6 Recording Sheet**.

| Greek Combining Forms | Certified Definition |
|---|---|
| archae/arche | primitive, ancient |
| cracy/crat | rule |
| demo | people |
| eco | house, home |
| graph | written or drawn |
| logy/logy/ology/ology | science, study |
| paleo | old, ancient |
| phob/phobia/phobic | irrational fear or hatred |
| phono | sound |
| photo | light |
| psych/psycho | mind or soul |
| techn | skill, craft |
| zoo | animal |

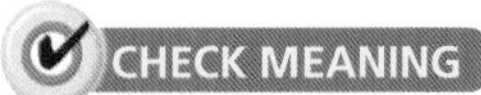


meaning of the words.

| Word | Greek Combining Form | Greek Combining Form | Suffix |
|---|---|---|---|
| demographer | demo: people | graph: written or drawn | er: one who does |
| Meaning: | a person who studies statistics about people like births, marriages, and deaths | | |
| demographic | demo: people | graph: written or drawn | ic: having the characteristic of |
| Meaning: | the statistics about people such as numbers of births or deaths | | |
| phonophobia | phono: sound | phobia: irrational fear or hatred | |
| Meaning: | an abnormal fear of sounds | | |
| photophobia | photo: light | phobia: irrational fear or hatred | |
| Meaning: | the fear of, or abnormal sensitivity to, light | | |

| Suffixes | Certified Definition |
|---|---|
| -al | related to |
| -er | one who does |
| -ic | having a characteristic |
| -ist | a person who works in a profession or studies a topic |

# cracy/crat, demo, phob/phobia/phobic, psych/psycho

## DAY 7 • Word Multiplier

### WORD MULTIPLIER

**Build words with *cracy/crat, demo, phob/phobia/phobic,* and *psych/psycho***

MATERIALS
- Day 7 Recording Sheet
- Notebook paper
- Greek Mat
- Cards:
  Greek Combining Forms: archae, arche, cracy, crat, demo, eco, graph, logy, log, ology, paleo, phob, phobia, phobic, phono, photo, psych, psycho, techn, zoo
  Suffixes: al, er, ic, ist
  Inflected Endings: s

**DIRECTIONS** Students work together to build words using their **Cards** and **Mats**.

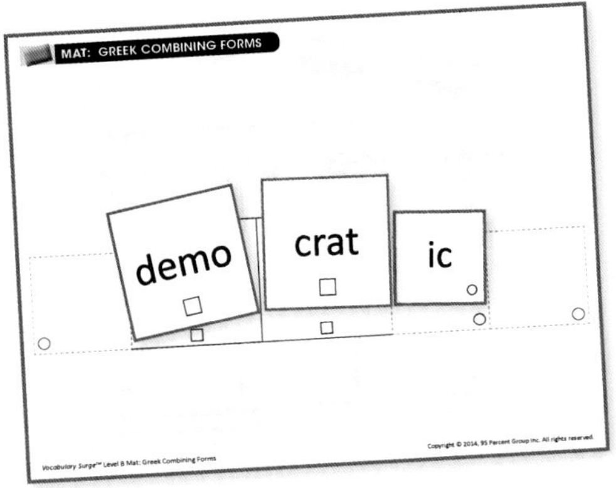


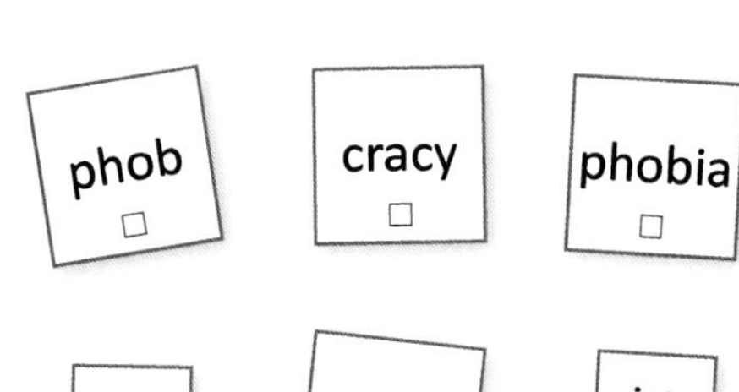


**WE DO** Let's combine **Cards** to build a word.

- I select cards ***demo, crat,*** and ***ic***.
- Where shall I place the Greek combining form ***demo***? In the box on the left side of the mat
- Why do we place it here? Because it is a Greek combining form
- Where shall I place the Greek combining form ***crat***? In the box to the right of ***demo***
- Why do we place it here? Because it is a Greek combining form
- Finally, where shall I place the suffix ***-ic***? To the right of ***crat***, matching the circle on the mat to the one on the card
- What word have we built? Democratic
- What is the definition of ***democratic***? Relating to a government where the people elect their leaders

**WORD MULTIPLIER**

| | | | |
|---|---|---|---|
| 1. | demo+cracy | democracy | noun |
| | Write the Meaning: | a government where the people elect their leaders | |
| 2. | demo+graph+er | demographer | noun |
| | Write the Meaning: | a person who studies statistics about people like births, marriages, and deaths | |
| 3. | phono+phobia | phonophobia | noun |
| | Write the Meaning: | the fear of sound | |
| 4. | photo+phob+ic | photophobic | adjective |
| | Write the Meaning: | a person who is afraid of, or abnormally sensitive to, light | |
| 5. | psych+ology+ist | psychologist | noun |
| | Write the Meaning: | a person who studies the human mind and behavior | |
| 6. | psycho+techn+ic+al | psychotechnical | adjective |
| | Write the Meaning: | relating to the use of the mind to develop technology | |

**YOU DO** Use your **Cards** and **Mats** to build more words. Complete the **Day 7 Recording Sheet** with your partner. Write additional words on notebook paper.

**Possible Words**: democrat, demographic, demophobia, demophobic, graphic, psychology, phonophobic, photophobia, psychological, technical, technology

## cracy/crat, demo, phob/phobia/ phobic, psych/psycho

# DAY 8 • Demonstrate Meaning

## BUILD MEANING

MATERIALS
- Whiteboards
- Markers

**DIRECTIONS** Complete the I Do and We Do whole class, and pair students to work on the You Do. Students can record their ideas on small whiteboards. Ask a few pairs to share their work with the class.

**I DO** Listen to me demonstrate understanding of the meaning of the Greek combining form ***demo***.

- The first word is ***democrat***. We know a ***democrat*** is a person who believes in equality or represents the Democratic Party. I'm going to think of examples of things that are ***democrats***.
  - Many elected seats in the United States Senate and Congress are filled by ***Democrats***.
  - Former Presidents Carter and Clinton are ***Democrats***.
- The second word is ***demographic***, which means relating to the study of a group of people. I'm going to think of examples of ***demographics*** used to describe people.
  - The government studies the ***demographics*** of the American people.
  - The ***demographics*** reveal that people are moving from rural areas to the city.

**WE DO** Let's try the next one together with the Greek combining form ***psych***.

- The first word is ***psychomotor***. The Greek combining form ***psych*** means mind or soul, the Latin root ***mot*** means to move, and the suffix ***-or*** means one who has a special characteristic. ***Psychomotor*** means a motor action controlled by the mind. The tossing of a basketball is a ***psychomotor*** movement.
  - Name something that might be studied in a ***psychomotor*** experiment.
- The second word is ***psychology***. The Greek combining form ***psych*** means mind or soul and the Greek combining form ***ology*** means science or study. ***Psychology*** means the science of the human mind and behavior.
  - Name something that might be studied in a ***psychology*** experiment.

**PROMPT IDEAS** ***psychomotor***
- catch a Frisbee
- brush your teeth
- write your name

**PROMPT IDEAS** ***psychology***
- how people learn a second language
- how people remember strings of numbers
- how groups behave in an emergency

**YOU DO** Now it's your turn. Work with a partner, and record your ideas on a whiteboard so you're ready to share with the class. You'll have five minutes to think of examples for two words that contain the Greek combining forms ***phob/phobia***.

- The two words are ***technophobia*** and ***bibliophobia***.
  - What does the Greek combining form ***techn*** mean? Machine What does the Greek combining form ***phobia*** mean? Irrational fear or hatred What does ***technophobia*** mean? Fear of machines
  - What does the Greek combining form ***biblio*** mean? Books What does the Greek combining form ***phobia*** mean? Irrational fear or hatred What does ***bibliophobia*** mean? Fear of books
  - Think of an example of something a person who has ***technophobia*** might fear.
  - Think of an example of something a person who has ***bibliophobia*** might fear.

**PROMPT IDEAS** ***technophobia***
- phone
- oven
- car

**PROMPT IDEAS** ***bibliophobia***
- dictionary
- magazine
- textbook

# archa~~e~~/arche, cracy/crat, demo, eco, pale/paleo, phob/phobia, psych, psycho, zoo

## DAY 9 • Review What You Learned

### STEP 1 REVIEW THE MEANING

MATERIALS
- Word parts projected on document camera, overhead projector, or PowerPoint™

**Review *archa~~e~~/arche, cracy/crat, demo, eco, pale/paleo, phob/phobia, psych/psycho,* and *zoo***

**DIRECTIONS** Display the morphemes so students can see them, and ask for the Certified Definition of each one.

**When I show you the word parts, think about the Certified Definitions we discussed as you prepare to answer.**

| Greek Combining Form | Certified Definition | Greek Combining Form | Certified Definition |
|---|---|---|---|
| **archa~~e~~/arche** | primitive, ancient | **cracy/crat** | rule |
| **eco** | house, home | **demo** | people |
| **pale/paleo** | old, ancient | **phob/phobia** | irrational fear, hatred |
| **zoo** | animal | **psych/psycho** | mind, soul |

### STEP 2 CHECK MEANING

MATERIALS
- Day 9 Recording Sheet

**DIRECTIONS** Read the following sentences to check that students understand the meanings of ***archa~~e~~/arche, cracy/crat, demo, eco, pale/paleo, phob/phobia, psych/psycho,*** and ***zoo***. Model the first sentence for students using the We Do step, below.

**WE DO** As I read this sentence, think about the Certified Definitions of the Greek combining form that fits the blank.

1. The ________ologist examined the tiny jade carving.

- Which Greek combining form do you think fits on the line? Arche
- What is the new word? Archeologist
- What do you think the word ***archeologist*** means? A person who studies ancient history

**YOU DO** Complete the rest of the sentences on the **Day 9 Recording Sheet** with your partner to find the Greek combining form that best fits on the line. Record the new words and their meanings.

CHECK MEANING

1. The arche **ologist** examined the tiny jade carving. archeologist
   Meaning: a person who studies ancient history
2. Eco **logy** and caring for Earth is the focus of our next field trip. ecology
   Meaning: the biological study of how organisms interact with their environments
3. James has demo **phobia** so he doesn't like eating in the crowded cafeteria. demophobia
   Meaning: the fear of crowds of people
4. The eco **biologist** studied how landfills have affected air and water quality. ecobiologist
   Meaning: a person who studies how organisms interact with their environment
5. The United States is a demo **cratic** country. democratic
   Meaning: relating to a system of government where the people elect their leaders
6. The zoo **logist** cradled the tiny panda in his hands. zoologist
   Meaning: a person who studies animals

Students write two sentences with missing Greek combining forms to challenge the class.

archaé/arche, cracy/crat, demo, eco, pale/paleo, phob/phobia/phobic, psych/psycho, zoo

# DAY 10 • 2nd Review Day

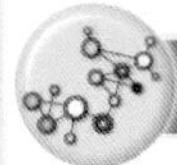

## STEP 1 MAKE CONNECTIONS

MATERIALS
- Day 10 Recording Sheet

**DIRECTIONS** Students pair up to write sentences with either one or two of the words that are provided.

**I am going to model how to use two words containing this week's Greek combining forms in a meaningful sentence. The words are *archeologist* and *archetypical*.**

- The ***arche*ologist** made an amazing discovery of an ***arche*typical** cliff dwelling.
- It is your turn to create five more sentences using the words on the top of the recording sheet.
- Sentences with two words get two points and sentences with one word get one point.

MAKE CONNECTIONS

| Words | | |
|---|---|---|
| archaic | ecological | bibliophobia |
| archeology | paleography | demophobic |
| archeologist | zoology | photophobia |
| archetype | zoologist | zoophobia |
| ecobiologist | democratic | psychologist |
| ecology | demographics | psychomotor |

1. Riding a bike is a psychomotor skill.
2. The lady wore dark sunglasses because she suffered from photophobia.
3. If I say that I'm bibliophobic, will I get excused from reading this book?
4. The social scientist studied birth rates, which was one key demographic statistic.
5. A person with zoophobia should not become a zoologist.

## STEP 2 CHALLENGE: MORPHEME MADNESS

MATERIALS
- Day 10 Recording Sheet
- Notebook paper
- Greek Mat
- Cards listed in the table below

**DIRECTIONS** Students pair up to use Cards and Mats to build words. Students record all of the words they build and then record the words' definitions.

| Word Parts | Cards |
|---|---|
| Greek Combining Forms | archaé, arche, biblio, cracy, crat, demo, eco, graph, logy, logý, ology, ologý, pale, paleo, phob, phobia, phobic, psych, psycho, techno, zoo |
| Inflected Endings | n/a |
| Prefixes | n/a |
| Suffixes | al, er, ic, ist, y |
| Connecting Letters | n/a |

**Now it's your turn to build words.**

- First, find a partner.
- Use the Cards and Mats to build words.
- Record the words and their definition on a separate sheet of paper.

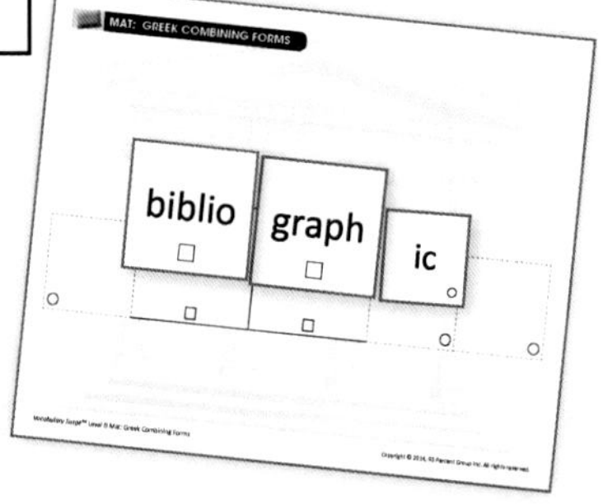


 

# Latin

| Latin Roots | Meaning | Lesson |
|---|---|---|
| anni, annu | year | 13 |
| art | something skillful or beautiful | 7 |
| aud | to hear, listen | 11 |
| cas | to fall or befall | 10 |
| cause, cause̸ | to cause; motive | 10 |
| cede, cede̸, ceed | to go, yield, or surrender | 11 |
| cern | to separate | 10 |
| cess | to go, yield, or surrender | 11 |
| cid, cide, cide̸ | to fall or befall | 10 |
| cis, cise, cise̸ | to cut | 10 |
| claim, clam | to declare, call, or cry out | 5 |
| cline, cline̸ | to lean | 6 |
| close, close̸ | to shut or close | 13 |
| clude, clude̸, clus | to shut or close | 13 |
| cogn | to know | 8 |
| corp | body | 13 |
| cred | to believe | 12 |
| cuse, cuse̸ | to cause; motive | 10 |
| dic, dict | to say or tell | 5 |
| dorm | to sleep | 13 |
| fac, fect, fic | to make or do | 7 |
| fact | something that is the truth or is known | 7 |
| feder | doctrine or belief | 12 |
| fer | to bear or yield | 11 |
| fid, fide, fide̸ | doctrine or belief | 12 |
| fin, fine, fine̸, finis | end, last | 13 |
| fix | to repair, or to make stationery | 7 |
| flect, flex | to bend or curve | 7 |
| flu, fluc, flux | to flow | 6 |
| form | to shape or mold | 7 |
| grad, grade, grade̸ | step, degree, walk | 8 |
| grate, grate̸ | thanks, pleasing | 11 |
| gress | step, degree, walk | 8 |
| jac, ject | to throw; lie | 6 |

# Latin

| Latin Roots | Meaning | Lesson |
|---|---|---|
| judge, judg~~e~~, judic | to rule or decide | 12 |
| jur, jus | law or right | 12 |
| leg | law | 12 |
| magna, magni | great | 11 |
| mot, mote, mot~~e~~ | to move | 8 |
| move, mov~~e~~ | to move | 8 |
| pend, pense, pens~~e~~ | to hang or weigh | 8 |
| pict | to paint | 7 |
| put, pute, put~~e~~ | to think | 8 |
| rect, recti, reg | straight or right | 6 |
| rupt | to break or burst | 5 |
| scribe, scrib~~e~~, script | to write | 7 |
| sec, sect, seg | to cut | 10 |
| sense, sens~~e~~, sent | to feel, perceive, or know | 12 |
| sist | to stand | 9 |
| spec, spect | to look, see, or watch | 8 |
| spir, spire, spir~~e~~ | to breathe | 9 |
| stat | to stand | 9 |
| tact | to touch | 9 |
| tain, ten | to hold | 9 |
| tang | to touch | 9 |
| tend, tent | to stretch or strain | 5 |
| tense, tens~~e~~ | to stretch or strain | 5 |
| tinu, tinue | to hold | 9 |
| vent | to come | 8 |
| verse, vers~~e~~, vert | to turn | 6 |
| vis, vise, vis~~e~~ | to see | 9 |
| vit, vita, viv | to live | 13 |
| voc, voke, vok~~e~~ | to call or voice | 5 |

 

# Greek Combining Forms

| Greek Combining Forms | Meaning | Lesson |
|---|---|---|
| auto | self, same | 14 |
| archaɇ, arche | primitive, ancient | 17 |
| ast, astro | star | 16 |
| biblio | book | 15 |
| bio | life | 15 |
| chron, chrono | time | 14 |
| cracy, crat | rule | 17 |
| demo | people | 17 |
| eco | house, home | 17 |
| geo | earth | 15 |
| gram, graph | written or drawn | 14 |
| hydr, hydra, hydro | water | 15 |
| lith, litho | stone | 15 |
| logy, logɏ | science, study | 16 |
| mechan | machine | 16 |
| micro | small | 15 |
| mono | one | 14 |
| morph, morpho | to change form, shape, structure | 16 |
| naut | sailor | 16 |
| neo | new, recent | 16 |
| nomy | a body of knowledge | 16 |
| ology | science,study | 16 |
| pale, paleo | old, ancient | 17 |
| phob, phobia, phobic | irrational fear or hatred | 17 |
| phon, phone, phono | sound | 14 |
| photo | light | 14 |
| poly | many | 16 |
| proto | earlist, original | 16 |
| psych, psycho | mind or soul | 17 |
| scope | to watch or see | 15 |
| spher, sphere, spherɇ | ball, globe, circle | 15 |
| techn, techno | skill, craft | 16 |
| tele | far, distant | 14 |
| wave | movement | 15 |
| zoo | animal | 17 |

# Prefixes

| Prefixes | Meaning | Lesson |
|---|---|---|
| ab | from or away | Review |
| ac, ad, af, ag, al, an | to, toward, in, or near | Review |
| anti | against, opposite | Review |
| ap, ar, as, at | to, toward, in, or near | Review |
| be | completely, thoroughly, or excessively | |
| bi | two (Latin) | 10 |
| cent, centi | 100 (Latin) | |
| col, com, con | together, with | Review |
| contra | against, opposite | Review |
| cor | together, with | Review |
| counter | contrary, opposite | |
| de | away from, down | 4 |
| dec, deca, deci | ten (Latin & Greek) | |
| di | two | |
| dif, dis | not, apart | Review |
| dys | bad or difficult (Latin & Greek) | |
| e, ex | out | Review |
| il | not | Review |
| il, im, in, ir | in, on or toward | Review |
| inner | in | |
| inter | between, among | |
| intra | within | |
| mal | bad or badly | |
| manu | make by hand | |
| mille, milli | 1000 (Latin) | |
| mis | bad, wrong | Review |
| multi | many | 10 |
| non | not | Review |
| ob, oc, op | down, against, or facing; to | 4 |
| per | through or completely | 5 |
| pre | before, earlier | |
| pro | forward, earlier, or prior to | 3 |
| re | back or again | |
| semi | half | 11 |

 

# Prefixes

| Prefixes | Meaning | Lesson |
|---|---|---|
| sub, suc, suf, sug, sup, sus | under, beneath or below | 3 |
| super | of superior quality or size | |
| trans | across, beyond | Review |
| un | not | Review |
| under | below, beneath | Review |
| uni | one | |

# Suffixes

| Suffixes | Meaning | Lesson |
|---|---|---|
| able | able, can do | Review |
| acy | state or quality | Review |
| ade | result of action (façade, cascade, decade, blockade) | |
| age | collection, mass, relationship | 8 |
| al | related to, like | Review |
| an | relating to | 1 |
| ance, ance̸ | action, state or quality (noun or adj) | 2 |
| ancy, ant | action, state or quality (noun or adj) | 2 |
| ar | relating to (Latin) | Review |
| ary | relating to (Latin) | 1 |
| ate, ate̸ | to cause or make, rank or office | 4 |
| cial | related to, like | Review |
| cian | one who has a certain skill or art | 3 |
| cide | to kill | |
| cious | full of or having | 1 |
| cy | state or quality | |
| en | made of, or to make | 12 |
| ence, ence̸, ency, ent | action, state, or quality (noun or adj) | 2 |
| eous | characterized by | |
| er | one who does, is from, or has a special characteristic (er-A/S, or-Latin) | Review |
| ery | relating to, place where, quality | 1 |
| ese | related to | 1 |
| est | comparative, the most or extreme, superlative degree | Review |

# Suffixes

| Suffixes | Meaning | Lesson |
|---|---|---|
| ful | full of, or full | |
| fy, ify | make or become | Review |
| ial | related to, like | Review |
| ian | one who has a certain skill or art | 1 |
| ible, ibl~~e~~ | able, can do | Review |
| ibly | alternate spelling of ably | |
| ic | having the characteristic of | Review |
| ile | relating to, suited for, or capable of | 2 |
| ine | relating to, resembling | 2 |
| inter | between or among | |
| ion | state of being, quality, action | Review |
| ious | characterized by, like | 1 |
| ish | origin, nature, or resembling | |
| ism | doctrine, belief | 12 |
| ist | one who performs a specific action | Review |
| ity | condition, quality | Review |
| ium | relating to status, ending for elements | |
| ive | showing a quality or tendency | 4 |
| ize, iz~~e~~ | become, change, make | 4 |
| ly | like | |
| ment | act of, state of, or result of an action | Review |
| ness | state of | |
| or | one who does | Review |
| ory | relating to (Latin) | 1 |
| ous | characterized by | 1 |
| ship | office, state, dignity, skill, quality, or profession | 5 |
| sion | state of being, quality, action | |
| ster | one who is associated with, participates in | 2 |
| tial | alternate spelling of al | Review |
| tion | state of being, quality, action | 12 |
| tious | full of or having | 1 |

 

# Suffixes

| Suffixes | Meaning | Lesson |
|---|---|---|
| tude | condition, state, or quality of | 3 |
| ture, ure | state of, process, function, or | 3 |
| ty | condition, quality | 12 |
| y | characterized by | 12 |

# Mats

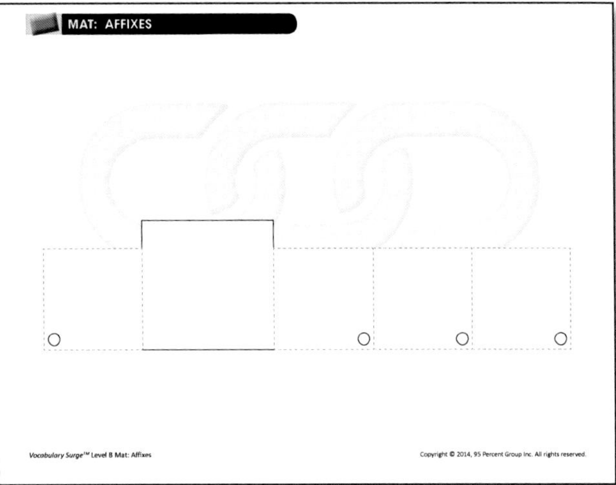


***Affixes***

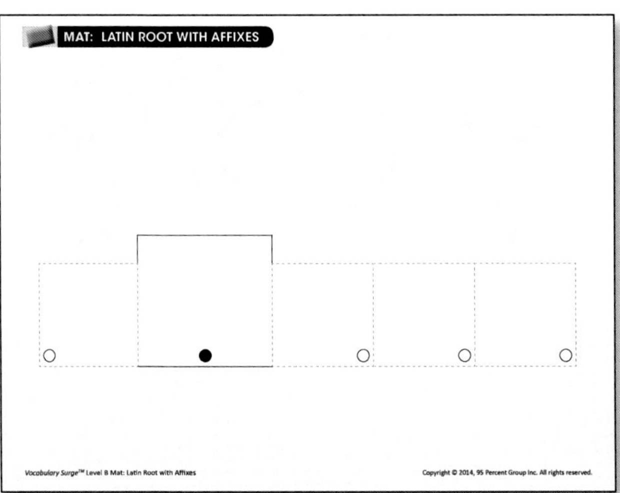


***Latin***

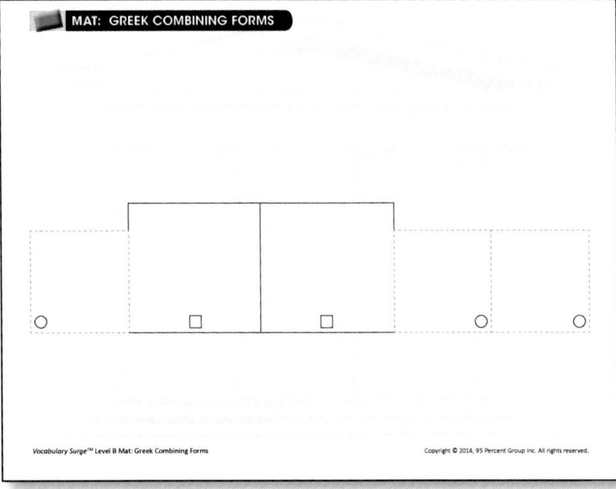


***Greek Combining Forms***

 

# Cards

### Seven Types of Word Cards (368 Total)

| Size | Symbol | | Number of Cards |
|---|---|---|---|
| Large | group Lesson 3 | Bases | 48 |
| | claim ● | Latin Roots | 126 |
| | photo □ | Greek Combining Forms | 55 |
| Medium | re ○ | Prefixes | 64 |
| | ize ○ | Suffixes | 69 |
| | ed ○ | Inflected Endings | 4 |
| Small | i | Connecting Letters | 2 |

# Review Lessons

This table provides a list of the prefixes and suffixes assumed to be understood by students in Level B. If students don't know the meanings of these affixes, teachers can download any of these twelve review lessons from the product secure website and provide instruction. Instructions for downloading can be found on the inside front cover.

| Prefixes | Meaning | Lesson |
|---|---|---|
| ad/ac/af/ag/al/an/ap/ ar/as/at | to, toward, in, or near | R7 |
| anti | against, opposite | R3 |
| con/com/col/cor | together, with | R5 |
| contra | against, opposite | R3 |
| dis/dif | not, apart | R1 |
| ex | out | R3 |
| in/im/ir | in, on or toward | R4 |
| in/il/im/ir | not | R2 |
| inner | in | R4 |
| inter | between, among | R5 |
| mis | bad, wrong | R2 |
| non | not | R1 |
| sub | under, beneath or below | R6 |
| trans | across, beyond | R6 |
| un | not | R1 |
| under | below, beneath | R6 |
| **Suffixes** | **Meaning** | **Lesson** |
| able/ible | able, can do | R9 |
| acy | state, condition, or quality | R10 |
| al/ial/cial/tial | related to, like | R11 |
| ar/er/or | one who does, is from; has a special characteristic | R8 |
| est | comparative, the most or extreme, superlative degree | R8 |
| ic | having the characteristic of | R11 |
| ify | make or become | R9 |
| ion/sion/tion | state of being, quality, action | R10 |
| ist | one who performs a specific action | R12 |
| ity | condition, quality | R12 |
| ium | relating to status, ending for elements | R11 |
| ment | act of, state of, or result of an action | R10 |

 

# Day 10 Morpheme Madness Word Building Activity

Below is an example of the document that can be downloaded from the product secure website. This document provides teachers with a list of words that can be built with the set of word cards listed in the Day 10 Morpheme Madness activity. Instructions for downloading can be found on the inside front cover.

Morpheme Madness Activity – Words that Students Can Build – Lesson 5

Below is a table containing the words that can be built with the 24 word card parts listed in the Morpheme Madness activity.

| Word | Word Cards |
|---|---|
| Latin Roots | claim, clam, dic, dict, rupt, tend, tens, tense (e slashed), tent, voc, voke, voke (e slashed) |
| Inflected Endings | ed, ing |
| Prefixes | contra, cor, dis, ex, in, inter, pre, re |
| Suffixes | ate, ate (e slashed), ion |

| Word | Word Cards | Meaning |
|---|---|---|
| **claim/clam – to declare, call, or cry out** | | |
| claim | claim | to declare, call, or cry out |
| claimed | claim + ed | declared, called, or cried out |
| claiming | claim + ing | declaring, calling, or crying out |
| exclamation | ex + clam + ate + ion | something that is emphasized or called out |
| exclaim | ex + claim | to emphasize or call out something |
| exclaimed | ex + claim | to have emphasized or called out something |
| exclaiming | ex + claim + ing | to be emphasizing or calling out something |
| reclaim | re + claim | to get back something lost or taken away |
| reclaimed | re + claim + ed | to get back something lost or taken away |
| reclaiming | re + claim + ing | taking back something lost or removed |
| **dic/dict – to say or tell** | | |
| dictate | dic + tate | to tell someone what to do |
| contradict | contra + dict | to say something that is the opposite of what was said before |
| contradicted | contra + dict + ed | to have said something opposite of before |
| contradicting | contra + dict + ing | saying something opposite of what was said before |
| predict | pre + dict | to tell something before it happens |
| predicted | pre + dict + ed | to have told something before it happened |
| predicting | pre + dict + ing | telling something before it happens |
| **Rupt – to break or burst** | | |
| corrupt | cor + rupt | to change to something that is dishonest or immoral |
| corrupted | cor + rupt + ed | to have changed to something dishonest or immoral |
| corrupting | cor + rupt + ing | changing to something dishonest or immoral |
| corruption | cor + rupt + ion | something that is dishonest or immoral |
| interrupt | inter + rupt | to break into a conversation or an event |
| **Tend – to stretch or strain** | | |
| tend | tend | to stretch or strain, pay attention |
| tended | tend + ed | paid attention to |
| tending | tend + ing | paying attention to |
| distend | dis + tend | to stretch or bulge |
| extend | ex + tend | to stretch out far |
| extended | ex + tend + ed | to have stretched out |
| extending | ex + tend + ing | stretching out |
| intend | in + tend | to have a purpose in mind |

*Vocabulary Surge: Unleashing the Power of Word Parts*™, Level B 

# Mats and Word Cards

Download Mats and Word Cards from the Product Secure Website (see inside front cover for instructions).

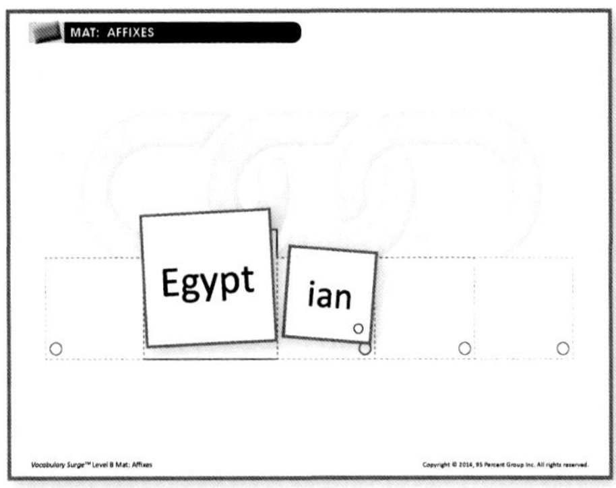


### *Bases for Affix Lessons*

| America<br>Lesson 1 | fish<br>Lesson 1 | hatch<br>Lesson 1 | Japan<br>Lesson 1 |
|---|---|---|---|
| hero<br>Lesson 2 | trick<br>Lesson 2 | young<br>Lesson 2 | class<br>Lesson 3 |
| Egypt<br>Lesson 3 | fail<br>Lesson 3 | floor<br>Lesson 3 | group<br>Lesson 3 |

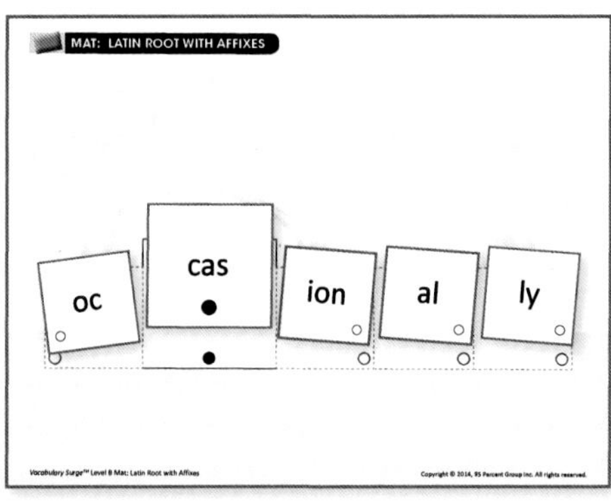


### *Latin Roots*

| anni | annu | art | aud |
|---|---|---|---|
| cas | cause | causȩ | cede |
| cedȩ | ceed | cern | cess |

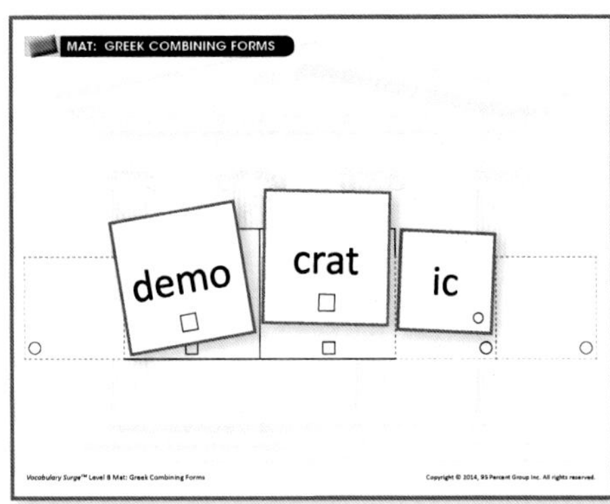


### *Greek Combining Forms*

| archaȩ | arche | ast | astro |
|---|---|---|---|
| biblio | bio | chron | chrono |
| cracy | crat | demo | eco |

### *Prefixes*

| ab | ac | ad | af | ag | al |
|---|---|---|---|---|---|
| an | anti | ap | ar | as | at |
| be | bi | cent | centi | col | com |
| con | contra | cor | counter | de | dec |

### *Suffixes*

| able | acy | ade | age | al | an |
|---|---|---|---|---|---|
| ance | ancȩ | ancy | ant | ar | ary |
| ate | atȩ | cial | cian | cide | cious |
| cy | en | ence | encȩ | ency | ent |

### *Inflected Endings and Connectives*

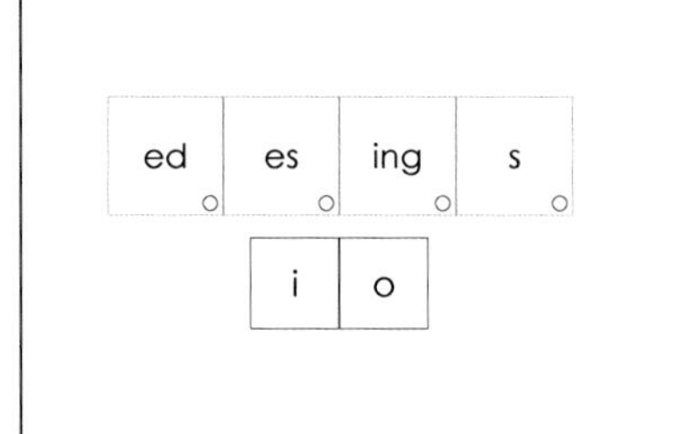


 